Houghton Mifflin

California

Math

 HOUGHTON MIFFLIN   BOSTON

GRADE 2 STUDENT RESOURCES VOLUME

ISBN-13: 978-0-547-17110-4

GRADE 2 STUDENT BOOK

ISBN-13: 978-0-618-82738-1

18 19 20 21 22 0877 18 17 16 15

4500521024

Houghton Mifflin

California Math

Authors & Consultants

Authors

Renee Hill
Mathematics Specialist
Riverside Unified School District
Riverside, CA

Matt Larson
Curriculum Specialist for
Mathematics
Lincoln Public Schools
Lincoln, NE

Miriam A. Leiva
Bonnie E. Cone Distinguished
Professor Emerita
Professor of Mathematics Emerita
University of North Carolina
Charlotte, NC

Jean M. Shaw
Professor Emerita of Curriculum and
Instruction
University of Mississippi
Oxford, MS

Dr. Lee Stiff
Professor of Mathematics Education
North Carolina State University
Raleigh, NC

Dr. Bruce Vogeli
Clifford Brewster Upton Professor of
Mathematics
Teachers College, Columbia
University
New York, NY

Consultants

Mental Math Strategies

Greg Tang
Author and Mathematics Consultant
Belmont, MA

English Language Learners

Dr. Russell M. Gersten
Executive Director, Institutional
Research Group & Professor
Emeritus
College of Education, University of
Oregon
Long Beach, CA

Lisette Estrella-Henderson
Director of District and School
Support
Solano County Office of Education
Fairfield, CA

Language and Vocabulary

Dr. Shane Templeton
Foundation Professor, Department
of Educational Specialties
University of Nevada at Reno
Reno, NV

Strategic Consultant

Dr. Liping Ma
Senior Scholar
Carnegie Foundation for the
Advancement of Technology
Palo Alto, CA

Special Projects

Catherine Valentino
Author-in-Residence
Houghton Mifflin
West Kingston, RI

Content Reviewers

Dr. W. Stephen Wilson
(Grades K–2)
Professor of Mathematics
Johns Hopkins University
Baltimore, MD

Dr. Kurt Kreith
(Grades 3–4)
Emeritus Professor of Mathematics
University of California at Davis
Davis, CA

Dr. Solomon Friedberg
(Grade 5)
Professor of Mathematics
Boston College
Chestnut Hill, MA

Dr. Bert Fristedt
(Grade 6)
Professor of Mathematics
University of Minnesota
Minneapolis, MN

California Reviewers

Grade K

Cynthia Dominguez
Highlands Elementary School
Saugus, CA

Dana Hight
Royal Oaks Elementary School
Visalia, CA

Patricia Mahoney
John Adams Elementary School
Madera, CA

Teresa Rogers
Skyline North Elementary School
Barstow, CA

Schelly Solko
Roy W. Loudon Elementary School
Bakersfield, CA

Julie Towne
Jurupa Vista Elementary School
Fontana, CA

Grade 1

Kirsten Marsh
Edgemont Elementary School
Moreno Valley, CA

Jill McCarthy
Edgemont Elementary School
Moreno Valley, CA

Brandee Ramirez
Myford Elementary School
Tustin, CA

Rebecca Solares
Cerritos Elementary School
Glendale, CA

Leanne Thomas
Scott Lane Elementary School
Santa Clara, CA

Sheila Vann
Folsom Hills Elementary School
Folsom, CA

Grade 2

Deborah Nelson
North Park Elementary School
Valencia, CA

Kathryn Smith
Quail Run Elementary School
San Ramon, CA

Angelica Yates
Allen at Steinbeck
Elementary School
San José, CA

Grade 3

Pamela Aurangzeb
Grapeland Elementary School
Etiwanda, CA

Veronica Fowler
Challenger School of Sports &
Fitness
Victorville, CA

Nancy Hayes
Toro Park School
Salinas, CA

Megan Heavens
North Park Elementary School
Valencia, CA

Caryl Lyons
Manuel L. Real Elementary School
Perris, CA

Stacey McKay
Glenn E. Murdock Elementary
School
La Mesa, CA

Peggy Morrill
Grapeland Elementary School
Etiwanda, CA

Kristine Salomonson
Freedom Elementary School
Clovis, CA

Susan Steubing
Folsom Hills Elementary School
Folsom, CA

These people helped make this book the best it can be.

California Reviewers

Grade 4

Cheryl Robertson
McPherson Magnet School
Orange, CA

JoAnna Trafecanty
North Park Elementary School
Valencia, CA

Grade 5

Karen Clarke
Manuel L. Real Elementary School
Perris, CA

Bonita DeAmicis
Highlands Elementary School
Saugus, CA

Gretchen Oberg
Ralph Dailard Elementary School
San Diego, CA

Grade 6

Judy Denenny
McPherson Magnet School
Orange, CA

Terri Parker
Leo B. Hart Elementary School
Bakersfield, CA

George Ratcliff
Joseph Casillas Elementary School
Chula Vista, CA

Patricia Wenzel
Cloverly Elementary School
Temple City, CA

Across Grade

Gina Chavez
California State University, Los
Angeles
Los Angeles, CA

Catherine De Leon
Washington Elementary School
Madera, CA

Cindy Ellis
Madera Unified School District
Madera, CA

Jenny Maguire
Orinda Union School District
Orinda, CA

Ernest Minelli
Selby Lane School
Redwood City, CA

Barbara Page
Modesto City Schools
Modesto, CA

Ian Tablit
Delano Union Elementary School
District
Delano, CA

Jeannie Tavolazzi
Grapeland Elementary School
Etiwanda, CA

Dina Tews
John J. Pershing Elementary School
Madera, CA

They really love
teaching math, too.

California Mathematics
Content Standards

What are Key Standards?

- The California Math standards are goals for what you will learn in math this year.

- The standards have five strands: Number Sense; Algebra and Functions; Measurement and Geometry; Statistics, Data Analysis, and Probability; Mathematical Reasoning.

- The symbol ⬤ means a standard is a KEY to success this year.

- Knowing and understanding the content standards means you can do well on tests.

How will this book help you succeed?

It's easy as one, two, three.

❶ Look for **Key Standards** in this book.

❷ Do your best work. Ask questions.

❸ Use the Key Standards Handbook on pages KSH1–KSH24.

Doing well feels terrific!

Number Sense

Standards You Will Learn	Some Places to Look
1.0 Students understand the relationship between numbers, quantities, and place value in whole numbers up to 1,000:	Lessons 3.1, 3.2, 3.3, 3.4, 4.1, 4.3, 4.4, 4.5, 10.3, 23.1, 23.2, 23.3, 23.4, 24.1, 24.2, 24.3, 24.4 Chapters 3, 23 Link
1.1 KEY Count, read, and write whole numbers to 1,000 and identify the place value for each digit.	Lessons 3.1, 3.2, 3.3, 3.4, 4.3, 23.1, 23.2, 23.3, 23.4, 24.1, 24.2, 24.4, Key Standards Handbook, p. KSH2; Chapters 3 Vocabulary; 23 Link; Chapter 4 Key Standards Review
1.2 Use words, models, and expanded forms (e.g., 45 = 4 tens + 5) to represent numbers (to 1,000).	Lessons 3.1, 3.2, 3.3, 3.4, 23.1, 23.2, 23.3, 23.4, 24.1 Chapter 23 Link
1.3 KEY Order and compare whole numbers to 1,000 by using the symbols <, =, >.	Lessons 4.1, 4.2, 4.3, 6.4, 24.2, 24.3, 24.4 Key Standards Handbook, p. KSH3; Chapter 4 Link; Chapters 5, 7, 25 Key Standards Review
2.0 Students estimate, calculate, and solve problems involving addition and subtraction of two- and three-digit numbers:	Lessons 8.1, 8.2, 8.3, 8.4, 9.1, 9.2, 9.3, 9.4, 9.5, 10.1, 10.2, 10.4, 10.5, 11.1, 11.2, 11.3, 12.1, 12.2, 12.3, 12.4, 13.1, 13.2, 13.3, 13.5, 25.1, 25.2, 25.3, 25.4, 25.5, 26.1, 26.2, 26.3, 26.4, 26.5, 27.1, 27.2, 27.3, 27.4, 27.5, 28.3, 28.4 Chapters 8, 9, 11, 25, 26, 27 Link
2.1 KEY Understand and use the inverse relationship between addition and subtraction (e.g., an opposite number sentence for 8 + 6 = 14 is 14 − 6 = 8) to solve problems and check solutions.	Lessons 1.3, 1.4, 9.2, 13.5, 28.3, 28.5 Key Standards Handbook, p. KSH4; Chapter 2 Key Standards Review
2.2 KEY Find the sum or difference of two whole numbers up to three digits long.	Lessons 1.1, 1.3, 1.4, 1.5, 8.1, 8.2, 8.3, 8.4, 9.1, 9.2, 9.3, 9.4, 9.5, 10.1, 10.3, 10.4, 11.1, 11.2, 11.3, 12.1, 12.1, 12.2, 12.3, 12.4, 13.1, 13.3, 13.4, 13.5, 18.5, 25.1, 25.2, 25.3, 25.4, 25.5, 26.1, 26.2, 26.3, 26.4, 26.5, 27.1, 27.2, 27.3, 27.4, 27.5, 28.3, 28.4 Key Standards Handbook, p. KSH5–KSH6; Chapters 8, 9, 11, 25, 26, 27 Link; Chapters 9, 10, 12, 13, 26, 27, 28 Key Standards Review

	Standards You Will Learn	**Some Places to Look**
2.3	Use mental arithmetic to find the sum or difference of two two-digit numbers.	Lessons 8.1, 10.1, 13.1, 25.1, 26.1 Go Far, Go Fast Mental Math Strategies, p. 207, p. 263
3.0 KEY	Students model and solve simple problems involving multiplication and division:	Lessons 20.1, 20.2, 20.3, 20.4, 20.5, 21.1, 21.2, 21.3, 21.4, 21.5, 22.1, 22.2, 22.3, 22.4, 22.5 Key Standards Handbook p. KSH7; Chapter 22, 23 Key Standards Review; Chapter 20 Link
3.1 KEY	Use repeated addition, arrays, and counting by multiples to do multiplication.	Lessons 20.1, 20.2, 20.3, 20.4, 20.5, 21.1, 21.2, 21.3, 21.4, 21.5 Key Standards Handbook, p. KSH8–KSH9; Chapter 22 Key Standards Review; Chapter 20 Link
3.2 KEY	Use repeated subtraction, equal sharing, and forming equal groups with remainders to do division.	Lessons 22.1, 22.2, 22.3, 22.4, 22.5 Key Standards Handbook, KSH10; Chapter 23 Key Standards Review
3.3 KEY	Know the multiplication tables of 2s, 5s, and 10s (to "times 10") and commit them to memory.	Lessons 20.3, 20.4, 21.1, 21.2, 21.3 Key Standards Handbook, p. KSH11
4.0	Students understand that fractions and decimals may refer to parts of a set and parts of a whole:	Lessons 16.1, 16.2, 16.3, 16.4, 16.5, 17.1, 17.2, 17.3, 17.4 Chapter 17 Challenge, p. 339
4.1 KEY	Recognize, name, and compare unit fractions from $\frac{1}{12}$ to $\frac{1}{2}$.	Lessons 16.1, 16.2, 16.3, 16.5, 17.1 Key Standards Handbook, p. KSH12; Chapter 17, 18 Key Standards Review
4.2 KEY	Recognize fractions of a whole and parts of a group (e.g., one-fourth of a pie, two-thirds of 15 balls).	Lessons 16.1, 16.2, 16.3, 16.4, 16.5, 17.1, 17.2, 17.3, 17.4 Key Standards Handbook, p. KSH13; Chapter 18 Key Standards Review
4.3 KEY	Know that when all fractional parts are included, such as four-fourths, the result is equal to the whole and to one.	Lessons 16.1, 16.3, 16.4, 17.2, 17.4 Key Standards Handbook, p. KSH14; Chapter 17 Key Standards Review

Number Sense (continued)

Standards You Will Learn	Some Places to Look
5.0 Students model and solve problems by representing, adding, and subtracting amounts of money:	Lessons 6.1, 6.2, 6.3, 6.4, 7.1, 7.2, 7.3, 7.4, 7.5, 10.4, 10.6, 13.4, 24.5, 24.6, 28.1, 28.2
5.1 KEY Solve problems using combinations of coins and bills.	Lessons 6.2, 6.3, 6.4, 6.5, 7.1, 7.2, 7.3, 7.4, 7.5, 24.5, 28.1, 28.2 Key Standards Handbook, p. KSH15; Chapter 6 Link; Chapter 7 Key Standards Review
5.2 KEY Know and use the decimal notation and the dollar and cent symbols for money.	Lessons 6.1, 6.2, 7.3, 7.4, 7.5, 10.4, 13.4, 24.5, 28.1, 28.2 Key Standards Handbook, p. KSH16; Chapter 8 Key Standards Review
6.0 Students use estimation strategies in computation and problem solving that involve numbers that use the ones, tens, hundreds, and thousands places:	Lessons 4.4, 10.2, 13.2, 23.2, 28.4, 28.5 Chapter 13 Vocabulary
6.1 Recognize when an estimate is reasonable in measurements (e.g., closest inch).	Lessons 18.1, 18.3, 18.4, 18.5

Algebra and Functions

Standards You Will Learn	Some Places to Look
1.0 Students model, represent, and interpret number relationships to create and solve problems involving addition and subtraction:	Lessons 1.2, 1.5, 2.6, 7.5, 8.5, 9.5, 10.5, 10.6, 12.2, 12.3, 12.4, 13.6, 15.5, 26.5, 27.1, 27.5, 28.3, 28.5
1.1 KEY Use the commutative and associative rules to simplify mental calculations and to check results.	Lessons 1.2, 10.5, 20.2, 21.1 Key Standards Handbook, p. KSH17; Chapter 2 Key Standards Review and Challenge
1.2 Relate problem situations to number sentences involving addition and subtraction.	Lessons 1.5, 2.6, 8.5, 9.5, 10.6, 11.4, 13.6, 15.5, 26.5, 27.5, 28.3, 28.5
1.3 Solve addition and subtraction problems by using data from simple charts, picture graphs, and number sentences.	Lessons 2.3, 2.6, 9.5, 10.6, 11.4, 12.4, 13.5, 13.6, 15.5, 25.3, 25.4, 26.3, 26.5, 27.1, 27.5, 28.1

Measurement and Geometry

	Standards You Will Learn	Some Places to Look
1.0	Students understand that measurement is accomplished by identifying a unit of measure, iterating (repeating) that unit, and comparing it to the item to be measured:	Lessons 18.1, 18.2, 18.3, 18.4, 18.5, 19.1, 19.2, 19.3, 19.4, 19.5, 19.6 Unit 7 Take-Home Book
1.1	Measure the length of objects by iterating (repeating) a nonstandard or standard unit.	Lessons 18.1, 18.2, 18.4
1.2	Use different units to measure the same object and predict whether the measure will be greater or smaller when a different unit is used.	Lessons 18.2, 18.4, 18.5
1.3 KEY	Measure the length of an object to the nearest inch and/or centimeter.	Lessons 18.3, 18.4, 18.5 Key Standards Handbook, p. KSH18; Chapter 18 Link; Chapter 19 Key Standards Review
1.4	Tell time to the nearest quarter hour and know relationships of time (e.g., minutes in an hour, days in a month, weeks in a year).	Lessons 19.1, 19.2, 19.3, 19.4, 19.5, 19.6
1.5	Determine the duration of intervals of time in hours (e.g., 11:00 a.m. to 4:00 p.m.).	Lessons 19.4, 19.6
2.0 KEY	Students identify and describe the attributes of common figures in the plane and of common objects in space:	Lessons 14.1, 14.2, 14.3, 14.4, 14.5, 15.1, 15.2, 15.3, 15.4, 15.5 Key Standards Handbook, p. KSH19; Chapter 15 Key Standards Review
2.1 KEY	Describe and classify plane and solid geometric shapes (e.g., circle, triangle, square, rectangle, sphere, pyramid, cube, rectangular prism) according to the number and shape of faces, edges, and vertices.	Lessons 14.1, 14.2, 14.3, 15.1, 15.2, 15.3, 15.4, 15.5 Key Standards Handbook, p. KSH20; Chapter 15 Link; Chapters 15, 16 Key Standards Review
2.2 KEY	Put shapes together and take them apart to form other shapes (e.g., two congruent right triangles can be arranged to form a rectangle).	Lessons 14.4, 14.5, 15.1 Key Standards Handbook, p. KSH21; Chapter 14 Link; Chapter 15 Key Standards Review; Chapter 15 Challenge, p. 303

Statistics, Data Analysis, and Probability

Standards You Will Learn	Some Places to Look
1.0 KEY Students collect numerical data and record, organize, display, and interpret the data on bar graphs and other representations:	Lessons 2.1, 2.2, 2.3, 2.4, 2.5, 2.6 Key Standards Handbook, p. KSH22-KSH23; Chapter 2 Math Music; Chapter 3 Key Standards Review; Chapter 3 Challenge; Chapter 12 Link
1.1 Record numerical data in systematic ways, keeping track of what has been counted.	Lessons 2.1, 2.6, 6.5, 7.2, 11.4
1.2 Represent the same data set in more than one way (e.g., bar graphs and charts with tallies).	Lessons 2.3, 2.4, 2.5
1.3 Identify features of data sets (range and mode).	Lessons 2.4, 2.5, 22.2 Chapter 2 Vocabulary; Chapter 3 Key Standards Review
1.4 Ask and answer simple questions related to data representations.	Lessons 2.1, 2.2, 2.3, 2.4, 2.5, 2.6, 8.5, 9.3, 9.5, 11.4, 15.5, 16.5, 19.6, 22.2, 25.3, 26.5, Chapter 3 Key Standards Revew; Chapter 4 Link
2.0 KEY Students demonstrate an understanding of patterns and how patterns grow and describe them in general ways:	Lessons 3.5, 5.1, 5.2, 5.3, 5.4, 5.5, 9.4, 15.5, 20.4, 23.1, 23.5, 25.1 Key Standards Handbook, p. KSH24; Chapter 6 Key Standards Review
2.1 Recognize, describe, and extend patterns and determine a next term in linear patterns (e.g., 4, 8, 12...; the number of ears on one horse, two horses, three horses, four horses).	Lessons 3.5, 5.1, 5.2, 5.3, 5.4, 5.5, 9.4, 15.5, 20.4, 23.5 Chapter 5 Vocabulary
2.2 Solve problems involving simple number patterns.	Lessons 3.5, 5.5, 12.1, 23.1, 23.5, 25.1 Chapter 20 Link; Unit 9 Take-Home Book

Mathematical Reasoning

	Standards You Will Learn	Some Places to Look
1.0	Students make decisions about how to set up a problem:	Lessons 1.5, 2.6, 5.4, 5.5, 7.5, 8.4, 8.5, 10.1, 10.5, 13.1, 15.5, 17.4, 18.2, 18.5, 20.5, 21.5, 23.5, 24.6, 26.5, 27.2
1.1	Determine the approach, materials, and strategies to be used.	Lessons 1.5, 2.3, 2.6, 4.5, 5.5, 8.4, 10.1, 13.1, 14.5, 17.4, 18.2, 18.5, 20.5, 22.5, 23.5, 26.5, 28.5
1.2	Use tools, such as manipulatives or sketches, to model problems.	Lessons 1.1, 3.1, 5.1, 6.1, 6.2, 6.3, 7.1, 7.2, 7.4, 7.5, 8.1, 9.1, 11.1, 11.2, 11.3, 12.1, 12.2, 13.1, 14.1, 14.2, 14.3, 14.4, 14.5, 15.1, 15.2, 15.3, 16.1, 16.2, 16.3, 16.5, 17.1, 17.2, 17.4, 18.1, 18.2, 18.3, 19.1, 20.1, 20.3, 22.1, 23.1, 23.2, 24.1, 24.3, 24.6, 25.1, 25.2, 25.3, 26.1, 26.2, 26.3, 27.1, 28.1
2.0	Students solve problems and justify their reasoning:	Lessons 1.1, 1.3, 1.4, 2.4, 2.5, 3.4, 4.2, 4.4, 5.2, 5.3, 6.2, 6.3, 6.4, 7.1, 7.5, 8.2, 9.4, 9.5, 10.1, 10.2, 10.4, 11.2, 11.3, 12.3, 12.5, 13.1, 13.2, 13.3, 13.4, 14.2, 14.3, 14.5, 15.4, 15.5, 16.4, 17.2, 17.4, 18.1, 18.2, 19.6, 21.2, 23.5, 24.2, 24.3, 24.5, 25.2, 25.4, 25.5, 27.2, 27.3, 27.5, 28.4, 28.5
2.1	Explain the reasoning used and justify the procedures selected.	Lessons 1.5, 2.1, 2.2, 2.6, 4.2, 4.3, 5.2, 7.1, 7.2, 7.4, 8.1, 8.2, 8.4, 9.4, 10.4, 10.5, 11.2, 11.3, 11.4, 14.5, 16.4, 16.5, 17.3, 18.1, 25.3, 27.2, 27.4, 28.1, 28.4
2.2	Make precise calculations and check the validity of the results from the context of the problem.	Lessons 1.5, 8.5, 9.5, 10.3, 13.3, 13.5, 18.5, 19.6, 21.5, 22.5, 25.5, 26.5, 27.2, 28.5
3.0	Students note connections between one problem and another.	Lessons 1.3, 8.1, 9.1, 10.4, 11.1, 13.4, 13.5, 14.1, 18.4, 21.1, 21.2, 21.3, 21.4, 25.1, 26.1, 28.2, 28.3

Key Standards Handbook

I like to solve problems in math.

This is what problem solving means to me.

I add, subtract, multiply and divide.

18 − ☐ = 13

I talk about math.

I find math all around me.

I think about math in different ways.

I connect math to other ideas.

I have fun with math!

Name _____

Numbers To 1,000

You can show a number as **hundreds**, **tens**, and **ones**.

Workmat 6

Hundreds	Tens	Ones

Hundreds	Tens	Ones
3	5	3

_____

Use Your Skills

1. Show 8 ▢ ,

3 ▭ ,

and 9 ▪ .

Write the number. _____

Hundreds	Tens	Ones

2. Compare In which number does the 2 have the greatest value? Write the number word for that number.

421   182   209   _____

3. Show 5 ▢ , 2 ▭ ,

and 9 ▪ .

Write the number. _____

Hundreds	Tens	Ones

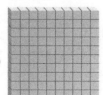

KEY **NS 1.1** Count, read, and write whole numbers to 1,000 and identify the place value for each digit.

Name _____

Compare and Order Numbers

Compare 314 and 321.

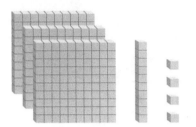 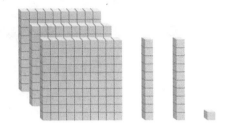

Compare hundreds. The hundreds are the same.
Compare tens. 1 ten is less than 2 tens.

So 314 is **less than** 321.

314 (<) 321

Compare the numbers. Then write the numbers from greatest to least.

125   298   129

298 > 129 > 125

> 298 is greater than 125 and 129.

> 129 is greater than 125.

> 125 and 129 both have 2 tens.

Use Your Skills

Compare the numbers.

Write >, <, or = in the ( ).

1. 294 ( ) 145   **2.** 314 ( ) 319

3. Write the numbers from least to greatest. 356   214   350   _____ < _____ < _____

4. Write the numbers from greatest to least. 892   298   928   _____ > _____ > _____

5. Explain How would you compare 176 and 165?

KEY **NS 1.3** Order and compare whole numbers to 1,000 by using the symbols <, =, >.

KSH3

Name _____

Relating Addition and Subtraction

You can **add** to check your **subtraction** .

Step 1 Subtract.

Tens	Ones
8	4
− 6	1
2	3

Step 2 Add the **difference** to the number you subtracted.

Tens	Ones
6	1
+ 2	3
8	4

The **sum** is the same as the number you subtracted from. The answer is correct.

Use Your Skills

Subtract. Then add to check your answer.

1. $\begin{array}{r} 65 \\ -\ 15 \end{array}$ + ▢ / ▢

2. $\begin{array}{r} 74 \\ -\ 63 \end{array}$ + ▢ / ▢

3. $\begin{array}{r} 48 \\ -\ 16 \end{array}$ + ▢ / ▢

4. $\begin{array}{r} 57 \\ -\ 12 \end{array}$ + ▢ / ▢

5. **Assess** Amy solved 14 + 23 = 37. Then she subtracted 23 from the sum. Is this a good way to check her work?

KEY **NS 2.1** Understand and use the inverse relationship between addition and subtraction (e.g., an opposite number sentence for 8+6=14 is 14−6=8) to solve problems and check solutions.

Name _____

Add to Find the Sum

Add 45 and 18.

Step 1

Add 5 ones and 8 ones.

Regroup 10 ones as 1 ten.

Tens	Ones
1 4 + 1	5 8
	3

Step 2

Add the tens.

Tens	Ones
1 4 + 1	5 8
6	3

Use Your Skills

Use Workmat 6 and Learning Tool 24.

Add.

1. 23
   + 69

2. 76
   + 13

3. 15
   + 65

4. 168
   + 107

5. 290
   + 315

6. 632
   + 208

7. **Generalize** How do you know when you need to regroup?

KEY NS 2.2 Find the sum or difference of two whole numbers up to three digits long.

Name _____

Subtract to Find the Difference

Find 32 – 16.

Step 1
Do you need more ones?

Tens	Ones
3	2
– 1	6

Step 2
Regroup 1 ten as 10 ones.

Tens	Ones
2 ~~3~~	12 ~~2~~
– 1	6

Step 3
Subtract the ones.

Tens	Ones
2 ~~3~~	12 ~~2~~
– 1	6
	6

Step 4
Subtract the tens.

Tens	Ones
2 ~~3~~	12 ~~2~~
– 1	6
1	6

Use Your Skills

Use Workmat 6 and Learning Tool 24. Subtract.

1. 75
  – 16

2. 32
  – 23

3. 69
  – 18

4. 473
  – 262

5. 734
  – 618

6. Justify Do you need to regroup to find 822 – 603? Explain why or why not.

KSH6

KEY **NS 2.2** Find the sum or difference of two whole numbers up to three digits long.

Name _____

Using Models to Multiply

You can use **equal groups** of counters to model
multiplication .

| 2 | 4 | 6 | 8 | 10 | 12 |

How many groups are there? _____

How many counters are in each group? _____ .

___6___ × ___2___ = ___12___

You can put counters into equal groups to model division.

Circle groups of 5 counters each.

How many groups are there? _____

___15___ ÷ ___5___ = ___3___

Use Your Skills

Use counters to model the problems.

Write the answer.

1. $4 \times 5 =$ _____   **2.** $7 \times 2 =$ _____   **3.** $3 \times 10 =$ _____

4. $18 \div 2 =$ _____   **5.** $12 \div 3 =$ _____   **6.** $10 \div 5 =$ _____

7. Apply Start with one group of 18 counters.
How many equal groups can you put them in?

KEY NS 3.0 Students model and solve simple problems involving multiplication and division.

KSH7

Name _____

Use Repeated Addition to Multiply

You can add equal groups to find a sum.

You can multiply equal groups to find the product.

Add.

$3 + 3 + 3 + 3 = 12$

Multiply.

$4 \times 3 = 12$

Use Your Skills

Find the product using repeated addition.

1. 3 pizzas with 8 slices each _____

2. 5 tables with 4 chairs each _____

3. 6 flowers with 8 petals each _____

4. **Apply** Lynn puts stickers in 3 rows. There are 5 stickers in each row. How could you multiply to find the total number of stickers? Write the number sentence.

Name _____

Use Arrays to Multiply

You can draw an array to help you multiply. An array is a drawing that shows objects in equal rows.

Janet planted 3 rows of tulips. In each row, she put 4 flowers. How many tulips did she plant in all?

Draw an array.

xxxx

xxxx

xxxx

3	×	4	=	12
number of rows		number of objects in each row		**product**

You can multiply in any order.

4	×	3	=	12
number of objects in each row		number of rows		**product**

Use Your Skills

Find the product using an array.
Skip count.

1. 4 shelves with 9 books each

2. 8 birdcages with 3 birds each

3. **Apply** Andre puts his rock collection on 4 shelves. There are 7 rocks on each shelf. Draw an array to show how to multiply. Then write a multiplication sentence.

KEY NS 3.1 Use repeated addition, arrays, and counting by multiples to do multiplication.

KSH9

Name _____

Divide into Equal Groups

How many groups of 3 can you make?

Step 1
Start with 6 shells.

Step 2
Circle groups of 3.

Step 3
Write a **division sentence** to show how many groups there are.
$6 \div 3 = 2$

Use Your Skills

1. Circle groups of 6.
Write the division sentence.

_____ ÷ _____ = _____

2. Subtract by 3s to divide.
Use the number line below.

$12 \div 3 =$ _____

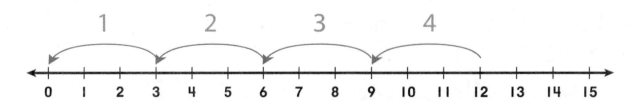

3. Apply How can 3 children share 9 crackers equally?

 KEY NS 3.2 Use repeated subtraction, equal sharing, and forming equal groups with remainders to do division.

Name _____

Multiply by 2, 5, and 10

There are 4 shirts. There are 5 buttons on each shirt.

How many buttons are there on 4 shirts?

You can skip count by 5 to add.

__5_,_10_,_15_,_20_

You can write a multiplication sentence to find the product.

__4_ × __5_ = _20_

There are _20_ buttons in all.

Use Your Skills

Write how many in all.

Then write the multiplication sentence.

1. 8 groups of 2 = _____   **2.** 3 groups of 10 = _____

_____ × _____ = _____   _____ × _____ = _____

Multiply

3. 3 × 2 = _____   **4.** 2 × 5 = _____   **5.** 2 × 10 = _____

6. 3 × 5 = _____   **7.** 9 × 2 = _____   **8.** 7 × 5 = _____

9. Relate What two ways can you use skip counting to find how many roses are in 5 groups of 10 roses?

KEY NS 3.3 Know the multiplication tables of 2s, 5s, and 10s (to "times 10") and commit them to memory.

KSH11

Name _____

Comparing Fractions

Look at the fraction strips.

Name the **fraction** of the strip that is colored.

Then use >, <, and = to compare the fractions.

$\frac{1}{2}$ (>) $\frac{1}{3}$

Use Your Skills

Look at the fraction strips.

Name the fraction of the strip that is colored.

Then use >, <, and = to compare the fractions.

1. $\frac{1}{12}$ 1   _____

    $\frac{1}{4}$ 1   _____   _____ ◯ _____

2. $\frac{1}{8}$ 1   _____

    $\frac{1}{10}$ 1   _____   _____ ◯ _____

3. **Extend** Sally is putting the measuring cups for $\frac{1}{4}$, $\frac{1}{2}$, and $\frac{1}{8}$ in order from least to greatest. Order the measuring cups.

KEY NS 4.1 Recognize, name, and compare unit fractions from $\frac{1}{12}$ to $\frac{1}{2}$.

Name _____

Fractions as Part of a Group

Write a fraction for the part of the circle that is red.

_____ red part

_____ parts in all

$\frac{1}{3}$ of the circle is red.

Write a fraction for the circles that are red.

_____ red circle

_____ circles in all

$\frac{1}{3}$ of the circles are red.

Use Your Skills

Write the fraction for the shaded part.

1. 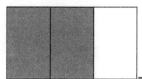 _____

2. 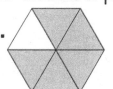 _____

3. 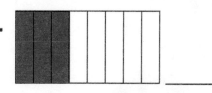 _____

Write the fraction for each part of the group.

4.  _____ blue triangles

 _____ red triangles

5. **Illustrate** Draw a pizza. Divide the pizza into 8 equal parts. Draw peppers on 3 slices. Which fractional part of the pizza has peppers?

KEY **NS 4.2** Recognize fractions of a whole and parts of a group (e.g., one-fourth of a pie, two-thirds of 15 balls).

Name _____

Name One Whole

Fractions can name one **whole** .

The whole circle is green.

$\frac{4}{4} = 1$

$\frac{4}{4}$ are green.

Use Your Skills

Write the fraction for the shaded part.

Circle the fractions that name one whole.

1. 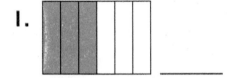 _____

2. 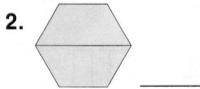 _____

3. 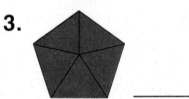 _____

4. **Conclude** Which fraction names one whole, $\frac{1}{6}$ or $\frac{6}{6}$? How do you know?

KEY NS 4.3 Know that when all fractional parts are included, such as four-fourths, the result is equal to the whole and to one.

Name _____

Money

Find the value of these coins.

Put your coins in order from greatest to least. Write the value of each coin. Count on. Write the value.

90¢

Use Your Skills

Find the value of the money to solve the problem.

1. Bill has the money below. How much does Bill have?

2. Anna used the coins below to buy a hair ribbon. How much did the ribbon cost?

3. Carl has $1.75. Mindy has the money below. Who has more money?

4. **Illustrate** Draw coins to show 67¢. Use the fewest coins.

KEY NS 5.1 Solve problems using combinations of coins and bills.

KSH15

Name _____

Use Money Symbols

A dollar bill equals 100¢.

Use a dollar sign and a decimal point to write amounts of one dollar or more.

The decimal point separates the dollars from the cents.

one dollar and
fifteen cents

115¢ $1.15

When you read the
money amounts aloud,
say "and" for the
decimal point.

Use Your Skills

Write the value of the money.

1.

2.

3.

4. Apply Use numbers to write the following money amount:
four dollars and twenty-eight cents.

KEY NS 5.2 Know and use the decimal notation and the dollar and cent symbols for money.

Name _____

Add in Any Order

You can add two numbers in any order and get the same sum.

_3_ + _5_ = _8_   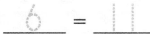 _5_ + _3_ = _8_

You can add three numbers in any order and get the same sum.

     _2_ + _3_ + _6_ = _11_

     _3_ + _2_ + _6_ = _11_

     _6_ + _3_ + _2_ = _11_

Use Your Skills

Write two addition sentences for each.

1.  ____ + ____ = ____   ____ + ____ = ____

2. ____ + ____ = ____   ____ + ____ = ____

3. **Formulate** How many addition sentences can you write with the addends 4, 9, and 3?

____ + ____ + ____ = ____   ____ + ____ + ____ = ____

____ + ____ + ____ = ____   ____ + ____ + ____ = ____

____ + ____ + ____ = ____   ____ + ____ + ____ = ____

KEY **AF 1.1** Use the commutative and associative rules to simplify mental calculations and to check results.

KSH17

Name _____

Measuring Length

Use a ruler to measure to the nearest inch.

0 1 2 3 4 5 6 7
inches

about ____5____ inches

Use a ruler to measure to the nearest **centimeter**.

0 1 2 3 4 5 6 7 8 9 10 11 12 13 14 15 16 17 18
centimeters

about ____10____ centimeters

Use Your Skills

Find these objects in your classroom.

Measure with an inch ruler.

Then measure with a centimeter ruler.

1. about _____ inches

   about _____ centimeters

2. about _____ inches

   about _____ centimeters

3. about _____ inches

   about _____ centimeters

4. **Estimate** Draw a line. Estimate how long it is in inches.
   Then use a ruler to find the length in inches.

Name _____

Plane and Solid Shapes

Flat shapes are called **plane shapes** .

They have **sides** , **angles** , and **vertices** .

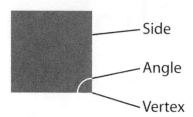
Side
Angle
Vertex

Three-dimensional shapes are called solid shapes.

They have **faces** , **edges** , and **vertices** .

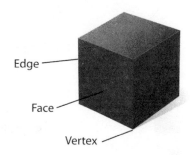
Edge
Face
Vertex

The face of a solid shape looks like a plane shape.

The face of the cube looks like a <u>square</u>.

Use Your Skills

Look at each solid shape. Circle the plane shape that matches a face of the solid shape. Then write the name of both shapes.

1.

   _____

   _____

2.

   _____

   _____

3.

   _____

   _____

4. **Predict** If you trace the face of a can of soup, what shape will you get?

KEY MG 2.0 Identify and describe the attributes of common figures in the plane and of common objects in space.

KSH19

Name _____

Identifying Plane and Solid Shapes

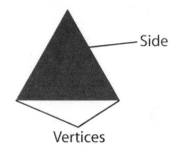

Side

Vertices

How many sides does a triangle have?
___3___ sides

How many vertices does a triangle
have? ___3___ vertices

How many faces does a rectangular
prism have? ___6___ faces

How many edges does a rectangular
prism have? ___12___ edges

How many vertices does a rectangular
prism have? ___8___ vertices

Use Your Skills

Read the clues.
Then draw a picture of the shape.

1. I am a solid
   shape. I have
   5 faces, 5 vertices,
   and 8 edges.
   What am I?

2. I am a plane
   shape. I have
   4 sides. All my
   sides are the same
   length. What am I?

3. I am a plane
   shape with
   6 sides. What
   am I?

4. I am a solid shape.
   I have no faces,
   vertices, or edges.
   What am I?

5. **Analyze** How is a sphere different from other solid shapes?

KEY **MG 2.1** Describe and classify plane and solid geometric shapes (e.g. circle, triangle, square, rectangle,
sphere, pyramid, cube, rectangular prism) according to the number and shape of faces, edges, and vertices.

Name _____

Change Shapes

You can cut apart shapes to make new shapes.

You can cut apart this square to make two <u>triangles</u>.

You can put two or more shapes together to make new shapes.

The rectangle is made up of three <u>squares</u>.

Use Your Skills

Draw one line to cut apart each shape to make two new shapes.

1.

2.

Put the shapes together to make a new shape.

3.

4.

5. Extend Which two solid shapes can you put together to make the shape of an ice cream cone?

KEY MG 2.2 Put shapes together and take them apart to form other shapes. (e.g., two congruent right triangles can be arranged to form a rectangle).

Name _____

Collecting Data

You can make a tally chart to keep count when you are collecting data.

Each **tally mark** represents I.

Ask 10 classmates which fruit they like best.

Make a tally mark on the chart for each answer.

Write the total number of votes for each fruit.

Fruits		
Fruit	**Tally Mark**	**Number**
Apple		
Orange		
Peach		
Banana		

Use Your Skills

Use the information in the tally chart to answer the question.

I. Which fruit was chosen most often? _____

2. Which fruit was chosen least often? _____

3. Did more classmates prefer bananas or peaches? _____

4. Extend Ask 5 more classmates to pick the fruit they like best. How does interviewing more people change your data?

KEY **SDAP 1.0** Students collect numerical data and record, organize, display, and interpret the data on bar graphs and other representations.

Name _____

Making Bar Graphs to Organize Data

Make a bar graph.

Use the information in the tally chart. Complete the bar graph.

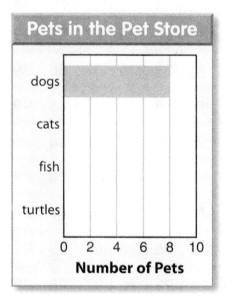

Use Your Skills

Use the information in the bar graph to answer the question.

1. How many fish does the pet store have? _____ fish

2. How many more dogs than cats are there? _____ dogs

3. The store has the same number of two pets.

Which pets are they? _____ and _____

4. Apply Suppose the pet store sells 4 dogs and buys 2 cats. How does this change the bar graph? Explain.

KEY **SDAP 1.0** Students collect numerical data and record, organize, display, and interpret the data on bar graphs and other representations.

Name _____

Identifying Number Patterns

You can use a hundred chart to find patterns.

1	2	3	4	5	6	7	8	9	10
11	12	13	14	15	16	17	18	19	20
21	22	23	24	25	26	27	28	29	30
31	32	33	34	35	36	37	38	39	40
41	42	43	44	45	46	47	48	49	50
51	52	53	54	55	56	57	58	59	60
61	62	63	64	65	66	67	68	69	70
71	72	73	74	75	76	77	78	79	80
81	82	83	84	85	86	87	88	89	90
91	92	93	94	95	96	97	98	99	100

Find the number 6.

Color it yellow.

Skip count by 2s. Color each number.

Stop when you color the number 42.

What pattern do you see?

Use Your Skills

Use a hundred chart to complete the patterns.

1. 5, 10, _____, _____, 25, _____

2. 10, 20, _____, 40, _____, _____

3. 4, 8, _____, 16, _____, 24

4. **Create** Make your own pattern. Show it to a classmate. Can he or she tell what comes next in the pattern?

KEY SDAP 2.0 Students demonstrate an understanding of patterns and how patterns grow and describe them in general ways.

Using the Table of Contents

These pages tell you about the book.

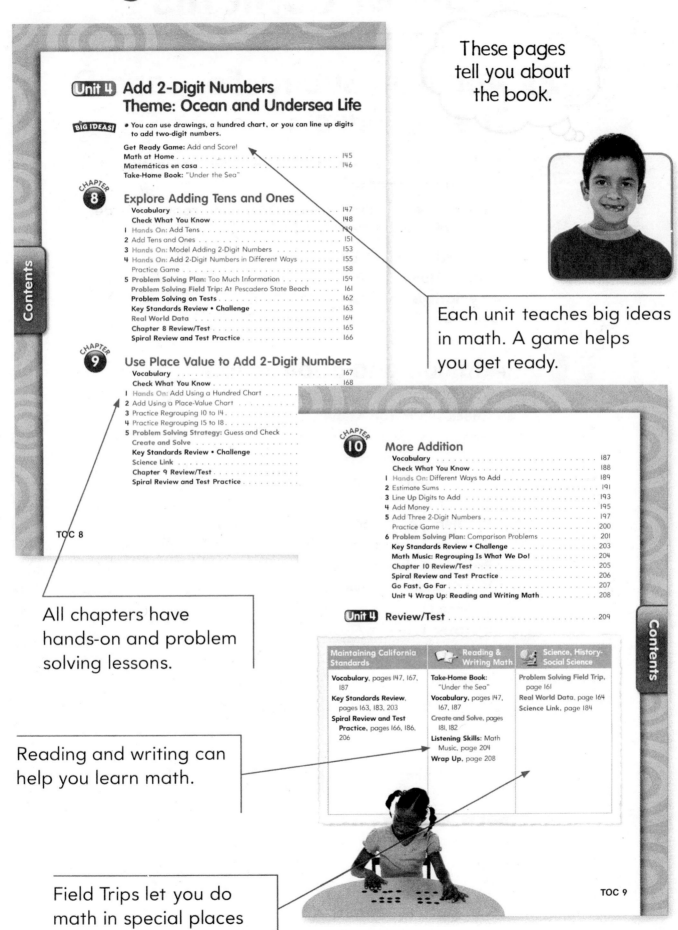

Each unit teaches big ideas in math. A game helps you get ready.

All chapters have hands-on and problem solving lessons.

Reading and writing can help you learn math.

Field Trips let you do math in special places in California.

TOC 9

Table of Contents

Contents

CHAPTER 2

Data and Graphs

Maintaining California Standards	**Reading & Writing Math**	**Science, History-Social Science**
Vocabulary, pages 3, 21	**Take-Home Book:** "Finding Ten"	**Problem Solving Field Trip,** page 15
Key Standards Review, pages 17, 37	**Vocabulary,** pages 3, 21	**Science Link,** page 18
Spiral Review and Test Practice, pages 20, 40	Create and Solve, pages 35, 36	
	Listening Skills: Math Music, page 38	
	Wrap Up, page 42	

Contents

Unit 2 Numbers and Patterns to 200
Theme: Performing Arts

BIG IDEAS!
- Each digit in a number has a different value based on its position.
- You can use place value to compare and order numbers.
- You can use number patterns to solve problems.

CHAPTER 3

Place Value

CHAPTER 4

Compare and Order Numbers to 200

Contents

TOC 4

CHAPTER
5

Number Patterns

Contents

 **Unit 3** **Money**
Theme: Shopping

 BIG IDEAS!
- Different combinations of coins can have the same value.
- When the value of money is more than the price, you can count on to give back change.

CHAPTER 6

Coins

Maintaining California Standards	Reading & Writing Math	Science, History-Social Science
Vocabulary, pages 103, 121 **Key Standards Review,** pages 117, 137 **Spiral Review and Test Practice,** pages 120, 140	**Take-Home Book:** "Money" **Vocabulary,** pages 103, 121 **Create and Solve,** pages 135, 136 **Listening Skills:** Math Music, page 138 **Wrap Up,** page 142	**Problem Solving Field Trip,** page 115 **Science Link,** page 118

Unit 4 Add 2-Digit Numbers
Theme: Ocean and Undersea Life

BIG IDEAS!

● You can use drawings, a hundred chart, or you can line up digits to add two-digit numbers.

CHAPTER 8

Explore Adding Tens and Ones

CHAPTER 9

Use Place Value to Add 2-Digit Numbers

Contents

CHAPTER 10 More Addition

Contents

Maintaining California Standards	Reading & Writing Math	Science, History- Social Science
Vocabulary, pages 147, 167, 187	**Take-Home Book:** "Under the Sea"	**Problem Solving Field Trip,** page 161
Key Standards Review, pages 163, 183, 203	**Vocabulary,** pages 147, 167, 187	**Real World Data,** page 164
Spiral Review and Test Practice, pages 166, 186, 206	**Create and Solve,** pages 181, 182	**Science Link,** page 184
	Listening Skills: Math Music, page 204	
	Wrap Up, page 208	

Unit 5 Subtract 2-Digit Numbers
Theme: Dinosaurs, Insects, and Collections

BIG IDEAS!
- You can use drawings, a hundred chart, or you can line up digits to subtract two-digit numbers.
- You can check a subtraction answer by adding.

Explore Subtracting Tens and Ones

Use Place Value to Subtract

Contents

CHAPTER 13

Relate 2-Digit Addition and Subtraction

Maintaining California Standards	Reading & Writing Math	Science, History-Social Science
Vocabulary, pages 213, 227, 245	**Take-Home Book:** "Our Big Sale"	**Problem Solving Field Trip,** page 239
Key Standards Review, pages 223, 241, 259	**Vocabulary,** pages 213, 227, 245	**Real World Data,** page 242
Spiral Review and Test Practice, pages 226, 244, 262	**Create and Solve,** pages 257, 258	**Science Link,** page 224
	Listening Skills: Math Music, page 260	
	Wrap Up, page 264	

Unit 6 Geometry and Fractions
Theme: Food

BIG IDEAS!

- You can name, describe, and compare shapes and combine or separate them to make other shapes.

- A fraction is a number that tells about part of a group, part of a whole, or a whole.

Shapes

More About Shapes

Fractions

CHAPTER 17

More About Fractions

 Contents

Maintaining California Standards	Reading & Writing Math	Science, History-Social Science
Vocabulary, pages 269, 289, 307, 325	**Take-Home Book:** "Shape Up at Pizza Palace"	**Problem Solving Field Trip,** pages 283, 337
Key Standards Review, pages 285, 303, 321, 339	**Vocabulary,** pages 269, 289, 307, 325	**Science Link,** pages 286, 304
Spiral Review and Test Practice, pages 288, 306, 324, 342	**Create and Solve,** pages 301, 302	**History-Social Science Link,** page 322
	Listening Skills: Math Music, page 340	
	Wrap Up, page 344	

 **Measurement**
Unit 7
Theme: School

 BIG IDEAS!
- You can measure length with different kinds of units.
- Minutes, hours, days, weeks, months, and years are units used to measure time.
- You can say the time on a clock by counting minutes or using fractions such as a "quarter-hour."

CHAPTER 18

Length

CHAPTER 19

Time and Calendar

Maintaining California Standards	Reading & Writing Math	Science, History-Social Science
Vocabulary, pages 349, 367 **Key Standards Review**, pages 363, 383 **Spiral Review and Test Practice**, pages 366, 386	**Take-Home Book:** "A New School for Paul Bunyan" **Vocabulary**, pages 349, 367 Create and Solve, pages 381, 382 **Listening Skills:** Math Music, page 384 **Wrap Up,** page 388	**Problem Solving Field Trip,** page 361 **Science Link,** page 364

Contents

Unit 8 Multiplication and Division
Theme: Insects and Nature

BIG IDEAS!

- When you multiply, you join equal groups.
- When you divide, you separate equal groups.
- When you divide, there are sometimes remainders that do not make an equal group.

Multiplication

Multiply by 2, 5, or 10

CHAPTER 22 Division

Contents

 **Unit 9** **Numbers and Patterns to 1,000**
Theme: Transportation

 BIG IDEAS!
- You can show how many ones, tens, and hundreds are in a number.
- You can use symbols such as +, =, <, and > to tell about numbers.
- You can use a decimal point and a dollar sign to show dollars and cents.

CHAPTER 23

Numbers to 1,000

Contents

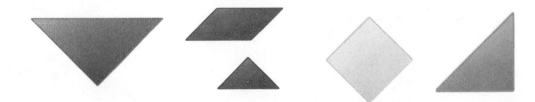

CHAPTER 24

Use Numbers to 1,000

Maintaining California Standards	Reading & Writing Math	Science, History-Social Science
Vocabulary, pages 449, 467 **Key Standards Review**, pages 463, 483 **Spiral Review and Test Practice**, pages 466, 486	**Take-Home Book:** "Auto Factory" **Vocabulary**, pages 449, 467 Create and Solve, pages 481, 482 **Listening Skills:** Math Music, page 484 **Wrap Up,** page 488	**Problem Solving Field Trip,** page 461 **Science Link,** page 464

Contents

Unit 10 Add and Subtract 3-Digit Numbers
Theme: Space

BIG IDEAS!

- When you add a three-digit number, you may have to regroup the ones, tens, or hundreds.

- When you subtract from a three-digit number, you may have to regroup the tens or hundreds.

- You can show a number sentence that relates to an addition or subtraction situation.

Add 3-Digit Numbers

Subtract 3-Digit Numbers

Contents

Maintaining California Standards	Reading & Writing Math	Science, History-Social Science
Vocabulary, pages 493, 511, 529, 547 **Key Standards Review,** pages 507, 525, 543, 563 **Spiral Review and Test Practice,** pages 510, 528, 546, 566	**Take-Home Book:** "You Can Be a Winner!" **Vocabulary,** pages 493, 511, 529, 547 **Create and Solve,** pages 523, 524 **Listening Skills:** Math Music, page 564 **Wrap Up,** page 568	**Problem Solving Field Trip,** pages 505, 561 **Science Link,** pages 508, 526 **History-Social Science Link,** page 544

Contents

Name _____

What I Know About Math

1. I can write the number that comes after 59.

_____

2. I can add two numbers

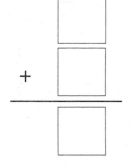

---

3. I can draw a line 3 inches long.

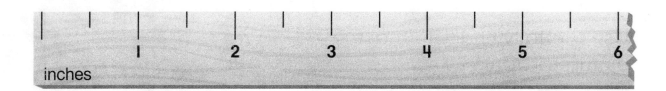

---

4. I can name these solid shapes. Match each figure with the correct name.

Sphere

Pyramid

Cube

5. I can find the value.

_____ ¢

---

6. I can color to show $\frac{1}{2}$.

 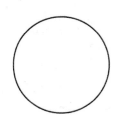

Take a Survey: Graphing

1. Ask 10 friends which of these animals from Africa is their favorite. Make a tally chart.

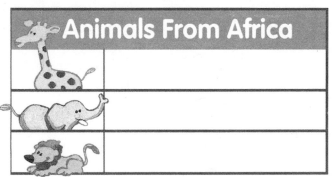 Animals From Africa	

2. Use the tally chart to make a picture graph.

Animals From Africa	
giraffe	
elephant	
lion	

Key: Each 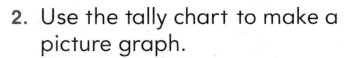 stands for 2 votes

3. Now make a bar graph from the picture graph.

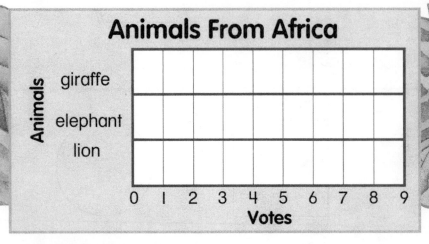

Animals From Africa

Animals: giraffe, elephant, lion
Votes: 0 1 2 3 4 5 6 7 8 9

Talk About It

4. Which is your favorite animal from Africa? How would the graph change if your vote were shown?

B2 BTS

Name _____

Number Patterns

You can make pairs with even numbers.

You can not make pairs with odd numbers.

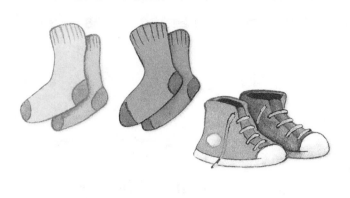

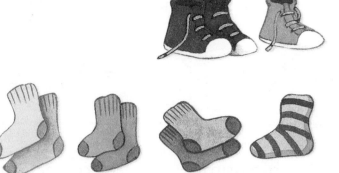

Write the odd numbers between 2 and 10.

1. _____ _____ _____ _____

Write the even numbers between 1 and 9.

2. _____ _____ _____ _____

Skip count by 2s from 2 to 16.

3. _____ _____ _____ _____ _____ _____ _____ _____

Skip count by 5s from 5 to 40.

4. _____ _____ _____ _____ _____ _____ _____ _____

Skip count by 10s from 10 to 80.

5. _____ _____ _____ _____ _____ _____ _____ _____

Talk About It

6. Is the number 15 an odd or an even number? How did you decide?

Rounding and Estimation

Use this number line to round numbers to the nearest 10.

1. 21 _____   2. 13 _____   3. 8 _____   4. 17 _____   5. 26 _____

Use this number line to round numbers to the nearest 10.

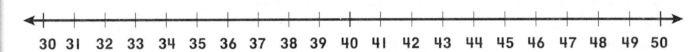

6. 42 _____   7. 36 _____   8. 44 _____   9. 35 _____   10. 31 _____

Round each number and estimate the sum.

11. 22 + 18 _____   12. 79 + 11 _____

13. 82 + 16 _____   14. 38 + 15 _____

Talk About It

15. How might rounding and estimation help you in a store?

Name _____

Count Coins

Draw a line between the same amounts of money.

1.

2.

3.

4.

Talk About It

5. What coins can you use to make 65¢?

Trading Bills

1. Cross out the bills that are **not** a fair trade for a $20 bill.

2. Match the money with the price.

$16.00

$12.00

$18.00

3. **Talk About It** What bills can you use to make $45?

B6 BTS

Name _____ _____

Basic Facts

You know the strategies that can help you with addition and subtraction facts.

Use counting on to solve.

1.	2.	3.	4.	5.
8 +2	6 +3	2 +9	3 +7	9 +3

Use doubles to solve.

6.	7.	8.	9.	10.
3 +3	7 +7	6 +6	5 +5	4 +4

Use counting back to solve.

11.	12.	13.	14.	15.
9 −2	11 −2	10 −3	12 −2	10 − 2

Use related facts to subtract.

16.	17.	18.	19.	20.
12 −9	14 −6	15 −7	11 −5	12 − 4

Talk About It

21. What strategy would you use to solve 12 − 3? Why?

Fact Families

Complete the fact family.

1.

17	
8	9

$$\begin{array}{r} 8 \\ +\ 9 \\ \hline \end{array}$$

$$\begin{array}{r} \\ +\ \\ \hline \end{array}$$

$$\begin{array}{r} 17 \\ -\ 8 \\ \hline \end{array}$$

$$\begin{array}{r} \\ -\ \\ \hline \end{array}$$

2.

18	
9	9

$$\begin{array}{r} 9 \\ +\ \\ \hline \end{array}$$

$$\begin{array}{r} 18 \\ -\ \\ \hline \end{array}$$

3.

16	
9	7

$$\begin{array}{r} 9 \\ +\ \\ \hline \end{array}$$

$$\begin{array}{r} 7 \\ +\ \\ \hline \end{array}$$

$$\begin{array}{r} 16 \\ -\ 9 \\ \hline \end{array}$$

$$\begin{array}{r} 16 \\ -\ \\ \hline \end{array}$$

Talk About It

4. Look at Exercise 2. Why are there only two facts?

Name _____

Missing Addends

Find and write the missing number.

1. $6 + \boxed{} = 13$

   $13 - 6 = \underline{}$

2. $5 + \boxed{} = 10$

   $10 - 5 = \underline{}$

3. $8 + \boxed{} = 11$

   $11 - 8 = \underline{}$

4. $9 + \boxed{} = 15$

   $15 - 9 = \underline{}$

5. $7 + \boxed{} = 12$

   $12 - 7 = \underline{}$

6. $4 + \boxed{} = 13$

   $13 - 4 = \underline{}$

7. $7 + \boxed{} = 14$

   $14 - 7 = \underline{}$

8. $6 + \boxed{} = 14$

   $14 - 6 = \underline{}$

9. $8 + \boxed{} = 16$

   $16 - 8 = \underline{}$

10. $3 + \boxed{} = 10$

    $10 - 3 = \underline{}$

11. $9 + \boxed{} = 12$

    $12 - 9 = \underline{}$

12. $7 + \boxed{} = 15$

    $15 - 7 = \underline{}$

Talk About It

13. Why can you use subtraction to check addition?

Patterns

Circle the one that is likely to come next.

1.

2.

3.

4.

Talk About It

5. How do you know which part of the pattern repeats?

Name _____

Measurement

1. Circle the object that is longer.

2. Circle the object that is shorter.

3. Circle the object that weighs more.

4. Circle the object that weighs less.

5. Circle the object that can hold less.

6. Circle that object that can hold more.

Talk About It

7. How can you compare the length of two objects?

Geometry

1. Color the spheres blue.
   Color the cubes green.
   Color the pyramids red.
   Color the cones yellow.

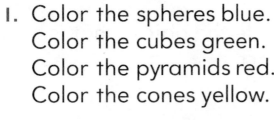
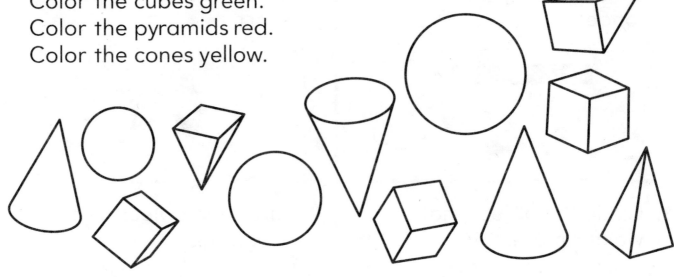

2. Color the triangles red.

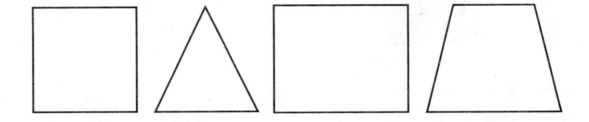

3. Color the squares yellow.

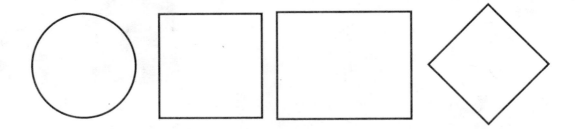

Talk About It

4. How do you know that the figures you colored in Problem 3 are squares?

Name _____

Duration and Sequence of Events

1. Circle the activity that usually lasts the longest.

2. Circle the activity that is over the quickest.

Circle the unit you would use to tell

3. the age of your classmate.

   hours   days   weeks   years

4. how long it takes to get to school.

   minutes   hours   days   weeks

5. how long you sleep at night.

   minutes   hours   weeks   months

6. how long a camping trip lasts.

   minutes   days   months   years

7. Write 1, 2, 3 to show the correct order.

Talk About It

8. Tell a story about 3 activities you do each day. Put them in order.

Telling Time

Show the time in two ways.

1. 7 o'clock

 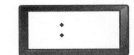

2. 5 o'clock

 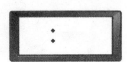

Write the time the clock shows.

3.

4.

Draw the time that comes 1 hour later.

5.

6.

Write the time that comes a half-hour later.

7. 8:00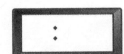

8.  4:30

Talk About It

9. Name some reasons you need to be able to tell time.

Unit

Houghton Mifflin
California Math

Addition, Subtraction, and Data

BIG IDEAS!

- You can use the idea that adding and subtracting are opposites to solve problems.

- You can use numbers from tables and graphs to understand facts about the real world.

Songs and Games

 Math Music Track 1
How Many Instruments?

eGames
www.eduplace.com/camap/

Literature

Read Aloud Big Book
- Hannah's Collections

Math Readers

First to Ten

How to Play

1. Each player will use one ten frame on the workmat.

2. Player 1 holds and drops all 10 counters. Place the counters that land red side up on the ten frame.

3. Say the addition and subtraction fact for 10 shown on the ten frame.

4. Player 2 takes a turn and does the same.

5. On Player 1's next turn, hold and drop the remaining counters.

6. Continue taking turns until one player has all 10 counters on their ten frame.

What You Need	
2 players	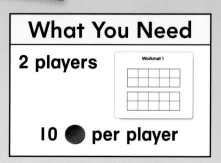
10 ● per player	

KEY NS 2.2 Find the sum or difference of two whole numbers up to three digits long.
Also **NS 2.0, MR 1.2, MR 2.2**

Education Place
Visit **www.eduplace.com/camap/** for eGames and Brain Teasers.

Math at Home

Dear Family,

My class is starting Unit I, **Addition, Subtraction, and Data.** I will be learning strategies to help me add and subtract facts. I will also learn how to make and read different kinds of graphs. You can help me learn these vocabulary words, and we can do the Math Activity together.

From,

_____

Vocabulary

fact family A group of related addition and subtraction facts that use the same numbers

$$6 + 9 = 15 \qquad 15 - 9 = 6$$
$$9 + 6 = 15 \qquad 15 - 6 = 9$$

The fact family above uses the numbers 6, 9, and 15.

bar graph Graph that shows data with colored bars

Favorite Fair Games

Number of Children

10
8
6
4
2
0
ring toss   sack race
Game

Education Place
Visit **www.eduplace.com/camaf/** for
- eGames and Brain Teasers
- Math at Home in other languages

Family Math Activity

Game for 2 players: Put 10 beans on a table. The first player closes his or her eyes. The second player hides some of the beans in his or her hand. The first player looks at the table, tells how many beans are hidden, and says a number sentence for the beans. Players take turns hiding the beans.

Literature

These books link to the math in this unit. Look for them at the library.

- **Math All Around: Sorting at the Ocean** by Jennifer Rozines Roy and Gregory Roy (*Marshall Cavendish*, 2006)
- **Math Appeal** by Greg Tang Illustrated by Harry Briggs
- **The Math Curse** by Jon Scieszka Illustrated by Lane Smith

Estimada familia:

Mi clase está comenzando la Unidad I, **Suma, resta y datos**. Aprenderé estrategias para realizar operaciones de suma y resta. También aprenderé a hacer y leer diferentes tipos de gráficas. Me pueden ayudar a aprender estas palabras de vocabulario y podemos hacer juntos la Actividad de matemáticas para la familia.

De:

_____

Vocabulario

familia de operaciones Grupo de operaciones relacionadas de suma y resta que usan los mismos números.

$$6 + 9 = 15 \qquad 15 - 9 = 6$$
$$9 + 6 = 15 \qquad 15 - 6 = 9$$

La familia de operaciones de arriba usa los números 6, 9 y 15.

gráfica de barras Gráfica en la que una barra de color muestra los datos.

Juegos de feria favoritos

(Número de niños vs. Juego: lanzamiento de anillos, carrera de costales)

Education Place
Visite **www.eduplace.com/camaf/** para
• Juegos en línea y acertijos
• Matemáticas en casa en otros idiomas

Actividad de matemáticas para la familia

Juego para 2 jugadores. Coloquen 10 frijoles en una mesa. El primer jugador cierra sus ojos. El segundo jugador agarra algunos frijoles y los esconde en su mano. Después, el primer jugador mira la mesa, dice cuántos frijoles están escondidos y dice un enunciado numérico para los frijoles. Los jugadores se turnan para esconder los frijoles.

Analízalo
Tienes 6 frijoles en tu mano porque 4 + 6 es igual a 10 frijoles.

Literatura

Estos libros hablan sobre las matemáticas de esta unidad. Búscalos en la biblioteca.

• **¿Cuántos osos hay?** por Cooper Edens (Atheneum, 1994)

• **Hagamos una gráfica** por Elena Martin

2

Finding Ten

written by Mike Mason

This Take-Home Book belongs to

Reading and Writing Math

This take-home book will help you review tens and ones.

When Keri got home, she got busy! Look at the great things she made for the sale!

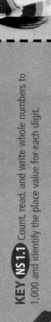

KEY **NS 1.1** Count, read, and write whole numbers to 1,000 and identify the place value for each digit.

Keri will make things for a craft fair.
Keri has a list of things she needs to
get for her crafts.
Can you read her list?

12 Stickers
24 buttons
35 beads
16 Stars
18 Clothespins

Keri needs 18 clothespins.
Clothespins are sold in sets of
ten or one at a time.
Circle the clothespins you think
Keri will buy.

Keri needs 12 stickers for her project.
The stickers are sold in sets of ten or one at a time.
Circle the stickers you think Keri will buy.

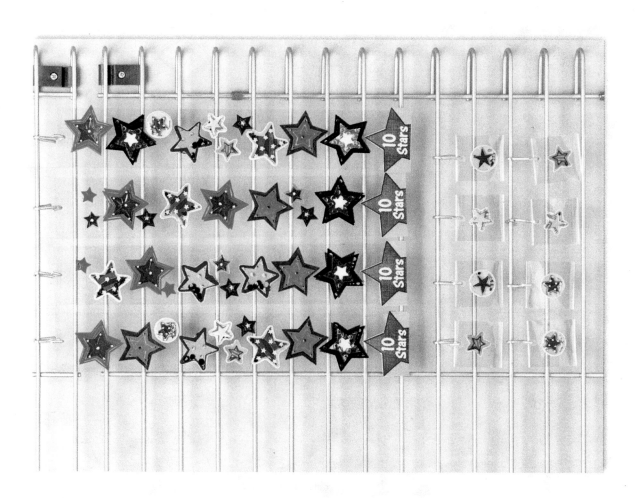

Keri needs 16 stars. Stars are sold in sets of ten or as single stars.
Circle the stars you think Keri will buy.

Keri needs 24 buttons. The buttons are sold in sets of ten or as single buttons. Circle the buttons you think Keri will buy.

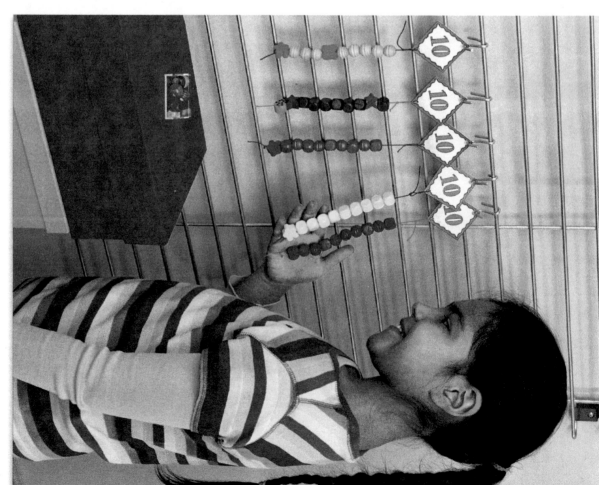

Next, Keri needs 33 beads. Beads are sold in sets of ten or as single beads. Circle the beads you think Keri will buy.

5

Addition and Subtraction

Vocabulary

Here are some vocabulary words you will learn in the chapter.

sum The result when numbers are added

$$4 + 3 = 7$$

↑
sum

addend The parts in an addition sentence

$$3 + 5 = 8$$

↑   ↑
addends

fact family All the addition and subtraction facts that use the same numbers

$$3 + 7 = 10 \qquad 10 - 3 = 7$$
$$7 + 3 = 10 \qquad 10 - 7 = 3$$

See English-Spanish Glossary pages 573–589.

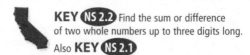 **KEY NS 2.2** Find the sum or difference of two whole numbers up to three digits long.
Also **KEY NS 2.1**

 **Education Place**
Visit **www.eduplace.com/camap/**
for the eGlossary and eGames.

three **3**

Name _____

Use the table to solve.

Fair Prizes	
balloons	6
pinwheels	3
ribbons	1
whistles	4

1. How many prizes are there in all?

   _____ prizes

2. How many pinwheels and whistles are there?

   _____ + _____ = _____ pinwheels and whistles

3. Which 2 prizes can you add to make 10?

   _____

   Write the number sentence.

   _____ + _____ = _____

4. Which 3 prizes can you add to make 10?

   _____

   Write the number sentence.

   _____ + _____ + _____ = _____

5. How many more whistles are there than ribbons?

   _____ – _____ = _____ more whistles

Use this page to review important skills needed for this chapter.

Chapter 1 Lesson 1

Make Ten to Add

 **Learn**

Making a 10 can help
you add 7, 8, and 9.

Find 9 + 4.
Use Workmat 1 and ⬤ ⚪.

Step 1

Show 9.
Then show 4.

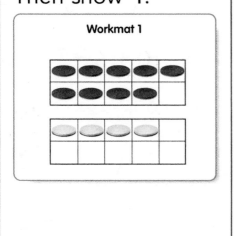

Workmat 1

Step 2

Move a counter
to make 10.

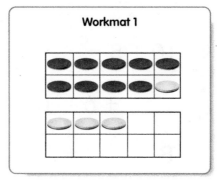

Workmat 1

9 + 4 is the same
as 10 + 3.

Step 3

Add. 9 + 4 = ___13___

▶ **Guided Practice**

Use Workmat 1 and ⬤ ⚪.
Add.

Think!
I add 2 to 8 to make 10.

1. 8 + 5 = ____

2. 9 + 7 = ____

3. 9
   +8

4. 5
   +9

5. 7
   +8

6. 7
   +4

7. 8
   +8

8. 8
   +6

9. (123) **Math Talk** How does making 10 help you
   add 9 + 7?

KEY NS 2.2 Find the sum or difference of two
whole numbers up to three digits long.
Also NS 2.0, MR 2.0

MR 1.2 Use tools, such as manipulatives or sketches,
to model problems.

five **5**

Remember!
Make 10 to help
you add.

Use Workmat 1 and ⬤ ⬭. Add.

10.	9	11.	8	12.	6	13.	7	14.	2	15.	8
	+6		+8		+8		+6		+9		+5
	15										

16.	9	17.	4	18.	9	19.	4	20.	5	21.	8
	+8		+8		+5		+9		+7		+6

Use Workmat 1 and ⬤ ⬭.
Complete each addition sentence.

22. 10 + ____ = 14

9 + ____ = 14

8 + 6 = ____

____ + 7 = 14

23. 10 + 5 = ____

____ + 6 = 15

8 + ____ = 15

7 + 8 = ____

24. 10 + 6 = ____

9 + ____ = 16

8 + ____ = 16

7 + 9 = ____

Problem Solving: Number Sense

Use the picture to solve.

25. Lim Sing has 15 tickets. Some of the tickets are in her pocket. The rest are shown below. How many tickets are in her pocket?

Draw or write to explain.

_____ tickets

🏠 **At Home** Ask your child to explain how making a 10 can help you find 8 + 4 and 9 + 2.

En casa Pida a su niño que explique cómo hacer una decena puede ayudarlo a hallar 8 + 4 y 9 + 2.

Chapter 1 Lesson 2

Add Three Numbers

▶ **Learn**

Objective
Add three numbers using the associative rule.

Vocabulary
sum

You can add numbers in different ways and get the same **sum.**

Find $2 + 3 + 8$.
Add two numbers first.
Then add the third number.

First find $2 + 8$.
The sum is 10.

The third addend is 3.
$10 + 3 = 13$.

Look for two addends that make 10. Add them first.

Workmat 1

Workmat 1

$2 + 3 + 8 = \underline{}$

▶ **Guided Practice**

Look for two numbers to add first.
Find the sum.

1. 4
    6
  + 2

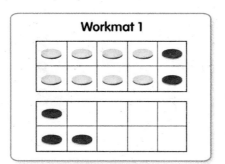
Think!
4 + 6 make 10.
Then I add 2 more.

2. 8
    6
  + 2

3. 6
    3
  + 2

4. 5
    8
  + 2

5. **(123) Math Talk** Can adding the numbers in any order help you check your answer? Explain how.

KEY AF 1.1 Use the commutative and associative rules to simplify mental calculations and to check results.
Also **MR 2.2**

AF 1.0 Model, represent, and interpret number relationships to create and solve problems involving addition and subtraction.

▶ Practice

Look for two numbers
to add first.
Find the sum.

Remember!
You can add numbers
in any order.

6. 4
    2
  +8
  ――
   14

7. 3
    1
  +5
  ――

8. 9
    0
  +1
  ――

9. 6
    7
  +3
  ――

10. 4
     2
   +4
   ――

11. 5
     1
   +9
   ――

12. 8
     0
   +2
   ――

13. 5
     5
   +5
   ――

14. 1
     4
   +6
   ――

15. 1
     4
   +9
   ――

16. 2
     8
   +3
   ――

17. 2
     7
   +0
   ――

18. 7 + 7 + 1 = _____

19. 2 + 3 + 4 = _____

20. 5 + 6 + 0 = _____

21. 8 + 1 + 9 = _____

22. 7 + 6 + 3 = _____

23. 6 + 7 + 4 = _____

Problem Solving: Reasoning

Use what you know about adding
in any order to find the missing numbers.

24. 3 + 2 + 4 = 2 + _7_

25. 6 + 0 + 2 = 0 + _____

26. 4 + 1 + 6 = 6 + _____

27. 5 + 2 + 1 = 1 + _____

28. 1 + 7 + 3 = 7 + _____

29. 2 + 4 + 5 = 5 + _____

At Home Ask your child to explain
two different ways to add 3 + 7 + 1.

En casa Pida a su niño que explique dos
maneras diferentes de sumar 3 + 7 + 1.

Name _____

Chapter 1 Lesson 3

Fact Families

 **Explore**

This **fact family** uses the numbers 8, 6, and 2.
8 is the whole. 6 and 2 are the parts.

Hands On ✋

Objective
Use a part-part-whole model to add and subtract.

Vocabulary
fact family

Step 1

Model the parts with ●.

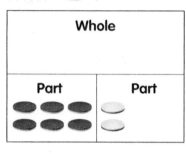

Now move all the ● ○ to show the whole.

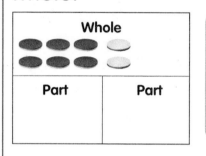

Whole	
8	
Part	**Part**
6	2

part + part = whole   _6_ + _2_ = _8_

Write **2** addition facts.   _2_ + _6_ = _8_

Step 2

Model the whole with ●.

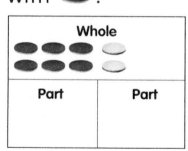

Now take away 6. How many ● are left?

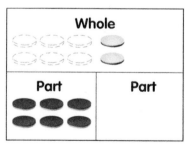

Whole	
8	
Part	**Part**
6	2

whole − part = part   _8_ − _6_ = _2_

Write **2** subtraction facts. _8_ − _2_ = _6_

You have written the fact family for the numbers 2, 6, and 8.

1. (123) **Math Talk** How many facts are in the fact family for 3, 3, and 6? Why?

 KEY NS 2.1 Understand and use the inverse relationship between addition and subtraction (e.g., an opposite number sentence for 8 + 6 = 14 is 14 − 6 = 8) to solve problems and check solutions.

MR 3.0 Note connections between one problem and another.
Also **NS 2.0, MR 1.2, MR 2.0, KEY NS 2.2**

▶ Extend

Use ⬤.
Write the fact families.

2. 9, 4, 5

Whole	
9	
Part	**Part**
4	5

___4___ + ___5___ = ___9___   ___5___ + ___4___ = ___9___

___9___ − ___4___ = ___5___   ___9___ − ___5___ = ___4___

3. 6, 3, 9

_____ + _____ = _____   _____ + _____ = _____

_____ − _____ = _____   _____ − _____ = _____

4. 7, 1, 8

_____ + _____ = _____   _____ + _____ = _____

_____ − _____ = _____   _____ − _____ = _____

5. 8, 6, 14

_____ + _____ = _____   _____ + _____ = _____

_____ − _____ = _____   _____ − _____ = _____

6. 4, 6, 10

_____ + _____ = _____   _____ + _____ = _____

_____ − _____ = _____   _____ − _____ = _____

7. Choose 3 numbers and write the fact family for those numbers.

_____

_____

At Home Ask your child to explain how he or she knows if four facts are in the same fact family.

En casa Pida a su niño que explique cómo sabe si cuatro operaciones pertenecen a la misma familia de operaciones.

Name _____

Missing Addends

Vocabulary
addend

▶ **Learn**

You can use related facts to find a missing **addend**.

Step 1

$7 + \boxed{} = 12$

Show the whole.

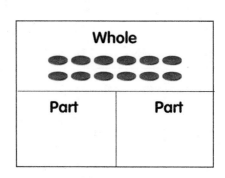

Whole
Part	Part

Step 2

Subtract the part you know.

$12 - 7 = \underline{}$

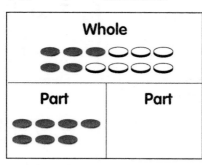

Whole
Part	Part

Step 3

How many are left? Write the missing addend.

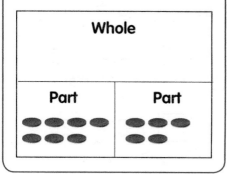

Whole
Part	Part

The missing addend is __5__.

▶ **Guided Practice**

Use a related fact to find the missing addend.

1. $3 + \boxed{} = 7$

   $7 - 3 = \underline{}$.

   The missing addend is _____.

   Think!
   I can subtract 3 from 7 to find the missing addend.

2. $9 + \boxed{} = 15$

   $15 - 9 = \underline{}$

   The missing addend is _____.

3. $7 + \boxed{} = 16$

   $16 - 7 = \underline{}$

   The missing addend is _____.

4. **123 Math Talk** What subtraction fact can you use to find the missing addend in $5 + \boxed{} = 11$?

KEY NS 2.1 Understand and use the inverse relationship between addition and subtraction (e.g., an opposite number sentence for 8 + 6 = 14 is 14 − 6 = 8) to solve problems and check solutions.

Also **KEY NS 2.2, NS 2.0, MR 3.0, MR 2.0**

▶ Practice

Use a related fact to find the missing addend.

5. $4 + \square = 13$

$13 - \underline{4} = \underline{9}$.

The missing addend is _____.

Whole
●●●●●● ●●●●●

Part	Part

6. $\square + 5 = 14$

$14 - \underline{} = \underline{}$

7. $3 + \square = 11$

$11 - \underline{} = \underline{}$

8. $\square + 8 = 12$

$12 - \underline{} = \underline{}$

9. $7 + \square = 13$

$13 - \underline{} = \underline{}$

10. $8 + \square = 15$

$15 - \underline{} = \underline{}$

11. $\square + 8 = 13$

$13 - \underline{} = \underline{}$

Problem Solving: Reasoning

Use the picture to solve.

12. Susie makes 15 finger puppets at the fair. Some of the puppets are in a box. The rest are shown below. How many puppets are in the box?

Draw or write to explain.

_____ puppets

At Home Have your child explain how to find the missing addend in $4 + \underline{} = 15$.

En casa Pida a su niño que explique cómo hallar el sumando que falta en $4 + \underline{} = 15$.

Name _____

Write a Number Sentence

▶ **Learn**

Objective
Write a number sentence to solve a problem.

There are 15 birdhouses for sale.
Only 8 birdhouses are sold.
How many birdhouses are not sold?

Understand

What do you know?
• 15 birdhouses are for sale.
• 8 birdhouses are sold.

Plan

Use the part-part-whole mat to show what you already know.

birdhouses	
15	
sold	not sold
8	

Solve

Solve for the other part.
Write a number sentence.

___15___ ◯ ___8___ = ___7___

___7___ birdhouses are not sold.

birdhouses	
15	
sold	not sold
8	7

Look Back

Does your answer make sense?
What helped you decide how to write the number sentence?

AF 1.2 Relate problem situations to number sentences involving addition and subtraction.
Also **AF 1.0, KEY NS 2.2, NS 2.0, MR 2.0, MR 2.2**

MR 2.1 Defend the reasoning used and justify the procedures selected.

1. 12 children make frames or cards. 9 children make frames. How many children make cards?

What do you know?

_____ children make frames or cards.

_____ children make frames.

What do you need to find?

_____

Write a number sentence.

_____ ◯ _____ = _____

Think!
12 is the whole.
9 is one part. I need to find the other part.

children	
_____	
frames	**cards**
_____	_____

_____ children

2. **Math Talk** How do you know when to write a subtraction sentence?

► **Problem Solving Practice**

Write a number sentence to solve.

3. There are 16 frames for sale. 9 are not sold. How many are sold?

_____ ◯ _____ = _____

_____ frames are sold.

frames	
_____	
not sold	**sold**
_____	_____

4. The students invite 5 people to the sale on Monday and 8 people on Tuesday. How many people are invited in all?

_____ ◯ _____ = _____

_____ people

both days	
_____	
Monday	**Tuesday**
_____	_____

At Home Ask your child to show an addition problem using a part-part-whole mat.

En casa Pida a su niño que muestre un problema de suma usando un tablero de parte-parte-entero.

Name _____

History-Social Science

State Indian Museum

California Field Trip

At the State Indian Museum

You can see and learn about California Native American history and way of life. You can learn how they make baskets and other artifacts. You can also see the clothes and instruments they use for dances.

Choose a way to solve.
Show your work.

1. There are **9** baskets in one case.
   There are **5** in another case.
   How many baskets are there in all?

   _____ baskets

basket

---

2. Max counts **10** headdresses in the museum. Janine counts **4** headdresses. How many do Max and Janine count in all?

   _____ headdresses

headdress

---

3. Cameron sees **12** photographs of Native American history. **5** are of people making baskets. How many photographs show people doing other activities?

   _____ photographs

photograph

KEY NS 2.2 Find the sum or difference of two whole numbers up to three digits long.
History-Social Science 2.1

MR 1.0 Make decisions about how to set up a problem.
Also **MR 1.1, MR 2.0**

fifteen **15**

Problem Solving on Tests
Listening Skills

Listen to your teacher read the problem.
Choose the correct answer.

Select a Strategy
Use a Hundred
    Chart
Draw a Picture
Use a Number
    Line
Act It Out

1. Which of the following numbers
   is between 3 and 5?

1	2	4	6
○	○	○	○

   Gr. 1 KEY **NS 1.1**

2. What number is 1 less than 56?

54	55	57	58
○	○	○	○

   Gr. 1 KEY **NS 2.3**

3.

2	5	7	9
○	○	○	○

   Gr. 1 KEY **NS 2.5**

4.

54	64	84	94
○	○	○	○

   Gr. 1 KEY **NS 2.3**

MR 1.0 Make decisions about how to set up
a problem.
MR 1.1 Determine the approach, materials, and
strategies to be used.

Education Place
Visit **www.eduplace.com/camap/** for
Test-Taking Tips and Extra Practice.

Name _____

 # Key Standards Review

Find the sum.

1.   6
   +2

2.   8
   +1

3.   7
   +4

4.   5
   +7

5.   6
   +5

6.   5
   +3

7.   7
   +7

8.   9
   +1

9.   10
   + 2

10.   6
    +6

11.   9
    +8

12.   10
    +10

Challenge   Number Sense

The key on the right shows how many points each letter is worth.

1. Find the sum for SPOT.

S   P   O   T
↓   ↓   ↓   ↓

1 + 3 + 2 + 4 = _____

O = 2
P = 3
S = 1
T = 4

2. Find the sum for TOPS.

T   O   P   S
↓   ↓   ↓   ↓

_____ + _____ + _____ + _____ = _____

Gr1 KEY NS 2.1 Know the addition facts (sums to 20) and the corresponding subtraction facts and commit them to memory.

seventeen 17

Rock Collections

Some people collect rocks as a hobby. Rocks can be made up of other smaller rocks. They can also be made of crystals. Solve.

1. Joe sorts his rock collection into three groups. How many rocks does Joe have all together?

   _____ + _____ + _____ = _____

   Joe has _____ rocks.

2. Maddy has different kinds of rocks in her collection. How many rocks does Maddy have in all?

   _____ + _____ + _____ = _____

   Maddy has _____ rocks.

3. Josh, Tom, and their father explore a California cavern. Josh sees 5 limestone rocks. Tom sees 3 limestone rocks. Their father sees 7 limestone rocks. How many do they see in all?

   _____ rocks

AF 1.0 Model, represent, and interpret number relationships to create and solve problems involving addition and subtraction.
Science ES 3.a

Name _____

Concepts and Skills

Add.   KEY NS 2.2

1. 5 + 7 = _____   2. 3 + 8 = _____   3. 4 + 9 = _____

Look for two numbers to add first. Find the sum.   KEY AF 1.1

4. 7 + 3 + 5 = _____   5. 4 + 6 + 8 = _____

Write the fact family.   KEY NS 2.1

6. 9, 2, 11   _____ + _____ = _____   _____ + _____ = _____

_____ – _____ = _____   _____ – _____ = _____

Find the missing addend.   KEY NS 2.1

7. [ ] + 7 = 13   8. 4 + [ ] = 12

13 – _____ = _____   12 – _____ = _____

Problem Solving   KEY NS 2.2, KEY NS 2.1, MR 2.0

9. Ana has 6 stuffed animals. She got more stuffed animals for her birthday. Now she has 13. How many stuffed animals did Ana get for her birthday?

_____ stuffed animals

Explain how you know.

_____

_____

Spiral Review and Test Practice

1. Which number is 1 more?　29

28	29	30	291
○	○	○	○

Gr.1 KEY NS 2.3 Page 29

2. What comes next in the pattern?

　○　　　　○　　　　○　　　　○

Gr.1 KEY SDAP 2.1 Page 207

3. What is the sum?

$$4 + 5 + 6$$

735	15	10	8
○	○	○	○

KEY AF 1.1 Page 7

4. Which is the missing addend?

$$\boxed{} + 7 = 12$$

12	7	5	4
○	○	○	○

KEY NS 2.1 Page 11

Education Place
Visit www.eduplace.com/camap/ for
Test-Taking Tips and Extra Practice.

Spiral Review

Vocabulary

Here are some vocabulary words you will learn in the chapter.

picture graph Uses symbols to show data

Fair Prizes	
soccer ball	★ ★ ★
jump rope	★
softball	★ ★

Key: Each ★ stands for 5 prizes.

bar graph Uses bars to show data

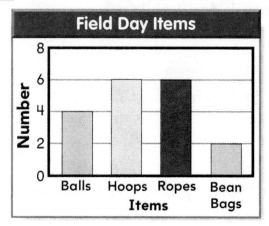

Field Day Items

mode The number in a data set that occurs the most

range The difference between the greatest and least numbers in a data set

See English-Spanish Glossary pages 573–589.

KEY SDAP 1.0 Collect numerical data and record, organize, display, and interpret the data on bar graphs and other representations. Also **SDAP 1.3**

Education Place
Visit www.eduplace.com/camap/ for the eGlossary and eGames.

twenty-one **21**

Name _____

1. Anna makes these tally marks to show how many children play hoops at field day. ⊬⊦ ||| How many tally marks does Anna make?

   _____ tally marks

2. Show how you would draw 6 tally marks. _____

Use the graph to solve.

3. What does this picture graph show?

   _____

4. Circle the sport that is chosen by the most children.

   jump rope   relay race   soccer

5. Circle the sport that is chosen by the fewest children.

   jump rope   relay race   soccer

Use this page to review important skills needed for this chapter.

Name _____

Make a Tally

▶ **Explore**

A **tally mark** is a way to keep track of what you are counting.

Ramon's school is having a fair.
Ask 10 classmates what prize they would like to win at a fair.
Make a tally mark on the chart for each answer.
Write the total number.

Tally Marks

| | stands for 1.

‖‖ stands for 5.

Prizes		
Prize	**Tally Marks**	**Number**
Pinwheel		_____
Balloon		_____
Toy Car		_____

Use the tally chart to answer the questions.

1. Which prize was chosen the most? _____

2. Which prize was chosen the least? _____

3. Did more classmates choose balloons or toy cars? _____

4. **123** **Math Talk** How does making tally marks help you keep track of your count?

SDAP 1.1 Record numerical data in systematic ways, keeping track of what has been counted. Also **SDAP 1.4, MR 2.1**

KEY SDAP 1.0 Collect numerical data and record, organize, display, and interpret the data on bar graphs and other representations.

twenty-three **23**

▶ **Extend**

Ask 10 classmates to choose which activity they would do at a fair.

Make a tally mark for each answer. Write the total number.

Fair Activities		
Activity	**Tally Marks**	**Number**
Games		_____
Crafts		_____
Music		_____

Use the tally chart to answer the questions.

5. How many classmates chose music?

   _____ classmates

6. Which activity was chosen the most?   _____

7. Which activity was chosen the least?   _____

8. Use the tally chart to complete the sentence.

   More children chose red balloons

   than _____ balloons.

9. How many more children chose green ballons than red?

   _____

Favorite Balloon Colors		
Color	**Tally Marks**	**Number**
red	||||	_4_
green	卌	_5_
blue			_1_

Name _____

Chapter 2 Lesson 2

Compare Data in Tables

▶ **Learn**

Objective
Compare data using tables.

Vocabulary
data

You can compare **data**, or information, in two tables.
The children in Jenny's class and Rick's class chose their favorite games at the street fair.

Look at the same line in each table. Then compare.

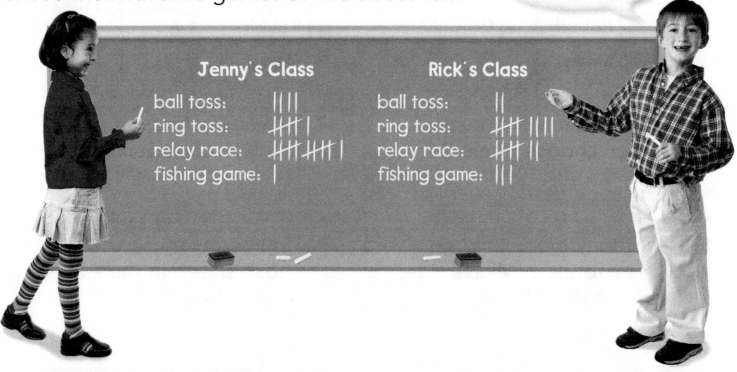

Jenny's Class

ball toss: ||||
ring toss: ||||
relay race: ||||||||||
fishing game: |

Rick's Class

ball toss: ||
ring toss: ||||||||
relay race: |||||||
fishing game: |||

▶ **Guided Practice**

Use the data to answer the questions.

1. In whose class did more children choose the relay race? _____

2. In whose class did more children choose the fishing game? _____

3. How many more children chose the ring toss in Rick's class than in Jenny's class? _____ children

4. How many more children chose the ball toss in Jenny's class than in Rick's class? _____ children

*Think!
I see more tallies for the relay race in Jenny's table.*

5. (123) **Math Talk** How did you find the answer for Exercise 3?

KEY SDAP 1.0 Collect numerical data and record, organize, display, and interpret the data on bar graphs and other representations.
Also **SDAP 1.4, MR 2.0, MR 2.1, MR 2.2**

AF 1.3 Solve addition and subtraction problems by using data from simple charts, picture graphs, and number sentences.

Practice

Remember!
When you use a table, read across the row.

These tables show children's favorite animals in the fair's petting zoo.

Use both tables to answer the questions.

Mina's Class	
Animal	**Number**
Pony	6
Rabbit	9
Sheep	3

Akio's Class	
Animal	**Number**
Pony	8
Rabbit	6
Sheep	5

6. In whose class did more children choose ponies?

Akio's class
_____

7. In whose class did more children choose rabbits?

_____

8. How many more children chose rabbits in Mina's class than in Akio's class?

_____ children

9. How many more children chose sheep in Akio's class than in Mina's class?

_____ children

10. How many children voted in Mina's class?

_____ children

11. How many children voted in all?

_____ children

Problem Solving: Reasoning

12. Use the clues to complete the table.
- There are 2 more cats than dogs.
- There are 4 dogs.
- The number of fish is the same as the number of birds.
- There are 12 pets in all.

Pets			
Cats	**Dogs**	**Fish**	**Birds**
_____	_____	_____	_____

At Home Ask your child to make tally charts sorting and counting the number of objects in two different rooms. Ask him or her to compare the information.

En casa Pida a su niño que haga tableros de conteo para clasificar y contar el número de objetos en dos ambientes diferentes de la casa. Pídale que compare la información.

Read a Picture Graph

Objective
Show data in tally charts and picture graphs.

Vocabulary
picture graph

▶ Learn

A **picture graph** uses pictures to show information. You can show the data from a tally chart in a picture graph.

Both tables show the same data.

Flags in the Parade

Color	Tally Marks
Blue	IIII
Red	HHT I
Green	IIII
Yellow	II

Flags in the Parade

Blue	⚑ ⚑
Red	⚑ ⚑ ⚑
Green	⚑ ⚑
Yellow	⚑

Key: Each ⚑ stands for 2 flags.

▶ Guided Practice

Use the picture graph to answer the question.

1. How many flags are red?

   I can skip count by 2s for each flag.

   _____ flags

2. How many flags are green?

   _____ flags

3. How many green flags and yellow flags are there in all?

   _____ green and yellow flags

4. How many more blue flags than yellow flags are there?

   _____ more blue flags

5. (123) **Math Talk** How can you use a picture graph to show tallies in a different way?

SDAP 1.2 Represent the same data set in more than one way (e.g., bar graphs and charts with tallies).
Also **KEY SDAP 1.0, SDAP 1.4, MR 1.1**

AF 1.3 Solve addition and subtraction problems by using data from simple charts, picture graphs, and number sentences.

twenty-seven **27**

Flora's class played music in the parade. The tally chart shows what they played.

In the Band	
Instrument	**Tally Marks**
Horn	~~IIII~~ III
Drum	IIII
Flute	IIII
Tuba	II

6. Use the tally chart to make a picture graph. Draw one ★ for every 2 tally marks.

In the Band	
Horn	☆
Drum	
Flute	
Tuba	

★ = 2 instruments

Use the picture graph to answer the questions.

7. How many more horns than drums were in the parade?

_____ more horns

8. If 2 more children play the tuba, how many ★ will you add to the picture graph?

_____ ★

Problem Solving: Data Sense

Use the picture graph.

9. How many clowns were happy?

_____

Clowns	
Happy	★ ★ ★
Sad	★

Each ★ stands for 5 clowns.

10. How would you find the total number of clowns?

_____

At Home Have your child tell you how he or she counted the number of happy clowns in the picture graph.

En casa Pida a su niño que le diga cómo contó el número de payasos alegres en la pictografía.

Chapter 2 Lesson 4

Read and Make a Bar Graph

 **Learn**

The tally chart shows how many children choose each snack on Field Day. The **bar graph** shows the same data.

Objective
Make and read bar graphs; compare data on a bar graph.

Vocabulary
bar graph

Field Day Snacks

watermelon	IIII
juice bar	HHI
apple	II

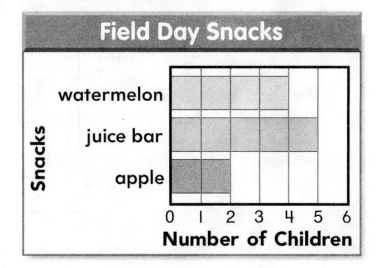

Field Day Snacks

Snacks: watermelon, juice bar, apple

Number of Children: 0 1 2 3 4 5 6

▶ **Guided Practice**

1. Use the tally chart to complete the bar graph.

Think!
I color I box inside the bar for each tally mark.

Favorite Snacks

cheese	III
pretzels	HHI
yogurt	II

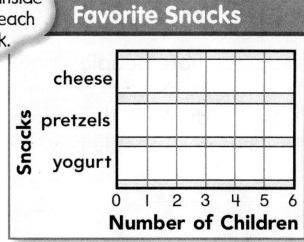

Favorite Snacks

Snacks: cheese, pretzels, yogurt

Number of Children: 0 1 2 3 4 5 6

2. Which snack is chosen most often? _____

3. **123** **Math Talk** How many children voted in all? How do you know?

 SDAP 1.2 Represent the same data set in more than one way (e.g., bar graphs and charts with tallies).
Also **KEY SDAP 1.0**, SDAP 1.1, MR 2.0
Prepares for SDAP 1.3

SDAP 1.4 Ask and answer simple questions related to data representations.

twenty-nine **29**

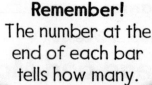

▶ Practice

Remember!
The number at the end of each bar tells how many.

Annie sells **5** lemonades.
She sells **2** more bottles of water than lemonade. Annie sells **3** juice boxes.
She sells **1** more milk than juice box.

4. Color the bar graph to show what Annie sold.

Annie's Drink Stand

5. How many more people buy water than juice boxes?

_____ more people

6. What is the total number of drinks that Annie sells?

_____ drinks

7. Which drink do the greatest number of people buy?

_____

8. Which drink do the least number of people buy?

_____

9. Annie wants to buy more drinks to sell another day. Which drink should she buy the most of? Why?

_____

At Home Have your child color a bar on the graph to show his or her favorite drink. Then read the revised graph together.

En casa Pida a su niño que coloree una barra en la gráfica de barras para mostrar su bebida favorita. Luego lean juntos la gráfica modificada.

30 |||

Range and Mode

 **Learn**

You can compare data to find how often something happens.

In the Pet Parade, each pony earns a score. The tally chart and the **line plot** show the ponies' scores.

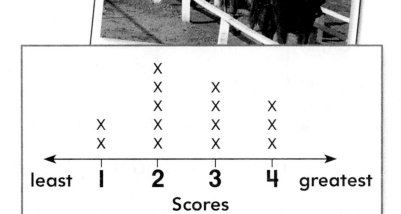

Pony Scores

Score	Number of Ponies
1			
2	卌
3					
4				

The **mode** is the score of the greatest number of ponies.

The **range** is the difference between the greatest and the least score.

▶ **Guided Practice**

Use the data above to answer the questions.

Think!
I can count the Xs above the 3.

1. How many ponies earned a score of 3? _____ ponies

2. Which score has the greatest number of Xs? mode: _____

3. What is the difference between the greatest and the least score?
   _____ – _____ = _____
   greatest least range

4. **(123) Math Talk** Is the range always greater than the mode? Explain.

SDAP 1.3 Identify features of data sets (range and mode).
Also **SDAP 1.2, KEY SDAP 1.0, AF 1.3, MR 2.0**

SDAP 1.4 Ask and answer simple questions related to data representations.

thirty-one **31**

▶ Practice

The children in the Pet Parade did a relay race with their ponies. The tally chart and line plot show their times.

Remember!
To find the mode, look for the greatest number of Xs.

Relay Race Times	
Time	**Number of Children**
5 min	l
6 min	lll
7 min	++++ l
8 min	lll l
9 min	l

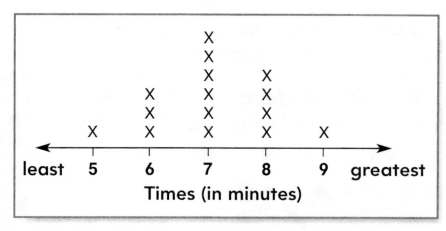

least   5   6   7   8   9   greatest
Times (in minutes)

Use the data to answer the questions.

5. How many children had a time of 6 minutes? ___3___ children

6. How many children had a time of 8 minutes? _____ children

7. Which time has the greatest number of Xs? mode: _____

8. Write a number sentence to find the range of the data. ____ ◯ ____ ◯ ____

Problem Solving: Data Sense

9. Make a picture graph and a bar graph to show the same data as the table.

Games Won	
Alice	15
Josh	5

Games Won

Alice
Josh
0   5   10   15
Number of Games

Games Won

Alice	
Josh	

Each ★ stands for 5 games.

At Home Ask your child to tell you how the bar graph and picture graph in Exercise 9 show the same information.

En casa Pida a su niño que le diga cómo la gráfica de barras y la pictografía del Ejercicio 9 muestran la misma información.

Chapter 2 Lesson 6

Use a Graph

 **Learn**

Use the data to add.

Each child chooses one Field Day event.

How many children choose the rope tug and ball throw events?

Find the data in the bar graph. Then add.

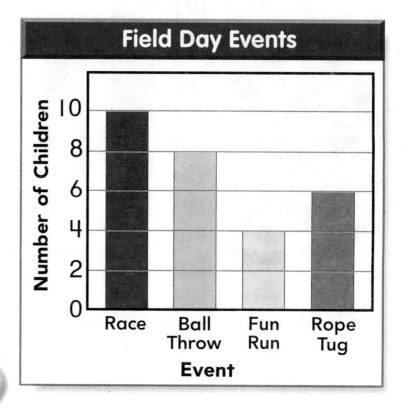

Field Day Events

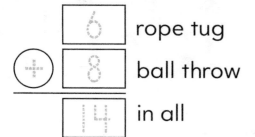

6	rope tug
8	ball throw
14	in all

Think!
6 children are in the rope tug and 8 children are in the ball throw.

Use the data to compare.

How many more children choose the race than the fun run?

Find the data in the bar graph. Subtract to compare.

Think!
10 children are in the race and 4 children are in the fun run.

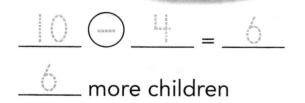

$$10 \bigcirc 4 = 6$$

_____ 6 _____ more children

 AF 1.3 Solve addition and subtraction problems by using data from simple charts, picture graphs, and number sentences.
Also **KEY SDAP 1.0**, AF 1.0, AF 1.2, MR 2.1

SDAP 1.4 Ask and answer simple questions related to data representations.

Use the data in the graph to solve.

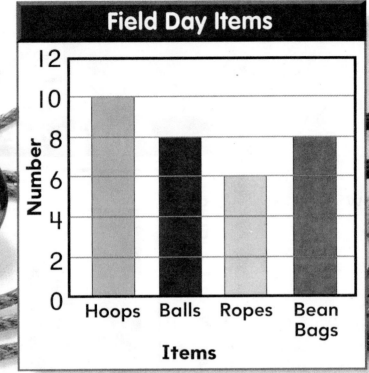

Field Day Items

1. How many more bean bags
   than ropes does the class
   have for Field Day?

   Think!
   I find the numbers
   on the graph. Then I
   subtract.

   Subtract to compare.

   _____ ◯ _____ = _____   _____ more bean bags

2. **123** **Math Talk** How would you find the item
   on the graph with the least amount?

3. The class has the same
   number of which items?   _____ and _____

4. How many more hoops than
   ropes does the class have?   _____ more hoops

At Home Place a set of 6 objects and
a set of 3 objects on a table. Ask your
child to show addition or subtraction
with them.

En casa Coloque un conjunto de 6 objetos y
un conjunto de 3 objetos en una mesa. Pida
a su niño que muestre la suma o la resta con
los objetos.

Name _____

Create and Solve

Problem Solving

Objective
Write problems and use strategies to solve.

Emilia and her friends buy hats at the fair.

1. Use the table. Make a tally chart to show the colors of their hats.

Hat Colors	
red	
green	
blue	
yellow	

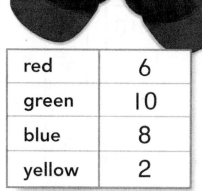

red	6
green	10
blue	8
yellow	2

2. How many red and green hats did the children buy?

   _____ + _____ = _____

3. Write an addition problem about hats at the fair. Use the data from the tally chart.

   _____

   _____

   _____

4. Write an addition sentence to solve your problem.

   _____ + _____ = _____

   Share your addition story with a classmate.

SDAP 1.4 Ask and answer simple questions related to data representations.
Also **SDAP 1.1, KEY SDAP 1.0 , MR 1.0, MR 1.1, AF 1.2, AF 1.0**

AF 1.3 Solve addition and subtraction problems by using data from simple charts, picture graphs, and number sentences.

Joanna asks people about their favorite ice cream flavor at the fair.

Favorite Ice Cream Flavors	
vanilla	4
chocolate	10
strawberry	8
bubble gum	2
mint	4

5. Color the graph to show the votes.

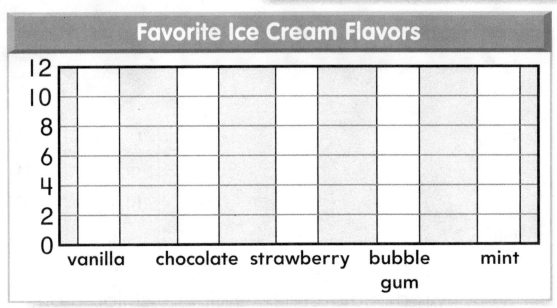

Favorite Ice Cream Flavors

12
10
8
6
4
2
0

vanilla   chocolate   strawberry   bubble gum   mint

6. How many more people voted for chocolate than for strawberry?

_____ – _____ = _____

7. Write subtraction problem about ice cream flavors. Use the data from the graph.

_____

_____

8. Write a subtraction sentence to solve your problem.

_____ – _____ = _____

Share your subtraction story with a classmate.

Key Standards Review

Write the fact family.

1.

Whole
7

Part	Part
3	4

_____ + _____ = _____

_____ – _____ = _____

_____ + _____ = _____

_____ – _____ = _____

Find the missing addend.

2. ☐ + 6 = 15

15 – _____ = _____

3. 2 + ☐ = 11

11 – _____ = _____

4. 9 + ☐ = 18

18 – _____ = _____

5. 7 + ☐ = 9

9 – _____ = _____

Challenge — Algebra

Solve.

1. 3 + ■ = 7 + 3   ■ = _____

2. ■ + 8 = ●   ● = _____

3. What is ● – ■ ?   _____ – _____ = _____

KEY NS 2.2 Find the sum or difference of two whole numbers up to three digits long.
Also KEY AF 1.1, KEY NS 2.1

How Many Instruments?

Math Music, Track 1
Tune: "John Jacob Jingleheimer Schmidt"

We watch the marching band go by.
See all the instruments?
See **30** big brass horns,
And **20** big bass drums,
Can you track the ones you see go by?
Da da da da da da da

You can make a tally chart.
Tally the instruments.
Record each one you see,
And when your chart's complete,
Count the tally marks for every one.
Da da da da da da da

Count up the tally marks you made.
Skip count if it helps you.
5, 10, 15, 20
Is one way you can count.
Count up all the tally marks you made.
Da da da da da da da

KEY SDAP 1.0 Collect numerical data and record, organize, display, and interpret the data on bar graphs and other representations.
Also **KEY NS 2.2**

Name _____

Concepts and Skills

Use the tally chart to complete the sentences.

KEY **SDAP 1.0**

Favorite Pet	
Dog	⊬⊬ l
Cat	lll
Hamster	ll

1. More children liked cats than _____.

2. Four more children chose _____ than chose hamsters.

Use both tables to answer the questions. KEY **SDAP 1.0**

3. In whose class did more children choose soccer?

_____

Alex's Gym Class	
Sport	**Number**
Soccer	7
Baseball	5
Basketball	8

Lia's Gym Class	
Sport	**Number**
Soccer	5
Baseball	6
Basketball	9

4. How many more children chose basketball in Lia's class than in Alex's class? _____

Problem Solving KEY **SDAP 1.0**, SDAP 1.3

Use the data in the graph.

5. Which color has the greatest number?

_____

6. Write a number sentence to help you find the range of the data.

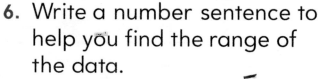

7. How many shirts are there in all?

_____ shirts in all

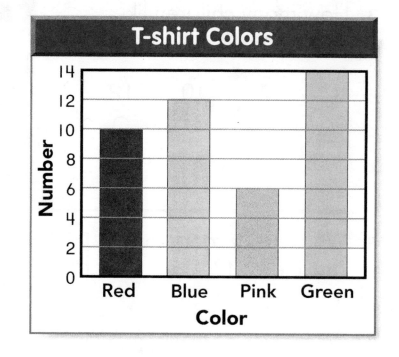

T-shirt Colors

Spiral Review and Test Practice

1. What is the fact family for 6, 2, and 8?

○ 6 − 2 = 4   2 + 4 = 6   6 − 4 = 2   4 + 2 = 6

○ 6 + 2 = 8   8 − 6 = 2   2 + 8 = 10   10 − 2 = 8

○ 6 + 2 = 8   2 + 6 = 8   6 + 8 = 14   8 + 6 = 14

○ 6 + 2 = 8   2 + 6 = 8   8 − 2 = 6   8 − 6 = 2

KEY **NS 2.1** Page 9

---

2. Use the tally chart to answer the question.

How many people voted in all?

Favorite Pet	
Dog	ᚼᚼ ‖
Cat	‖‖‖
Fish	‖

10   11   12   13
○   ○   ○   ○

KEY **SDAP 1.0**, SDAP 1.4 Page 25

---

3. How many children like apples best?

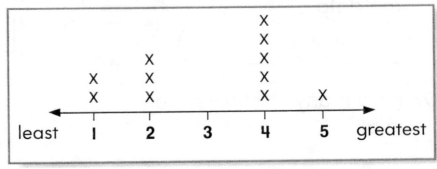

Favorite Snack	
Chips	♀
Juice	♀ ♀ ♀
Apples	♀ ♀ ♀ ♀

Key: Each ♀ stands for 3 children.

4   7   10   12
○   ○   ○   ○

SDAP 1.4, KEY **SDAP 1.0** Page 27

---

4. What is the range of the line plot?

1   2
○   ○

4   5
○   ○

```
                              X
                              X
                    X         X
          X         X         X
          X         X         X         X
      ◄───┼─────────┼─────────┼─────────┼─────────┼──────►
   least  1         2         3         4         5    greatest
```

SDAP 1.3, KEY **SDAP 1.0**, SDAP 1.4 Page 31

 **Education Place**
Visit **www.eduplace.com/camap/** for
Test-Taking Tips and Extra Practice.

Spiral Review

Name _____

Greg Tang's Go Fast, Go Far

Subtract to 10

> Subtract a few before the rest. Making 10 is always best!

> I think of 5 as 2 + 3, then subtract in 2 easy steps. First I subtract 12 − 2 = 10. Then I subtract 10 − 3 = 7.

1. $12 - 5 = \boxed{7}$

   $\boxed{2}$ $\boxed{3}$

   Make 10. Subtract the rest.

2. $14 - 6 = \square$

   $\square$ $\square$

   Make 10. Subtract the rest.

3. $15 - 7 = \square$

   $\square$ $\square$

   Make 10. Subtract the rest.

4. $13 - 5 = \square$

   $\square$ $\square$

5. $15 - 6 = \square$

   $\square$ $\square$

Great Job!

Take It Further: Now try doing all the steps in your head!

6. $17 - 8 = \square$

7. $12 - 4 = \square$

Reading and Writing Math

Jenny asked her classmates to choose a team color for field day. She used tally marks to show their choices.

Word Bank
bar graph
data
sum
tally marks

1. Complete the bar graph from the data in the tally chart.

Field Day Colors	
blue	‖‖‖
green	‖
red	‖‖‖

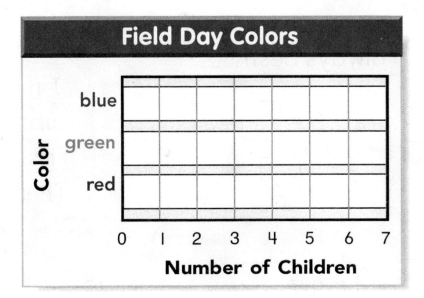

Field Day Colors

(bar graph with Color axis showing blue, green, red and Number of Children axis 0–7)

2. How many children chose a team color for field day? Add to find the sum.

_____ + _____ + _____ = _____

_____ children

3. **Writing Math** Write another question about the data. Exchange questions with a classmate and solve.

_____

_____

SDAP 1.2 Represent the same data in more than one way (e.g., bar graphs and charts with tallies).
Also AF 1.3, SDAP 1.4, AF 1.2, KEY SDAP 1.0, AF 1.0

Name _____

Concepts and Skills

Make ten to add.   KEY **NS 2.2**

1. $5 + 6 =$ _____

2. $2 + 8 =$ _____

Look for two numbers to add first. Find the sum.   KEY **AF 1.1**

3. $4 + 5 + 5 =$ _____

4. $6 + 2 + 8 =$ _____

Write the fact family.   KEY **NS 2.1**

5. 6, 2, 8   _____ + _____ = _____   _____ + _____ = _____

   _____ – _____ = _____   _____ – _____ = _____

6. 9, 1, 10   _____ + _____ = _____   _____ + _____ = _____

   _____ – _____ = _____   _____ – _____ = _____

Find the missing addend.   KEY **NS 2.1**

7. ☐ $+ 6 = 12$

8. $4 +$ ☐ $= 11$

9. ☐ $+ 7 = 7$

10. $2 +$ ☐ $= 11$

Use the tally chart to complete the sentence.   KEY **SDAP 1.0**

11. More children liked dogs than _____.

12. Two more children liked _____ than liked birds.

Favorite Pet	
Dog	IIII
Cat	HHt
Bird	II

Use the data in the picture graph to answer the questions. KEY SDAP 1.0

13. How many children chose juice?

_____

14. How many more children chose apples than chose chips?

_____

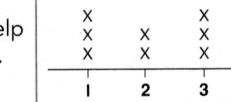

Favorite Snack

Chips	⚲
Carrots	⚲ ⚲
Juice	⚲ ⚲ ⚲ ⚲
Apple	⚲ ⚲ ⚲

Key: Each ⚲ stands for 2 children.

Use the line plot to answer the questions. SDAP 1.3

15. What is the mode?

_____

16. Write a number sentence to help you find the range of the data.

_____ ◯ _____ ◯ _____

```
                              X
                              X
              X       X       X
        X     X       X       X       X
        X     X       X       X       X
        X     X       X       X       X
        ┬─────┬───────┬───────┬───────┬
        1     2       3       4       5
```

Problem Solving

Use the data in the bar graph. MR 2.0, KEY SDAP 1.0

17. How many more green than blue backpacks are there?

_____

Explain how you solved.

_____

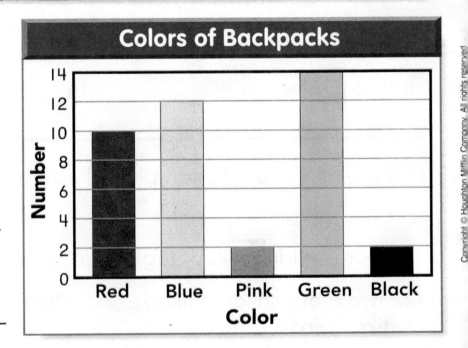

Colors of Backpacks

Unit 2

Numbers and Patterns to 200

BIG IDEAS!

- Each digit in a number has a different value based on its position.

- You can use place value to compare and order numbers.

- You can use number patterns to solve problems.

Songs and Games

 Math Music Track 2
Skip Count in a Snap

eGames
www.eduplace.com/camap/

Literature

Read Aloud Big Book
- Underwater Counting

Math Readers

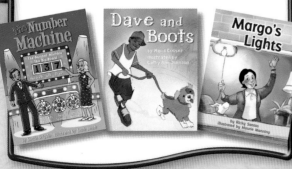

Three in a Row

How to Play

1. Each player makes a set of number cards, cuts them out, and puts them in a pile.

2. Take turns picking a card from your pile.

3. Match the cards to the game board.

4. Play until someone gets three in a row.

What You Need
2 players

41	82	55
24	95	74
36	18	63

4 tens 1 one	80 + 2	← 13 14 15 16 17 **18** 19 20 21 22 23 →
(base-ten blocks)	9 tens 5 ones	70 + 4
← 50 51 52 53 54 **55** 56 57 58 59 60 →	(base-ten blocks)	60 + 3

KEY NS 1.1 Count, read, and write whole numbers to 1,000 and identify the place value for each digit.
Also **NS 1.0, NS 1.2, MR 1.2**

Education Place
Visit **www.eduplace.com/camap/** for eGames and Brain Teasers.

Math at Home

Dear Family,

My class is starting Unit 2, **Numbers and Patterns to 200.** I will be learning how to find place value, regroup, compare, and order numbers up to 200. You can help me learn these vocabulary words, and we can do the Math Activity together.

From,

_____

Vocabulary

place value The value of a digit depends on where it is in a number.

125

1 is in the hundreds place.
2 is in the tens place.
5 is in the ones place.

regroup In addition, trade 10 ones for 1 ten.

greater than (>), less than (<), equal to (=)
Words or symbols used to compare numbers

7 > 5	7 is greater than 5.
3 < 7	3 is less than 7.
7 = 7	7 is equal to 7.

 Education Place
Visit **www.eduplace.com/camaf/** for
• eGames and Brain Teasers
• Math at Home in other languages

Family Math Activity

Game for two players. Make a set of cards with the digits 0–9, five cards that read *tens*, and five that read *ones.* Shuffle each set. Place face down. Each player draws 2 number cards to make a 2-digit number. Then one of the cards from the *ones* and *tens* set is turned up. The player with the greater digit in that place value wins the round. Replace and shuffle again.

0 1 2 3 4 5 6 7 8 9
tens   ones

Literature

These books link to the math in this unit. Look for them at the library.

• **Count on Pablo**
by Barbara deRubertis
Illustrated by
Rebecca Thornburgh
(*The Kane Press*, 2005)

• **Math All Around: Patterns in Nature**
by Jennifer Rozines Roy and Gregory Roy

Matemáticas en casa

Estimada familia:

Mi clase está comenzando la Unidad 2, **Números y patrones hasta el 200**. Aprenderé a hallar el valor de posición, a reagrupar, comparar y ordenar números hasta el 200. Me pueden ayudar a aprender estas palabras de vocabulario y podemos hacer juntos la Actividad de matemáticas para la familia.

De:

_____

Vocabulario

valor de posición El valor de un dígito depende del lugar que ocupa en un número.

125

1 está en el lugar de las centenas.

2 está en el lugar de las decenas.

5 está en el lugar de las unidades.

reagrupar En la suma, cambiar 10 unidades por 1 decena

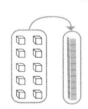

mayor que (>), menor que (<), igual a (=)
Palabras o símbolos para comparar números

7 > 5	7 es mayor que 5.
3 < 7	3 es menor que 7.
7 = 7	7 es igual a 7.

Education Place
Visite **www.eduplace.com/camaf/** para
- Juegos en línea y acertijos
- Matemáticas en casa en otros idiomas

Actividad de matemáticas para la familia

Juego para 2 jugadores: Hagan un conjunto de cartas con los dígitos del 0 al 9, cinco cartas que digan *decenas* y cinco que digan *unidades*. Barajen y coloquen boca abajo cada conjunto. Cada jugador toma 2 cartas para hacer un número de 2 dígitos. Se voltea una de las cartas de *unidades* y *decenas*. El jugador con el dígito mayor en ese valor de posición gana ese turno. Devuelvan las cartas y barajen nuevamente.

0 1 2 3 4 5 6 7 8 9

decenas   unidades

Literatura

Estos libros hablan sobre las matemáticas de esta unidad. Búscalos en la biblioteca.

- **¿Qué sigue, Nina?**
  por Sue Kassirer
  (Kane Press, 2005)
- **La caja de los botones**
  por Margarette S. Reid
- **Cuenta con Pablo**
  por Barbara de Rubertis

The Big Show

written by Timothy Johnson

illustrated by Bernard Adnet

This Take-Home Book belongs to

_____

Reading and Writing Math

This take-home book will help you review patterns.

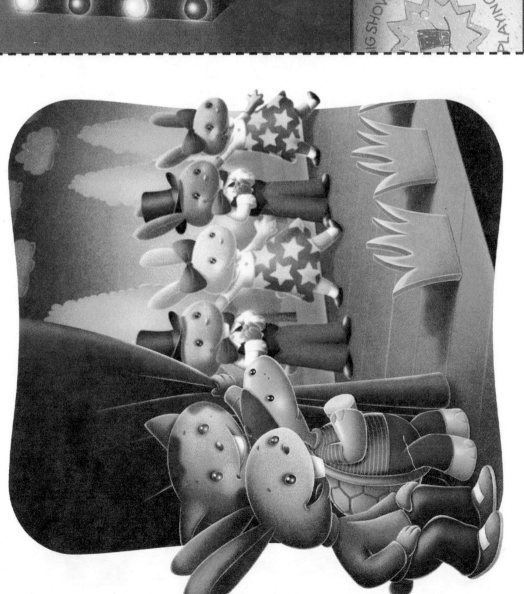

The show has begun
And so has the fun!
Please take a seat!
This show can't be beat!

KEY SDAP 2.0 Demonstrate an understanding of patterns and how patterns grow and describe them in general ways.

Everyone gets ready.
It's opening night.
But something is wrong
with a few of the lights.

Find the pattern. Use red and yellow
crayons to color the missing lights.

The seats all fill up,
lined up in straight rows.
Friends point out the patterns
as they wait for the show.

Can you find the patterns in the theater?

The stage lights you see
have a nice pattern too!
And Turtle would like
some help just from you!

Use crayons to help fix Turtle's lights.

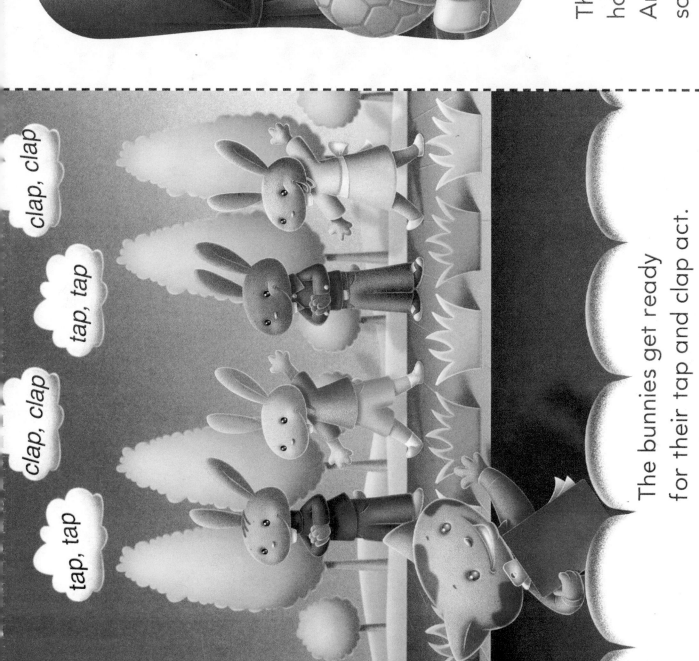

clap, clap

tap, tap

clap, clap

tap, tap

The bunnies get ready
for their tap and clap act.
You clap, tap their pattern.
It's really a snap.

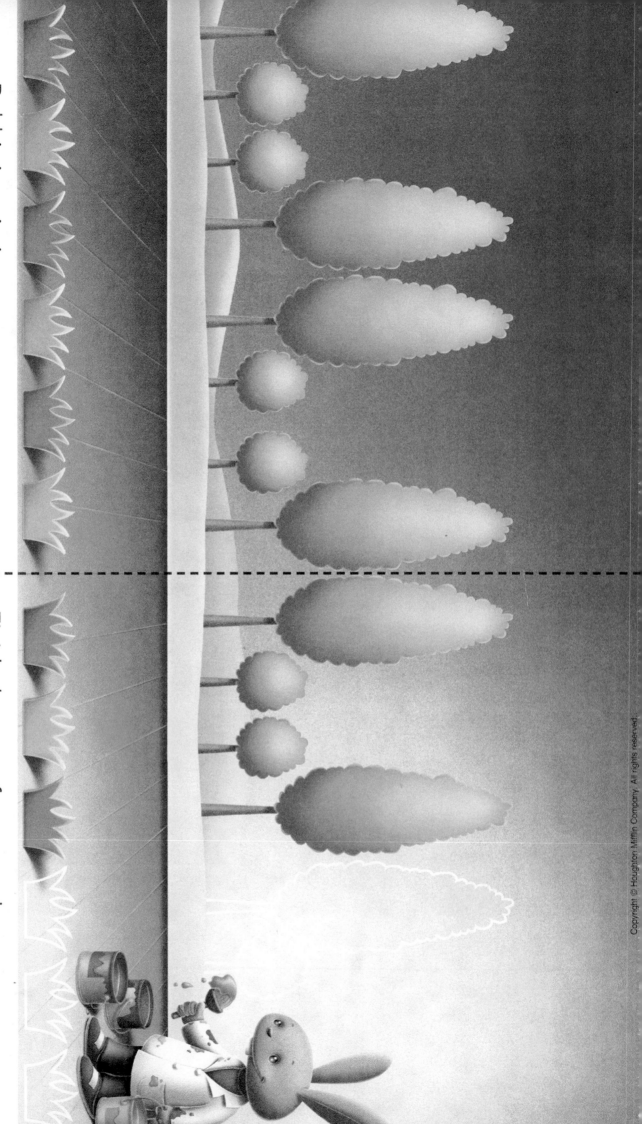

Rabbit is painting.
It's the back drop you know.
Can you finish the back drop
in time for the show?

Finish the row of trees and grass.

4

5

Place Value

Vocabulary

Here are some vocabulary words you will learn in the chapter.

regroup Rename 10 ones as 1 ten

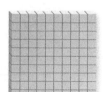

10 ones are the same as 1 ten.

digit Any of the numbers 0, 1, 2, 3, 4, 5, 6, 7, 8, 9

136   In the number 136,
↑↑↑   the three digits are 1, 3, and 6.

place value The value of the place where a digit is

125

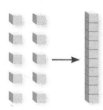 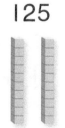 

1 hundred = 100   2 tens = 20   5 ones = 5

See English-Spanish Glossary pages 573–589.

 KEY **NS 1.1** Count, read, and write whole numbers to 1,000 and identify the place value for each digit.

 **Education Place**
Visit **www.eduplace.com/camap/** for the eGlossary and eGames.

Name _____

1. Show the number **83** as tens and ones.

Tens	Ones

2. Show the number **58** as tens and ones.

Tens	Ones

3. Which number has more tens, **64** or **27**? How do you know?

   _____ has more tens because

   _____

4. Circle the value of the **7** in the number **27**.

   70   7

5. Circle the value of the **3** in the number **39**.

   30   3

Use this page to review important skills needed for this chapter.

Chapter 3 Lesson 1

Place Value to 200

▶ **Explore**

10 **tens** = 1 **hundred**

Hands On

Objective
Use models to show numbers to 200.

Vocabulary
tens
hundreds

Show one hundred thirty-four.

Workmat 6		
Hundreds	Tens	Ones

Draw a quick picture.

Draw ☐ for ▦
Draw | for |
Draw ∘ for ▪

Write the number.

134

~~134~~

Use Workmat 6 with ▦ , ▭ , and ▪.
Show the number. Then draw a quick picture and write the number.

1. twenty-three

quick picture

_____

Think!
I need to draw
2 tens and 3 ones.

2. one hundred fifty-seven

quick picture

_____

3. one hundred five

quick picture

_____

4. (123) **Math Talk** How is 35 different from 53? Explain.

KEY NS 1.1 Count, read, and write whole numbers to 1,000 and identify the place value for each digit.
Also **NS 1.0, MR 1.2**

NS 1.2 Use words, models, and expanded forms (e.g., 45 = 4 tens + 5) to represent numbers (to 1,000).

Use Workmat 6 with , and .
Complete the table.

	Show the number.	Draw a quick picture.	Write the number.
5.	one hundred thirteen		_____
6.	one hundred twenty		_____
7.	ninety-nine		_____
8.	one hundred eighty-one		_____
9.	fifty-six		_____
10.	one hundred forty-eight		_____

At Home Have your child draw quick pictures for numbers you find on nutrition labels or calendars.

En casa Pida a su niño que haga dibujos rápidos para números que encuentre en tablas de nutrición o calendarios.

Name _____

Expanded Form

 **Learn**

To find the value of a **digit,** find the value of the **place** it is in.

What are the values of the digits in 158?

Find the place of each digit.

Hundreds	Tens	Ones
1	5	8

Show the values of the digits with Secret Code Cards.

100   50   8

1 0 0   5 0   8

Write the number in expanded form.

___100___ + ___50___ + ___8___

Write the number. ___158___

The 1 is in the hundreds place. Its value is 100.

The 5 is in the tens place. Its value is 50.

The 8 is in the ones place. Its value is 8.

Objective
Write numbers in expanded form.

Vocabulary
digit
place

▶ **Guided Practice**

Show the number with Secret Code Cards.
Circle the value of the red digit.

1.   163

Think!
I represent the 6 with my 60 Secret Code Card.

   60   6

2.   102

   10   100

3.   94

   40   4

4.   124

   20   200

5.   17

   70   7

6. **(123)** **Math Talk** Why does the number 50 have a zero in the ones place?

NS 1.2 Use words, models, and expanded forms (e.g., 45 = 4 tens + 5) to represent numbers (to 1,000).
Also NS 1.0, MR 2.0

KEY NS 1.1 Count, read, and write whole numbers to 1,000 and identify the place value for each digit.

fifty-one 51

Use Secret Code Cards.
Complete the table.

Find the place of each digit.	Write the expanded form.	Write the number.
7. one hundred eleven Hundreds | Tens | Ones 1 | 1 | 1	100 + 10 + 1	111
8. sixty-seven Hundreds | Tens | Ones	____ + ____	____
9. one hundred thirty-five Hundreds | Tens | Ones	____ + ____ + ____	____
10. one hundred twenty-one Hundreds | Tens | Ones	____ + ____ + ____	____
11. fourteen Hundreds | Tens | Ones	____ + ____	____

Problem Solving: Logical Reasoning

12. I have more ones than tens.
The value of my tens digit is 70.
What two numbers could I be?

_____ or _____

Draw or write to explain.

Chapter 3 Lesson 3

Regroup Tens or Ones

 **Learn**

When you have 10 or more ones,
you need to **regroup**.

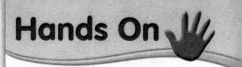
Objective
Regroup ten ones as
I ten.

Vocabulary
regroup

Step 1	Step 2	Step 3
Show 35 as 2 tens 15 ones. 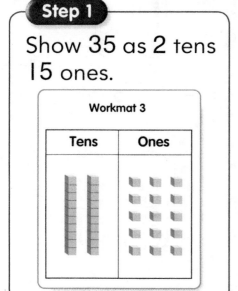	There are 15 ones. Regroup 10 ones as I ten. 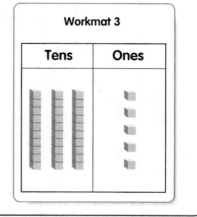	This shows 35 as 3 tens and 5 ones.

▶ **Guided Practice**

Use Workmat 3 with _____ and ▪ .
Show the tens and ones.
Regroup. Write the number.

1.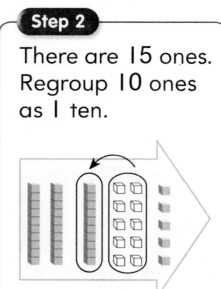

Think!
Regroup 12 ones as
I ten and 2 ones.

_____ tens _____ ones **Regroup** ⟩ _____ tens _____ ones [ ]

2. 5 tens 10 ones **Regroup** ⟩ _____ tens _____ ones [ ]

3. (123) **Math Talk** What does it mean to regroup?

KEY NS 1.1 Count, read, and write whole numbers to 1,000 and identify the place value for each digit.
Also **NS 1.2, NS 1.0**

MR 1.2 Use tools, such as manipulatives or sketches, to model problems.

fifty-three **53**

▶ Practice

Use Workmat 3 with ▭▭▭▭ and ▪.
Show the tens and ones.
Regroup. Write the number.

Remember!
Regroup 10 ones
as 1 ten.

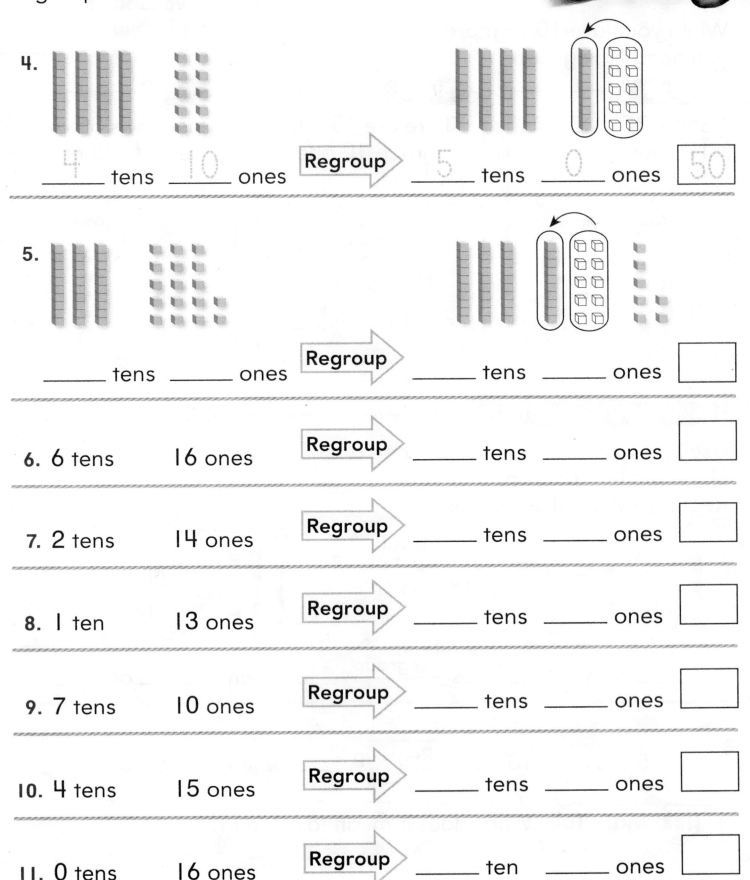

4. ___4___ tens ___10___ ones → **Regroup** → ___5___ tens ___0___ ones [50]

5. _____ tens _____ ones → **Regroup** → _____ tens _____ ones [ ]

6. 6 tens   16 ones → **Regroup** → _____ tens _____ ones [ ]

7. 2 tens   14 ones → **Regroup** → _____ tens _____ ones [ ]

8. 1 ten   13 ones → **Regroup** → _____ tens _____ ones [ ]

9. 7 tens   10 ones → **Regroup** → _____ tens _____ ones [ ]

10. 4 tens   15 ones → **Regroup** → _____ tens _____ ones [ ]

11. 0 tens   16 ones → **Regroup** → _____ ten _____ ones [ ]

At Home Have your child count a handful of objects, such as cereal or macaroni, by making groups of 10.

En casa Pida a su niño que cuente un puñado de objetos, como cereal o macarrones, haciendo grupos de 10.

54 ||||| ° ° ° °

Name _____

Different Ways to Show Numbers

 **Learn**

Objective
Represent numbers in different forms (words, models, expanded form).

You can show a number in different ways.
These are some of the ways to show 34.

3 tens 4 ones   30 + 4

▶ **Guided Practice**

Circle the way that shows the number.

1. | 31 | 3 tens 1 one

Think!
I know that the number 31 has 3 tens.

---

2. | 54 | 50 + 4

---

3. | 45 | 40 + 50   4 tens 5 ones

---

4. | 29 |    9 tens 2 ones

---

5. | 157 |    1 hundred 5 tens 2 ones

---

6.  **Math Talk** What is another way you can show the number 157? Explain.

 NS 1.2 Use words, models, and expanded forms (e.g., 45 = 4 tens + 5) to represent numbers (to 1,000).
Also **KEY** NS 1.1, **MR 2.0**

NS 1.0 Understand the relationship between numbers, quantities, and place value in whole numbers up to 1,000.

Remember!
Think about how many tens and ones are in the number.

Circle two ways to show the number.

7. 72 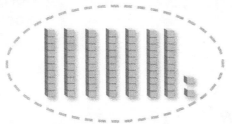 2 tens 7 ones (70 + 2)

8. 33 3 tens 3 ones 30 + 3

9. 167 7 tens 6 ones  100 + 60 + 7

10. 28  60 + 7

11. 156 100 + 50 + 6 I hundred 5 tens 6 ones

12. 43 4 + 30 4 tens 3 ones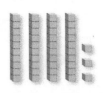

Problem Solving: Number Sense

13. Show 199 in two different ways.

At Home Ask your child to draw pictures to show 135 in two ways.

En casa Pida a su niño que dibuje dos formas de mostrar el número 135.

Chapter 3 Lesson 5

Find a Pattern

▶ **Learn**

Music cards are sold in packs. There are 3 cards in each pack. How many cards are in 5 packs?

Understand

What do you know?
- There are 3 cards in a pack.
- There are 5 packs.

Plan

You can make a table to find a pattern.

I pack has __3__ cards.

2 packs have __6__ cards.

Number of Packs	1	2	3	4	5
Number of Cards	3	6			

Solve

You can use the table to extend the pattern and find out how many cards are in 5 packs.

How many cards are in 5 packs?

__15__ cards

Number of Packs	1	2	3	4	5
Number of Cards	3	6	9	12	15

Look Back

Does your answer make sense?
What is the pattern?

KEY SDAP 2.0 Demonstrate an understanding of patterns and how patterns grow and describe them in general ways.
Also **SDAP 2.1, MR 2.0**

SDAP 2.2 Solve problems involving simple number patterns.

Remember!
Understand
Plan
Solve
Look Back

1. There are **2** children at each music stand. How many children are at **6** music stands?

   What do you need to find out?

   _____

   _____

   How many children are at **2** music stands?   _____

   How many children are at **3** music stands?   _____

   Complete the table.

   There are _____ children at **6** music stands.

Stands	1	2	3	4	5	6
Children	2					

2. **(123) Math Talk** How can a table help you find a pattern?

3. There are **3** people in each car. How many people are in **7** cars?

   _____ people

Cars	1	2	3	4	5	6	7
People							

4. Each dance group has **10** dancers. How many dancers are in **5** groups?

   _____ dancers

Groups	1	2	3	4	5
Dancers					

At Home Make a pattern using coins or cups. Ask your child to identify the pattern.

En casa Cree un patrón usando monedas o vasos. Pida a su niño que identifique el patrón.

Name _____

 # Key Standards Review

The bar graph shows how many children bought each kind of snack.

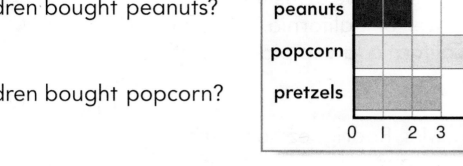

Fair Snacks

1. How many children bought peanuts?

   _____ children

2. How many children bought popcorn?

   _____ children

3. How many children bought pretzels?

   _____ children

4. What snack was bought the most? What is the mode?

   _____ mode: _____

5. Write a subtraction sentence to find the range of the data.

   _____ – _____ = _____

Data

Use the clues to complete the graph.

- Anna rode the ferris wheel 4 times.

- Billy rode the ferris wheel more times than Anna.

- George rode the ferris wheel more times than Billy.

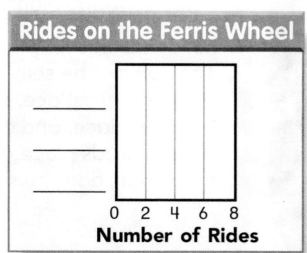

Rides on the Ferris Wheel

Number of Rides

KEY **SDAP 1.0** Collect numerical data and record, organize, display, and interpret the data on bar graphs and other representations. Also **SDAP 1.3, SDAP 1.4**

fifty-nine **59**

California Poppy

The California Poppy is a bright orange flower. It is the state flower of California. It is against California law to pick or destroy it.

Solve.

Draw or write to explain.

1. Mrs. Rodriguez has some poppy seeds. The number has a 1 in the hundreds place, a 7 in the tens place, and an 8 in the ones place. How many seeds does she have?

_____ seeds

2. The number of poppy plants in the park has a 5 in the tens place, a 1 in the hundreds place, and a 2 in the ones place. How many poppy plants are in the park?

_____ poppy plants

3. Mr. Johnson sells plant pots. The number he sells has a 4 in the ones place, a 6 in the tens place, and a 1 in the hundreds place. How many pots does he sell?

_____ pots

KEY **NS 1.1** Count, read, and write whole numbers to 1,000 and identify the place value for each digit.
Also **NS 1.0, NS 1.2**
Science **LS 2.e**

Name _____

Concepts and Skills

Use Workmat 6 with 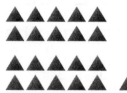, 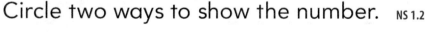, and . KEY **NS 1.1**

	Show the number.	Draw a quick picture.	Write the number.
1.	one hundred eighty-six		_____

Complete the chart. KEY **NS 1.1**

	Find the place of each digit.	Write the expanded form.	Write the number.
2.	one hundred eight **Hundreds | Tens | Ones**	_____ + _____ + _____	_____

Regroup the ones.
Write the number. KEY **NS 1.1**

3. 4 tens and 15 ones   regroup _____ tens _____ ones

4. 8 tens and 12 ones   regroup _____ tens _____ ones

Circle two ways to show the number. NS 1.2

5.

| 21 | 2 tens 1 one

Problem Solving   KEY **NS 1.1**, MR 2.0

6. Maureen says she is thinking of a number that has
3 hundreds, 5 ones, and 8 tens.

What number is Maureen thinking of? How do you know?

_____

Spiral Review and Test Practice

1. Which is the missing addend? $9 + \boxed{} = 12$

   3   9   12   15
   ○   ○   ○   ○

KEY **NS 2.1** Page 11

Use the graph to answer.

2. Which number sentence shows how many more red T-shirts there are than green ones?

   $14 - 8 = 6$ $14 - 6 = 8$
        ○   ○

   $12 + 14 = 26$ $14 - 12 = 2$
        ○   ○

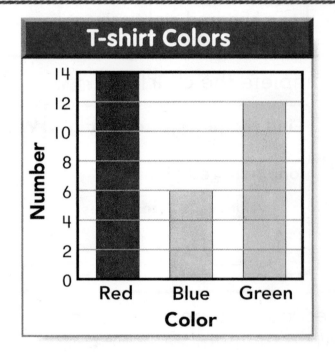

T-shirt Colors

Number / Color: Red, Blue, Green

3. How many blue and green T-shirts are there?

   6   12   18   20
   ○   ○   ○   ○

KEY **SDAP 1.0**, SDAP 1.4 Page 29

4. What is another way to show one hundred seventeen?

   $100 + 1 + 7$ $100 + 10 + 7$ $100 + 70 + 0$ 10017
        ○   ○   ○   ○

NS 1.2, KEY **NS 1.1**, NS 1.0 Page 51

5. What is another way to show 23?

   2 tens and 3 ones $2 + 3$ 2 ones and 3 ones
        ○   ○   ○   ○

NS 1.2, NS 1.0 Page 55

Education Place
Visit www.eduplace.com/camap/ for
Test-Taking Tips and Extra Practice.

Spiral Review

Compare and Order Numbers to 200

Vocabulary

Here are some vocabulary words you will learn in the chapter.

greater than (>), less than (<), equal to (=)
Words and symbols used to compare numbers

152 > 136	152 is greater than 136.
136 < 152	136 is less than 152.
152 = 152	152 is equal to 152.

before, after, between Words used to order numbers

145 146 147 148 149 150 151 152 153 154 155 156 157 158 159 160

147 is before 148   152 is between 151 and 153   160 is after 159

round To find the nearest ten

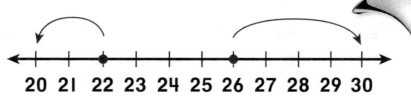

20 21 22 23 24 25 26 27 28 29 30

22 is closer to 20.
22 rounds to 20.

26 is closer to 30.
26 rounds to 30.

See English-Spanish Glossary pages 573–589.

KEY NS 1.3 Order and compare whole numbers to 1,000 by using the symbols <, =, >.
Also **KEY NS 1.1**

Education Place
Visit www.eduplace.com/camap/ for the eGlossary and eGames.

Name _____

✓ Check What You Know

Use the tickets to solve.

1. Which concert ticket number comes before 23?

   ticket number _____

2. Which concert ticket number comes between 49 and 86?

   ticket number _____

3. What is the order of the ticket numbers from least to greatest?

   _____, _____, _____, _____, _____

4. Which ticket numbers are greater than 18 but less than 57?

   _____ and _____

5. Create a new ticket number that is less than 23 but greater than 18.

   _____

Use this page to review important skills needed for this chapter.

Chapter 4 Lesson 1

Compare Numbers to 200

▶ **Explore**

You can use place value to compare numbers.

Objective
Use place value to compare numbers to 200.

Vocabulary
greater than
less than
equal to

Compare 32 and 27.
Show each digit with
Secret Code Cards.

32   27

30 2   20 7
3 0 2   2 0 7

First compare tens.
30 is **greater than** 20.
So, 32 is greater than 27.

Compare 34 and 38.
Show each digit with
Secret Code Cards.

34   38

30 4   30 8
3 0 4   3 0 8

First compare tens.
30 is **equal to** 30.

If the tens are equal,
compare ones.
4 is **less than** 8.
So, 34 is less than 38.

Compare the numbers.
Write the value of each digit.
Circle to complete the sentence.

1.   46   49

    _40_ _6_ _40_ _9_

    46 is (less than) 49
           greater than

2.   78   75

    ____ ____ ____ ____

    78 is less than 75
           greater than

3. **(123) Math Talk** Compare 56 and 48. Did you have
   to compare all the digits? Why or why not?

KEY NS 1.3 Order and compare whole numbers
to 1,000 by using the symbols <, =, >.
Also **NS 1.2, NS 1.0, MR 1.2, MR 2.1**

KEY NS 1.1 Count, read, and write whole
numbers to 1,000 and identify the place value for
each digit.

sixty-five **65**

You can compare three-digit numbers the same way.

Remember!
Start with hundreds.
If there are no hundreds, start with tens.

Compare 146 and 141.

146   141

| 1 0 0 | 4 0 | 6 | | 1 0 0 | 4 0 | 1 |

First compare hundreds. If the hundreds are equal, compare tens. If the tens are equal, compare ones. 146 is greater than 141.

Use Secret Code Cards to compare the numbers.
Write the value of each digit.
Circle to complete the sentence.

4.   114   133

_____ _____ _____   _____ _____ _____

114 is   less than   133
         greater than

5.   127   122

_____ _____ _____   _____ _____ _____

127 is   less than   122
         greater than

6.   163   136

_____ _____ _____   _____ _____ _____

163 is   less than   136
         greater than

7.   185   167

_____ _____ _____   _____ _____ _____

185 is   less than   167
         greater than

At Home Name two numbers less than 200. Ask your child to tell which is greater and explain how he or she knows.

En casa Diga dos números que sean menores que 200. Pregunte a su niño cuál es mayor y pídale que explique cómo lo sabe.

Compare Numbers to 200

 **Learn**

Use these symbols to compare numbers.

> greater than
< less than
= equal to

I want to eat the greater number.

45 < 46
45 is less than 46.

Compare 134 and 125.

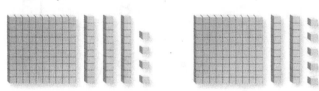

First compare hundreds.
One hundred is equal to one hundred.
100 = 100

If the hundreds are equal, compare the tens. 30 is greater than 20.

134 > 125

▶ **Guided Practice**

Think!
First I compare the tens.
Since they are the same,
I compare the ones.

Write the numbers and compare.
Write >, <, or =.

1.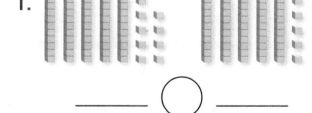

_____ ◯ _____

2.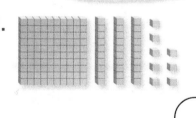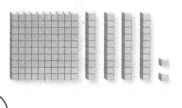

_____ ◯ _____

Compare the numbers using >, <, or =.

3. 87 ◯ 68   4. 65 ◯ 59   5. 27 ◯ 41

6. (123) **Math Talk** Compare 173 and 177. Did you have to compare all the digits? Why or why not?

KEY NS 1.3 Order and compare whole numbers to 1,000 by using the symbols <, =, >.
Also **NS 1.0, MR 2.1, MR 2.0**

KEY NS 1.1 Count, read, and write whole numbers to 1,000 and identify the place value for each digit.

sixty-seven **67**

Write the numbers. Compare.
Write >, <, or =.

Remember!
> means greater than.
< means less than.
= means equal to.

7.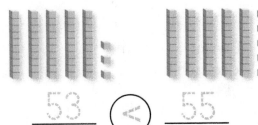

_53_ (<) _55_

8.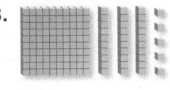

____ ◯ ____

Compare the numbers using >, <, or =.

9. 43 ◯ 43

10. 62 ◯ 57

11. 85 ◯ 88

12. 124 ◯ 129

13. 89 ◯ 95

14. 152 ◯ 135

15. 73 ◯ 64

16. 123 ◯ 117

17. 118 ◯ 131

18. 155 ◯ 145

19. 81 ◯ 81

20. 192 ◯ 179

21. 22 ◯ 29

22. 166 ◯ 177

23. 54 ◯ 68

24. 133 ◯ 128

25. 142 ◯ 152

26. 105 ◯ 99

27. Find the sums. Then compare
the numbers using >, <, or =.

$$\begin{array}{r} 14 \\ +\ 3 \\ \hline \end{array}$$
$$\begin{array}{r} 11 \\ +\ 6 \\ \hline \end{array}$$

____ ◯ ____

Problem Solving: Logical Reasoning

28. Antonio is thinking of a number
between 100 and 200. It has
3 tens and 6 ones. Kim is thinking
of a number between 100 and 200.
It has 6 tens and 3 ones. Who is
thinking of a greater number?

Draw or write to explain.

_____ is thinking of a greater number.

Chapter 4 Lesson 3

Order Numbers to 200

Objective
Order whole numbers to 200.

 **Learn**

Order 37, 29, and 32 from least to greatest.

Tens	Ones

Tens	Ones
3	7

Tens	Ones

Tens	Ones
2	9

Tens	Ones

Tens	Ones
3	2

Step 1
Compare the tens. There are fewer tens in 29 than 32 or 37. So 29 is the least number.

Step 2
Compare the ones. Seven ones is greater than 2 ones. So 37 is the greatest number. The numbers from least to greatest are 29, 32, 37.

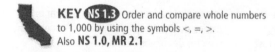 **Guided Practice**

Draw quick pictures.
Order the numbers from least to greatest.
Then order the numbers from greatest to least.

Think!
I compare the tens place first.

	52 64 46	least to greatest	greatest to least
1.		46 52 64	___ ___ ___
2.	135 153 114	___ ___ ___	___ ___ ___
3.	48 84 45	___ ___ ___	___ ___ ___

4. **123 Math Talk** How did you decide what was the least number in Exercise 3?

KEY NS 1.3 Order and compare whole numbers to 1,000 by using the symbols <, =, >. Also **NS 1.0, MR 2.1**

KEY NS 1.1 Count, read, and write whole numbers to 1,000 and identify the place value for each digit.

▶ Practice

Draw quick pictures. Write the numbers in order from least to greatest. Then order the numbers from greatest to least.

				least to greatest	greatest to least
5.	36	53	63	36 53 63	_____ _____ _____
6.	114	150	127	_____ _____ _____	_____ _____ _____
7.	84	48	54	_____ _____ _____	_____ _____ _____
8.	121	136	119	_____ _____ _____	_____ _____ _____

Problem Solving: Reasoning

9. Jay won 132 tickets. Lenny won 141 tickets. Chris won 137 tickets. Who won the most tickets?

_____

10. Circle the numbers that are shown from greatest to least.

A. 46, 54, 77, 78, 83

B. 56, 49, 23, 20, 17

C. 85, 63, 58, 92, 11

D. 49, 68, 57, 25, 36

Chapter 4 Lesson 4

Round to the Nearest Ten

▶ **Learn**

You can use a number line to **round** a number to the nearest ten.
Round 43 to the nearest ten.

If a number has a 5 in the ones place, round up to the nearest ten.

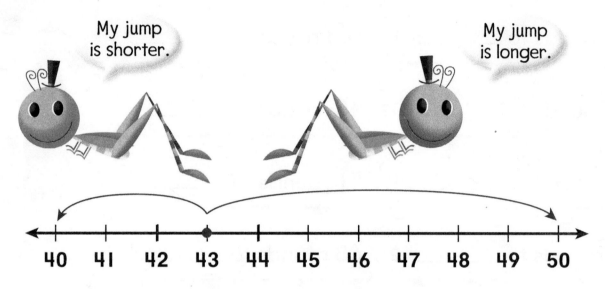

My jump is shorter.

My jump is longer.

40 41 42 43 44 45 46 47 48 49 50

Round to the closer number.
43 is closer to 40. 43 rounds to 40.

▶ **Guided Practice**

Round the number to the nearest ten.
Use Workmat 4 to help.

Think!
Find 14. Is it closer to 10 or 20?

1. 14 rounds to _____.

2. 27 rounds to _____.

3. 35 rounds to _____.

4. 173 rounds to _____.

5. 58 rounds to _____.

6. 182 rounds to _____.

7. 61 rounds to _____.

8. 99 rounds to _____.

9. **(123) Math Talk** How do you round a number to the nearest ten?

NS 6.0 Use estimation strategies in computation and problem solving that involve numbers that use ones, tens, hundreds, and thousands places.

Also **MR 2.0, NS 1.0, KEY NS 1.1**

Remember!
Find the shorter jump on the number line to round to the nearest ten.

Round the number to the nearest ten.
Use Workmat 4 to help.

10. 22 rounds to __20__.   11. 137 rounds to _____.

12. 34 rounds to _____.   13. 24 rounds to _____.

14. 36 rounds to _____.   15. 128 rounds to _____.

16. 43 rounds to _____.   17. 45 rounds to _____.

18. 167 rounds to _____. 19. 51 rounds to _____.

20. 59 rounds to _____.   21. 68 rounds to _____.

22. 163 rounds to _____. 23. 154 rounds to _____.

24. 75 rounds to _____.   25. 186 rounds to _____.

26. 94 rounds to _____.   27. 199 rounds to _____.

Problem Solving: Logical Reasoning

28. I am a number between 160 and 170.
I round to 160.
My tens digit is 4 more than
my ones digit.
What number am I?

Draw or write to explain.

I am _____.

At Home Have your child explain how he or she would round 26 to the nearest ten.

En casa Pida a su niño que explique cómo redondearía 26 a la decena más cercana.

Reasonable Answers

▶ **Learn**

There are 7 children in the puppet club.
More children join the club.
How many children are in the club now?

4 children   7 children   10 children

Understand
What do you know?
- There are 7 children in the puppet club.
- More children join the club.

Plan
Circle what you need to find out.

How many more children join the club?

How many children are in the club now?

Will the answer be more than, less than, or equal to 7?   _more than 7_

Solve
Look for clues in the problem.

4 children   7 children   (10 children)

There are ___10___ children in the club now.

Look Back
Is your answer reasonable?
How do you know?

Objective
Choose the most reasonable answer.

Think!
First there are 7 children in the club. Then more join, so the answer must be greater than 7.

NS 1.0 Understand the relationship between numbers, quantities, and place value in whole numbers up to 1,000.
Also **MR 2.0**

AF 1.0 Model, represent, and interpret number relationships to create and solve problems involving addition and subtraction.

▶ Guided Problem Solving

1. 12 children are selling tickets.
   More girls than boys are selling tickets.
   How many girls are selling tickets?

   4 girls   8 girls   12 girls

   What do you know?

   There are _____ children selling tickets.

   There are _____ girls than boys.

   If there are 4 girls, then there are _____ boys.

   If there are 12 girls, then there are _____ boys.

   If there are 8 girls, then there are _____ boys.

Think!
I can test
each answer.

   Choose the most reasonable answer.

   There are _____ girls selling tickets.

2. **123 Math Talk** How can you tell that
   your answer is reasonable?

▶ Problem Solving Practice

Circle the most reasonable answer.   Draw or write to explain.

3. Molly has 15 puppets. She gives some
   to Pam. How many puppets does
   Molly have left?

   9 puppets   15 puppets   18 puppets

4. Eddie buys 4 tickets on Monday.
   On Tuesday he buys some more.
   How many tickets does Eddie
   buy in all?

   2 tickets   4 tickets   6 tickets

 At Home Have your child explain
why his or her answer is reasonable in
Exercise 4.

En casa Pida a su niño que explique por
qué es razonable la respuesta que le dio al
Ejercicio 4.

Name _____

California Field Trip

At the San Francisco Opera

An opera is like a play, but the actors sing the words. At the opera, you can hear songs and see colorful costumes. You can even take a tour of the opera house!

Choose a way to solve. Show your work.

History-Social Science

An opera performance

1. The opera has **58** masks backstage. They have more in storage. How many masks does the opera have? Circle a reasonable answer.

   50 masks   **100** masks

mask

2. Tim has **10** opera programs to give out. He gives out **5** programs. How many programs does he have left?

   _____ programs

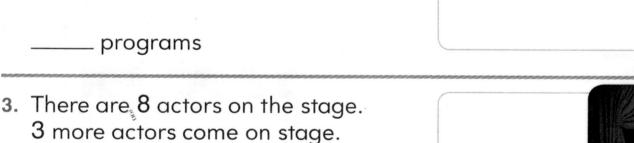

program

3. There are **8** actors on the stage. **3** more actors come on stage. How many actors are on the stage now?

   _____ actors

stage

NS 2.0 Estimate, calculate, and solve problems involving addition and subtraction of two- and three-digit numbers.
Also **NS 1.0, MR 1.0, MR 1.1**

AF 1.0 Model, represent, and interpret number relationships to create and solve problems involving addition and subtraction.

Problem Solving on Tests
Listening Skills

Listen to your teacher read the problem.
Choose the correct answer.

Select a Strategy
Use Mental Math
Write a Number
Sentence
Use a Graph

1. There are 3 children onstage.
   2 more join them. Then 7 more come onstage.
   How many children are there in all?

   12   10   7   5
   ○   ○   ○   ○

   KEY **AF 1.1**

2. Which number sentence can be used to check
   the answer to the problem in the box?

   $4 + 3 = 7$

   $7 + 3 = 10$ $2 + 5 = 7$ $7 - 4 = 3$ $10 - 3 = 7$
       ○   ○   ○   ○

   KEY **NS 2.1**

3.
   13   10   7   6
   ○   ○   ○   ○

Horn Players	
Girls	卌 II
Boys	卌 卌 III

   KEY **SDAP 1.0**

4.
   2   6   8   10
   ○   ○   ○   ○

Trips to the Opera

SDAP 1.4

MR 1.0 Make decisions about how to set up a problem.
MR 1.1 Determine the approach, materials, and
strategies to be used.

Education Place
Visit **www.eduplace.com/camap/** for
Test-Taking Tips and Extra Practice.

Key Standards Review

Complete the chart.

Word Form	Expanded Form	Number
1. eighty-four	_____ + _____	_____
2. twenty-nine	_____ + _____	_____
3. _____	_____ + _____ + _____	155
4. _____	100 + 90 + 3	_____
5. _____	100 + 70 + 6	_____

Challenge   Number Sense

The Egyptians used these symbols for numbers.

1. How would you write 2?

   _____

2. How would you write 20?

   _____

3. How would you write 200?

   _____

KEY **NS 1.1** Count, read, and write whole numbers to 1,000 and identify the place value for each digit.
Also **NS 1.2**

The United Nations

The United Nations is an international organization founded in 1945 that makes decisions about global peace and safety.

Students from Mrs. Grady's class made a chart to show how many countries were members of the UN in each year.

Year	Member countries of the UN
2000	189
1970	124
1990	157
1960	98
1980	150

Solve.

Draw or write to explain.

1. Use <, >, or = to compare the number of member countries in the years 1980 and 1990.

   _____ ◯ _____

2. Today there are 192 countries in the United Nations. Use <, >, or = to compare this number to the members in 2000.

   _____ ◯ _____

3. Rewrite the number of member countries in order from least to greatest.

   _____, _____, _____,

   _____, _____

KEY NS 1.3 Order and compare whole numbers to 1,000 by using the symbols <, =, >.
Also KEY SDAP 1.0, NS 1.0, SDAP 1.4
History-Social Science 3.2

Concepts and Skills

1. Compare the numbers.
   Write the value of the digits.
   Circle to complete the sentence. **KEY NS 1.3**

   184   153

                          less than

   _____ _____ _____   _____ _____ _____
                          greater than
        184 is   153.

Compare the numbers using >, <, or =. **KEY NS 1.3**

2. 78 ◯ 72   3. 126 ◯ 131

Draw quick pictures. Write the numbers
in order from least to greatest.
Then order the numbers from greatest to least. **KEY NS 1.3**

4.   49   19   33

   least to greatest   greatest to least

   _____ _____ _____   _____ _____ _____

Use Workmat 4. Round the number to the nearest ten. **NS 6.0**

5. 35 rounds to _____   6. 82 rounds to _____

Problem Solving **KEY NS 1.3, MR 2.0**

7. Ricky is thinking of a number
   between 100 and 200. It has 8 tens
   and 6 ones. Blanche is thinking of
   a number between 100 and 200.
   It has 6 tens and 8 ones. Who is
   thinking of a greater number? Why?

_____

1. Which is the missing addend?   ☐ + 4 = 13

   4   9   13   17
   ○   ○   ○   ○

KEY NS 2.1, KEY NS 2.2 Page 11

Use the table to answer the questions.

Favorite Sport	
Sport	Number
Soccer	7
Baseball	4
Basketball	9

2. How many people voted in all?

   7   11   13   20
   ○   ○   ○   ○

3. How many more people like basketball than baseball?

   4   5   9   13
   ○   ○   ○   ○

KEY SDAP 1.0, SDAP 1.4 Page 25

4. Use the line plot to answer the question.

   What is the mode of the data?

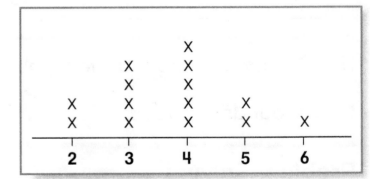

   2   3   4   5
   ○   ○   ○   ○

KEY SDAP 1.0, SDAP 1.4 Page 31

5. Which symbol makes this comparison true?   68 ◯ 62

   >   <   =   +
   ○   ○   ○   ○

KEY NS 1.3, KEY NS 1.1, NS 1.0 Page 67

Education Place
Visit www.eduplace.com/camap/ for
Test-Taking Tips and Extra Practice.

Spiral Review

Number Patterns

Vocabulary

Here are some vocabulary words you will learn in the chapter.

skip count Count using repeated addition of the same number

     2, 4, 6, 8, 10   You can count by 2s.
     5, 10, 15, 20, 25   You can count by 5s.
     10, 20, 30, 40, 50   You can count by 10s.

even number A number that has none left over when you make groups of 2

6 is an even number.

odd number A number that has 1 left over when you make groups of 2

7 is an odd number.

See English-Spanish Glossary pages 573–589.

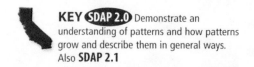

KEY SDAP 2.0 Demonstrate an understanding of patterns and how patterns grow and describe them in general ways. Also **SDAP 2.1**

Education Place
Visit www.eduplace.com/camap/ for the eGlossary and eGames.

Solve. Use the picture.

1. How many children are in the line? _____ children

2. How many groups of 2 can you make? _____

   Are there any children left over? _____

   How many? _____

3. If one more child joins the line,
   how many children would there be? _____

   How many groups of 2 could you make? _____

   Would there be any children left over? _____

4. Skip count by 5s to 35.

   5, 10, _____, _____, _____, _____, _____

5. Skip count by 2s. Write the missing numbers.

   2, 4, _____, 8, _____, _____, 14, _____, 18, _____

Use this page to review important skills needed for this chapter.

82

Count by 2s

▶ **Explore**

You can use a **hundred chart** to
skip count by 2s.
Put a ● on 2.
Add 2 more by moving the ●
to the number that is 2 more.

Hands On 🖐

Objective
Use a hundred chart
to count by 2s.

Vocabulary
hundred chart

1. Skip count by 2s. Color the
   numbers ◀ ━ ▶. Keep skipping
   and coloring until you reach 100.

I start on 2. Then
I keep adding
2 more.

1	2	3	4	5	6	7	8	9	10
11	12	13	14	15	16	17	18	19	20
21	22	23	24	25	26	27	28	29	30
31	32	33	34	35	36	37	38	39	40
41	42	43	44	45	46	47	48	49	50
51	52	53	54	55	56	57	58	59	60
61	62	63	64	65	66	67	68	69	70
71	72	73	74	75	76	77	78	79	80
81	82	83	84	85	86	87	88	89	90
91	92	93	94	95	96	97	98	99	100

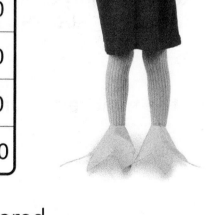

2. (123) **Math Talk** Look at the numbers you colored.
   What pattern do you see?

SDAP 2.1 Recognize, describe, and extend patterns and
determine a next term in linear patterns (e.g., 4, 8, 12...;
the number of ears on one horse, two horses, three horses,
four horses).

KEY SDAP 2.0 Demonstrate an understanding of
patterns and how patterns grow and describe them in
general ways.
Also **MR 1.2,** Prepares for **KEY NS 3.1, KEY NS 3.3**

Remember!
Skip counting by 2s is the same as adding 2 more.

You can start on any number when you count by 2s.

1	2	3	4	5	6	7	8	9	10
11	12	13	14	15	16	17	18	19	20
21	22	23	24	25	26	27	28	29	30
31	32	33	34	35	36	37	38	39	40
41	42	43	44	45	46	47	48	49	50
51	52	53	54	55	56	57	58	59	60
61	62	63	64	65	66	67	68	69	70
71	72	73	74	75	76	77	78	79	80
81	82	83	84	85	86	87	88	89	90
91	92	93	94	95	96	97	98	99	100

3. Start on 1. Color it ◖━━◗. Keep adding 2 and saying the number. Color the numbers.

4. Start on 4. Draw an ✕. Keep adding 2 and saying the number. Draw an ✕ on the numbers.

Use the hundred chart to complete the pattern.

5. 2, 4, 6, _____, _____, 12, _____, 16, _____, _____

6. 80, _____, 84, _____, 88, _____, 92, _____, 96, _____

At Home Ask your child to use the hundred chart to count by 2s to 50.

En casa Pida a su niño que use la tabla de números hasta el cien para contar de 2 en 2 hasta 50.

Name _____

Chapter 5 Lesson 2

Count by 5s

▶ Learn

You can use a hundred chart to skip count by 5s.
Start on 5. Color it ▭◯▶.
Add 5 more. Color the number.
Keep adding 5 to skip count by 5s.

▶ Guided Practice

1. Skip count by 5s. Color the numbers ▭◯▶.

Think!
I start on 5.
Then I keep adding 5 more.

Use the hundred chart to complete the pattern.

1	2	3	4	5	6	7	8	9	10
11	12	13	14	15	16	17	18	19	20
21	22	23	24	25	26	27	28	29	30
31	32	33	34	35	36	37	38	39	40
41	42	43	44	45	46	47	48	49	50
51	52	53	54	55	56	57	58	59	60
61	62	63	64	65	66	67	68	69	70
71	72	73	74	75	76	77	78	79	80
81	82	83	84	85	86	87	88	89	90
91	92	93	94	95	96	97	98	99	100

2. 5, 10, 15, _____, _____, 30, _____, 40, 45, _____

3. 60, 65, _____, 75, _____, _____, 90, _____, _____

4. **(123) Math Talk** Which number is likely to come next in this pattern: 25, 30, 35, 40? How do you know?

SDAP 2.1 Recognize, describe, and extend patterns and determine a next term in linear patterns (e.g., 4, 8, 12...; the number of ears on one horse, two horses, three horses, four horses).

Also **KEY SDAP 2.0**, MR 2.0, MR 2.1
Prepares for **KEY NS 3.1**, **KEY NS 3.3**

► **Practice**

Use the hundred chart.

Remember!
You can start on any number when you count by 5s.

1	2	3	4	5	6	7	8	9	10
11	12	13	14	15	16	17	18	19	20
21	22	23	24	25	26	27	28	29	30
31	32	33	34	35	36	37	38	39	40
41	42	43	44	45	46	47	48	49	50
51	52	53	54	55	56	57	58	59	60
61	62	63	64	65	66	67	68	69	70
71	72	73	74	75	76	77	78	79	80
81	82	83	84	85	86	87	88	89	90
91	92	93	94	95	96	97	98	99	100

5. Start on 2. Color it ▭▭▭. Skip count by 5s. Color the numbers.

6. Write a rule for the pattern in Exercise 5.

_____

Use the hundred chart to complete the pattern.

7. 12, 17, 22, _____, 32, _____, _____, 47, 52, _____

8. Complete the pattern.

   70, 75, 80, 85, 90, 95, 100, _____, _____

Problem Solving: Visual Thinking

9. Marco made this pattern. How should he color the last 3 boxes? Circle the answer. Tell how you know.

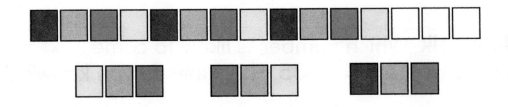

At Home Ask your child to count by 5s to 100.

En casa Pida a su niño que cuente de 5 en 5 hasta 100.

Name _____

Chapter 5 Lesson 3

Count by 10s

▶ **Learn**

You can use a hundred chart to skip count by 10s.
Start on 10. Color it ◖▬▬◗.

1	2	3	4	5	6	7	8	9	10
11	12	13	14	15	16	17	18	19	20
21	22	23	24	25	26	27	28	29	30
31	32	33	34	35	36	37	38	39	40
41	42	43	44	45	46	47	48	49	50
51	52	53	54	55	56	57	58	59	60
61	62	63	64	65	66	67	68	69	70
71	72	73	74	75	76	77	78	79	80
81	82	83	84	85	86	87	88	89	90
91	92	93	94	95	96	97	98	99	100

▶ **Guided Practice**

1. Skip count by 10s. Color the numbers ◖▬▬◗.

   Think!
   I start on 10.
   Then I keep adding 10 more.

2. Use the hundred chart to complete the pattern.

   10, 20, _____, _____, _____,

   _____, _____, _____, _____

Look at the numbers in the pattern you completed. Answer the questions.

3. How are the numbers the same?

   _____

4. How are the numbers different?

   _____

5. (123) **Math Talk** What pattern do you see in the first digits of the numbers?

SDAP 2.1 Recognize, describe, and extend patterns and determine a next term in linear patterns (e.g., 4, 8, 12...; the number of ears on one horse, two horses, three horses, four horses).

Also **KEY** SDAP 2.0, MR 2.0
Prepares for **KEY** NS 3.1, **KEY** NS 3.3

▶ Practice

You can start on any number when you count by 10s.

6. Start on 3. Color it ◀━━▶. Skip count by 10s. Color the numbers.

Use what you know about skip counting to answer the questions.

1	2	3	4	5	6	7	8	9	10
11	12	13	14	15	16	17	18	19	20
21	22	23	24	25	26	27	28	29	30
31	32	33	34	35	36	37	38	39	40
41	42	43	44	45	46	47	48	49	50
51	52	53	54	55	56	57	58	59	60
61	62	63	64	65	66	67	68	69	70
71	72	73	74	75	76	77	78	79	80
81	82	83	84	85	86	87	88	89	90
91	92	93	94	95	96	97	98	99	100

7. What number is 10 more than 40? _____

8. What number is 10 more than 70? _____

9. What number is 10 less than 60? _____

10. What number is 10 less than 150? _____

Problem Solving: Number Sense

11. Danielle skip counted by 2s, 5s, and 10s on a hundred chart. Each time she skip counted, she circled the numbers. She found a number that she circled three times. What could the number be? Explain.

_____

_____

 At Home Ask your child to start with 4 and skip count by 10s. **En casa** Pida a su niño que cuente salteado de 10 en 10, empezando por el 4.

Name _____

Even and Odd Numbers

▶ **Learn**

Objective
Identify even and odd numbers.

Vocabulary
even
odd

You can make groups of **2** to decide if a number is **even** or **odd**.

A number is even when you make groups of **2** and there are none left over.

A number is odd when you make groups of **2** and there is I left over.

| 8 | |
| 11 | |

▶ **Guided Practice**

Draw groups of **2** to show the number. Circle **even** or **odd**.

Think!
When I draw groups of 2 for I5 I have one left over.

1. | 15 | |

   even   odd

2. | 22 | |

   even   odd

3. | 34 | |

   even   odd

4. **(123)** **Math Talk** How could you use skip counting to help you find the even numbers on a hundred chart?

SDAP 2.1 Recognize, describe, and extend patterns and determine a next term in linear patterns (e.g., 4, 8, 12...; the number of ears on one horse, two horses, three horses, four horses).

SDAP 2.2 Solve problems involving simple number patterns.
Also **MR 2.0, MR 1.0, MR 1.1, KEY** SDAP 2.0

eighty-nine **89**

Draw groups of **2** to show the number. Circle **even** or **odd**.

Remember!
If there is 1 left over, the number is odd.

5. | 9 |

00 00 00 00 .

even (odd)

6. | 18 |

even   odd

---

7. Color the even numbers ◖━◗.
   Color the odd numbers ◖━◗.

51	52	53	54	55	56	57	58	59	60
61	62	63	64	65	66	67	68	69	70
71	72	73	74	75	76	77	78	79	80
81	82	83	84	85	86	87	88	89	90
91	92	93	94	95	96	97	98	99	100

Problem Solving: Logical Reasoning

8. Nam has a secret number.
   The number has two digits.
   It is less than 13. It is odd.
   What is Nam's secret number?
   Tell how you know.

   _____

At Home Put a handful of small items, such as buttons, on a table. Ask your child to tell you if the number of items is even or odd.

En casa Coloque un puñado de objetos pequeños, como botones, en una mesa. Pida a su niño que le diga si el número de objetos es par o impar.

Create and Solve

Problem Solving 5

Objective
Write problems an
use strategies to
solve them.

Dana and Alex are playing a guessing
game with a hundred chart.
Dana writes this riddle:

When I skip count by
5s, I land on the secret
number. The secret
number is more than
5 and less than **20**.
The secret number is
odd. What is the secret
number?

1	2	3	4	5	6	7	8	9
11	12	13	14	15	16	17	18	19
21	22	23	24	25	26	27	28	29
31	32	33	34	35	36	37	38	39
41	42	43	44	45	46	47	48	49
51	52	53	54	55	56	57	58	59
61	62	63	64	65	66	67	68	69
71	72	73	74	75	76	77	78	79
81	82	83	84	85	86	87	88	89
91	92	93	94	95	96	97	98	99

1. Solve Dana's riddle.
   Tell how you found
   the answer.

   The secret number is

   _____.

2. Write your own number riddle.
   Use clues from the hundred chart.

   _____

   _____

   _____

3. Write the answer to your riddle.

   The secret number is _____.

   Share your riddle with a classmate.

SDAP 2.2 Solve problems involving simple number
patterns.
Also **SDAP 2.1, MR 1.0, MR 1.1, MR 2.0**

KEY SDAP 2.0 Demonstrate an understanding
of how patterns grow and describe them in general
ways.

Bobby makes a table to show some number patterns.

Number	Pattern
1	4, 6, 8, 10, 12, 14, 16, 18
2	3, 8, 13, 18, 23, 28, 33, 38
3	3, 5, 7, 9, 11, 13, 15, 17
4	12, 22, 32, 42, 52, 62, 72, 82
5	4, 9, 14, 19, 24, 29, 34, 39

Bobby writes this riddle:

The rule for the pattern is that I skip count by 10s. Which pattern number is it?

4. Solve Bobby's riddle.
   Tell how you found the answer.
   You can use the hundred chart to help.

   The pattern is number _____.

5. Write your own riddle about one of Bobby's patterns.

   _____

   _____

   _____

6. Write the answer to your riddle.

   The pattern is number _____.

   Share your riddle with a classmate.

Name _____

 # Key Standards Review

Use >, <, or = to compare.

1. 78 ◯ 87

2. 43 ◯ 34

3. 109 ◯ 190

4. 56 ◯ 49

5. 175 ◯ 157

6. 183 ◯ 193

7. 123 ◯ 133

8. 175 ◯ 100 + 70 + 5

9. 150 ◯ 100 + 50

Challenge   Number Sense

1. Use the clues to find the scores.

   Team A has a score between 30 and 40. The tens and ones digits are the same.

   Team B also has a score between 30 and 40. The ones digit is one less than the tens digit.

   Team A's score is _____.

   Team B's score is _____.

Team A   Team B

_____   _____

2. Use <, >, or = to compare the scores.

   Team A   Team B

   _____ ◯ _____

 KEY **NS 1.3** Order and compare whole numbers to 1,000 by using the symbols <, =, >.

ninety-three **93**

Skip Count in a Snap

 Math Music, Track 2
Tune: original

Skip count, skip count, count with me.
What will all the numbers be?
If they're even, do one clap.
If they're odd, do one snap.
Think of numbers that you know.
Count by 5s. Ready? Set. Go!

> 5, 10, 15—That's the way.
> 20, 25, 30—Shout hooray!
> 35, 40, 45—Don't be late.
> 50, 55, 60—You're doing great!
> 65, 70, 75—Right on cue.
> Count by 5s. That's what we do!

Skip count, skip count, count with me.
What will all the numbers be?
If they're even, do one clap.
If they're odd, do one snap!
Think of numbers that you know.
Count by 10s. Ready? Set. Go!

> 10, 20, 30—Keep on going.
> 40, 50, 60—The numbers keep growing!
> 70, 80, 90—Have some fun.
> Count by 10s and then you're done!

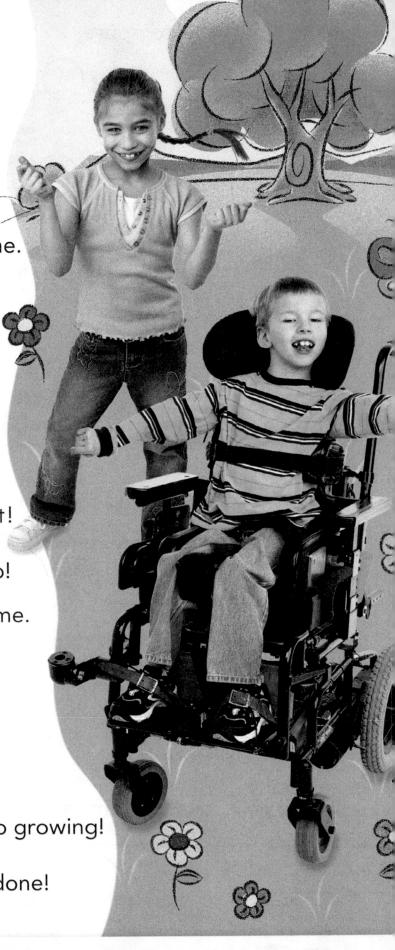

 SDAP 2.1 Recognize, describe, and extend patterns and determine a next term in linear patterns (e.g., 4, 8, 12 . . .; the number of ears on one horse, two horses, three horses, four horses).

Name _____

Concepts and Skills

Use the hundred chart to
complete the pattern. **KEY SDAP 2.0**

1	2	3	4	5	6	7	8	9	10
11	12	13	14	15	16	17	18	19	20
21	22	23	24	25	26	27	28	29	30
31	32	33	34	35	36	37	38	39	40
41	42	43	44	45	46	47	48	49	50
51	52	53	54	55	56	57	58	59	60
61	62	63	64	65	66	67	68	69	70
71	72	73	74	75	76	77	78	79	80
81	82	83	84	85	86	87	88	89	90
91	92	93	94	95	96	97	98	99	100

1. 10, 12, _____, 16, _____, _____,

   22, 24, _____

2. 34, _____, 38, _____, _____, 44,

   46, _____, 50

Follow the pattern.
Write the missing numbers. **KEY SDAP 2.0**

3. 17, 20, 23, _____, _____, 32

4. 41, 36, 31, _____, 21, _____

Answer the questions. **KEY SDAP 2.0**

5. What number is 10 more

   than 50? _____

6. What number is 10 less

   than 120? _____

Draw groups of 2 to show the number. Circle even or odd. **SDAP 2.1**

7. 23

   even   odd

8. 30

   even   odd

Problem Solving SDAP 2.1, MR 2.0

9. What is wrong with this number pattern?

   5, 8, 11, 14, 18, 20, 23

   _____

   _____

1. Which is the sum? $1 + 5 + 5 =$ _____

   10 ○   11 ○   12 ○   155 ○

KEY **AF 1.1** Page 7

2. Which is the number shown in the chart?

Hundreds	Tens	Ones
1	2	8

   ○ one hundred eighty-two   ○ two hundred eighteen

   ○ eight hundred twenty-one   ○ one hundred twenty-eight

NS 1.2, KEY **NS 1.1**, NS 1.0 Page 51

3. Which is another way to show 58?

   ○ 5 ones and 8 ones   ○ 5 tens and 8 tens

   ○ 5 tens and 8 ones   ○ 8 tens and 5 ones

NS 1.2, NS 1.0 Page 55

4. Which shows the numbers in order from greatest to least?   36   57   22

   22, 57, 36 ○   22, 36, 57 ○   57, 22, 36 ○   57, 36, 22 ○

KEY **NS 1.3**, KEY **NS 1.1**, NS 1.0 Page 69

5. Follow the pattern. Which is the missing number?   15, 19, 23, _____, 31

   24 ○   26 ○   27 ○   31 ○

KEY **SDAP 2.0**, SDAP 2.1 Page 85

Education Place
Visit www.eduplace.com/camap/ for
Test-Taking Tips and Extra Practice.

Spiral Review

Greg Tang's Go Fast, Go Far

Unit 2 Mental Math Strategies

Add Up

> Adding is a clever act, even when you must subtract.

> Starting at 8, I add 2 to make 10, then I add 1 more to make 11. The answer is 2 + 1 = 3!

1. $11 - 8 \rightarrow 8 + \boxed{3} = 11$

$\boxed{2} + \boxed{1}$

Make 10.　　Add the rest.

2. $13 - 9 \rightarrow 9 + \boxed{} = 13$

$\boxed{} + \boxed{}$

Make 10.　　Add the rest.

3. $14 - 8 \rightarrow 8 + \boxed{} = 14$

$\boxed{} + \boxed{}$

Make 10.　　Add the rest.

4. $11 - 7 \rightarrow 7 + \boxed{} = 11$

$\boxed{}\ \boxed{}$

5. $15 - 8 \rightarrow 8 + \boxed{} = 15$

$\boxed{}\ \boxed{}$

Take It Further: Now try doing all the steps in your head!

Good For You!

6. $17 - 8 = \boxed{}$

7. $15 - 9 = \boxed{}$

Reading and Writing Math

Complete the word web to show the
number 152 in different ways.

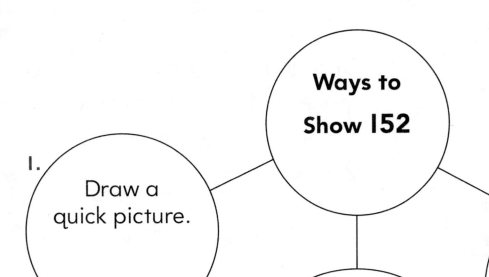

Ways to Show 152

1. Draw a quick picture.

2. Write the place of each digit.

Hundreds	Tens	Ones

3. Show the number in expanded form.

_____ + _____ + _____

4. **Writing Math** Write **7** or **3** for the missing
   digit to make the comparison true.
   Then explain your answer.

   ☐ 3 < 73

   _____

   7 ☐ > 73

   _____

|||||||||°°°°°

KEY NS 1.1 Count, read, and write whole numbers to
1,000 and identify the place value for each digit.
Also **KEY** NS 1.3, NS 1.2

Name _____

Concepts and Skills

Complete the chart. KEY **NS 1.1**

Find the place of each digit.	Write the expanded form.	Write the number.
1. two hundred nineteen Hundreds | Tens | Ones	_____ + _____ + _____	_____
2. one hundred seven Hundreds | Tens | Ones	_____ + _____ + _____	_____

Circle two ways to show the number. NS 1.2

3. | 31 | 3 tens 1 one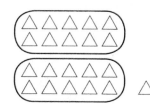

4. | 50 | 50 + 0   5 ones

Compare using >, <, or =.   KEY **NS 1.3**

5. 88 ◯ 90   6. 126 ◯ 97   7. 180 ◯ 108

Draw quick pictures. Write the numbers in order from least to greatest. Then order the numbers from greatest to least. KEY NS1.3

36   33   19

8. least to greatest   greatest to least

_____ _____ _____   _____ _____ _____

Write the missing numbers. KEY SDAP 2.0

9. 50, 52, _____, _____, 58, 60, 62

Draw groups of 2 to show the number.
Circle even or odd.   SDAP 2.2

10. 13   11. 12

     even   odd   even   odd

Problem Solving

Solve.   MR 2.0, KEY SDAP 2.0

12. What is wrong with this number pattern?

15, 20, 25, 30, 40, 45, 50

_____

_____

Unit

3

Money

BIG IDEAS!

- Different combinations of coins can have the same value.

- When the value of money is more than the price, you can count on to give back change.

Songs and Games

Math Music Track 3
Let's Go Shopping

eGames
www.eduplace.com/camap/

Literature

Read Aloud Big Book
- Coin Counting Book

Math Readers

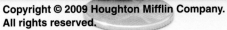

Coin Race

How to Play

1. Put counters on START.

2. Take turns spinning the spinner. Move forward to the next space with the coin you spin.

3. Continue taking turns until one player reaches FINISH.

What You Need

2 players

START

FINISH

FINISH

NS 5.0 Model and solve problems by representing, adding, and subtracting amounts of money. Also **MR 1.2**

Dear Family:

My class is starting Unit 3, **Money.** I will be learning how to identify coins, count money, and make change. You can help me learn these vocabulary words, and we can do the Math Activity together.

From:

_____

Vocabulary

 penny A coin worth 1¢

 nickel A coin worth 5¢

 dime A coin worth 10¢

 quarter A coin worth 25¢

 half-dollar A coin worth 50¢

 **dollar** A bill worth $1.00 or 100 cents

$1.00
↑ ↑
dollar sign   decimal point

 Education Place
Visit **www.eduplace.com/camaf/** for
• eGames and Brain Teasers
• Math at Home in other languages

Family Math Activity

Play store. Put some pennies, nickels, dimes, and quarters in a bag. Each person takes a handful of coins. Take turns being store clerk and customer. One person gives the price of an item, and the other has to decide if he or she has enough money to buy it. If the customer has enough money, he or she must buy the item. The clerk will give change back. Then trade roles.

Literature

These books link to the math in this unit. Look for them at the library.

• **The Coin Counting Book** by Rozanne Lanczack Williams (*Charlesbridge Publishing, 2001*)

• **How Much is that Guinea Pig in the Window?** by Joanne Rocklin Illustrated by Meredith Johnson

• **The Lunch Line** by Karen Berman Nagel Illustrated by Jerry Zimmerman

Estimada familia:

Mi clase está comenzando la Unidad 3, **Dinero**. Aprenderé a identificar monedas, contar dinero y hacer cambio. Me pueden ayudar a aprender estas palabras de vocabulario y podemos hacer juntos la Actividad de matemáticas para la familia.

De:

_____

Vocabulario

moneda de un centavo
Moneda que vale 1¢.

moneda de cinco centavos
Moneda que vale 5¢.

moneda de diez centavos
Moneda que vale 10¢.

moneda de veinticinco centavos
Moneda que vale 25¢.

moneda de medio dólar
Moneda que vale 50¢.

dólar Billete que vale $1.00 ó 100 centavos.

$1.00
↑ ↑
signo de dólar   punto decimal

Education Place
Visite **www.eduplace.com/camaf/** para
• Juegos en línea y acertijos
• Matemáticas en casa en otros idiomas

Actividad de matemáticas para la familia

Jueguen a la tienda. Coloquen algunas monedas de un centavo, de cinco centavos, de diez centavos y de veinticinco centavos en una bolsa. Cada persona toma un puñado de monedas. Túrnense para ser el vendedor y el cliente. Una persona da el precio de un objeto y la otra tiene que decidir si tiene suficiente dinero para comprarlo. Si el cliente tiene suficiente dinero, debe comprar el objeto. El vendedor dará el cambio. Luego intercambien roles.

Literatura

Estos libros hablan sobre las matemáticas de esta unidad. Búscalos en la biblioteca.

• **Alexander, que era rico el domingo pasado**
por Judith Viorst
(*Live Oak Media*, 2005)

UNIT 3

Money

written by Mike Mason

This Take-Home Book belongs to

_____

Reading and Writing Math

This take-home book will help you review money.

The year is 1967.
Stamps are 5¢.
I need 4 stamps.
Circle the coins I will
use to pay for my stamps.

KEY NS 5.1 Solve problems with combinations of coins and bills.

8

2

The year is 1899.

A quart costs 20¢. I need two quarts.
Circle the coins I will use to pay for the milk.

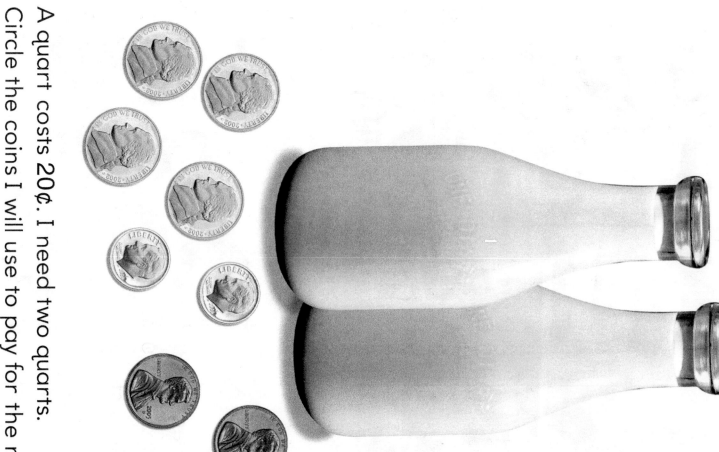

7

I just got a loaf of bread for 5¢.
I got a dozen eggs for 10¢.
Circle the coins you think I used to pay for
the eggs and bread.

The year is 1947.
Mom sent me to the store to buy milk.

The year is 1927.
My dad is buying gas for the car.

Gas costs 15¢ a gallon.
Dad will buy 1 gallon of gas.
Circle the coins he will use to pay
for gas.

Vocabulary

Here are some vocabulary words you will learn in the chapter.

cent sign (¢) A symbol used to show money value

45¢
↑
cent sign

 penny A coin worth 1¢

 **nickel** A coin worth 5¢

 dime A coin worth 10¢

 **quarter** A coin worth 25¢

 **half-dollar** A coin worth 50¢

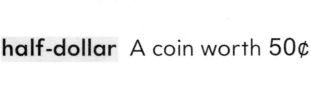

75¢

See English-Spanish Glossary pages 573–589.

 **KEY NS 5.1** Solve problems using combinations of coins and bills.
Also **KEY NS 5.2**

Education Place
Visit **www.eduplace.com/camap/**
for the eGlossary and eGames.

one hundred three **103**

Name _____

 Check What You Know

Solve. Use the picture.

1. How many pennies are there? _____ pennies

   What is the value of 10 pennies? _____

2. How many pennies equal the value of 1 nickel?

   _____ pennies

   What is the value of 1 nickel? _____

3. How many pennies equal the value of 1 dime?

   _____ pennies

   What is the value of 1 dime? _____

4. How many pennies equal the value of 1 quarter?

   _____ pennies

5. How many nickels equal the value of 1 quarter?

   _____ nickels

Use this page to review important skills needed for this chapter.

Identify Coins

 **Explore**

Think!
A ¢ symbol after a
number means "cents."

Each **coin** has a value.

Hands On 🖐

Objective
Identify coins and
order them by value.

Vocabulary
coin
half-dollar
quarter
dime
nickel
penny

half-dollar	quarter	dime	nickel	penny
50¢	25¢	10¢	5¢	1¢

You can order coins by their value. Find a coin
in your coin set to match each picture.

1. Put the coins in order from greatest value
   to least value. Draw the coins in order.
   Write their names.

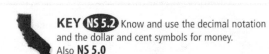

_____ _____ _____ _____

2. **(123)** **Math Talk** How do you know how to put
   a nickel, quarter, and dime in order from
   greatest to least value?

KEY NS 5.2 Know and use the decimal notation
and the dollar and cent symbols for money.
Also **NS 5.0**

MR 1.2 Use tools, such as manipulatives or sketches,
to model problems.

one hundred five **105**

Use your coin set or Learning Tool 18.
Find a coin to match the value.
Write the name of the coin.

Remember!
¢ is a cent sign.

3. 25¢

_____

4. 5¢

_____

5. 10¢

_____

6. 50¢

_____

7. 1¢

_____

Use your coin set or Learning Tool 18 to
find a coin to match each picture. Write
the coin values. Draw the coins in order
from greatest to least value.

8.

_____   _____   _____   _____

9.

_____   _____   _____   _____

10.

_____   _____   _____   _____

At Home Show your child some
coins. Ask him or her to identify the
coins and tell their values.

En casa Muestre a su niño algunas monedas.
Pídale que las identifique y que diga su valor.

Name _____

Count Coins

▶ **Learn**

Find the value of these coins.

Start with the coin of the greatest value.

Put your coins in order to find the value. Write the value of each coin. Count on. Write the total value.

25¢ 25¢ 25¢ 10¢ 5¢

25¢ 50¢ 75¢ 85¢ 90¢

The total value is __90¢__.

▶ **Guided Practice**

1. Use any five coins. Sort the coins. Write the value of each coin. Count on. Write the total.

Think!
I need to use the ¢ symbol.

◯ ◯ ◯ ◯ ◯

____ ____ ____ ____   total = ____

2. **Math Talk** What combination of coins could you use to make 25¢?

KEY NS 5.1 Solve problems using combinations of coins and bills.
Also NS 5.0, MR 1.2, MR 2.0

KEY NS 5.2 Know and use the decimal notation and the dollar and cent symbols for money.

one hundred seven **107**

▶ Practice

Use coins or Learning Tool 18.
Count on to find the value of the coins.

3.

96¢

4.

_____

5.

_____

6.

_____

7.

_____

8.

_____

Problem Solving: Visual Thinking

9. Rachel has **3** quarters. Brian has
7 dimes. Who has the group
of coins with the greater value?

_____

Draw or write to explain.

At Home Find items advertised for
99¢ or less. Ask your child to tell which
coins could be used to buy each item.

En casa En anuncios, busque objetos que
cuesten 99¢ o menos. Pida a su niño que
le diga qué monedas pueden usarse para
comprar cada objeto.

Chapter 6 Lesson 3

Equal Amounts

 **Learn**

Different sets of coins can make **equal** amounts.

 **Hands On**

Objective
Show equal amounts with different coin combinations.

Vocabulary
equal

25¢   25¢

25¢

▶ **Guided Practice**

Use your coin set or Learning Tool 18. Show two ways to make 50¢. Draw the coins.

Think!
I can show 50¢ with quarters, dimes, nickels, and pennies.

1. 50¢

2. 50¢

3. **123** **Math Talk** Would it take more nickels or more dimes to make 50¢? How do you know?

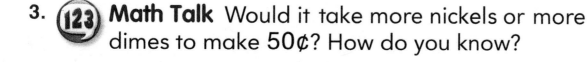

KEY **NS 5.1** Solve problems using combinations of coins and bills.
Also KEY **NS 5.2**, MR 1.2, MR 2.0

NS 5.0 Model and solve problems by representing, adding, and subtracting amounts of money.

one hundred nine **109**

Remember!
You can count on to
find the value of a set
of coins.

Use your coin set or Learning
Tool 18. Show two ways to
make the amount shown.
Draw the coins.

76¢

4. 76¢

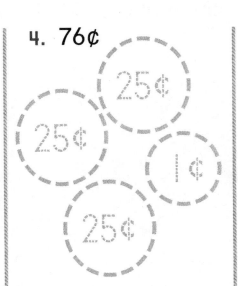

25¢ 25¢ 1¢ 25¢

5. 76¢

6. 97¢

7. 97¢

97¢

Problem Solving: Number Sense

Draw or write to explain.

8. Reema has **22¢**. She has only 1 dime.
Draw the coins she could have.

Compare Money Amounts

Objective
Compare the values
of sets of coins.

Vocabulary
greater than (>)
less than (<)
equal (=)

 **Learn**

Compare the values
of two sets of coins.

__60__¢ ⊘(>) __50__¢   __30__¢ (<) __65__¢

60¢ is **greater than** 50¢.   30¢ is **less than** 65¢.

▶ **Guided Practice**

Write the value of the sets of coins.
Compare the sets.
Write >, <, or =.

> **Think!**
> When the values
> are the same, they
> are equal (=).

1.

_____¢ ◯ _____¢

2.

_____¢ ◯ _____¢

3. (123) **Math Talk** Do 5 coins always have a greater
value than 3 coins? How do you know?

 **KEY** NS 5.1 Solve problems using combinations
of coins and bills.
Also **KEY** NS 1.3, NS 5.0, MR 2.0

KEY NS 5.2 Know and use the decimal notation
and the dollar and cent symbols for money.

one hundred eleven **111**

Write the value of the sets of coins.
Compare the sets.

4.

42 ¢ (>) 26 ¢

5.

_____ ¢ ( ) _____ ¢

6.

_____ ¢ ( ) _____ ¢

7.

_____ ¢ ( ) _____ ¢

Problem Solving: Reasoning

8. Jenny has **2** quarters, **2** dimes, and a nickel. How much more money does she need to buy the bag?

_____ ¢

90¢

Draw or write to explain.

Chapter 6 Lesson 5

Make a List

 **Learn**

Lisa wants to buy a top for 35¢.
She has 1 quarter, 3 dimes, and 7 nickels.
How many ways can she make 35¢?

Problem Solving
Strategy

Objective
Make a list to show
the same amount in
different ways.

Think!
I have to make
sure each total adds
up to 35¢.

Understand
What do you know?
• A top costs 35¢.
• Lisa has 1 quarter, 3 dimes,
  and 7 nickels.

Plan
Use coins to make a list.
Find all the ways to make
the money amount.

Solve
Complete the list.

There are ___6___ ways to make
35¢ with Lisa's coins.

Make 35¢

25¢	10¢	5¢
1	1	
		2

Look Back
Did you answer the question?
How do you know you found
all the ways?

KEY NS 5.1 Solve problems using combinations of coins and bills.
Also **NS 5.0, MR 1.0, MR 1.1, MR 2.0, MR 2.2**

SDAP 1.1 Record numerical data in systematic ways, keeping track of what has been counted.

Remember!
Understand
Plan
Solve
Look Back

1. Henry wants to buy a toy car for 40¢. He has quarters, dimes, and nickels. Show five ways that he can make 40¢.

   What do you know?

   The toy car costs _____¢.

   Henry has quarters, dimes, and nickels.

Make 40¢		
25¢	10¢	5¢

2.  **Math Talk** How did you find 5 ways to make 40¢?

Make a list to solve.

3. Ella wants a doll. She has dimes and nickels. Show three ways Ella can make 25¢.

Make 25¢	
10¢	5¢

4. Mario wants a book. He has quarters, dimes, and nickels. Show four ways he can make 30¢.

Make 30¢		
25¢	10¢	5¢

 At Home Have your child explain how to find three ways to make 20¢ with nickels and dimes.

En casa Pida a su niño que explique cómo hacer una lista para hallar tres maneras de juntar 20¢ usando monedas de cinco y diez centavos.

Name _____

California Field Trip

At the Kern County Museum

You can learn about California history. You can take a tour of a one-room school. You can walk on a big map of the United States. You can shop for toys at the General Store.

Making adobe bricks

Choose a way to solve. Show your work.

1. At the General Store, Tara wants to buy a postcard that costs 50¢. She has quarters, dimes, and nickels. What are three ways she can make 50¢?

   _____

   _____

postcard

2. Mike wants to buy a marble that costs 30¢. He has dimes and nickels. What are three ways he can make 30¢?

   _____

   _____

marble

3. Vanessa buys jacks for 60¢ and a paper doll for 30¢. How much does she spend in all?

   _____

jacks

KEY NS 5.1 Solve problems using combinations of coins and bills. Also **MR 1.0, MR 1.1**

NS 5.0 Model and solve problems by representing, adding, and subtracting amounts of money.

Problem Solving on Tests
Listening Skills

Listen to your teacher read the problem.
Choose the correct answer.

Select a Strategy
Find a Pattern
Use a Graph
Reasonable
  Answers
Act It Out

1. What is likely to come next in the pattern?

6, 12, 18, 24, _____

18	28	30	32
○	○	○	○

SDAP 2.1

2. A number has 7 ones, three tens, and one hundred. What is the number?

731	317	173	137
○	○	○	○

KEY NS 1.1

3.

90¢	70¢	65¢	55¢
○	○	○	○

NS 5.0

4.

20	30	50	80
○	○	○	○

Games at the Store

checkers	□		
bingo	□	□	□
cards	□		
tic-tac-toe	□	□	□	□

Key: Each □ = 10 games

KEY SDAP 1.0

MR 1.0 Make decisions about how to set up a problem.
MR 1.1 Determine the approach, materials, and strategies to be used.

Education Place
Visit www.eduplace.com/camap/ for
Test-Taking Tips and Extra Practice.

Name _____

 # Key Standards Review

Write the missing numbers.

Skip count by 2s.

1. 70, 72, _____, 76, _____, 80, _____

2. 52, 54, _____, _____, 60, _____

Skip count by 5s.

3. 30, 35, _____, _____, 50, _____

4. 65, _____, _____, 80, _____, 90

Skip count by 10s.

5. 30, 40 _____, _____, _____, 80

6. 45, _____, 65, _____, _____, 95

Challenge   **Patterns**

The Mayas used these numbers to count to 10. Can you find a pattern? Use the pattern to show how the Mayas wrote the number 11.

•	• •	• • •	• • • •	▬
1	2	3	4	5

| • | • • | • • • | • • • • | ▬ |
▬	▬	▬	▬	▬
6	7	8	9	10

 KEY SDAP 2.0 Demonstrate an understanding of patterns and how patterns grow and describe them in general ways.

The California Quarter

The first California quarter came out in 2005. Quarters and other coins are made at mints. The quarter is made of the metals nickel and copper. One roll of metal at the mint is as long as **5** football fields!

Solve.

1. Krissy has **3** California quarters, **1** nickel, and **2** pennies. How much money does she have?

   _____

2. She wants to buy the pencil. Does she have enough money to buy it?

   _____

   50¢

3. Krissy's dad gives her the coins shown. How much money does he give her?

   _____

KEY NS 5.1 Solve problems using combinations of coins and bills.
Also **NS 5.0**
Science ES 3.e

Name _____

Concepts and Skills

Write the coin values. Draw the coins in order
from greatest value to least value. KEY NS 5.2

1.

   _____   _____   _____   _____

Show two ways to make the amount. Draw the coins. KEY NS 5.1

2. 35¢

Write the value of the sets of coins. Compare the sets. KEY NS 5.1

3.

    _____ ¢ ◯ _____ ¢

Problem Solving KEY NS 5.1, NS 5.0, MR 2.0

4. Mara has 2 quarters, 1 dime, and
   2 pennies. She wants to buy a purse
   that is 75¢. How much more money
   does she need? Why?

   _____

1. Which number sentence completes this fact family?

$3 + 2 = 5$ $2 + 3 = 5$ $5 - 2 = 3$

$5 + 2 = 7$ ○ $5 + 3 = 8$ ○ $5 - 1 = 4$ ○ $5 - 3 = 2$ ○

KEY **NS 2.1** Page 9

2. Which is this number? 7 tens, 0 ones

7 ○   17 ○   70 ○   77 ○

NS 1.2, NS 1.0 Page 55

3. Which is this number rounded to the nearest ten?   45

40 ○   45 ○   50 ○   100 ○

NS 6.0 Page 71

4. What number is 10 more than 60?

50 ○   60 ○   61 ○   70 ○

KEY **SDAP 2.0**, SDAP 2.1 Page 87

5. What is the value of the coins?

61¢ ○   60¢ ○   46¢ ○   34¢ ○

KEY **NS 5.1**, KEY **NS 5.2**, NS 5.0 Page 107

Education Place
Visit www.eduplace.com/camap/ for
Test-Taking Tips and Extra Practice.

120 ☐ll   Spiral Review

Dollar and Coins

Vocabulary

Here are some vocabulary words you will learn in the chapter.

change The amount of money you get back when you pay more than the price

dollar An amount of money equal to 100 cents

 =

dollar sign ($) A symbol usually used to show money that is equal to one dollar or more

decimal point Separates the dollars and cents when writing an amount of money

$1.00
↑ ↑
dollar sign   decimal point

See English-Spanish Glossary pages 573–589.

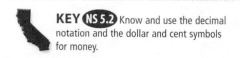 **KEY NS 5.2** Know and use the decimal notation and the dollar and cent symbols for money.

Education Place
Visit **www.eduplace.com/camap/** for the eGlossary and eGames.

one hundred twenty-one **121**

Name _____

✔ Check What You Know

Solve. Use the picture.

1. Complete the table using the coins shown above.

Type of Coin	Number of Coins	Total Value
penny	_____	_____ ¢
nickel	_____	_____ ¢
dime	_____	_____ ¢
quarter	_____	_____ ¢

2. If you add the nickels and quarters together, how much money is that in all?

   _____ ¢ + _____ ¢ = _____ ¢

3. What is the total amount shown by all the coins?   _____ ¢

4. If you take away a dime and a nickel, how much do you have left?   _____ ¢

5. If you add a nickel, how much money do you have in all? $ _____

Use this page to review important skills needed for this chapter.

Name _____

Use Coins to Show an Amount

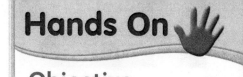

Hands On

Objective
Make an exact amount.

► **Learn**

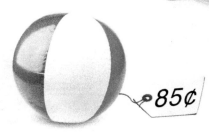

37¢   85¢   50¢   70¢

Luis wants to buy the car. He chooses the coins to make the exact amount.

Count: 25¢, 35¢, 36¢, 37¢

Ana wants to buy the hat. She needs more coins to make the exact amount.

Count: 25¢, 35¢, 45¢, 55¢, 60¢
Ana needs 10¢ more.

► **Guided Practice**

Use coins to show the price.
Circle the coins you used.

Think!
I start counting with the quarter.

1.

50¢

2.

65¢

3. **123** **Math Talk** Are **3** quarters and **3** pennies enough to pay for a toy that costs **83¢**? How do you know?

KEY NS 5.1 Solve problems using combinations of coins and bills.
Also **MR 1.2, KEY** NS 5.2, **MR 2.0, MR 2.1**

NS 5.0 Model and solve problems by representing, adding, and subtracting amounts of money.

► **Practice**

Use coins to show the price.
Circle the coins you used.

Remember!
Start with the coins
of greatest value.
Count on.

4.
42¢

5.
46¢

6.
65¢

Problem Solving: Reasoning

7. Sam wants to buy the hat.
   Show how to pay the exact
   amount with three coins.

8. Did everyone in your
   class show the same
   coins? Why?

55¢

Draw or write to explain.

124

Objective
Make an amount using the fewest coins.

Use Money

▶ Learn

Josh pays for the book with the fewest coins possible. What coins does he use?

 40¢

Step 1	Step 2
Find the coin of the greatest value. Try a quarter.	Count on until you reach 40¢.

Step 1: _25_ ¢

Step 2: _35_ ¢   _40_ ¢

Josh uses a _quarter_, a _dime_, and a _nickel_.

▶ Guided Practice

Think!
Which coin should I start with to show 56¢?

Draw the fewest coins that show the amount.

1.  56¢

2.  19¢

3. (123) **Math Talk** How do you decide which coin you can start with to use the fewest coins?

KEY NS 5.1 Solve problems using combinations of coins and bills.
Also **MR 1.2, KEY** NS 5.2, MR 2.0, MR 2.1, SDAP 1.1

NS 5.0 Model and solve problems by representing, adding, and subtracting amounts of money.

one hundred twenty-five **125**

Draw the fewest coins that show the amount.

4.

75¢

 50¢   25¢

5.

81¢

6.

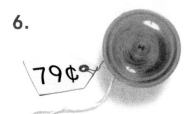

79¢

7.

99¢

Problem Solving: Data Sense

8. Find the fewest coins that show each amount. Complete the table to show how many of each coin are needed.

	Half-Dollar	Quarter	Dime	Nickel	Penny
29¢					
82¢					

At Home Have your child use the fewest coins to show 16¢, 32¢, 58¢, and 95¢.

En casa Pida a su niño que use la menor cantidad de monedas para mostrarle 16¢, 32¢, 58¢ y 95¢.

Name _____

One Dollar

▶ **Learn**

100¢ has the same value as one **dollar.**
Use a **dollar sign ($)** and a **decimal point (.)**
when you write one dollar.

Objective
Identify coin combinations equal to a dollar and record them using the proper notation.

Vocabulary
dollar
dollar sign ($)
decimal point (.)

one dollar

100¢ or $1.00
↑ ↑
dollar sign decimal point

one dollar

100¢ or $1.00

The decimal point goes between the dollar and the cents.

▶ **Guided Practice**

Draw more coins to make one dollar.

Write the amount.

1.

100¢

$1.00

Think!
2 quarters equal 50¢.
How many more quarters do I need?

2.

_____

_____

3. **123** **Math Talk** What other coins could you use to show one dollar?

KEY NS 5.2 Know and use the decimal notation and the dollar and cent symbols for money.
Also **NS 5.0, MR 2.0**

KEY NS 5.1 Solve problems using combinations of coins and bills.

one hundred twenty-seven **127**

▶ Practice

Write the value of the coins.
Circle the sets of coins
that equal one dollar.

Remember!
Use a dollar symbol
and a decimal point to
write one dollar.

4.

$1.00

_____

5.

_____

6.

_____

7.

_____

Problem Solving: Reasoning

8. Tara has **2** quarters and **4** dimes.
Does she have **$1.00** or less than
$1.00?

_____

Draw or write to explain.

At Home Show your child coins that
are equal to and less than $1.00. Ask
your child to find the total.

En casa Muestre a su niño grupos de
monedas que sean iguales y menores que
$1.00. Pida a su niño que halle el total.

Name _____

Make Change

 **Learn**

When you pay more money than
the price, you get **change.**

Beth buys:

43¢

She pays:

50¢

Make change.
Count on from the price
to the amount Beth paid.

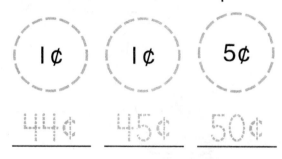

(1¢) (1¢) (5¢)

44¢   45¢   50¢

The change is _____7¢_____.

▶ **Guided Practice**

Write the amount paid.
Draw coins and count on to find the change.

Think!
I can count on from
17¢ to 20¢.

	Amount Paid	Price	Draw Coins to Count On	Change
1.	_____¢	17¢	_____¢ _____¢ _____¢	_____¢

2. **(123) Math Talk** You have 75¢. Will you get more
change if you buy something for 56¢ or for
36¢? How do you know?

KEY NS 5.1 Solve problems using combinations
of coins and bills.
Also **KEY NS 5.2**, MR 1.2, MR 2.0, MR 2.1

NS 5.0 Model and solve problems by representing,
adding, and subtracting amounts of money.

one hundred twenty-nine **129**

Write the amount paid. Draw coins and count on to find the change.

	Amount Paid	Price	Draw Coins to Count On			Change
3.	50 ¢	10¢	(5¢) (10¢) (25¢) 15 ¢	25 ¢	50 ¢	40 ¢
4.	____ ¢	63¢	____ ¢	____ ¢	____ ¢	____ ¢
5.	$ ____	93¢	____ ¢	____ ¢ $ ____		____ ¢
6.	$ ____	$1.04	$ ____	$ ____	$ ____	____ ¢

Problem Solving: Reasoning

7. Jamie pays for this puppet with a dollar. He gets 3 coins back as change. What coins does he get?

84¢

Draw or write to explain.

Name _____

Chapter 7 Lesson 4

▶ **Practice**

Write the amount paid.
Draw coins and count on to find the change.

	Amount Paid	Price	Draw Coins to Count On	Change
8.	_____ ¢	20¢	_____ ¢ _____ ¢	_____ ¢
9.	_____ ¢	15¢	_____ ¢ _____ ¢	_____ ¢
10.	_____ ¢	55¢	_____ ¢ _____ ¢	_____ ¢
11.	$_____	90¢	$_____	_____ ¢
12.	$_____	60¢	_____ ¢ _____ ¢ $_____	_____ ¢

KEY **NS 5.1** Solve problems using combinations of coins and bills.
Also KEY **NS 5.2**

Go for the Money

How to Play

What You Need

2 players

Coin set

1. Put game pieces on Start.

2. Take turns tossing the number cube. Move that many spaces.

3. Follow the directions on the space where you land.

4. The first player to collect $1.00 wins.

START

Take 10¢.

Take 20¢.

Take 3 nickels.

Take 2 dimes.

Put back 1 nickel.

Put back 15¢.

Skip a turn.

Take 2 nickels.

Take 1 dime.

Put back 10¢.

Take 25¢.

NS 5.0 Model and solve problems by representing, adding, and subtracting amounts of money.

Education Place
Visit www.eduplace.com/camap/ for more games.

Name _____

Act It Out

 **Learn**

Tom has **4** dimes, **2** nickels, and **2** pennies. Does he have enough money to buy the toy?

55¢

Objective
Use money to solve problems in amounts up to and including $1.00.

Understand

What do you know?

• Tom has **4** dimes, **2** nickels, and **2** pennies.

• The toy costs **55¢**.

Plan

Act out the problem to solve.
Use coins to show Tom's money.
Find the total amount.

Tom has ___52¢___.

Solve

Compare the amount Tom has
to the price of the toy.
Tom has **52¢**. The toy costs ___55¢___ .

52¢ (<) 55¢

Does Tom have enough money to buy the toy? ___No___

Look Back

Does your answer make sense?
What helped you decide if Tom could buy the toy?

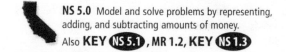 **NS 5.0** Model and solve problems by representing, adding, and subtracting amounts of money.
MR 2.0 Solve problems and justify reasoning.
Also **KEY NS 5.1** , **MR 1.2, KEY NS 1.3**

one hundred thirty-three **133**

Guided Problem Solving

Use coins to act out the problem.
Solve.

Remember!
Understand
Plan
Solve
Look Back

1. Ron has **2** dimes and **3** nickels.
   He wants to buy the puzzle.
   Does he have enough money?

   Use coins to act out the problem.
   Write the total amount Ron has.

   _____

   Compare the amount that Ron
   has with the price of the puzzle.

   Ron _____ buy the puzzle.

   _____ ◯ _____

2. **123** **Math Talk** How do you know if Ron
   has enough money to buy the puzzle?

Problem Solving Practice

Use coins. Solve.

3. Sara has **2** quarters, **1** nickel, and
   1 penny. How much money does she
   have? How much more does she need
   to buy a jump rope that costs **78¢**?

   _____

   _____

   Draw or write to explain.

4. Tami earns **25¢** to set the table
   and **10¢** to walk the dog. If she
   does each job **2** times, how much
   will she earn altogether?

   _____

At Home Show one quarter and
several dimes and nickels. Ask if there is
enough to buy an item that costs 80¢.

En casa Muestre una moneda de 25 centavos
y varias monedas de 10 centavos y de 5
centavos. Pregunte si hay suficiente para
comprar un objeto que cueste 80¢.

Create and Solve

Bethany has 4 quarters, 3 dimes,
4 nickels, and 5 pennies.

Objective
Write problems
and use strategies
to solve them.

$1.00   15¢   15¢   52¢

1. Bethany wants to buy a hat and a balloon.
   Does she have enough money?
   Circle your answer.
   Use coins to help you solve.

   yes   no

2. Write an addition problem about Bethany's coins
   and the objects above.

   _____

   _____

   _____

   _____

3. Write an addition sentence to solve your problem.

   _____ + _____ = _____

   Share your addition story with a classmate.

AF 1.0 Model, represent, and interpret number
relationships to create and solve problems involving
addition and subtraction.

NS 5.0 Model and solve problems by representing,
adding, and subtracting amounts of money.
Also **KEY NS 5.1**, **KEY NS 5.2**, AF 1.2,
MR 1.0, MR 1.1

one hundred thirty-five **135**

Awon has **2** quarters, **3** dimes, **2** nickels, and **2** pennies. He buys a juice box. How much money does he have left? Use coins to help you solve.

15¢   50¢   20¢   60¢

4. Write a number sentence to solve.

_____¢ – _____¢ = _____¢

5. Write a subtraction problem about Awon's coins and the objects above.

_____

_____

_____

_____

6. Write a subtraction sentence to solve your problem.

_____ – _____ = _____

Share your subtraction story with a classmate.

Name _____

 # Key Standards Review

Use the coins shown to answer the questions.

1. Write the total value of the coins. _____

2. If you added a dime to the coins above, how much money would there be in all? _____

3. If you took away 2 nickels from the coins above, how much money would be left? _____

4. Marco has 2 quarters and 5 nickels. Use <, >, or = to compare his total coin value to the coins above.

   Marco's coins   Coins above

   _____ ◯ _____

Challenge   **Money**

Write the values of the missing coins to make each side of the puzzle adds up to 40¢.

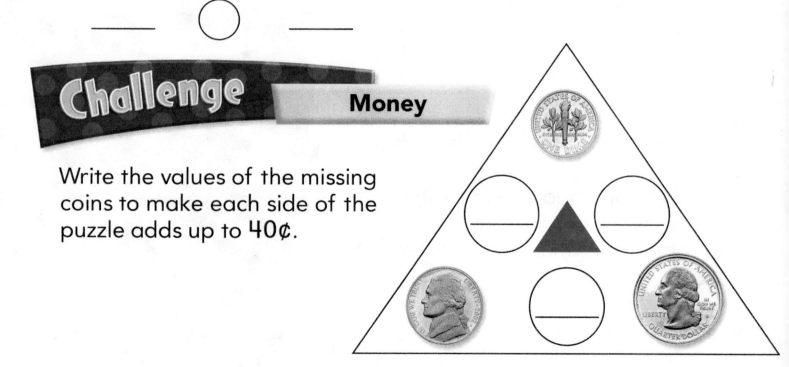

KEY **NS 5.1** Solve problems using combinations of coins and bills.
Also KEY **NS 1.3**

one hundred thirty-seven **137**

Let's Go Shopping

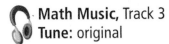 **Math Music,** Track 3
Tune: original

Let's go shopping at the store.
We'll buy two toys, and then no more!
Blue car, red car—fast and new—
There's one for me and one for you.
Count out coins to buy each one—
After paying, we'll have fun!

Counting pennies. Count each one.
1, 2, 3, 4—have some fun!
Counting nickels—there are plenty!
5, 10, 15, now comes 20!
Counting dimes—they are so nifty—
10, 20, 30, 40, 50!
Counting quarters, shout and holler—
25, 50, 75, $1.00!

80 cents will buy each one.
Skip count coins and then we're done!
25, 50, 75, 80—
A car for Hong and one for Katie!
Can you count another way?
Use some coins, then shout *Hooray!*

KEY NS 5.1 Solve problems using combinations of coins and bills.

Name _____

Concepts and Skills

Circle the coins that make the exact amount. KEY NS 5.1

1.

Write the value of the coins. KEY NS 5.2

2.

$_____

Write the amount paid.
Draw coins and count on to find the change. KEY NS 5.1

3.

Amount Paid	Price	Draw Coins to Count On	Change
_____ ¢	72¢	_____ ¢ _____ ¢ _____ ¢	_____ ¢

Problem Solving KEY NS 5.1, NS 5.0

4. Valerie wants to buy a pen that costs 45¢. Show how to pay the exact amount with three coins.

1. Which shows the numbers in order from least to greatest?

36   57   22

| 36, 57, 22 | 57, 36, 22 | 22, 57, 36 | 22, 36, 57 |
| ○ | ○ | ○ | ○ |

KEY **NS 1.3**, KEY **NS 1.1**, NS 1.0 Page 69

---

2. Which picture shows an even number?

           ●

| ○ | ○ | ○ | ○ |

SDAP 1.2 Page 89

---

3. Which group of coins is worth more than the coins shown?

| ○ | ○ | ○ | ○ |

KEY **NS 5.1**, NS 5.0 Page III

---

4. Which set of coins shows the price?

75¢

| ○ | ○ | ○ | ○ |

KEY **NS 5.1**, NS 5.0 Page 125

Education Place
Visit www.eduplace.com/camap/ for
Test-Taking Tips and Extra Practice.

Spiral Review

Name _____

Greg Tang's Go Fast, Go Far

Make 10s

No need for paper or a pen. First make a multiple of 10!

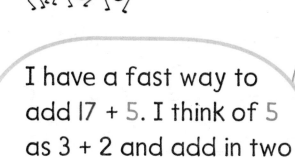

I have a fast way to add 17 + 5. I think of 5 as 3 + 2 and add in two steps. First I add 17 + 3 to make 20. Then I add the rest. 20 + 2 = 22.

1. 17 + 5 = ☐ 22

    [3] + [2]
    Make 20.   Add the rest.

2. 26 + 7 = ☐

    ☐ + ☐
    Make 30.   Add the rest.

3. 49 + 8 = ☐

    ☐ + ☐
    Make 50.   Add the rest.

4. 15 + 8 = ☐

    ☐ ☐

5. 28 + 4 = ☐

    ☐ ☐

Great Job!

Take It Further: Now try doing it in your head!

6. 53 + 8 = ☐   7. 74 + 8 = ☐

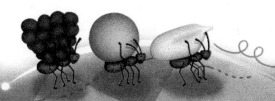

Reading and Writing Math

Choose a word from the word bank for each blank. Use each word only once.

Word Bank
dime
dollar
half-dollar
nickel
penny
quarter

1. 100¢ has the same value as one _____.

2. A _____ is worth 50¢.

3. There are 5 cents in a _____.

4. A _____ is worth 1¢.

5. A _____ is worth more than a _____.

6. **Writing Math** Which of these amounts would you rather have? Explain your answer.

_____

_____

KEY NS 5.1 Solve problems using combinations of coins and bills.
Also **KEY** NS 5.2, MR 2.1

Name _____

Concepts and Skills

Find the value of the coins. **NS 5.0**

1.    _____

Show two ways to make the amount.
Draw the coins. **KEY NS 5.1**

2. 34¢

Write the value of each set of coins.
Compare. **KEY NS 5.1**

3.

_____¢   ◯   _____¢

Circle the coins that make the exact amount. **KEY NS 5.1**

4.  45¢

Draw the fewest coins that show the amount. **KEY NS 5.1**

5.

45¢

Write the total value of the coins.
Circle the coins that add up to one dollar. **KEY NS 5.1**

6.

_____

Write the amount paid. Draw coins
and count on to find the change. **KEY NS 5.1**

	Amount Paid	Price	Draw Coins to Count On	Change
7.	_____ ¢	89¢	_____ ¢ _____ ¢	_____ ¢

Problem Solving

Solve. NS 5.0

8. Hillary has 48¢. She has only
I quarter. Draw the coins she
could have.

Unit

4

Add 2-Digit Numbers

BIG IDEAS!

- You can use drawings, a hundred chart, or you can line up digits to add two-digit numbers.

Songs and Games

Math Music Track 4
Regrouping Is
What We Do!

eGames
www.eduplace.com/camap/

Literature

Read Aloud Big Book
- Wishes and Swishes

Math Readers

Nature's Numbers
by Amy Lohn
illustrated by John Revell

Click! Flash!
Bunnies
by Eduardo Baro
illustrated by Jeff Mack

The Roadside Stand
FRESH VEGETABLES
by Asa Endo
illustrated by Mircea Catusanu

Add and Score!

How to Play

1. Place the number cards face down.

2. Choose two cards. Add the numbers to find the sum. Score 1 point each time you add two 2-digit numbers. Keep the cards.

3. Take turns until all the number cards have been used.

4. The player with the most points wins.

What You Need

2 players
Learning Tool 30

50 20 5 10 30
6 7 40 8 9

KEY NS 2.2 Find the sum or difference of two whole numbers up to three digits long.
Also **NS 2.0, NS 2.3, MR 1.2**

Education Place
Visit **www.eduplace.com/camap/**
for eGames and Brain Teasers.

Math at Home

Dear Family,

My class is starting Unit 4, **Add 2-Digit Numbers.** I will be learning different strategies to help me add 2-digit numbers, such as estimating sums and regrouping ones. You can help me learn these vocabulary words, and we can do the Math Activity together.

From,

_____

Vocabulary

sum The result of addition

$$24 + 53 = 77$$

$$\begin{array}{r} 24 \\ +53 \\ \hline 77 \end{array}$$

sum ⟶ 77

estimate A rounded answer that is close to an exact answer

29 ——round to nearest ten——> 30

+21 ——round to nearest ten——> +20

estimate ⟶ 50

regroup In addition, trade 10 ones for 1 ten.

 Education Place
Visit **www.eduplace.com/camaf/** for
• eGames and Brain Teasers
• Math at Home in other languages

Family Math Activity

Use a paper and a pencil to make spinners. Spin each spinner to make a 2-digit number. Spin again to make another 2-digit number. Have your child tell an addition story using the 2 numbers. Then have them tell you if they need to regroup to find the sum.

Literature

These books link to the math in this unit. Look for them at the library.

• **A Collection for Kate**
  by Barbara deRubertis
  Illustrated by Gioia Fiammenghi
  (*The Kane Press*, 1999)

• **Mall Mania**
  by Stuart J. Murphy
  Illustrated by Renée Andriani

• **The King's Commissioners**
  by Aileen Friedman
  Illustrated by Susan Guevara

Matemáticas en casa

Estimada familia:

Mi clase está comenzando la Unidad 4, **Suma de números de 2 dígitos**. Aprenderé diferentes estrategias para sumar números de 2 dígitos, como estimar sumas y reagrupar unidades. Me pueden ayudar a aprender estas palabras de vocabulario y podemos hacer juntos la Actividad de matemáticas para la familia.

De:

_____

Vocabulario

suma El resultado de la suma.

$$24 + 53 = 77$$

$$\begin{array}{r} 24 \\ + 53 \\ \hline 77 \end{array}$$

↑
suma ⟶

estimación Respuesta aproximada que es cercana a una respuesta exacta.

29	redondear a la decena más cercana ⟶	30
+21	redondear a la decena más cercana ⟶	+20
	estimación ⟶	50

reagrupar En la suma, intercambiar 10 unidades por 1 decena.

Education Place
Visite **www.eduplace.com/camaf/** para
• Juegos en línea y acertijos
• Matemáticas en casa en otros idiomas

Actividad de matemáticas para la familia

Usen papel y lápiz para hacer ruedas giratorias. Giren cada rueda para crear un número de 2 dígitos. Gírenlas de nuevo para crear otro número de 2 dígitos. Pida a su niño que cuente un cuento de suma usando los 2 números. Luego pregúntele si necesita reagrupar para hallar la suma y por qué.

Literatura

Estos libros hablan sobre las matemáticas de esta unidad. Búscalos en la biblioteca.

• **¡Qué montón de tamales!** por Gary Soto y Ed Martinez (Putnam Juvenile, 1996)

• **Cincuenta en la cebra** por Nancy Maria Grande Tabor

UNIT
4

Under the Sea

Written by Tim Johnson

This Take-Home Book belongs to

Reading and Writing Math

This take-home book will help you review addition through 20.

Mask

Flippers

Snorkel

KEY **NS 2.2** Find the sum or difference of two whole numbers up to three digits long.

12

My family went on a trip where we could snorkel.

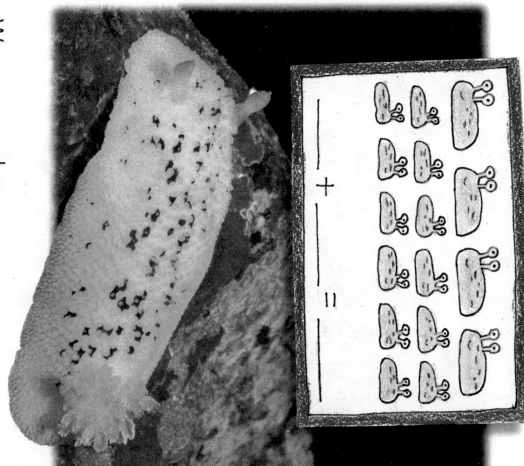

We saw sea lemons.
They are a kind of slug.
We saw 12 small ones and 4 big ones.
How many sea lemons did we see in all?

_____ sea lemons

Snorkeling is great fun. We saw
many things that live in the sea.

We saw two spiny lobsters hiding in rocks.
Each lobster had 10 legs.
How many legs did we see in all?

10

____ + ____ = ____ legs

We saw two groups of clownfish.
How many in all did we see?

_____ clownfish

We saw two red rock crabs.
Each had 8 legs and 2 claws.
How many legs do 2 crabs have in all?

_____ + _____ = _____ legs

We saw sea stars, too.
5 were big and 2 were small.
How many sea stars did we see in all?

___ + ___ = ___ sea stars

We found many different kinds of shells.

Circle two groups of shells.
Write an addition fact about the groups.

___ + ___ = ___ shells

The bluebar goby is beautiful.
We saw two groups of them.
One group had 4 and the other had 5.

How many did we see in all?

_____ bluebar gobies

Explore Adding Tens and Ones

Vocabulary

Here are some vocabulary words you will learn in the chapter.

ones Single objects
You can use ones blocks to count by ones.

6 ones

tens Groups of ten objects
You can use tens rods to count by tens.

4 tens

regroup Rename 10 ones as 1 ten

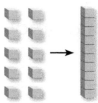

10 ones are the same as 1 ten.

See English-Spanish Glossary pages 573–589.

 **KEY** NS 2.2 Find the sum or difference of two whole numbers up to three digits long.

 **Education Place**
Visit **www.eduplace.com/camap/** for the eGlossary and eGames.

one hundred forty-seven **147**

Name _____

 **Check What You Know**

Count by 10s.

1. 32, 42, 52, _____, _____, _____, _____

2. 16, 26, _____, _____, _____, _____

3. 7 dolphins are swimming.
   3 more join the group.
   How many dolphins are there now?

   _____ + _____ = _____ dolphins

4. 5 seagulls are flying.
   10 seagulls are on the shore.
   How many seagulls are there in all?

   _____ + _____ = _____ seagulls

5. 10 sea lions are sitting on a rock.
   There are 2 sea otters and 8 fish nearby.
   How many animals are there in all?

   _____ + _____ + _____ = _____ animals

Use this page to review important skills needed for this chapter.

Name _____

Add Tens

When you **add** tens, think of an addition fact. When you add, you find the **sum**.

Paul took some tens rods.
He has 4 tens and 2 tens.
What is the value of his tens rods?

Hands On

Objective
Use basic facts and mental math to add tens.

Vocabulary
add
sum

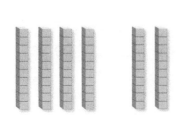

$4 + 2 = \underline{6}$

$4 \text{ tens} + 2 \text{ tens} = \underline{6}$ tens

$40 + 20 = \underline{60}$
$\uparrow$
sum

▶ **Explore** ━━━━━━━━━━━━━━━━━━━━━━━━━━

Use a basic fact to help.
Use ▭▭▭▭. Draw a quick picture.

Think!
What addition fact can help me add the tens?

1. Take some ▭▭▭▭ .
   Make **2** groups.
   Draw your tens.

   Record.

   _____ tens + _____ tens = _____ tens

   _____ + _____ = _____

2. Take some ▭▭▭▭ .
   Make **2** groups.
   Draw your tens.

   Record.

   _____ tens + _____ tens = _____ tens

   _____ + _____ = _____

3. **Math Talk** How does $2 + 6$ help you find $20 + 60$?

NS 2.3 Use mental arithmetic to find the sum or difference of two two-digit numbers.
Also **NS 2.0, MR 1.2, MR 3.0, MR 2.1, MR 2.0**

KEY NS 2.2 Find the sum or difference of two whole numbers up to three digits long.

> ▶ **Extend**

Complete the addition sentences.
Use 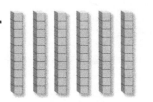.
Use a basic fact to help.

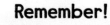

Remember!
Think about addition
facts to help you
add tens.

4.

6 + 3 = _____

6 tens + 3 tens = _____ tens

60 + 30 = _____

5.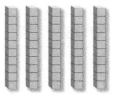

5 + 2 = _____

5 tens + 2 tens = _____ tens

50 + 20 = _____

---

6. 4 tens + 1 ten = _____ tens

_____ + _____ = _____

7. 2 tens + 6 tens = _____ tens

_____ + _____ = _____

---

8. 5 tens + 3 tens = _____ tens

_____ + _____ = _____

9. 4 tens + 4 tens = _____ tens

_____ + _____ = _____

---

10. 1 ten + 6 tens = _____ tens

_____ + _____ = _____

11. 3 tens + 2 tens = _____ tens

_____ + _____ = _____

---

12. 5 tens + 4 tens = _____ tens

_____ + _____ = _____

13. 3 tens + 3 tens = _____ tens

_____ + _____ = _____

---

14. 1 ten + 1 ten = _____ tens

_____ + _____ = _____

15. 2 tens + 7 tens = _____ tens

_____ + _____ = _____

At Home Use dimes to show an
addition sentence such as 30 + 40 = 70.
Now ask your child to make another
addition sentence.

En casa Use monedas de diez centavos para
mostrar un enunciado de suma como 30 + 40 = 70.
Ahora pida a su niño que haga otro enunciado
de suma.

Chapter 8 Lesson 2

Add Tens and Ones

▶ **Learn**

Objective
Add 2-digit and
1-digit numbers
with and without
regrouping.

There are **26** penguins on an iceberg.
Then **8** more penguins come. How
many penguins are there in all?

Add **26** and **8**.

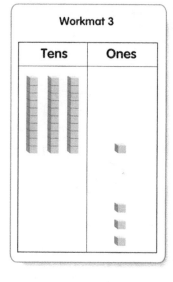

Step 1

Show **26** and **8**. Add
6 ones and 8 ones.

Workmat 3

Tens	Ones

Tens	Ones
2	6
+	8

Step 2

Regroup 10 ones
as 1 ten.

Workmat 3

Tens	Ones

Tens	Ones
2	6
+	8

Step 3

Add the tens.

Workmat 3

Tens	Ones

Tens	Ones
1	
2	6
+	8
3	4

There are _____ penguins.

KEY NS 2.2 Find the sum or difference of two
whole numbers up to three digits long.
Also **NS 2.0, MR 2.0, MR 2.1**

one hundred fifty-one **151**

Think!
Do I have 10 or more ones?
Do I need to regroup?

Add.

1.

Tens	Ones
4	5
+	3

2.

Tens	Ones
	5
+ 3	7

3.

Tens	Ones
5	6
+	7

4. **123** **Math Talk** What does the 1 in the ☐ represent in Exercise 3?

► **Practice**

Add.

5.

Tens	Ones
3	4
+	7

6.

Tens	Ones
	8
+ 2	9

7.

Tens	Ones
4	5
+	9

8.

Tens	Ones
7	7
+ 1	3

Problem Solving: Number Sense

9. Don has 24 goldfish. Rosa has some goldfish, too. Don adds to find how many they have together. He has to regroup when he adds. Does Rosa have 6, 3, or 5 goldfish?

Draw or write to explain.

_____ goldfish

Name _____

Chapter 8 Lesson 3
Model Adding 2-Digit Numbers

▶ **Learn**

You can use ▪ and ▭ to model addition with 2-digit numbers.

$46 + 14 =$ _____

Step 1

Show 46 and 14.

Step 2

Add. Regroup if you need to.

Step 3

Show your answer. Record.

$46 + 14 =$ _60_

▶ **Guided Practice**

Use ▭ and ▪ to add.

1. $16 + 27 =$ _____

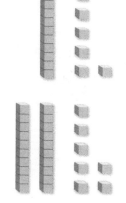

Think!
I need to regroup the ones.

2. $32 + 25 =$ _____

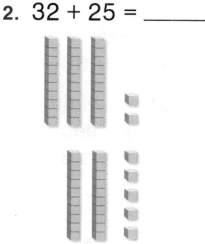

3. (123) **Math Talk** Do you need to regroup when you add 25 and 46? Why or why not?

KEY NS 2.2 Find the sum or difference of two whole numbers up to three digits long.
Also **NS 2.0, NS 1.2, MR 2.0**

MR 1.2 Use tools, such as manipulatives or sketches, to model problems.

▶ Practice

Use  and ▪ to add.
Show your work.

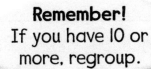
Remember!
If you have 10 or
more, regroup.

4. 52 + 38 = __90__

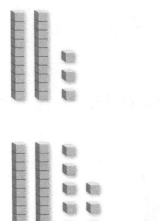

5. 23 + 28 = _____

6. 63 + 25 = _____

7. 45 + 19 = _____

8. 59 + 37 = _____

9. 22 + 17 = _____

Problem Solving: Number Sense

10. 37 sea otters are swimming.
22 sea otters are sleeping.
How many sea otters are
there in all?

Draw or write to explain.

_____ sea otters

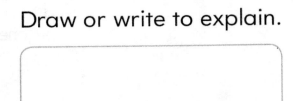

At Home Ask your child how he or
she found the sums on this page and
how he or she knew when to regroup.

En casa Pregunte a su niño cómo halló las
sumas de esta página y cómo supo cuándo
reagrupar.

Add 2-Digit Numbers in Different Ways

Hands On

Objective
Add 2-digit numbers with and without regrouping.

▶ **Learn**

You can add 2-digit numbers in different ways.

$62 + 29 =$ _____

Way 1

You can use 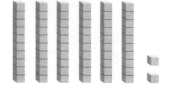 and 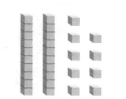.

Add the tens. $60 + 20 = 80$
Add the ones. $2 + 9 = 11$

Regroup if you need to.

Add the totals to find the sum.

$62 + 29 =$ _9 1_

Way 2

You can also use Secret Code Cards.

⁶⁰6 0 ²2 ²⁰2 0 ⁹9

Add the tens.

⁶⁰6 0 $+$ ²⁰2 0 $=$ ⁸⁰8 0

Add the ones.

²2 $+$ ⁹9 $=$ ¹⁰1 0 $+$ ¹1

Add the tens and ones.

⁸⁰8 0 $+$ ¹⁰1 0 $+$ ¹1 $=$ _9 1_

▶ **Guided Practice**

Add. Choose a way to solve.

1. $14 + 47 =$ _____

Think!
I have 11 ones. I need to regroup.

2. $54 + 23 =$ _____

3. 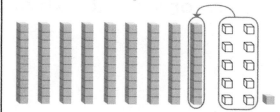 **Math Talk** How did you solve Exercise 1?

KEY NS 2.2 Find the sum or difference of two whole numbers up to three digits long.
Also NS 2.0, NS 1.2, MR 1.1, MR 2.0, MR 2.1

MR 1.2 Use tools, such as manipulatives or sketches, to model problems.

Add. Use Secret Code Cards
or to solve.

Remember!
Add the tens. Then
add the ones. Regroup
if you need to.

4. 36 + 58 = _94_ 5. 38 + 17 = _____ 6. 49 + 22 = _____

7. 20 + 34 = _____ 8. 19 + 63 = _____ 9. 26 + 44 = _____

10. 71 + 23 = _____ 11. 55 + 31 = _____ 12. 33 + 18 = _____

Problem Solving: Logical Reasoning

13. Carmen and Anil use Secret Code
    Cards to show how many seashells
    they have.

Carmen

40		8
4	0	8

Anil

30		?
3	0	?

Draw or write to explain.

If they add their seashells together,
they have:

80		7
8	0	7

What number is missing from Anil's
Secret Code Card?

_____

At Home Write two 2-digit numbers
less than 50. Ask your child to explain
how to find their sum.

En casa Escriba dos números de 2 dígitos,
menores que 50. Pida a su niño que explique
cómo hallar su suma.

▶ **Practice**

Add.
Circle the method you used.

14. 37 + 42 = _____

   Place-value blocks   Secret Code Cards   My own way

15. 64 + 29 = _____

   Place-value blocks   Secret Code Cards   My own way

16. 51 + 43 = _____

   Place-value blocks   Secret Code Cards   My own way

17. 62 + 28 = _____

   Place-value blocks   Secret Code Cards   My own way

18. 48 + 35 = _____

   Place-value blocks   Secret Code Cards   My own way

KEY **NS 2.2** Find the sum or difference of two whole numbers up to three digits long. Also **NS 2.0, MR 1.0**

MR 1.1 Determine the approach, materials, and strategies to be used.

Regroup and Score

How to Play

1. Place the Number Cards face down.

2. Choose two Number Cards. Add the numbers to find the sum. If you need to regroup, you score 1 point. Keep the cards.

3. Take turns until all the number cards have been used.

4. The player with the most points wins.

What You Need

2 Players
Number Cards
(Learning Tools 13–15)

56	24	18	25
12	30	26	37
23	35	27	40
16	14	32	19

KEY NS 2.2 Find the sum or difference of two whole numbers up to three digits long.

Education Place
Visit www.eduplace.com/camap/ for more games.

Too Much Information

 **Learn**

Problem Solving
Plan

Objective
Identify information you do not need in a word problem.

Sometimes a problem has more information than you need.

Miri, Zach, and Erin count fish at the aquarium. Miri counts clownfish, Zach counts sardines, and Erin counts angelfish. How many fish do Miri and Erin count in all?

Understand

What do you know?

- Miri counts ____20____ clownfish.

- Zach counts ____15____ sardines.

- Erin counts ____30____ angelfish.

Plan

Cross out the information you do not need.

Miri counts clownfish.

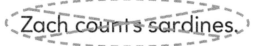 Zach counts sardines.

Erin counts angelfish.

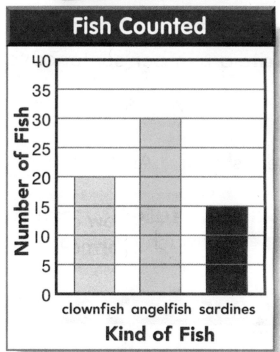

Fish Counted

Solve

Write a number sentence.

____30____ + ____20____ = ____50____

Look Back

Did you answer the question?
Did you need all the information?

Miri and Erin count ____50____ fish.

SDAP 1.4 Ask and answer simple questions related to data representations.
Also **NS 2.0, AF 1.3, KEY NS 2.2, AF 1.0, MR 2.0, MR 2.2**

AF 1.2 Relate problem situations to number sentences involving addition and subtraction.

Remember!
Understand
Plan
Solve
Look Back

1. Kenesha takes pictures of the bat rays.
   Andrew takes pictures of the sea stars.
   Bill takes pictures of the sharks.
   How many pictures do Kenesha
   and Andrew take all together?

   Use the graph.

   Kenesha takes _____ pictures
   of bat rays.

   Andrew takes _____ pictures
   of sea stars.

   Is there any information you do
   not need?

   _____

   Write a number sentence to add.

   _____ + _____ = _____

   Kenesha and Andrew take _____ pictures in all.

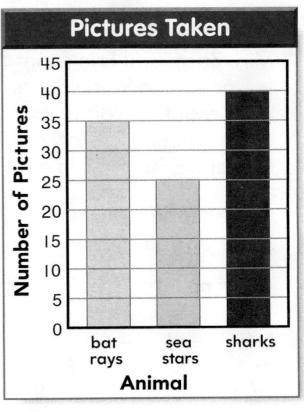

Pictures Taken

2. (123) **Math Talk** How can you tell if you have
   too much information?

Cross out information you do not need.

3. There are **30** first-graders,
   40 second-graders, and
   4 teachers in line for the aquarium.
   How many children are in line?

   _____ children

Draw or write to explain.

At Home Ask your child to identify
the extra information in Exercise 3.

En casa Pida a su niño que identifique la
información adicional en el Ejercicio 3.

160 ▯║║║║

Problem Solving

California Field Trip

At Pescadero State Beach

You can see plants and animals at the edge of the ocean. You can see cliffs and sandy coves. You can look at tide pools. In the tide pools, you can see crabs, sea stars, and small fish.

Choose a way to solve. Show your work.

Pescadero State Beach

1. Gina counts **42** sea anemones and **34** fish. Nick counts **20** sea anemones. How many sea anemones do Gina and Nick count in all?

sea anemone

_____ sea anemones

2. There are **20** hermit crabs in the cove. Then **13** more crawl in. **3** children watch the crabs. How many hermit crabs are in the cove now?

hermit crab

_____ hermit crabs

3. On their way out to sea, the children see **12** dolphins and **3** whales on the boat ride. On the ride back, they see **13** more dolphins. How many dolphins do they see in all?

dolphin

_____ dolphins

KEY **NS 2.2** Find the sum or difference of two whole numbers up to three digits long.
Also **NS 2.0, AF 1.0, MR 1.0, MR 1.1**

one hundred sixty-one **161**

Problem Solving on Tests
Listening Skills

Listen to your teacher read the problem.
Choose the correct answer.

Select a Strategy
Use a Model
Write a Number
   Sentence
Draw a Picture

1. Which number sentence does
   NOT belong to the fact family?

$2 + 5 = 7$ $7 - 5 = 2$ $2 + 7 = 9$ $7 - 2 = 5$
   ○   ○   ○   ○

KEY **NS 2.1**

2. Choose the correct number to complete
   the comparison.

$$108 < \boxed{}$$

81   88   100   180
○   ○   ○   ○

KEY **NS 1.3**

3.
   50¢   65¢   70¢   75¢
   ○   ○   ○   ○

KEY **NS 5.1**

4.
   8   12   20   40
   ○   ○   ○   ○

SDAP 2.1

MR 1.0 Make decisions about how to set up a problem.
MR 1.1 Determine the approach, materials, and
strategies to be used.

Education Place
Visit www.eduplace.com/camap/ for
Test-Taking Tips and Extra Practice.

Key Standards Review

Shawna has the coins shown below.
Use the coins to answer the questions.

1. Write the total value of the coins. $ _____

2. How many different ways can
   Shawna make 25¢ with her coins?   _____ ways
   Draw the coins to show the ways.

3. Shawna wants to buy a beach ball
   for 87¢. She pays $1.00. How much   _____
   change does she get back?

 **Money**

Chris buys sunglasses and a hat.
He pays $1.00 and gets back
15¢ as change. How much does
the hat cost?

Item	Price
Sunglasses	$0.60
Hat	?

$ _____

KEY NS 5.2 Know and use the decimal notation
and the dollar and cent symbols for money.
Also **KEY** NS 5.1

one hundred sixty-three **163**

Sara's Seashells

The bar graph shows the shells that Sara has collected. Use the graph to solve the problems.

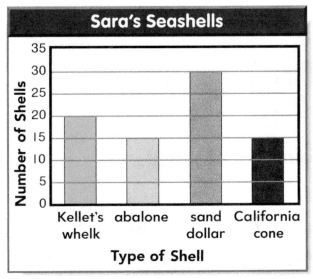

1. How many of each type of seashell has Sara collected?

   _____ Kellet's whelks   _____ sand dollars

   _____ abalones   _____ California cones

2. How many sand dollars and abalones does Sara have?   _____

3. How many California cones and Kellet's whelks does Sara have?   _____

4. Of which two shells does Sara have the same number?   _____

5. How many seashells does Sara have all together? _____

KEY NS 2.2 Find the sum or difference of two whole numbers up to three digits long.
Also **NS 2.0**
Science LS 2.d

Name _____

Concepts and Skills

Complete the addition sentences.
Use ▨▨▨▨▨ and a basic fact to help. NS 2.3

1. 3 tens + 4 tens = _____ tens

   _____ + _____ = _____

2. 5 tens + 1 ten = _____ tens

   _____ + _____ = _____

Use Workmat 3 with ▨▨▨▨▨ and ▮. Add. KEY NS 2.2

3. 23
   + 5

4. 46
   + 7

5.   8
   +43

6. 89
   + 9

7. 16 + 41 = _____

8. 38 + 59 = _____

9. 25 + 9 = _____

10. 48 + 49 = _____

11. 9 + 75 = _____

12. 47 + 30 = _____

Use Secret Code Cards or ▨▨▨▨▨ and ▮ to help. Add. KEY NS 2.2

13. 27 + 45 = _____

14. 50 + 27 = _____

15. 49 + 29 = _____

16. 9 + 83 = _____

17. 67 + 28 = _____

18. 88 + 11 = _____

Problem Solving KEY NS 2.2, MR 1.0

19. Sheryl has 17 turtles. Maria has some turtles, too. To find how many they have together, you need to regroup. Does Maria have 1, 2, or 5 turtles?

   _____

Spiral Review and Test Practice

1. Which symbol makes this comparison true?   78 ◯ 72

    <   +   =   >
    ◯   ◯   ◯   ◯

KEY NS 1.3, **KEY NS 1.1**, NS 1.0 Page 67

---

2. Follow the pattern. Which two numbers complete this pattern?

42, 47, 52, _____, _____ 67, 72

   53, 54   57, 58   57, 62   53, 66
     ◯   ◯   ◯   ◯

KEY SDAP 2.0, SDAP 2.1 Page 85

---

3. Which group of coins is worth $1.00?

    ◯   ◯   ◯   ◯

KEY NS 5.2, **KEY NS 5.1**, NS 5.0 Page 127

---

4. What is the sum?
$$\begin{array}{r} 43 \\ + \ 5 \\ \hline \end{array}$$

   45   48   93   435
   ◯   ◯   ◯   ◯

KEY NS 2.2 Page 151

Education Place
Visit www.eduplace.com/camap/ for
Test-Taking Tips and Extra Practice.

Spiral Review

Use Place Value to Add 2-Digit Numbers

Vocabulary

Here are some vocabulary words you will learn in the chapter.

hundred chart You can use a hundred chart to add.

$$28 + 50 = 78$$

1	2	3	4	5	6	7	8	9	10
11	12	13	14	15	16	17	18	19	20
21	22	23	24	25	26	27	28	29	30
31	32	33	34	35	36	37	38	39	40
41	42	43	44	45	46	47	48	49	50
51	52	53	54	55	56	57	58	59	60
61	62	63	64	65	66	67	68	69	70
71	72	73	74	75	76	77	78	79	80
81	82	83	84	85	86	87	88	89	90
91	92	93	94	95	96	97	98	99	100

place-value chart You can use a place-value chart to record two-digit addition with and without regrouping.

Tens	Ones
1	
4	5
+ 1	7
6	2

See English-Spanish Glossary pages 573–589.

KEY NS 2.2 Find the sum or difference of two whole numbers up to three digits long.

Education Place
Visit www.eduplace.com/camap/ for the eGlossary and eGames.

one hundred sixty-seven **167**

Name _____

 # Check What You Know

Use the data to solve.
Write number sentences.

Fish Counted	
striped fish	42
blue fish	23
hermit crabs	15

1. How many fish are
   there in all?

   _____ + _____ = _____ fish in all

2. How many hermit crabs and blue fish are there?

   _____ + _____ = _____ hermit crabs and blue fish

3. How many hermit crabs and striped fish
   are there?

   _____ + _____ = _____ hermit crabs and striped fish

4. If 13 more blue fish are counted, how many
   blue fish will there be?

   _____ + _____ = _____ blue fish

5. If 21 more striped fish are counted,
   how many striped fish will there be?

   _____ + _____ = _____ striped fish

Use this page to review important skills needed for this chapter.

Chapter 9 Lesson 1

Add Using a Hundred Chart

Hands On ✋

Objective
Use a hundred chart and count on by tens to add.

▶ **Learn**

You can add tens on the hundred chart. Each square is 10 more than the square above it. Find 35 + 20.

Step 1

Find 35 on Workmat 5.

Step 2

Count on by tens to add 20. Look for the pattern.
35, 45, 55

35 + 20 = ____55____

1	2	3	4	5	6	7	8	9	10
11	12	13	14	15	16	17	18	19	20
21	22	23	24	25	26	27	28	29	30
31	32	33	34	35	36	37	38	39	40
41	42	43	44	45	46	47	48	49	50
51	52	53	54	55	56	57	58	59	60
61	62	63	64	65	66	67	68	69	70
71	72	73	74	75	76	77	78	79	80
81	82	83	84	85	86	87	88	89	90
91	92	93	94	95	96	97	98	99	100

▶ **Guided Practice**

Add. Use the hundred chart on Workmat 5.

Think!
Find 62. Count on by tens to add 30.

1. 30 + 62 = _____

2. 20 + 77 = _____

3. 40 + 54 = _____

4. 45 + 10 = _____

5. 18 + 70 = _____

6. 68
   +10

7. 15
   +60

8. 40
   +49

9. 13
   +20

10. 30
    +34

11. (123) **Math Talk** What patterns do you see as you count on tens to add?

KEY NS 2.2 Find the sum or difference of two whole numbers up to three digits long.
Also **NS 2.0, MR 1.2, MR 3.0**

Use the hundred chart or Workmat 5. Add.

Remember!
Move down one row for each ten you add.

12. $16 + 10 =$ ___26___

13. $20 + 34 =$ _____

14. $69 + 30 =$ _____

15. $80 + 13 =$ _____

16. $24 + 60 =$ _____

17. $40 + 32 =$ _____

1	2	3	4	5	6	7	8	9	10
11	12	13	14	15	16	17	18	19	20
21	22	23	24	25	26	27	28	29	30
31	32	33	34	35	36	37	38	39	40
41	42	43	44	45	46	47	48	49	50
51	52	53	54	55	56	57	58	59	60
61	62	63	64	65	66	67	68	69	70
71	72	73	74	75	76	77	78	79	80
81	82	83	84	85	86	87	88	89	90
91	92	93	94	95	96	97	98	99	100

18.
$$\begin{array}{r} 28 \\ +20 \\ \hline \end{array}$$

19.
$$\begin{array}{r} 10 \\ +55 \\ \hline \end{array}$$

20.
$$\begin{array}{r} 12 \\ +30 \\ \hline \end{array}$$

21.
$$\begin{array}{r} 60 \\ +34 \\ \hline \end{array}$$

22.
$$\begin{array}{r} 43 \\ +50 \\ \hline \end{array}$$

23.
$$\begin{array}{r} 21 \\ +10 \\ \hline \end{array}$$

24.
$$\begin{array}{r} 20 \\ +39 \\ \hline \end{array}$$

25.
$$\begin{array}{r} 40 \\ +11 \\ \hline \end{array}$$

26.
$$\begin{array}{r} 16 \\ +70 \\ \hline \end{array}$$

27.
$$\begin{array}{r} 50 \\ +50 \\ \hline \end{array}$$

Algebra Readiness: Missing Addends

Choose a number to complete the addition sentence.

20   30   40   50   60

28. $36 +$ _____ $= 56$

29. $47 +$ _____ $= 97$

30. _____ $+ 28 = 58$

31. _____ $+ 53 = 93$

Copyright © Houghton Mifflin Company. All rights reserved.

 At Home Ask your child to explain how to add 45 and 20 on the hundred chart shown above.

En casa Pida a su niño que explique cómo sumar 45 y 20 en la tabla de números hasta el cien que se muestra arriba.

Chapter 9 Lesson 2

Add Using a Place-Value Chart

Objective
Add two-digit numbers and record the addition on a place-value chart.

► **Learn**

Add 17 and 25.

Step 1
Show 17 and 25.

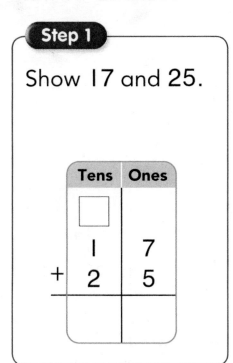

Step 2
Add the ones. Regroup 10 ones as 1 ten.

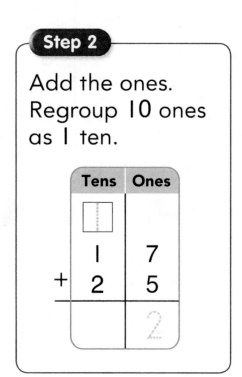

Step 3
Add the tens.

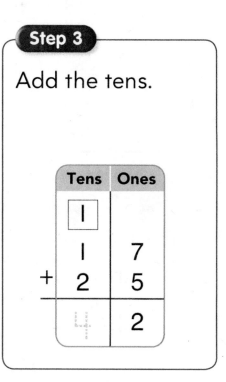

► **Guided Practice**

Add. Record your work.

1.

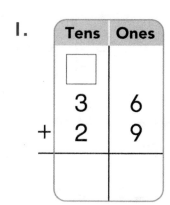

Tens	Ones
3	6
+ 2	9

Think!
How many tens can I make from 15 ones?

2.

Tens	Ones
5	4
+ 2	6

3.

Tens	Ones
4	2
+ 1	5

4. 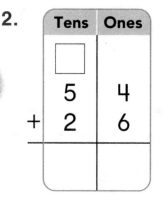 **Math Talk** Why do you record another ten after you regroup?

 **KEY NS 2.2** Find the sum or difference of two whole numbers up to three digits long.
Also **KEY NS 2.1**, MR 2.0

NS 2.0 Estimate, calculate, and solve problems involving addition and subtraction of two- and three-digit numbers.

▶ Practice

Add. Record your work.

Remember!
When you regroup ones, remember to record the ten you make.

5.

Tens	Ones
2	8
+ 3	2
6	0

6.

Tens	Ones
4	5
+	8

7.

Tens	Ones
3	3
+ 1	8

8.

Tens	Ones
2	5
+ 4	5

9.

Tens	Ones
5	4
+ 3	7

10.

Tens	Ones
6	1
+ 2	8

11.

Tens	Ones
2	9
+ 2	1

12.

```
    3   2
  + 2   6
 _____
```

13.

```
    2   6
  + 5   7
 _____
```

14.

```
    1   9
  + 3   5
 _____
```

15.

```
    3   7
    1   1
  + 2   3
 _____
```

Algebra Readiness: Missing Addends

Choose a number from the box to complete the addition facts.

23 30 42 51 65

16. 46 + _____ = 97

17. 33 + _____ = 56

18. _____ + 28 = 58

19. _____ + 53 = 95

At Home Write a two-digit addition problem such as 38 + 56. Ask your child to explain how to find the sum.

En casa Escriba un problema de suma de dos dígitos como 38 + 56. Pida a su niño que explique cómo hallar la suma.

Name _____

Practice Regrouping 10 to 14

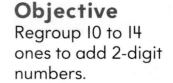

Objective
Regroup 10 to 14 ones to add 2-digit numbers.

▶ **Learn**

If there are 10, 11, 12, 13, or 14 ones, regroup 10 ones as 1 ten.

At the beach, Morgan's class found 34 brown shells and 16 white shells. How many shells did they see in all?

Step 1

Find 34 + 16.

How many tens and ones are there?

___4___ tens

___10___ ones

Step 2

Do you need to regroup?

(yes)   no

Step 3

Record the sum.

Tens	Ones
1	
3	4
+ 1	6
5	0

▶ **Guided Practice**

Complete the chart to help you add.

		Add the tens. Add the ones.	Do you need to regroup?	What is the sum?
1.	55 + 26	_____ tens _____ ones	yes no	_____
2.	19 + 40	_____ tens _____ ones	yes no	_____

3. (123) **Math Talk** What is the greatest number of ones you can have without regrouping? Explain.

KEY NS 2.2 Find the sum or difference of two whole numbers up to three digits long. Also **NS 2.0, SDAP 1.4, MR 2.0**

► **Practice**

Add.

4.
```
    3 | 5
  + 2 | 5
    6 | 0
```

5.
```
    2 | 2
  + 6 | 0
```

6.
```
    2 | 4
  + 3 | 7
```

7.
```
    3 | 6
  + 5 | 6
```

8.
```
    3 | 3
  + 4 | 7
```

9.
```
    5 | 4
  + 1 | 9
```

10.
```
    3 | 8
  + 3 | 6
```

11.
```
    4 | 3
  + 2 | 0
```

12.
```
    4 | 8
  + 3 | 3
```

13.
```
    2 | 6
  + 1 | 5
```

14.
```
    4 | 5
    3 | 4
  + 1 | 3
```

Problem Solving: Data Sense

15. How many children saw fish?

    _____ children

16. How many children saw shells
    and seaweed?

    _____ children

At the Beach — Things to See / Number of Children

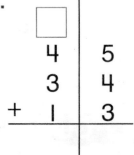

At Home Ask your child to solve
exercises such as 25 + 26 and 34 +
15. Ask your child to explain when
regrouping is necessary.

En casa Pida a su niño que resuelva
ejercicios como 25 + 26 y 34 + 15. Pídale que
explique cuándo es necesario reagrupar.

Chapter 9 Lesson 4

Practice Regrouping 15 to 18

▶ **Learn**

If there are 15, 16, 17, or 18 ones, regroup 10 ones as 1 ten.

How many fish in all?

Type of Fish	Number of Fish
Angelfish	29
Clownfish	38

Tens	Ones
[1] 2	9
+ 3	8
6	7

_67_ fish

▶ **Guided Practice**

Add.

1.

Tens	Ones
[ ] 4	8
+ 3	8

Think!
If 8 + 8 is more than 10 ones, I have to regroup.

2.

Tens	Ones
[ ] 2	9
+ 6	8

3. 10
   +27

4. 57
   +38

5. 29
   +57

6. 38
   +18

7. 36
   +12

8. (123) **Math Talk** Did you need to regroup in Exercises 2 and 3? Explain why or why not.

KEY **NS 2.2** Find the sum or difference of two whole numbers up to three digits long.
Also NS 2.0, SDAP 2.1, KEY **SDAP 2.0**, MR 2.0, MR 2.1

► **Practice**

Remember!
Decide whether you
need to regroup.

Add.

9. 29
    +59
    ‗‗‗
    88

10. 17
    +29

11. 46
    +22

12. 38
    +29

13. 79
    +17

14. 53
    +34

15. 31
    +25

16. 49
    +19

17. 68
    +28

18. 27
    +58

19. 19
    +48

20. 39
    +59

21. 19
    +36

22. 68
    +29

23. 38
    +48

24. 26
    13
    + 7

Problem Solving: Reasoning

25. There are **8** shells in a box.
    Kayla buys **5** boxes.
    How many shells does she buy?
    Complete the table to help you.

Boxes	1	2	3	4	5
Shells	8	16			

_____ shells

At Home Give your child two
numbers that are both less than 50.
Have your child explain how to add
them.

En casa Dé a su niño dos números que sean
menores que 50. Pida a su niño que explique
cómo sumarlos.

▶ **Practice**

Add.

26. 39
    +48

27. 48
    +28

28. 62
    +14

29. 13
    +28

30. 39
    +36

31. 35
    +23

32. 58
    +37

33. 32
    +25

34. 68
    +12

35. 41
    +34

36. 59
    +27

37. 69
    +21

KEY **NS 2.2** Find the sum or difference of two
whole numbers up to three digits long.
Also **NS 2.0**

Toss a number cube two times.
Write the numbers in the ones column.
Add.

38. 2 [5]
    + 4 [6]
    ‾‾‾‾‾
       [7] [ ]

39. 3 [ ]
    + 5 [ ]
    ‾‾‾‾‾

40. 1 [ ]
    + 6 [ ]
    ‾‾‾‾‾

41. 7 [ ]
    + 1 [ ]
    ‾‾‾‾‾

42. 3 [ ]
    + 3 [ ]
    ‾‾‾‾‾

43. 8 [ ]
    +   [ ]
    ‾‾‾‾‾

44. 4 [ ]
    + 1 [ ]
    ‾‾‾‾‾

45. 3 [ ]
    + 2 [ ]
    ‾‾‾‾‾

46. 5 [ ]
    +   [ ]
    ‾‾‾‾‾

47. 1 [ ]
    + 1 [ ]
    ‾‾‾‾‾

48. 2 [ ]
    + 5 [ ]
    ‾‾‾‾‾

49. 7 [ ]
    +   [ ]
    ‾‾‾‾‾

At Home Ask your child to explain whether he or she needs to regroup 78 + 12.

En casa Pida a su niño que explique si necesita reagrupar para hallar 78 + 12.

Guess and Check

 **Learn**

Mateo buys 2 different books.
The two books have 40 pages in all.
Which two books does Mateo buy?

Objective
Use Guess and Check
to solve problems.

Understand

What do you know?

- Mateo buys 2 different books.
- Each book has a different number of pages.
- The two books have 40 pages in all.

Title	Number of Pages
Seahorses	10
Lion Fish	15
Dolphins	25
The Sea Turtle	34

Plan

Choose 2 different books.
Try Dolphins and The Sea Turtle.
How can you check your guess?

add

Solve

Add to check.

Dolphins   25
The Sea Turtle + 34
                  59

Think!
59 > 40
Try again.
Look for ones digits
that add to ten.

Lion Fish   15
Dolphins   + 25
               40

Think!
The sum is 40.
I am done.

Mateo buys books titled _____ and _____.

Look Back

Did you answer the question?
Does your answer make sense?

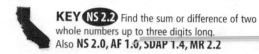

KEY NS 2.2 Find the sum or difference of two
whole numbers up to three digits long.
Also NS 2.0, AF 1.0, SDAP 1.4, MR 2.2

MR 2.0 Solve problems and justify reasoning.

Guided Problem Solving

Remember!
Understand
Plan
Solve
Look Back

1. Pedro buys **52** shells. Which 2 bags does he buy?

   Tell what you know.

   Try Bag B and Bag C.

   Try your guess. _23 + 34 = 57_

   There are too many shells.

   Try again.

   _____ and _____

   Try your guess. _____ + _____ = _____

   Pedro buys Bag _____ and Bag _____.

2. **Math Talk** How did you decide which bags to choose for your guess in Exercise 1?

Problem Solving Practice

Guess and check to solve.

3. Max spills **57** shells. Which two bags does he spill?

   Bag _____ and Bag _____

4. The gift shop sells two bags of shells. **65** shells in all are sold. Which two bags are sold?

   Bag _____ and Bag _____

At Home Have your child use objects in your home to write a guess and check problem for you to solve.

En casa Pida a su niño que use objetos de la casa para escribir un problema de estimar y comprobar para que usted lo resuelva.

Name _____

Create and Solve

1. Jeremy sees 14 stingrays and 19 jellyfish at the aquarium. How many stingrays and jellyfish does he see?

   Jeremy sees _____ stingrays and jellyfish.

2. Write an addition number story for 25 + 17.

   _____

   _____

   _____

3. Draw a picture about your story.

4. Write a number sentence to solve.

KEY NS 2.2 Find the sum or difference of two whole numbers up to three digits long.
Also **NS 2.0, AF 1.2, AF 1.3, SDAP 1.4, MR 1.0, MR 1.1**

AF 1.0 Model, represent, and interpret number relationships to create and solve problems involving addition and subtraction.

one hundred eighty-one **181**

5. The picture graph shows the number of fish in 4 tanks. Molly buys 18 fish. Which 2 tanks of fish does she buy?

Fish in Tanks	
Tank	**Number of Fish**
A	🐟🐟🐟🐟
B	🐟🐟🐟🐟🐟🐟
C	🐟🐟
D	🐟🐟🐟🐟🐟

Each 🐟 stands for **2** fish.

Molly buys Tank _____ and Tank _____.

6. Write your own addition story about the tanks of fish.

_____

_____

_____

_____

7. Write a number sentence to solve.

_____ ◯ _____ = _____

Share your addition story with a classmate.

Key Standards Review

Find the sum.

1. 73 + 20 = _____   2. 36 + 40 = _____   3. 14 + 54 = _____

4. 21 + 32 = _____   5. 68 + 30 = _____   6. 57 + 32 = _____

7. 13 + 45 = _____   8. 61 + 33 = _____   9. 25 + 74 = _____

Challenge   Number Sense

Find each sum. Then use the table below to match each sum to a letter. The word you spell is the highest mountain in California. It is more than 2 miles high!

_____ _____ _____ _____ _____ _____ _____

33 + 34   40 + 20   51 + 10   32 + 33   31 + 31   27 + 32   13 + 55

Sum	58	59	60	61	62	63	64	65	66	67	68
Letter	A	E	H	I	N	O	S	T	U	W	Y

The highest mountain in California is Mount _____.

KEY **NS 2.2** Find the sum or difference of two whole numbers up to three digits long.

Science Link

Sea Turtles

Sea turtles are found in warm seas all over the world. They come on land to lay their eggs. A sea turtle egg takes about 45–70 days to hatch.

Solve.

Draw or write to explain.

1. An olive ridley turtle is 26 inches long. A green sea turtle is 37 inches long. How many inches is that all together?

   _____ inches

2. A green turtle lays 48 eggs. A black turtle lays 43 eggs. How many eggs do the turtles lay in all?

   _____ eggs

3. Loggerhead turtles' jaws are made for crushing and grinding. One loggerhead eats 15 crabs and 29 shrimp. How many sea animals does it eat?

   _____ sea animals

KEY NS 2.2 Find the sum or difference of two whole numbers up to three digits long.
Also NS 2.0
Science LS 2.a

Name _____

Concepts and Skills

Add. Use Workmat 5. **KEY NS 2.2**

1. 52 + 20 = _____

2. 30 + 15 = _____

3. 35 + 30 = _____

4. 49 + 10 = _____

Use Workmat 3 with ▬▬▬ and ▪. Add. **KEY NS 2.2**

5. 48
  +13

6. 72
  +19

7. 19
  +29

8. 50
  +28

Add. **KEY NS 2.2**

9.
Tens	Ones
□	
5	6
+ 2	4

10.
Tens	Ones
□	
3	9
+ 5	2

11. 19
  +67

12. 39
  +29

13. 58
  + 8

14. 61
  +29

Problem Solving **KEY NS 2.2, MR 2.0**

15. Write the number that completes the addition sentence.

29 + _____ = 79

16. Explain how you found the answer.

_____

_____

Spiral Review and Test Practice

1. Which number is odd?

20	25	30	40
○	○	○	○

SDAP 2.1 Page 89

---

2. Which symbol goes in the ○ to make this true?

>	=	+	<
○	○	○	○

KEY NS 5.1, NS 5.0, KEY NS 1.3 Page 111

---

3. Rod buys a pen for 63¢.
He pays with these coins.

How much change should Rod get?

70¢	63¢	10¢	7¢
○	○	○	○

KEY NS 5.1, KEY NS 5.2, NS 5.0 Page 129

---

4. What is the sum?

$$\begin{array}{r} 58 \\ +13 \\ \hline \end{array}$$

61	71	73	78
○	○	○	○

KEY NS 2.2, NS 2.0 Page 171

Education Place
Visit www.eduplace.com/camap/ for
Test-Taking Tips and Extra Practice.

Spiral Review

More Addition

Vocabulary

Here are some vocabulary words you will learn in the chapter.

sum The result of addition

$$16 + 32 = 48$$

$$\begin{array}{r} 16 \\ + 32 \\ \hline 48 \end{array}$$

sum ⟶ 48

round To find the nearest ten

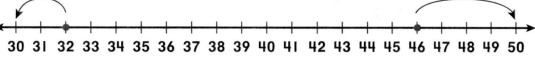

30 31 32 33 34 35 36 37 38 39 40 41 42 43 44 45 46 47 48 49 50

32 is closer to 30.   46 is closer to 50.
32 rounds to 30.   46 rounds to 50.

estimate A rounded answer that is close to an exact answer

46 ⟶ round to nearest ten ⟶ 50

+32 ⟶ round to nearest ten ⟶ +30

80 ⟵ estimate

See English-Spanish Glossary pages 573–589.

KEY NS 2.2 Find the sum or difference of two whole numbers up to three digits long. Also **NS 6.0**

Education Place
Visit **www.eduplace.com/camap/** for the eGlossary and eGames.

one hundred eighty-seven **187**

Name _____

# ✓ Check What You Know

Solve. Use the number line.

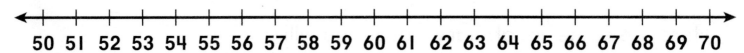

50 51 52 53 54 55 56 57 58 59 60 61 62 63 64 65 66 67 68 69 70

1. Is 57 closer to 50 or 60?

   57 is closer to _____.

2. Use the nearest tens to estimate the sum
   of 57 + 62.

   _____ + _____ = _____

3. Find the exact sum of 57 + 62.

   _____ + _____ = _____

4. Is 68 closer to 60 or 70?

   68 is closer to _____.

5. Use the nearest tens to estimate the sum
   of 68 + 54.

   _____ + _____ = _____

   Find the exact sum of 68 + 54.

   _____ + _____ = _____

Use this page to review important skills needed for this chapter.

Chapter 10 Lesson 1

Different Ways to Add

▶ **Learn**

Objective
Choose an appropriate way to add.

Choose a way to find 64 + 20.

mental math

hundred chart

place-value blocks

paper and pencil

▶ **Guided Practice**

Circle the way you would choose to add.

1. 34 + 38
   paper and pencil
   mental math

Think!
Can I do all the steps in my head?

2. 27 + 56
   place-value blocks
   mental math

3. 65 + 26
   mental math
   hundred chart

4. 45 + 30
   mental math
   paper and pencil

5. 60 + 7
   place-value blocks
   mental math

Add. Explain the way you find the sum.

6. 27 + 15 _____

_____

7. **(123)** **Math Talk** Is mental math the fastest way to add 60 + 20? Why or why not?

KEY NS 2.2 Find the sum or difference of two whole numbers up to three digits long. Also **NS 2.3, NS 2.0, MR 1.1, MR 1.2, MR 2.0**

MR 1.0 Make decisions about how to set up a problem.

one hundred eighty-nine **189**

Choose a way to add. Add. Explain the way you find the sum.

8. 46 + 28 = _74_

9. 57 + 30 = _____

_____

_____

_____

_____

10. 39 + 42 = _____

11. 90 + 6 = _____

_____

_____

_____

_____

Reading Math: Vocabulary

Circle the problem that asks you to find the sum.
Complete the number sentences.

12. 30 = 40 − _____

13. 19 + 36 = _____

14. 5 − _____ = 2

15. 17 + _____ = 22

Estimate Sums

Objective
Estimate the sum of 2-digit addends by rounding.

Vocabulary
estimate
round

▶ **Learn**

When you do not need an exact sum, you can **estimate.**

Estimate the sum of 21 and 35.

Step 1

Round each addend to the nearest ten.

21 is closer to 20. Round down.

35 is exactly in the middle of 30 and 40. Round up.

20 21 22 23 24 25 26 27 28 29 30 31 32 33 34 35 36 37 38 39 40

Step 2

Add the tens to estimate the sum.   _20_ + _40_ = _60_

▶ **Guided Practice**

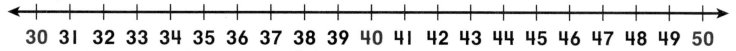

Round each addend to the nearest ten.
Estimate the sum.

30 31 32 33 34 35 36 37 38 39 40 41 42 43 44 45 46 47 48 49 50

Think!
38 is closer to 40
so I round up.

1. 45 + 38

_____ + _____ = _____

2. 27 + 36

_____ + _____ = _____

3.  **Math Talk** Libby estimated that the sum of
59 + 28 is 70. What error did she make?
What is a better estimate?

NS 6.0 Use estimation strategies in computation and
problem solving that involve numbers that use the
ones, tens, hundreds, and thousands places.
Also **MR 2.0**

NS 2.0 Estimate, calculate, and solve problems
involving addition and subtraction of two- and
three-digit numbers.

one hundred ninety-one **191**

▶ Practice

Round each addend to the nearest ten. Estimate the sum.

Remember!
When a number is exactly in the middle of two tens, round up.

```
 10  11  12  13  14  15  16  17  18  19  20  21  22  23  24  25  26  27  28  29  30
```

```
 30  31  32  33  34  35  36  37  38  39  40  41  42  43  44  45  46  47  48  49  50
```

4. 42 + 25

___40___ + ___30___ = ___70___

5. 37 + 49

_____ + _____ = _____

6. 22 + 48

_____ + _____ = _____

7. 15 + 44

_____ + _____ = _____

8. 19 + 34

_____ + _____ = _____

9. 42 + 36

_____ + _____ = _____

10. 7 + 18

_____ + _____ = _____

11. 25 + 47

_____ + _____ = _____

Problem Solving: Number Sense

12. Tony needs 16 starfish stickers and 32 shell stickers to make a design on his notebook. About how many stickers does he need in all?

Draw or write to explain.

about _____ stickers

🏠 **At Home** Give your child two numbers, such as 57 and 31. Ask your child to round the numbers to the nearest ten and add them.

En casa Dé a su niño dos números, como 57 y 31. Pida a su niño que redondee los números a la decena más cercana y que los sume.

Line Up Digits to Add

Objective
Align place values to solve addition problems.

▶ **Learn**

Find 46 + 8.

Remember to regroup.

Step 1
Rewrite 46 + 8. Line up the ones and the tens.

Tens	Ones
⬚	⬚
4	6
+	8

Step 2
Add the ones. Add the tens.

Tens	Ones
1	⬚
4	6
+	8
5	4

▶ **Guided Practice**

Rewrite the addends. Add.

1. 37 + 6

Tens	Ones
⬚	⬚
+	

Think!
I line up the 7 and the 6 in the ones column.

2. 59 + 16

Tens	Ones
⬚	⬚
+	

3. 7 + 62

Tens	Ones
⬚	⬚
+	

4. 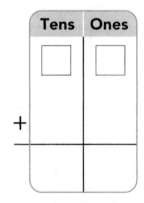 **Math Talk** Scott rewrites 49 + 5. Then he adds and gets a sum of 99. What did he do wrong?

KEY NS 2.2 Find the sum or difference of two whole numbers up to three digits long.
Also **NS 2.0, KEY NS 1.1, NS 1.0, MR 2.2**

Rewrite the addends. Add.

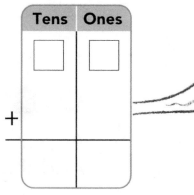
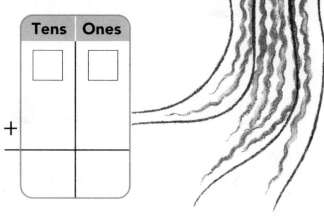

5. 18 + 72

Tens	Ones
1	8
+ 7	2
9	0

6. 63 + 25

Tens	Ones
+	

7. 5 + 39

Tens	Ones
+	

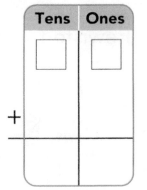

8. 48 + 39

Tens	Ones
+	

9. 59 + 15

Tens	Ones
+	

10. 86 + 4

Tens	Ones
+	

11. 27 + 34

Tens	Ones
+	

12. 8 + 56

Tens	Ones
+	

13. 65 + 19

Tens	Ones
+	

14. 29 + 65

Tens	Ones
+	

15. 23 + 67

Tens	Ones
+	

Problem Solving: Number Sense

16. The gift shop needs 75 toys. The shop gets a box of boats and a box of fish. Does the shop have enough toys? _____

47 31 24

Chapter 10 Lesson 4

Add Money

▶ Learn

You can add money the same way
you add numbers.

Ellis goes to the beach gift shop.
He buys a set of fish postcards for
33¢ and a toy dolphin for 48¢.
How much money does Ellis spend?

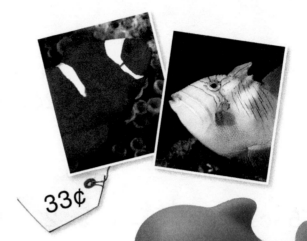

33¢

48¢

Step 1

Write the prices. Line up
the tens and ones.

$$
\begin{array}{r}
33¢ \\
+\ 48¢ \\
\hline
\end{array}
$$

Step 2

Add.
Regroup if you need to.

$$
\begin{array}{r}
33¢ \\
+\ 48¢ \\
\hline
81¢
\end{array}
$$

33¢ + 48¢ = ___81¢___

▶ Guided Practice

Rewrite the numbers to line up
the tens and ones. Add.

Think!
52¢ + 18¢ is
like 52 + 18.

1. 52¢ + 18¢

+ _____

2. 17¢ + 8¢

+ _____

3. (123) **Math Talk** How is adding 56 + 39 like
adding 56¢ + 39¢?

▶ Practice

Rewrite the numbers.
Add.

Remember!
Write the ¢ in your answer.

4. 47¢ + 5¢
$$\begin{array}{r} 47¢ \\ +\ 5¢ \\ \hline 52¢ \end{array}$$

5. 26¢ + 47¢ + _____

6. 32¢ + 44¢ + _____

7. 53¢ + 28¢ + _____

8. 22¢ + 75¢ + _____

9. 58¢ + 12¢ + _____

10. 67¢ + 25¢ + _____

11. 12¢ + 78¢ + _____

12. 33¢ + 65¢ + _____

13. 7¢ + 74¢ + _____

14. 35¢ + 52¢ + _____

15. 29¢ + 53¢ + _____

16. 84¢ + 9¢ + _____

17. 22¢ + 33¢ + _____

18. 64¢ + 36¢ + _____

Problem Solving: Reasoning

19. Kento has **63¢**. Becca has **28¢**.
They want to buy a beach ball that
costs **90¢**. Do they have enough to
buy the ball?

yes   no

Draw or write to explain.

|||||||||○○○○○

🏠 **At Home** Help your child cut out two
grocery ads for items, each less than
50¢. Ask your child to find the total
cost of the two items.

En casa Ayude a su niño a recortar dos
anuncios de supermercado, de productos que
cuesten menos de 50¢ cada uno. Pida a su niño
que halle el costo total de los dos productos.

Name _____

Add Three 2-Digit Numbers

▶ **Learn**

There are 17 girls and 23 boys on a whale watch.
There are also 13 adults.
How many people are on the whale watch?

Add 17, 23, and 13 to find the answer. You can use two ways.

Make a ten.	Use a fact you know.
$\begin{matrix} 17 \\ 23 \\ +13 \\ \hline 53 \end{matrix}$ $> 7 + 3 = 10$	$\begin{matrix} 17 \\ 23 \\ +13 \\ \hline 53 \end{matrix}$ $> 3 + 3 = 6$

There are ___53___ people on the whale watch.

▶ **Guided Practice**

Add.

1. $\begin{matrix} 16 \\ 24 \\ +\ 2 \\ \hline \end{matrix}$ **Think!** I can make a ten with 6 + 4.

2. $\begin{matrix} 22 \\ 32 \\ +\ 5 \\ \hline \end{matrix}$

3. $\begin{matrix} 45 \\ 14 \\ +24 \\ \hline \end{matrix}$

4. $\begin{matrix} 27 \\ 15 \\ +22 \\ \hline \end{matrix}$

5. $\begin{matrix} 16 \\ 26 \\ +11 \\ \hline \end{matrix}$

6. $\begin{matrix} 25 \\ 8 \\ +24 \\ \hline \end{matrix}$

7. $\begin{matrix} 17 \\ 12 \\ +\ 3 \\ \hline \end{matrix}$

8. $\begin{matrix} 15 \\ 20 \\ +34 \\ \hline \end{matrix}$

9. $\begin{matrix} 42 \\ 8 \\ +14 \\ \hline \end{matrix}$

10. **(123) Math Talk** How did you add the ones in Exercise 9?

 KEY AF 1.1 Use the commutative and associative rules to simplify mental calculations and to check results.
Also **AF 1.0, MR 2.1, MR 1.0**

NS 2.0 Estimate, calculate, and solve problems involving addition and subtraction of two- and three-digit numbers.

Add.

Remember!
Look for a ten or
a fact you know.

11. 19
      6
    +21
    ‾‾‾‾
     46

12. 66
     19
    + 4
    ‾‾‾‾

13. 17
     30
    +52
    ‾‾‾‾

14. 61
      3
    +13
    ‾‾‾‾

15. 27
     12
    +57
    ‾‾‾‾

16. 28
     11
    + 2
    ‾‾‾‾

17. 41
      9
    +27
    ‾‾‾‾

18.   2
     18
    +28
    ‾‾‾‾

19. 12
     13
    +41
    ‾‾‾‾

20. 34
     32
    + 7
    ‾‾‾‾

21. 14
     30
    +14
    ‾‾‾‾

22. 53
     17
    + 8
    ‾‾‾‾

23. 21
     42
    + 3
    ‾‾‾‾

24. 18
      4
    +36
    ‾‾‾‾

25.   6
     34
      3
    +25
    ‾‾‾‾

Algebra Readiness: Number Sentences

Complete the number sentences.
Do the work inside the ( ) first.

26. $(12 + 4) + 10 =$ _____

    _16_ $+ 10 =$ _____

27. $12 + (4 + 10) =$ _____

    $12 +$ _____ $=$ _____

28. Can you add numbers in any order?
    Why or why not?

_____

_____

At Home Tell a story using three
2-digit numbers. Ask your child to add
and explain how to find the sum.

En casa Cuente un cuento usando tres
números de 2 dígitos. Pida a su niño que
sume y explique cómo hallar la suma.

Name _____

▶ **Practice**

29.   23
       7
    +35

30.   57
      22
    +10

31.   64
       9
    +26

32.   38
      21
    +14

33.   46
      37
    +11

34.   73
      15
    + 2

35.   35
      21
    +13

36.   43
      19
    +25

37.   42
      28
    +12

38.   31
       3
    +33

39.   54
      17
    +15

40.   64
       8
    +12

41.   27
      38
    +31

42.   39
      26
    +23

43.   83
      11
    + 4

44.   33
      44
    +23

KEY **NS 2.2** Find the sum or difference of two whole numbers up to three digits long. Also **NS 2.0**

one hundred ninety-nine **199**

Add It Up!

How to Play

1. Mix the cards. Place them face down. Each player takes three cards.

2. Add the three numbers and find the sum.

3. The player with the greatest sum gets 1 point. When all the cards are used, mix them up and use them again.

4. The first player to get 10 points wins!

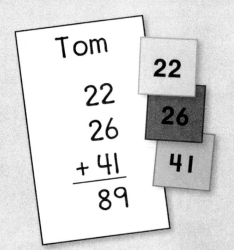

$$
\begin{array}{r}
\text{Tom} \\
22 \\
26 \\
+\ 41 \\
\hline
89
\end{array}
$$

NS 2.0 Students estimate, calculate, and solve problems involving addition and subtraction of two- and three-digit numbers.

Education Place
Visit www.eduplace.com/camap/ for more games.

Comparison Problems

 **Learn**

Naomi wants to buy a pail and shovel for her trip to the beach. How much money does she need?

Understand
What do you know?
- The pail costs 37¢.
- The shovel costs 33¢.

Item	Price
beach ball	25¢
pail	37¢
shovel	33¢
towel	45¢

Plan
How can you find how much money Naomi needs?

add

Use comparison bars. Write the parts you know.

Pail	Shovel
37	33
?	

Solve
Write a number sentence. Then solve.

$$37¢ + 33¢ = 70¢.$$

Naomi needs __70¢__ to buy the pail and shovel.

Think!
I know that the two parts are 37¢ and 33¢ from the table. I need to find the whole.

Look Back
Did you answer the question? How can you check your answer?

Problem Solving
Plan

Objective
Use comparison bars to solve problems.

KEY NS 2.2 Find the sum or difference of two whole numbers up to three digits long. Also **NS 2.0, NS 5.0, AF 1.2, AF 1.0, MR 2.0, MR 2.1, MR 2.2**

AF 1.3 Solve addition and subtraction problems by using data from simple charts, picture graphs, and number sentences.

Item	Price
goggles	18¢
hat	34¢
sunglasses	26¢
umbrella	42¢

1. Greg wants to buy a beach umbrella and goggles. How much money does he need?

What do you know?

The umbrella costs _____.

The goggles cost _____.

Write the parts you know in the comparison bars.

Write a number sentence. Then solve.

Remember!
Understand
Plan
Solve
Look Back

_____ + _____ = _____

Greg needs _____ to buy the umbrella and goggles.

Umbrella	Goggles

?

2. (123) **Math Talk** How did you use comparison bars to solve the problem?

Use comparison bars. Solve.

Draw or write to explain.

3. Travis wants to buy a hat and sunglasses. How much money does he need?

_____

4. Amy buys a hat and goggles. How much does she spend?

_____

At Home Ask your child to find out which two prices add up to 68¢.

En casa Pida a su niño que halle cuáles son los dos precios que suman 68¢.

Key Standards Review

Find the sum.

1. 38 + 54 = _____   2. 26 + 44 = _____   3. 57 + 24 = _____

4. 63 + 19 = _____   5. 45 + 45 = _____   6. 65 + 29 = _____

7. 35 + 56 = _____   8. 79 + 17 = _____   9. 38 + 28 = _____

Challenge   Number Sense

Alex and Tanya play a game of beanbag toss.
Tanya gets a score of 71.
Alex gets a score of 40.

1. What two numbers does Tanya land on?

_____ and _____

2. What two numbers does Alex land on?

_____ and _____

KEY **NS 2.2** Find the sum or difference of two
whole numbers up to three digits long.

two hundred three **203**

Regrouping Is What We Do!

🎧 **Math Music,** Track 4
Tune: original

Keisha has 19 fish.
Eduardo has 22.
How many fish are there in all?
Regroup—that's what we do!

When there are more than 10 ones—
Regroup—that's what we do.
Regroup 10 ones as 1 ten.
Regrouping is what we do!

Allie has 24 fish.
Hugo has 38.
How many fish are there in all?
Regroup—you'll do just great!

KEY NS 2.2 Find the sum or difference of two whole numbers up to three digits long.

Name _____

Concepts and Skills

Choose a way to add. Add.
Explain the way you find the sum. KEY **NS 2.2**

1. 26 + 67 = _____

_____

Round each addend to the nearest ten.
Estimate the sum. NS 6.0

2. 32 + 16

3. 49 + 25

_____ + _____ = _____   _____ + _____ = _____

4. Rewrite the
addends. Add.
29 + 42 KEY **NS 2.2**

Tens	Ones
☐	
+	

5. Rewrite the
numbers. Add.
34¢ + 19¢ KEY **NS 5.2**

6. Add. KEY **AF 1.1**

```
  15
  23
+ 46
```

Problem Solving NS 5.0, MR 2.0

7. Jamal has 27¢. Mina has 54¢. They
   want to buy a jump rope that costs
   95¢. Do they have enough to buy the
   jump rope? Explain how you know.

_____

_____

Spiral Review and Test Practice

1. Follow the pattern. What are the two missing numbers?

8, 12, 16, _____, _____, 28, 32

17, 18 ○   17, 27 ○   20, 21 ○   20, 24 ○

KEY **SDAP 2.0**, SDAP 2.1 Page 85

2. Find the fewest coins that show the amount.

 90¢

 ○    ○   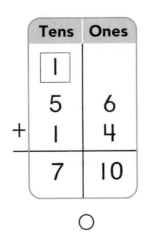 ○    ○

KEY **NS 5.1**, NS 5.0 Page 125

3. Which model shows 56 + 14?

Tens	Ones
☐	
5	6
+ 1	4
6	0

○

Tens	Ones
1	
5	6
+ 1	4
7	10

○

Tens	Ones
1	
5	6
+ 1	4
4	2

○

Tens	Ones
1	
5	6
+ 1	4
7	0

○

KEY **NS 2.2**, NS 2.0 Page 173

4. Round each addend to the nearest ten. Which is the best estimate for the sum?   52 + 16

50 ○   60 ○   70 ○   80 ○

NS 6.0, NS 2.0 Page 191

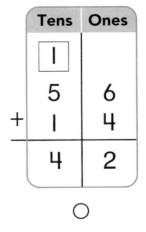 **Education Place**
Visit www.eduplace.com/camap/ for
Test-Taking Tips and Extra Practice.

Spiral Review

Greg Tang's Go Fast, Go Far

Unit 4 Mental Math Strategies

Partial Sums

Partial sums are fast to do. First break each number into two!

I think of 25 as 20 + 5 and 23 as 20 + 3.
Then I add.
20 + 20 = 40.
5 + 3 = 8.
Then I add 40 + 8 = 48.

1. 25 + 23 = ☐40☐ + ☐8☐ = ☐48☐

2. 14 + 12 = ☐20☐ + ☐ = ☐

3. 31 + 36 = ☐ + ☐ = ☐

4. 47 + 42 = ☐ + ☐ = ☐

5. 26 + 22 = ☐ + ☐ = ☐

6. 35 + 14 = ☐ + ☐ = ☐

7. 17 + 11 = ☐ + ☐ = ☐

8. 43 + 45 = ☐ + ☐ = ☐

Take It Further: Now try doing all the steps in your head!

9. 33 + 15 = ☐

10. 55 + 24 = ☐

Reading and Writing Math

The table below shows how many stickers Mimi has.

Kind of Sticker	Number of Stickers
Shell	29
Starfish	16

Word Bank
add
estimate
ones
regroup
round

Choose a word from the word bank for each blank.

1. To find the total number of stickers,

   you need to _____ 29 + 16.

2. When you have 10 or more _____, you

   have to _____ them to make another ten.

3. When you _____ a sum, you _____
   each number to the nearest ten before you add.

Writing Math Think about ways to add 29 + 16.
Which way would you use? Circle *Yes* or *No*.
Then tell why or why not.

	Would you use:	Tell why or why not.
4.	mental math? Yes No	
5.	tens and ones blocks? Yes No	

KEY NS 2.2 Find the sum or difference of two whole numbers up to three digits long.
Also **MR 1.1**

Name _____

Concepts and Skills

Complete the addition sentences.
Use a basic fact to help. NS 2.3

1. 3 tens + 6 tens = _____ tens   _____ + _____ = _____

Use Workmat 3 with ▭▭▭▭▭▭ and ▪ .
Add. KEY NS 2.2

2.   42
   + 5

3.   67
   + 7

4.   38
   +18

5.   77
   +19

6. 46 + 41 = _____

7. 49 + 28 = _____

8. 56 + 30 = _____

9. 40 + 47 = _____

Add. KEY NS 2.2

10.

Tens	Ones
☐	
4	8
+ 3	7

11.

Tens	Ones
☐	
1	6
+ 5	6

Add. KEY NS 2.2

12.   19
   +67

13.   39
   +29

Choose a way to add. Add.
Explain the way you find the sum. KEY NS 2.2, MR 2.1

14. 37 + 20 = _____

How I solved: _____

Round each addend to the nearest ten.
Estimate the sum. NS 6.0

15. 33 + 28

_____ + _____ = _____

33 + 28 is about _____.

16. 59 + 29

_____ + _____ = _____

59 + 29 is about _____.

Add. KEY NS 5.2

17. 44¢ + 39¢ = _____

18. 73¢ + 18¢ = _____

Add. KEY AF 1.1

19.   15
       26
     + 55

Problem Solving

Solve. KEY NS 2.2

20. Eric counted 49 cars on his way
    to school. On his way home, he
    counted 27 more cars. How
    many cars did Eric count in all?

_____

Draw or write to explain.

Unit 5

Subtract 2-Digit Numbers

BIG IDEAS!

- You can use drawings, a hundred chart, or you can line up digits to subtract two-digit numbers.

- You can check a subtraction answer by adding.

Songs and Games

Math Music Track 5
How Many Will Be Left?

eGames
www.eduplace.com/camap/

Literature

Read Aloud Big Book
- The Mystery of the Missing Eggs

Math Readers

The Cereal Box Mystery
by Caterina Mateo
Illustrated by Rene King Moreno

Comic Books for Sale
by Michael Sellers
Illustrated by Catherine Lucas

Lots of Box Tops
by Gary LoPresti
illustrated by Barry Gott

Subtract from 99

How to Play

1. Write the number 99 at the top of a piece of paper.

2. Take turns drawing a number card from the bag.

3. Subtract the number from 99. Write the difference on the paper.

4. Take turns drawing new number cards. Subtract each new number from the last difference on your paper.

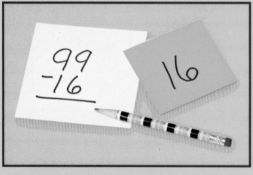

$$\begin{array}{r} 99 \\ -16 \\ \hline \end{array}$$

16

5. The player with the lesser difference after four turns wins.

What You Need

2 players
Learning Tool 31

0	1	2	3	4	5	6
7	8	9	10	11	12	13
14	15	16	17	18	19	20
21	22	23	24	25		

KEY **NS 2.2** Find the sum or difference of two whole numbers up to three digits long.
Also **NS 2.0, MR 1.2, MR 2.2**

Education Place
Visit **www.eduplace.com/camap/**
for eGames and Brain Teasers.

Math at Home

Dear Family,

My class is starting Unit 5, **Subtract 2-Digit Numbers.** I will be learning different strategies to help me subtract 2-digit numbers, such as estimating differences and regrouping tens. You can help me learn these vocabulary words, and we can do the Math Activity together.

From,

_____

Vocabulary

difference The result of subtraction

$$15 - 10 = 5$$

$$\begin{array}{r} 15 \\ -10 \\ \hline 5 \end{array}$$

difference ⟶

estimate A rounded answer that is close to an exact answer

29 → round to nearest ten → 30
−21 → round to nearest ten → −20
                    estimate ⟶ 10

regroup In subtraction, trade 1 ten for 10 ones.

 Education Place
Visit **www.eduplace.com/camaf/** for
• eGames and Brain Teasers
• Math at Home in other languages

Family Math Activity

Make up a subtraction number sentence using 2 two-digit numbers, such as 52−36. Have your child tell you a story to go with the number sentence. Then have your child tell if he or she needed to regroup to subtract and why or why not. Add to check the answer.

Literature

These books link to the math in this unit. Look for them at the library.

• **Shark Swimathon**
  by Stuart J. Murphy
  Illustrated by Lynne Cravath
  (HarperCollins, 2001)
• **Lights Out!**
  by Lucille Recht Penner
  Illustrated by Jerry Smath
• **Panda Math**
  by Ann Whitehead Nagda

Matemáticas en casa

Estimada familia:

Mi clase está comenzando la Unidad 5, **Resta de números de 2 dígitos**. Aprenderé diferentes estrategias para restar números de 2 dígitos, como estimar diferencias y reagrupar decenas. Me pueden ayudar a aprender estas palabras de vocabulario y podemos hacer juntos la Actividad de matemáticas para la familia.

De:

_____

Vocabulario

diferencia El resultado de la resta.

$$15 - 10 = 5$$

diferencia

$$\begin{array}{r} 15 \\ -10 \\ \hline 5 \end{array}$$

diferencia ⟶

estimación Respuesta aproximada que es cercana a una respuesta exacta.

29 → redondear a la decena más cercana → 30

−21 → redondear a la decena más cercana → −20

estimación ⟶ 10

reagrupar En la resta, cambiar 1 decena por 10 unidades.

Actividad de matemáticas para la familia

Invente un enunciado numérico de resta usando 2 números de dos dígitos, como 52−36. Pida a su niño que le cuente un cuento que vaya con el enunciado numérico. Luego pregúntele si tuvo que reagrupar para restar y por qué. Sume para comprobar la respuesta.

Literatura

Estos libros hablan sobre las matemáticas de esta unidad. Búscalos en la biblioteca.

- **Katy no tiene bolsa**
  por Emmy Paine
  (*Rebound by Sagebrush*, 2000)

- **Primeros números**
  por Jo Litchfield

Education Place
Visite **www.eduplace.com/camaf/** para
- Juegos en línea y acertijos
- Matemáticas en casa en otros idiomas

UNIT
5

Our Big Sale

written by Tim Johnson

This Take-Home Book belongs to

_____

Bugs

Dinosaurs

Reading and Writing Math

This take-home book will help you review subtraction concepts.

Imagine you go to a sale. You see these 10 dinosaurs for sale. Circle the ones you would buy. How many would be left?

____ − ____ = ____

____ would be left

KEY **NS 2.2** Find the sum or difference of two whole numbers up to three digits long.

8

Kim and Daren set up a store.
They want to sell their collections of
bugs and dinosaurs.
"Come to our big sale," they call.

Kim places the rest of her bug
collection on the table.
José wants to buy 9 of the bugs.
How many will be left to sell?

_____ − _____ = _____

_____ left to sell

Daren has 6 T-Rex dinosaur toys.
Bill comes to buy 2. How many will
be left to sell?

_____ − _____ = _____

_____ left to sell

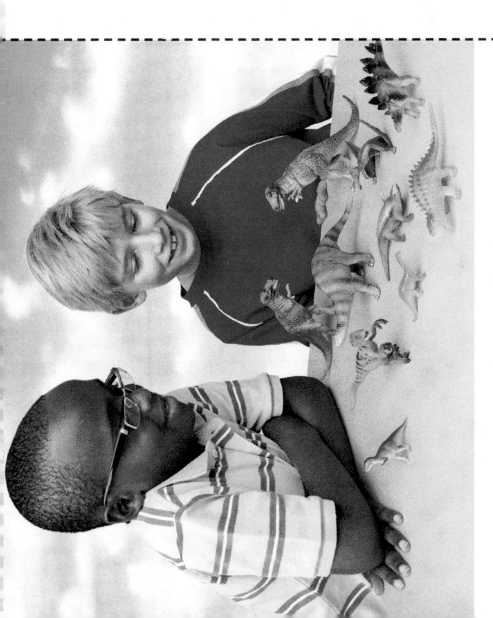

Along comes Ben. He looks at the
dinosaurs Daren still has for sale.
How many are in the collection?
If Ben buys 5, how many will be
left to sell?

_____ − _____ = _____

_____ left to sell

Tina likes Kim's ladybug collection.

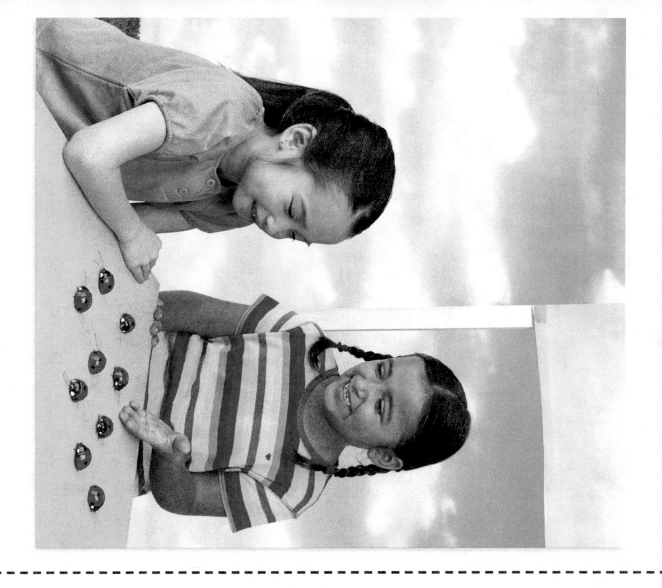

If Tina buys 7 of Kim's ladybugs, how many will Kim have left?

_____ − _____ = _____

_____ left

Explore Subtracting Tens and Ones

Vocabulary

Here are some vocabulary words you will learn in the chapter.

subtract Take away part of a group

$$7 - 3 = 4$$

minus sign

difference The result in a subtraction problem

$$7 - 3 = 4$$

difference

subtract tens You can take away groups of ten to solve a subtraction problem.

$$90 - 30 = 60$$

See English-Spanish Glossary pages 573–589.

KEY NS 2.2 Find the sum or difference of two whole numbers up to three digits long.

Education Place
Visit **www.eduplace.com/camap/** for the eGlossary and eGames.

two hundred thirteen **213**

Name _____

Check What You Know

Write the number sentence.

1. Ted makes 13 paper airplanes. Alan makes 7 paper airplanes. How many more paper airplanes does Ted make?

   _____ − _____ = _____ more paper airplanes

2. Jeff makes 9 paper boats. Dora makes 5 paper boats. How many more paper boats does Jeff make?

   _____ − _____ = _____ more paper boats

3. Clara makes 18 flags. She tapes 9 flags to the window. How many flags are not taped to the window?

   _____ − _____ = _____ flags

4. Pearl draws 12 trees on her picture. She cuts 8 of them out. How many trees are not cut out of the picture?

   _____ − _____ = _____ trees

5. Kayla makes 15 flowers. Steve makes 6 flowers. How many more flowers does Kayla make?

   _____ − _____ = _____ more

Use this page to review important skills needed for this chapter.

Name _____

Subtract Tens

Hands On

Objective
Use tens rods and basic facts to subtract tens.

▶ **Explore**

When you subtract tens, you can use a subtraction fact to help.

Patty has **50** pennies. She wants to know how many she will have left if she gives her brother **30** pennies.

Step 1

Use five tens rods to show **50** pennies. Move **3** tens to the side. How many tens rods do you have left? _____

Step 2

What number do two tens rods stand for? _____
Write a subtraction fact that helps solve the problem.

$$5 - 3 = 2$$

So, $50 - 30 = 20$.

Patty will have **20** pennies left.

1. Use 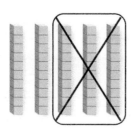 and quick pictures. Use a basic fact to help you.

Think!
A subtraction fact can help me subtract the tens.

Take some ▭▭▭▭ .

Draw your tens. Subtract some tens by crossing out.

Record.

_____ tens ⁻ _____ tens ⁼ _____ tens

_____ ⁻ _____ ⁼ _____

2. **123** **Math Talk** How does $7 - 2$ help you find $70 - 20$?

KEY NS 2.2 Find the sum or difference of two whole numbers up to three digits long. Also **NS 2.0, MR 2.0, MR 3.0**

MR 1.2 Use tools, such as manipulatives or sketches, to model problems.

> **Extend**

Use 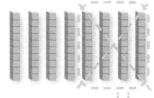.
Complete each subtraction sentence.
Use a basic fact to help.

3. Find 80 − 40.

8 − 4 = _____

8 tens − 4 tens = _____ tens

80 − 40 = _____

4. Find 60 − 30.

6 − 3 = _____

6 tens − 3 tens = _____ tens

60 − 30 = _____

Complete the subtraction sentences.
Use 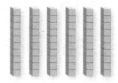 to help.

5. 5 tens − 1 ten = _____ tens

_____ − _____ = _____

6. 7 tens − 2 tens = _____ tens

_____ − _____ = _____

7. 9 tens − 3 tens = _____ tens

_____ − _____ = _____

8. 4 tens − 2 tens = _____ tens

_____ − _____ = _____

9. 5 tens − 2 tens = _____ tens

_____ − _____ = _____

10. 7 tens − 3 tens = _____ tens

_____ − _____ = _____

11. 9 tens − 7 tens = _____ tens

_____ − _____ = _____

12. 8 tens − 1 ten = _____ tens

_____ − _____ = _____

13. How can knowing how to subtract tens help you subtract 27 from 37? Write the subtraction problem.

_____

At Home Give your child up to 9 dimes. Create subtraction sentences, such as 8 dimes − 3 dimes = 5 dimes.

En casa Dé a su niño hasta 9 monedas de diez centavos. Creen enunciados de resta, como 8 monedas de diez centavos − 3 monedas de diez centavos = 5 monedas de diez centavos.

Name _____

Subtract 2-Digit Numbers

▶ **Learn**

Hands On ✋

Objective
Subtract 2-digit numbers using models and drawings.

Jim has 45 toy dinosaurs.
He gives 13 dinosaurs away.
How many dinosaurs does Jim have left?

Step 1

Show 45 with  and ▪.

Model the problem with a quick picture.

Step 2

Take away 13. Cross out 13 blocks.

Cross out 1 ten and 3 ones in your drawing.

Step 3

Count the tens and ones that are left.

__3__ tens

__2__ ones

45 – 13 = __32__

Jim has __32__ dinosaurs left.

▶ **Guided Practice**

Model with and ▪ or draw a picture. Subtract.

1. 37 – 15 = _____

Think!
I need to subtract 1 ten and 5 ones.

2. 48 – 31 = _____

3. 64 – 23 = _____

4. 25 – 12 = _____

5. **(123) Math Talk** How does showing a number as tens and ones help you subtract?

KEY NS 2.2 Find the sum or difference of two whole numbers up to three digits long. Also **NS 2.0, MR 2.0, MR 2.1**

MR 1.2 Use tools, such as manipulatives or sketches, to model problems.

Model or draw to subtract.
Find each difference.

Remember!
Find how many ones and
tens you have left.

6. $76 - 45 = \underline{}$

7. $39 - 15 = \underline{}$

8. $84 - 41 = \underline{}$

9. $28 - 14 = \underline{}$

10. $36 - 24 = \underline{}$

11. $57 - 32 = \underline{}$

12. $48 - 25 = \underline{}$

13. $68 - 24 = \underline{}$

14. $55 - 33 = \underline{}$

15. $100 - 70 = \underline{}$

Problem Solving: Number Sense

Read the clues. Write the number.

Draw or write to explain.

16. Maria has 42 dinosaur stickers.
When Maria and Jordan add
their stickers together, they have
75 stickers in all. How many
stickers does Jordan have?

_____ stickers

At Home Give your child 5 dimes and
9 pennies. Ask him or her to name the
amount and show how to subtract 14¢.

En casa Dé a su niño 5 monedas de diez
centavos y 9 monedas de un centavo. Pídale
que nombre la cantidad y muestre cómo
restar 14¢.

Subtract 2-Digit Numbers With Regrouping

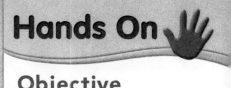

Hands On

Objective
Subtract with and without regrouping.

 **Learn**

Joon has 31 butterfly pictures.
He gives 7 pictures to his sister.
How many pictures does Joon have left?

If there are not enough ones to subtract, regroup 1 ten as 10 ones.
Model the subtraction with ▬▬▬ and ▪.

Step 1	**Step 2**	**Step 3**
Show 3 tens and 1 one.	Regroup 1 ten as 10 ones.	Take away 7 ones.

Step 3:

How many are left?

__2__ tens __4__ ones = __24__

 **Guided Practice**

Think!
Do I have enough ones to subtract?

Subtract.
Use ▬▬▬ and ▪ to help.

	Show the greater number.	Subtract the smaller number.	Do you need to regroup?	How many tens and ones are left?	What is the difference?
1. 42 – 7	42	7	yes no	_____ tens _____ ones	_____

2. 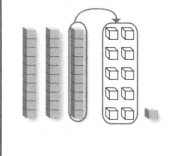 **Math Talk** How do you know when you need to regroup?

 KEY NS 2.2 Find the sum or difference of two whole numbers up to three digits long.
Also NS 2.0, MR 1.2, MR 2.0

MR 2.1 Defend the reasoning used and justify the procedures selected.

▶ Practice

Subtract.
Use and 🔲 to help.

Remember!
Regroup if you do not have enough ones to subtract.

3. 33 – 8

_____2_____ tens _____5_____ ones

_____25_____

4. 56 – 37

_____ tens _____ ones

_____

5. 37 – 7

_____ tens _____ ones

_____

6. 65 – 13

_____ tens _____ ones

_____

7. 24 – 17

_____ tens _____ ones

_____

8. 72 – 9

_____ tens _____ ones

_____

9. 98 – 35

_____ tens _____ ones

_____

10. 100 – 6

_____ tens _____ ones

_____

Problem Solving: Reasoning

11. Rita has 25¢.
She gives her friend 8¢.
How much money does
Rita have left?

Rita has _____¢ left.

Draw or write to explain.

At Home Have your child explain how he or she knew whether to regroup in Exercises 4 and 5.

En casa Pida a su niño que explique cómo supo si debía reagrupar en los Ejercicios 4 y 5.

Make a Table

 **Learn**

Kelly collects things she finds around the house. The pictures show what she finds. Count the objects and complete the table.

How many more buttons than paper clips does Kelly have?

Understand
What do you know?
Look for the information in the table.

- Kelly has 12 paper clips.
- Kelly has 26 buttons.

Plan
Will you add or subtract?

subtract

Think!
I need to compare two amounts, so I will subtract.

Kelly's Collection	
Object	**Number**
buttons	
paper clips	
keys	

Solve
Subtract to solve.

$$26 - 12 = 14$$

Look Back
Did you answer the question?
Does your answer make sense?

KEY NS 2.2 Find the sum or difference of two whole numbers up to three digits long. Also **NS 2.0, SDAP 1.1, SDAP 1.4, MR 2.0, MR 2.1, MR 2.2, AF 1.2**

AF 1.3 Solve addition and subtraction problems by using data from simple charts, picture graphs, and number sentences.

two hundred twenty-one **221**

▶ Guided Problem Solving

1. Joshua collects buttons. The picture shows his collection. Complete the table. How many orange and green buttons does Joshua have?

Remember!
Understand
Plan
Solve
Look Back

What do you know?

Joshua has _____ orange buttons

and _____ green buttons.

Will you add or subtract?

Think!
I need to find a total.

_____

Write a number sentence.

_____ + _____ = _____

Joshua has _____ orange and green buttons.

Joshua's Collection

Color	Number
orange	
blue	
green	

2. (123) **Math Talk** How did making a table help you solve?

▶ Problem Solving Practice

Use the table to solve.

3. How many more blue buttons than orange buttons does Joshua have?

_____ more blue buttons

Draw or write to explain.

4. How many more blue buttons than green buttons does Joshua have?

_____ more blue buttons

 At Home Have your child create an addition problem using the data in the table.

En casa Pida a su niño que haga un problema de suma usando los datos de la tabla.

Key Standards Review

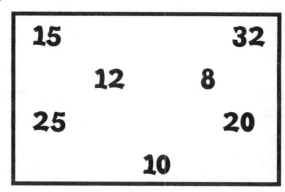

20 21 22 23 24 25 26 27 28 29 30 31 32 33 34 35 36 37 38 39 40

Round each addend to the nearest ten.
Estimate the sum.

1. 32 + 38

_____ + _____ = _____

2. 26 + 33

_____ + _____ = _____

3. 39 + 21

_____ + _____ = _____

4. 35 + 36

_____ + _____ = _____

Add.

5. 25¢ + 56¢ = _____

6. 68¢ + 14¢ = _____

7. 89¢ + 5¢ = _____

8. 36¢ + 48¢ = _____

Challenge   Number Sense

Choose the correct number from the box.

You say this number when you
start at zero and count by 5s.
You say this number when
you start at zero and count by 2s.
This number is double another
number in the box.

15		32
	12	8
25		20
	10	

What is the number?

_____

KEY NS 2.2 Find the sum or difference of two
whole numbers up to three digits long.
Also **SDAP 2.2**

two hundred twenty-three **223**

Native American Flutes

Flutes have been part of Native American music for hundreds of years. Flutes are made of many kinds of wood, such as redwood. Music is made by covering holes, blowing into the flute, and creating a vibration.

Write a number sentence. Solve.   Draw or write to explain.

1. Mr. Roberts sells 13 flutes in May. He sells 25 flutes in June. How many more flutes does he sell in June than in May?

   _____ – _____ = _____

2. 59 people play the flute. 33 people play the guitar. How many more people play the flute?

   _____ – _____ = _____

3. Mr. Roberts cleans 10 flutes in the morning. He cleans 17 in the afternoon. How many more flutes does he clean in the afternoon?

   _____ – _____ = _____

KEY **NS 2.2** Find the sum or difference of two whole numbers up to three digits long.
Also **NS 2.0**
Science PS 1.g

Name _____

Concepts and Skills

Complete the subtraction sentence. Use a quick picture or ▬▬▬▬ to help.   KEY **NS 2.2**

1. 8 tens − 5 tens = _____ tens

   _____ − _____ = _____

Model and draw to subtract. Find the difference.   KEY **NS 2.2**

2. 38 − 15 = _____

Subtract. Use ▬▬▬▬ and ▪ to help.   KEY **NS 2.2**

3. 52 − 8

   _____ tens   _____ ones

   _____

4. 35 − 29

   _____ tens   _____ ones

   _____

Problem Solving   KEY **NS 5.1**, NS 5.0, MR 2.0

5. Tina has 63¢. She gives her sister Lucy 24¢. How much money does Tina have left?

   _____

Spiral Review and Test Practice

1. Which number is 10 more than 60?

   50 ○   60 ○   70 ○   6010 ○

   KEY **NS 2.0**, NS 2.3 Page 189

2. Find the value of the sets of coins.
   Which symbol makes this true?

   \> ○   = ○   < ○   – ○

   KEY **NS 5.1**, NS 5.0, NS 1.3 Page 111

3. What is the sum?

$$\begin{array}{r} 24 \\ +\ 5 \\ \hline \end{array}$$

   28 ○   29 ○   30 ○   245 ○

   KEY **NS 2.2** Page 151

4. What is the sum?

$$\begin{array}{r} 29 \\ +67 \\ \hline \end{array}$$

   86 ○   89 ○   96 ○   98 ○

   KEY **NS 2.2**, NS 2.0 Page 175

Education Place
Visit **www.eduplace.com/camap/** for
Test-Taking Tips and Extra Practice.

Spiral Review

Use Place Value to Subtract

Vocabulary

Here are some vocabulary words you will learn in the chapter.

hundred chart

You can use a hundred chart to subtract.

$$96 - 40 = 56$$

1	2	3	4	5	6	7	8	9	10
11	12	13	14	15	16	17	18	19	20
21	22	23	24	25	26	27	28	29	30
31	32	33	34	35	36	37	38	39	40
41	42	43	44	45	46	47	48	49	50
51	52	53	54	55	56	57	58	59	60
61	62	63	64	65	66	67	68	69	70
71	72	73	74	75	76	77	78	79	80
81	82	83	84	85	86	87	88	89	90
91	92	93	94	95	96	97	98	99	100

regroup Trade 1 ten for 10 ones

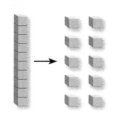

1 ten is the same as 10 ones.

See English-Spanish Glossary pages 573–589.

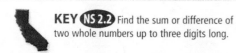
KEY **NS 2.2** Find the sum or difference of two whole numbers up to three digits long.

Education Place
Visit **www.eduplace.com/camap/** for the eGlossary and eGames.

two hundred twenty-seven **227**

Name _____

 **Check What You Know**

Solve. Use the table.

Collections	
stamps	56
rocks	40
buttons	20
keys	14

1. How many stamps are in the collection?

   _____ stamps

   _____ tens   _____ ones

2. How many more rocks than buttons are there?

   _____ – _____ = _____ more rocks

3. If 10 buttons were taken out of the button box, how many buttons would be left?

   _____ – _____ = _____ buttons

4. How many more stamps than rocks are in the collection?

   _____ – _____ = _____ more stamps

5. What is the difference between the number of stamps and the number of keys?

   _____ – _____ = _____

Use this page to review important skills needed for this chapter.

Name _____

Subtract Using a Hundred Chart

 **Learn**

Hands On 🖐

Objective
Use a hundred chart and count back by tens to subtract.

Use the hundred chart.
Find 57 – 30.

Step 1

Find 57 on the hundred chart.

Step 2

Move up 3 rows to subtract 30.

57, 47, 37, 27

57 – 30 = _27_

1	2	3	4	5	6	7	8	9	10
11	12	13	14	15	16	17	18	19	20
21	22	23	24	25	26	27	28	29	30
31	32	33	34	35	36	37	38	39	40
41	42	43	44	45	46	47	48	49	50
51	52	53	54	55	56	57	58	59	60
61	62	63	64	65	66	67	68	69	70
71	72	73	74	75	76	77	78	79	80
81	82	83	84	85	86	87	88	89	90
91	92	93	94	95	96	97	98	99	100

▶ **Guided Practice**

Use Workmat 5 and a ⬭.
Subtract.

Think!
Put a counter on 89.
Move up 2 rows.

1. 89 – 20 = _____

2. 35 – 10 = _____

3. 77 – 40 = _____

4. 95 – 30 = _____

5. 43 – 30 = _____

6. 70 – 60 = _____

7. 88 – 20 = _____

8. 64 – 50 = _____

9. 39
   –20

10. 62
    –50

11. 56
    –50

12. 93
    –50

13. 58
    –40

14. (123) **Math Talk** Look at 61, 51, 41, and 31 on the hundred chart. Describe the pattern. What number comes next?

KEY NS 2.2 Find the sum or difference of two whole numbers up to three digits long. Also **NS 2.0, SDAP 2.2**

MR 1.2 Use tools, such as manipulatives or sketches, to model problems.

two hundred twenty-nine **229**

Remember!
Move up one row to
subtract a ten.

Use the hundred chart or Workmat 5.
Subtract.

15. 31 − 10 = _21_

16. 65 − 40 = _____

17. 74 − 30 = _____

18. 89 − 70 = _____

19. 55 − 20 = _____

20. 29 − 10 = _____

1	2	3	4	5	6	7	8	9	10
11	12	13	14	15	16	17	18	19	20
21	22	23	24	25	26	27	28	29	30
31	32	33	34	35	36	37	38	39	40
41	42	43	44	45	46	47	48	49	50
51	52	53	54	55	56	57	58	59	60
61	62	63	64	65	66	67	68	69	70
71	72	73	74	75	76	77	78	79	80
81	82	83	84	85	86	87	88	89	90
91	92	93	94	95	96	97	98	99	100

21.   44
       −20

22.   67
       −40

23.   92
       −60

24.   17
       −10

25.   90
       −80

26.   63
       −40

27.   31
       −20

28.   86
       −50

29.   79
       −30

30.   100
        −20

Algebra Readiness: Number Sentences

31. Circle the number sentence
that is not correct.
Why is it wrong?

59 + 20 = 79   59 − 20 = 39

20 + 59 = 79   20 − 59 = 39

Draw or write to explain.

At Home Ask your child to show you
how to find 94 − 50 on the hundred
chart.

En casa Pida a su niño que le muestre cómo
hallar 94 − 50 en la tabla de números hasta
el cien.

Name _____

Subtract Using a Place-Value Chart

 **Learn**

Objective
Subtract a one-digit number from a two-digit number with and without regrouping.

Linda has 43 bug postcards.
If she gives her sister 5 postcards,
how many will she have left?

Find 43 – 5.

Step 1	**Step 2**	**Step 3**
Show 43.	Regroup 1 ten as 10 ones.	Subtract the ones. Subtract the tens.

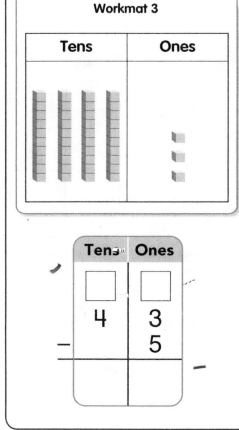

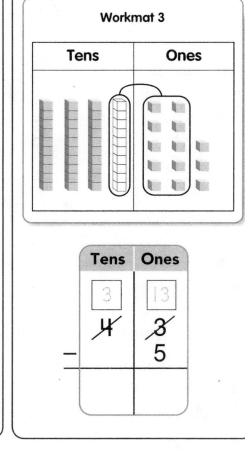

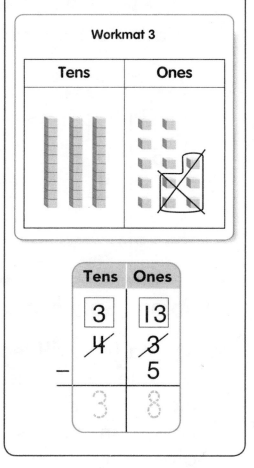

Linda has _____ cards left.

KEY NS 2.2 Find the sum or difference of two whole numbers up to three digits long. Also **NS 2.0, AF 1.0**

MR 1.2 Use tools, such as manipulatives or sketches, to model problems.

two hundred thirty-one **231**

Use Workmat 3 with ▭▭▭ and ▪.
Subtract. Record each step.

1.

Tens	Ones
☐	☐
3	2
−	4

Think!
Do I need to regroup to subtract 4 ones from 2 ones?

2.

Tens	Ones
☐	☐
5	0
−	6

3.

Tens	Ones
☐	☐
4	6
−	3

4. **Math Talk** What does the 10 you wrote in the ☐ represent in Exercise 2?

▶ **Practice**

Use Workmat 3 with ▭▭▭ and ▪.
Record the subtraction.

Remember!
Regroup when there are not enough ones.

5.

Tens	Ones
4	10
5	0
−	4
4	6

6.

Tens	Ones
☐	☐
6	5
−	8

7.

Tens	Ones
☐	☐
8	8
−	3

8.

Tens	Ones
☐	☐
4	5
−	6

Problem Solving: Mental Math

9. Marita finds 34 leaves. She gives some leaves to the caterpillars. Now Marita has 5 leaves left. How many leaves does Marita give away?

Draw or write to explain.

_____ leaves

🏠 **At Home** Tell your child your age. Have your child find the difference between your age and his or her age.

En casa Diga a su niño cuántos años tiene usted. Pida a su niño que halle la diferencia entre la edad de usted y la de él.

Chapter 12 Lesson 3

Practice Regrouping with 10 to 14

 **Learn**

Sometimes when you
subtract, you regroup
to make more ones.

Gabe has 40 bug pencils
in his collection. He gives
13 pencils to his brother.
How many pencils does
Gabe have left?

_27_ pencils

Tens	Ones
☐	☐
4	0
− 1	3

Regroup
1 ten as
10 ones.

Tens	Ones
3	10
4̸	0̸
− 1	3
2	7

▶ **Guided Practice**

Subtract. Regroup if you need to.

1.

Tens	Ones
☐	☐
5	0
− 3	5

Think!
Can I subtract
5 ones or do I need
to regroup?

2.

Tens	Ones
☐	☐
4	1
− 1	6

3.

Tens	Ones
☐	☐
5	3
− 3	6

4.

Tens	Ones
☐	☐
5	2
− 2	3

5.

Tens	Ones
☐	☐
3	2
− 1	7

6.

Tens	Ones
☐	☐
7	0
− 5	4

7.

Tens	Ones
☐	☐
8	1
− 1	3

8. (123) **Math Talk** What numbers can you subtract from
21 without regrouping? How do you know?

KEY NS 2.2 Find the sum or difference of two
whole numbers up to three digits long.
Also **AF 1.0, MR 2.0, SDAP 1.3, SDAP 1.4,
KEY SDAP 1.0**

NS 2.0 Estimate, calculate, and solve problems
involving addition and subtraction of two- and
three-digit numbers.

two hundred thirty-three **233**

► Practice

Subtract.
Regroup if you need to.

Remember!
After you regroup, rewrite
the number of tens.

9.

Tens	Ones
2	14
3̸	4̸
− 1	5
	9

10.

Tens	Ones
☐	☐
6	2
− 4	4

11.

Tens	Ones
☐	☐
4	3
− 1	1

12.

Tens	Ones
☐	☐
3	1
− 2	6

13.

Tens	Ones
☐	☐
4	0
− 3	2

14.

Tens	Ones
☐	☐
5	4
− 3	5

15.

Tens	Ones
☐	☐
6	3
− 2	7

16.

Tens	Ones
☐	☐
5	0
− 1	9

Problem Solving: Reasoning

17. Which color butterfly was
seen most often?

_____

18. How many more blue
butterflies were seen than
brown butterflies?

_____ more blue butterflies

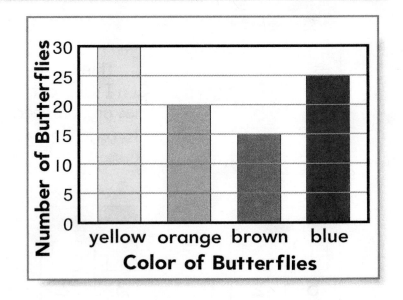

19. Write a subtraction problem using the information
in the graph. Then solve.

_____

_____

At Home Ask your child to solve
number sentences such as 60 – 27 and
51 – 34. Ask your child how he or she
found the answer.

En casa Pida a su niño que resuelva enunciados
numéricos como 60 – 27 y 51 – 34. Anime a su
niño a explicar cómo halló la respuesta.

Name _____

Chapter 12 Lesson 4

Practice Regrouping with 15 to 18

 **Learn**

Sometimes when you subtract, you regroup to make 15, 16, 17, or 18 ones.

Brandon counts 36 caterpillars in a tree. 19 caterpillars are green. How many caterpillars are not green?

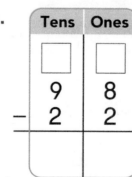

Tens	Ones
□	□
3	6
− 1	9

Regroup 1 ten as 10 ones.

Tens	Ones
2	16
3̷	6̷
− 1	9
	7

_____17_____ caterpillars are not green.

Objective
Practice subtraction with regrouping.

▶ **Guided Practice**

Subtract. Regroup if you need to.

1.
Tens	Ones
□	□
8	7
− 1	8

Think!
Can I subtract 8 ones from 7 ones?

2.
Tens	Ones
□	□
7	5
− 3	9

3.
Tens	Ones
□	□
6	5
− 2	8

4.
Tens	Ones
□	□
7	6
− 1	7

5.
Tens	Ones
□	□
9	6
− 4	9

6.
Tens	Ones
□	□
9	8
− 2	2

7.
Tens	Ones
□	□
5	6
− 1	8

8. **123** **Math Talk** Will you ever need to regroup to make 19 ones? Why or why not?

KEY NS 2.2 Find the sum or difference of two whole numbers up to three digits long. Also **AF 1.3, AF 1.0**

NS 2.0 Estimate, calculate, and solve problems involving addition and subtraction of two- and three-digit numbers.

two hundred thirty-five **235**

Subtract. Regroup if you need to.

Remember!
Always subtract the bottom number from the top number.

9.
Tens	Ones
4	17
5̶	7̶
− 2	8
2	9

10.
Tens	Ones
□	□
4	6
− 2	8

11.
Tens	Ones
□	□
3	8
− 1	9

12.
Tens	Ones
□	□
6	6
− 2	9

13.
Tens	Ones
□	□
2	5
− 1	7

14.
Tens	Ones
□	□
7	8
− 3	9

15.
Tens	Ones
□	□
3	6
− 2	5

16.
Tens	Ones
□	□
4	5
− 1	8

17.
Tens	Ones
□	□
7	7
− 5	9

18.
Tens	Ones
□	□
8	6
− 1	8

19.
Tens	Ones
□	□
5	8
− 3	9

20.
Tens	Ones
□	□
6	7
− 4	8

Algebra Readiness: Number Sentences

21. Someone spilled juice on the scientist's records. Fill in the numbers that can no longer be read.

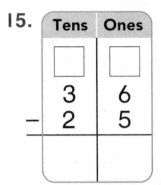

Insects Seen	Number of Insects		
	Saturday	Sunday	Total
Dragonflies	____	19	83
Bees	73	21	____
Grasshoppers	67	____	94
Butterflies	71	11	____

At Home Give your child two 2–digit numbers. Ask him or her to subtract the lesser number from the greater. Did your child regroup?

En casa Dé a su niño dos números de 2 dígitos. Pídale que reste el número menor del mayor. ¿Reagrupó su niño?

Name _____

Chapter 12 Lesson 5

Reasonable Answers

▶ **Learn**

Problem Solving
Plan

Objective
Decide whether an answer is reasonable.

Mia has **53** stamps in her collection.
She gives **24** stamps to Jeremy.
She gives some more stamps to Annie.
How many does Mia have left?

15 stamps   30 stamps   45 stamps

Understand
What do you know?
- Mia has **53** stamps.
- She gives **24** stamps to Jeremy.
- She gives some more stamps to Annie.

What do you need to find out?

how many stamps Mia has left

Plan
You can subtract to help find a
reasonable answer.

$$53$$
$$-24$$
$$\overline{\hspace{0.3cm}29\hspace{0.3cm}}$$

Mia has ___29___ stamps left
after she gives **24** to Jeremy.

Think!
I can subtract 53 – 24
to find out how many stamps
Mia has after she gives
Jeremy some.

Solve
Circle the most reasonable answer.

(15 stamps)   30 stamps   45 stamps

Think!
If Mia gives Annie some
of her 29 stamps, I know she
cannot have more than
29 stamps left.

Look Back
Is your answer reasonable?
How do you know?

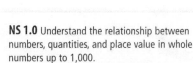 **KEY NS 2.2** Find the sum or difference of two
whole numbers up to three digits long.
Also **AF 1.0, NS 2.0, MR 2.0, MR 2.2**

NS 1.0 Understand the relationship between
numbers, quantities, and place value in whole
numbers up to 1,000.

two hundred thirty-seven **237**

Remember!
Understand
Plan
Solve
Look Back

1. Caleb has **48** cups in his collection. Alex has **27** cups in his collection. Danny has more cups than Alex but fewer than Caleb. How many cups does Danny have?

   20 cups   **35** cups   **60** cups

   What do you need to find out?

   _____

Think!
I have to pick the number that is between 27 and 48.

Circle the most reasonable answer.

20	35	60
cups	cups	cups

2. (123) **Math Talk** How did you choose a reasonable answer?

▶ **Problem Solving Practice**

Circle the most reasonable answer.

Draw or write to explain.

3. Lucia has **61** crayons. She gives **37** crayons to her brother. She also gives some crayons to her sister. How many crayons does Lucia have left?

10	30	50
crayons	crayons	crayons

4. Nathan has **35** stickers. Beth has **24** stickers. Tom has fewer stickers than Beth. How many stickers does Tom have?

40	30	20
stickers	stickers	stickers

At Home Ask your child to explain how he or she chose a reasonable answer in Exercise 3.

En casa Pida a su niño que explique cómo eligió una respuesta razonable para el Ejercicio 3.

California Field Trip

Science

Blackbird Pond

At the Shipley Nature Center

You can see many kinds of birds, such as brown pelicans, great blue herons, mallards, and California quail. At Blackbird Pond, you can see willow trees. There is also a butterfly garden.

Choose a way to solve. Show your work.

1. There are 51 mallards swimming in Blackbird Pond. Some mallards fly out of the pond. How many mallards are left?

mallard

| 70 mallards | 55 mallards | 35 mallards |

2. Volunteers at the nature center count 49 downy woodpeckers in one year. In the second year, they count 16 fewer downy woodpeckers. How many woodpeckers do they count in the second year?

_____ woodpeckers

downy woodpecker

3. Laura counts 37 monarch butterflies. Carlos counts 25 monarch butterflies. How many more butterflies does Laura count?

_____ more butterflies

monarch butterfly

KEY NS 2.2 Find the sum or difference of two whole numbers up to three digits long.
Also **AF 1.0, NS 2.0, MR 1.0, MR 1.1**
Science LS 2.a

two hundred thirty-nine **239**

Problem Solving on Tests
Listening Skills

Listen to your teacher read the problem.
Choose the correct answer.

Select a Strategy
Act It Out
Write a Number
Sentence
Reasonable
Answers

1. Allie has 50¢. She has 1 quarter, 2 dimes,
   and one other coin. What is the fourth coin?

   dime   quarter   nickel   penny
   ○   ○   ○   ○   NS 5.0

2. Luca has 35 butterfly pictures. Shannon
   has 7 butterfly pictures. How many butterfly
   pictures do they have in all?

   32   42   52   62
   ○   ○   ○   ○   KEY NS 2.2

3.
   92   82   72   62
   ○   ○   ○   ○

   KEY NS 2.2

4.
   about 50   about 60   about 70   about 80
   ○   ○   ○   ○

   NS 6.0

MR 1.0 Make decisions about how to set up a problem.
MR 1.1 Determine the approach, materials, and
strategies to be used.

Education Place
Visit **www.eduplace.com/camap/** for
Test-Taking Tips and Extra Practice.

Key Standards Review

Find the difference.

1. 95 − 30 = _____   2. 72 − 20 = _____   3. 89 − 43 = _____

4. 53 − 11 = _____   5. 86 − 53 = _____   6. 74 − 23 = _____

7. 73 − 50 = _____   8. 58 − 26 = _____   9. 44 − 13 = _____

Challenge   **Number Sense**

This is what a checkerboard looks like before you begin a game. Use the game board to answer the questions.

1. How many spaces are on the board in all?

   _____ spaces

2. How many checkers are on spaces on the board?

   _____ checkers

3. Write a number sentence to show how many spaces do not have checkers on them.

   _____ − _____ = _____ spaces

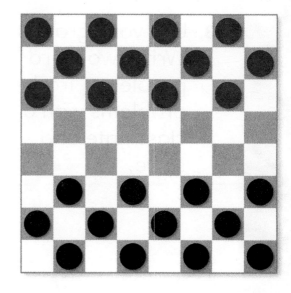

KEY NS 2.2 Find the sum or difference of two whole numbers up to three digits long.

two hundred forty-one **241**

California Trees

Marta visits Muir Woods in Marin County, California. The fog makes this forest damp and cool all year round. The tall redwood trees provide shade for the shorter trees.

Heights of Trees	
California Buckeye	30 feet
Red Alder	60 feet
Coast Live Oak	50 feet
California Bay Laurel	80 feet

Marta makes a table to show how tall some trees can grow. She wants to show the results as both a picture graph and a bar graph.

1. Use the data in the table to make a picture graph.

Heights of Trees	
California Buckeye	
Red Alder	
Coast Live Oak	
California Bay Laurel	

Key: Each ● = 10 feet

2. Use the data in the table to make a bar graph.

3. Use your graphs. Write two word problems. Trade problems with a classmate and solve.

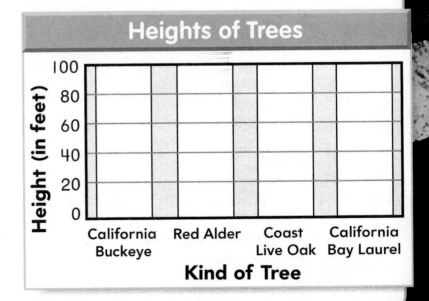

Heights of Trees

KEY SDAP 1.0 Collect numerical data and record, organize, display, and interpret the data on bar graphs and other representations.
Also **SDAP 1.2**
Science LS 2.e, IE 4.e

Name _____

Concepts and Skills

Use the hundred chart or Workmat 5.
Subtract. **KEY** **NS 2.2**

1	2	3	4	5	6	7	8	9	10
11	12	13	14	15	16	17	18	19	20
21	22	23	24	25	26	27	28	29	30
31	32	33	34	35	36	37	38	39	40
41	42	43	44	45	46	47	48	49	50
51	52	53	54	55	56	57	58	59	60
61	62	63	64	65	66	67	68	69	70
71	72	73	74	75	76	77	78	79	80
81	82	83	84	85	86	87	88	89	90
91	92	93	94	95	96	97	98	99	100

1. $65 - 30 =$ _____

2. $82 - 70 =$ _____

Subtract. Regroup if you need to. **KEY** **NS 2.2**

3.
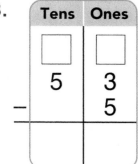

4.
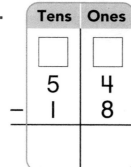

5.
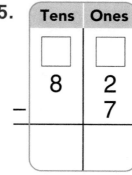

6.

Tens	Ones
□	□
7	5
− 2	9

Problem Solving **KEY** **NS 2.2**, MR 2.0

7. There is an ocean fish exhibit at the aquarium. There were **20** blue fin tuna and **15** hammerhead sharks. Then, they released **18** fish back to the ocean. How many fish are left in the exhibit?

_____ fish

Explain how you know.

_____

_____

Draw or write to explain.

_____

Spiral Review and Test Practice

1. Which is 77 rounded to the nearest ten?

  70   75   77   80
  ○   ○   ○   ○

NS 6.0 Page 71

---

2. Which is the value of the coins?

  60¢   75¢ $1.00 $1.60
  ○   ○   ○   ○

KEY NS 5.2, KEY NS 5.1, NS 5.0 Page 127

---

3. What is the sum?

$$44¢ + 9¢ = \underline{\hspace{2cm}}$$

  449¢   44¢   49¢   53¢
  ○   ○   ○   ○

NS 5.0, KEY NS 5.2, KEY NS 2.2, NS 2.0 Page 195

---

4. Which is the difference?

$$\begin{array}{r} 42 \\ -\ 7 \\ \hline \end{array}$$

  49   45   40   35
  ○   ○   ○   ○

KEY NS 2.2 Page 233

Education Place
Visit **www.eduplace.com/camap/** for
Test-Taking Tips and Extra Practice.

  Spiral Review

Relate 2-Digit Addition and Subtraction

Vocabulary

Here are some vocabulary words you will learn in the chapter.

round To find the nearest ten

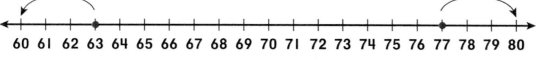

60 61 62 63 64 65 66 67 68 69 70 71 72 73 74 75 76 77 78 79 80

63 is closer to **60**.
63 rounds down to **60**.

77 is closer to **80**.
77 rounds up to **80**.

estimate A rounded answer that is close to an exact answer

$$48 \xrightarrow[\text{nearest ten}]{\text{round to}} 50$$
$$-31 \xrightarrow[\text{nearest ten}]{\text{round to}} -30$$
$$20 \leftarrow \text{estimate}$$

check subtraction You can check subtraction with addition.

$$\begin{array}{r} 74 \\ -25 \\ \hline 49 \end{array} \qquad \begin{array}{r} 49 \\ +25 \\ \hline 74 \end{array}$$

See English-Spanish Glossary pages 573–589.

 **KEY NS 2.2** Find the sum or difference of two whole numbers up to three digits long.
Also **KEY NS 2.1**, NS 6.0

 **Education Place**
Visit **www.eduplace.com/camap/**
for the eGlossary and eGames.

Name _____

✓ Check What You Know

Solve. Use the number line.

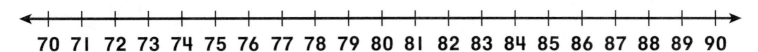

70 71 72 73 74 75 76 77 78 79 80 81 82 83 84 85 86 87 88 89 90

1. Does 86 round to 80 or 90?

   86 rounds to _____.

2. Use the nearest tens to estimate the difference of 86 − 73.

   _____ − _____ = _____

3. Find the exact difference of 86 − 73.

   _____ − _____ = _____

4. Does 85 round to 80 or 90?

   85 rounds to _____.

5. Use the nearest tens to estimate the difference of 85 − 75.

   _____ − _____ = _____

   Find the exact difference of 85 − 75.

   _____ − _____ = _____

Use this page to review important skills needed for this chapter.

Name _____

Different Ways to Subtract

 Hands On

Objective
Choose an appropriate computation method.

▶ **Learn**

Different ways to subtract:
- mental math
- hundred chart
- tens and ones blocks
- paper and pencil

Choose a way to find
55 − 39.

I can use pencil and paper to solve this.

▶ **Guided Practice**

Circle the way you would use to subtract.
Find the difference.

1. 36 − 10 = _____

   mental math

   paper and pencil

Think!
Can I count back in my head to subtract 10 from 36?

2. 41 − 32 = _____

   tens and ones blocks

   mental math

3. 87 − 43 = _____

   paper and pencil

   tens and ones blocks

4. 58 − 30 = _____

   mental math

   hundred chart

5. 96 − 37 = _____

   mental math

   tens and ones blocks

Explain how you find the difference.

6. 47 − 13 _____

_____

7.  **Math Talk** Why might it be faster to use mental math than paper and pencil to find 73 − 30?

KEY NS 2.2 Find the sum or difference of two whole numbers up to three digits long.
Also **NS 2.0, MR 1.2, NS 2.3, MR 1.0, MR 2.0**

MR 1.1 Determine the approach, materials, and strategies to be used.

two hundred forty-seven **247**

▶ Practice

Circle the way you would use to subtract.
Find the difference.

Remember!
Choose the way that works best for you.
• mental math
• hundred chart
• tens and ones
• paper and pencil

8. 72 − 15 = _57_

mental math

(paper and pencil)

9. 67 − 17 = _____

hundred chart

mental math

10. 92 − 58 = _____

paper and pencil

mental math

11. 57 − 22 = _____

tens and ones blocks

paper and pencil

12. 41 − 39 = _____

hundred chart

mental math

Subtract. Explain how you find the difference.

13. 42 − 19

_____

_____

_____

14. 58 − 7

_____

_____

_____

15. 84 − 37

_____

_____

_____

16. 88 − 79

_____

_____

_____

Problem Solving: Number Sense

17. Billy has **80** dinosaur stickers. He gives **30** away. Sonya asks Billy for **60** stickers. Does he have enough to give her? Explain how you know.

Draw or write to explain.

At Home Have your child show different ways to find 58 − 20 and explain which way he or she would use.

En casa Pida a su niño que muestre diferentes maneras de hallar 58 − 20 y que explique qué manera usaría.

Estimate Differences

 **Learn**

Objective
Estimate differences by rounding to the nearest ten.

Vocabulary
round

When you do not need an exact answer, you can estimate.

Estimate the difference of 35 – 22.

Step 1

Round each number to the nearest ten.

22 is closer to 20.
Round down.

35 is in the middle of 30 and 40. Round up.

20 21 **22** 23 24 25 26 27 28 29 30 31 32 33 34 **35** 36 37 38 39 40

Step 2

Subtract the tens to estimate the difference.

40 – 20 = _20_

▶ **Guided Practice**

Round each number to the nearest ten.
Estimate the difference.

1. 49 – 35

_____ – _____ = _____

Think!
Both numbers have 5 or more ones, so I round up.

2. 41 – 32

_____ – _____ = _____

3. 45 – 28

_____ – _____ = _____

4. **(123)** **Math Talk** How did you find the nearest ten for each number in Exercise 3?

NS 6.0 Use estimation strategies in computation and problem solving that involve numbers that use the ones, tens, hundreds, and thousands places. Also **MR 2.0**

NS 2.0 Estimate, calculate, and solve problems involving addition and subtraction of two– and three–digit numbers.

two hundred forty-nine **249**

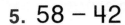 **Practice**

Round each number to the nearest ten.
Estimate the difference.

Remember!
Round down if the number has less than 5 ones.

5. 58 − 42

_60_ − _40_ = _20_

6. 53 − 41

____ − ____ = ____

7. 49 − 43

____ − ____ = ____

8. 57 − 34

____ − ____ = ____

9. 59 − 47

____ − ____ = ____

10. 44 − 41

____ − ____ = ____

11. 45 − 18

____ − ____ = ____

12. 37 − 21

____ − ____ = ____

13. 49 − 33

____ − ____ = ____

14. 46 − 24

____ − ____ = ____

15. Estimate 56 − 24.

____ − ____ = ____

Find the exact difference.

56 − 24 = ____

Problem Solving: Reasoning

16. Karen estimates 57 − 11 this way:

50 − 10 = 40

Is her estimate reasonable?
Explain.

Draw or write to explain.

 At Home Ask your child to demonstrate how to round to the nearest ten and estimate to find 42 − 23.

En casa Pida a su niño que demuestre cómo redondear a la decena más cercana y cómo estimar para hallar 42 − 23.

Line Up Digits to Subtract

▶ Learn

Find 85 − 59.

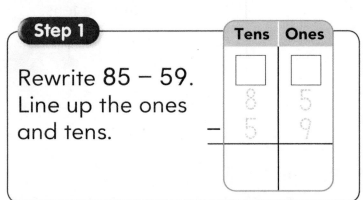

Step 1

Rewrite 85 − 59. Line up the ones and tens.

Tens	Ones
8	5
− 5	9

Step 2

Subtract the ones. Subtract the tens.

Tens	Ones
7	15
8̸	5̸
− 5	9
2	6

▶ Guided Practice

Write the numbers in vertical form. Subtract.

1. 46 − 7

Tens	Ones
□	□
−	

Think!
Do I write the 7 in the ones or the tens column?

2. 63 − 7

Tens	Ones
□	□
−	

3. 84 − 55

Tens	Ones
□	□
−−	

4. 81 − 32

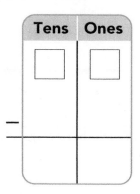

Tens	Ones
□	□
−	

5. 77 − 58

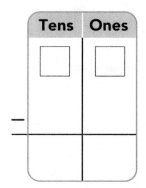

Tens	Ones
□	□
−	

6. 78 − 69

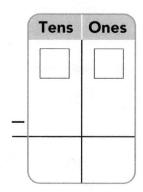

Tens	Ones
□	□
−	

7. 65 − 4

Tens	Ones
□	□
−−	

8. (123) **Math Talk** Brenda rewrites 72 − 6.
She subtracts and gets a difference of 12.
What did she do wrong?

KEY NS 2.2 Find the sum or difference of two whole numbers up to three digits long. Also **MR 2.2, MR 2.0**

NS 2.0 Estimate, calculate, and solve problems involving addition and subtraction of two- and three-digit numbers.

two hundred fifty-one **251**

Write the numbers in vertical form. Subtract.

9. 36 − 9

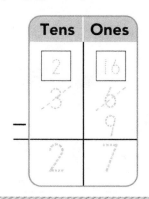

Tens	Ones
2	16
3	6
−	9
2	7

10. 58 − 24

Tens	Ones

11. 68 − 32

Tens	Ones

Remember!
Line up the ones and the tens.

12. 64 − 47

Tens	Ones

13. 42 − 3

Tens	Ones

14. 71 − 25

Tens	Ones

15. 38 − 17

Tens	Ones

16. 96 − 34

Tens	Ones

17. 81 − 4

Tens	Ones

18. 60 − 35

Tens	Ones

19. 45 − 27

Tens	Ones

Problem Solving: Reasoning

20. Tanya has 45 beads. She uses 17 to make a necklace. She uses 13 to make a bracelet. How many beads does Tanya have left?

Draw or write to explain.

_____ beads

At Home Have your child show you how to rewrite 53 − 16 and 63 − 7 and then find the differences.

En casa Pida a su niño que muestre cómo escribir 53 − 16 y 63 − 7 de otra manera y que halle las diferencias.

Chapter 13 Lesson 4

Add and Subtract Money

▶ **Learn**

You can add and subtract money like whole numbers. Just remember to write the ¢ sign.

Cameron wants to buy 2 ladybug postcards. How much do 2 ladybug postcards cost?

$$\begin{array}{r} 15 \\ +15 \\ \hline 30 \end{array} \qquad \begin{array}{r} 15¢ \\ +15¢ \\ \hline 30¢ \end{array}$$

If Cameron pays with 50¢, how much change does he get back?

$$\begin{array}{r} 50 \\ -30 \\ \hline 20 \end{array} \qquad \begin{array}{r} 50¢ \\ -30¢ \\ \hline 20¢ \end{array}$$

15¢

▶ **Guided Practice**

Add or subtract.

1. $\begin{array}{r} 54¢ \\ -16¢ \\ \hline \end{array}$
  Think!
  54¢ – 16¢ is like 54 – 16.

2. $\begin{array}{r} 19¢ \\ +7¢ \\ \hline \end{array}$

3. $\begin{array}{r} 71¢ \\ -37¢ \\ \hline \end{array}$

4. $\begin{array}{r} 41¢ \\ -32¢ \\ \hline \end{array}$

Rewrite the numbers. Then add or subtract.

5. 39¢ + 43¢

6. 94¢ – 6¢

7. 50¢ – 13¢

8. 51¢ + 19¢

$$\begin{array}{r} 3\ 9¢ \\ +\ 4\ 3¢ \\ \hline \end{array}$$

9. 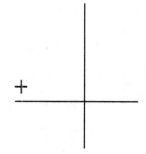 **Math Talk** How is adding money similar to adding numbers?

KEY NS 5.2 Know and use the decimal notation and the dollar and cent symbols for money. Also NS 2.0, NS 5.0, MR 3.0, MR 2.0

KEY NS 2.2 Find the sum or difference of two whole numbers up to three digits long.

▶ **Practice**

Remember!
Write the ¢ sign
in your answer.

Add or subtract.

10. 80¢
    −37¢
    43¢

11. 25¢
    +46¢

12. 33¢
    +50¢

13. 72¢
    − 6¢

14. 65¢
    −45¢

15. 58¢
    −39¢

16. 44¢
    + 8¢

17. 55¢
    +27¢

18. 34¢
    −16¢

19. 60¢
    −37¢

Solve.

29¢

45¢

20. Adriana has **8** dimes.
    She buys an album and a
    bag of marbles. How much
    money does she have left?

    _____ ¢

21. If Adriana buys **2** albums
    instead, how much money
    does she have left?

    _____ ¢

Problem Solving: Reasoning

22. Cindy has **7** dimes.
    She buys two marbles.
    How much money does
    she have left?

    _____ ¢

Draw or write to explain.

14¢

At Home Give your child a few coins.
Ask him or her if there is enough
money to buy the bag of marbles
shown above.

En casa Dé a su niño algunas monedas.
Pregúntele si hay suficiente dinero para
comprar la bolsa de canicas que se muestra
arriba.

Check Subtraction

► Learn

You can add to check your subtraction.

Step 1

Subtract.

Tens	Ones
4	6
5	6
− 1	8
3	8

Step 2

Start with the difference.
Add the number you subtracted.

Tens	Ones
1	
3	8
+ 1	8
5	6

If the sum equals the number you
subtracted from, your answer is correct.

► Guided Practice

Subtract. Check by adding.

Think!
13 is the difference,
so I can add 13 and
19 to check.

1.
```
   32
 − 19
```
+ ☐
____

2.
```
   81
 − 66
```
+ ☐
____

3.
```
   72
 − 64
```
+ ☐
____

4. **(123) Math Talk** Why can you use addition to
check subtraction?

KEY NS 2.1 Understand and use the inverse
relationship between addition and subtraction
(e.g., an opposite number sentence for 8 + 6 = 14 is
14 − 6 = 8) to solve problems and check solutions.

MR 2.2 Make precise calculations and check the
validity of the results in the context of the problem.
Also **KEY NS 2.2**, NS 2.0, MR 3.0, AF 1.3

► **Practice**

Subtract. Then add to check.

Remember!
Add the difference and the number you subtracted to check.

5.
```
   68
 - 42
   26
```
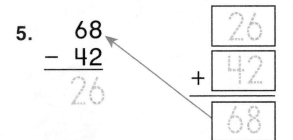
```
  26
+ 42
  68
```

6.
```
   40
 -  5
```
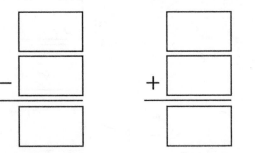
```
+
```

7.
```
   54
 - 19
```
```
+
```

8.
```
   85
 -  6
```
```
+
```

9.
```
   49
 - 28
```
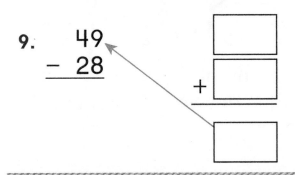
```
+
```

10.
```
   74
 - 10
```
```
+
```

11. 53 bees are buzzing in the meadow. 7 bees fly away. How many bees are left?

```
  -          +
```

12. 98 bees are in the hive. 51 bees fly out. How many bees are left in the hive?

```
  -          +
```

Algebra Readiness: Number Sentences

13. 43 + ▲ = 82

What is ▲? _____

14. 96 − ■ = 14

What is ■? _____

Name _____

Create and Solve

Objective
Write problems and use strategies to solve them.

The table shows the prices for packs of bird cards.

1. How much more does the Super Pack cost than the Extra Pack?

   The Super Pack costs _____¢ more.

2. Write your own subtraction problem about the bird cards. Use the prices in the table.

Card Prices	
Super Pack	80¢
Big Pack	60¢
Extra Pack	35¢
Basic Pack	22¢

_____

_____

_____

_____

_____

3. Write the subtraction sentence.
   Line up the digits to subtract.
   Solve.

   _
   _____

   Share your subtraction problem with a classmate.

KEY NS 2.2 Find the sum or difference of two whole numbers up to three digits long. Also **AF 1.0, NS 2.0, AF 1.2, SDAP 1.4, NS 5.0, MR 1.0, MR 1.1**

AF 1.3 Solve addition and subtraction problems by using data from simple charts, picture graphs, and number sentences.

The table shows the prices for toy insects.

Toy Insect Prices	
Insect	**Price**
Ladybug	49¢
Grasshopper	35¢
Butterfly	26¢
Cricket	42¢
Ant	18¢

4. Melissa wants to buy a ladybug and a cricket. How much will she spend in all?

   Melissa will spend _____ ¢.

5. Write your own addition problem about the toy insects. Use the prices in the table.

   _____

   _____

   _____

   _____

   _____

6. Write the addition sentence.
   Line up the digits to add.
   Solve.

   + _____

   Share your addition problem with a classmate.

Key Standards Review

Find the difference.

1. 75 − 37 = _____   2. 85 − 39 = _____   3. 53 − 14 = _____

4. 45 − 28 = _____   5. 92 − 56 = _____   6. 73 − 66 = _____

7. 81 − 65 = _____   8. 53 − 39 = _____   9. 84 − 69 = _____

 **Number Sense**

Write 6, 7, 8, and 9 in the first set of boxes to get the greatest possible difference.

Write 6, 7, 8, and 9 in the second set of boxes to get the least possible difference.

1. **Greatest**   2. **Least**

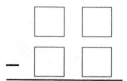 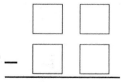

KEY NS 2.2 Find the sum or difference of two whole numbers up to three digits long.

two hundred fifty-nine **259**

How Many Will Be Left?

🎧 **Math Music,** Track 5
Tune: original

Let's subtract two numbers.
What's one thing you might do?
If you don't have enough ones—
Regroup! It might help you.
Regroup 1 ten as ten ones—
To see if this helps you!

Juan collects **26** stamps
And gives **19** to me.
How many stamps will he have left?
Regroup and we will see!

Sue collects **32** bugs
And gives **15** to me.
How many bugs will she have left?
Regroup and we will see!

Keb collects **44** rocks
And gives **16** to me.
How many rocks will he have left?
Regroup and we will see!

KEY NS 2.2 Find the sum or difference of two whole numbers up to three digits long.

Name _____

Concepts and Skills

Subtract.
Explain how you found the difference. KEY **NS 2.2**, MR 2.0

1. $56 - 4 = $ _____

_____

_____

Round each number to the nearest ten. Estimate the difference. NS 6.0

2. $78 - 24$

_____ – _____ = _____

3. $45 - 33$

_____ – _____ = _____

Write the numbers in vertical form.
Subtract. KEY **NS 2.2**

4. $87 - 29$

Tens	Ones
☐	☐
–	

Add or subtract. KEY **NS 2.2**

5. $56¢$
   $+ 15¢$

6. $72¢$
   $- 34¢$

Subtract. Then add to check. KEY **NS 2.1**

7. 94
   $- 37$

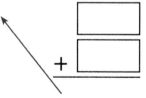

8. 91
   $- \ 8$

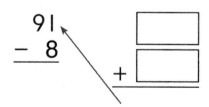

Problem Solving KEY **NS 5.1**, MR 2.0

9. Rhonda has 3 quarters. She buys a toy horse for
   56¢. How much money does Rhonda have left? _____

Spiral Review and Test Practice

1. If Pam pays for the item below with these coins, what is her change?

71¢

4¢ ○   6¢ ○   8¢ ○   10¢ ○

KEY NS 5.1, KEY NS 5.2, NS 5.0 Page 129

2. What is the sum?

$$\begin{array}{r} 5 \\ 23 \\ +56 \\ \hline \end{array}$$

84 ○   79 ○   74 ○   28 ○

KEY AF 1.1, AF 1.0, KEY NS 2.2, NS 2.0 Page 197

3. Which is the difference?

$$\begin{array}{r} 84 \\ -15 \\ \hline \end{array}$$

71 ○   79 ○   69 ○   61 ○

KEY NS 2.2 Page 233

4. Round each number to the nearest ten. Which is an estimate for the difference?   78 − 12

90 ○   80 ○   70 ○   60 ○

NS 6.0, KEY NS 2.2, NS 2.0 Page 249

Education Place
Visit www.eduplace.com/camap/ for
Test-Taking Tips and Extra Practice.

Spiral Review

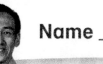

Greg Tang's Go Fast, Go Far

Unit 5 **Mental Math Strategies**

Partial Differences

Partial differences are quick.
Subtracting pieces is the trick!

I break the numbers into pieces. Then I subtract the pieces. $30 - 20 = 10$ and $8 - 4 = 4$. The answer is $10 + 4 = 14$.

1. $38 - 24 = \boxed{10} + \boxed{4} = \boxed{14}$

2. $45 - 23 = \boxed{20} + \boxed{} = \boxed{}$

3. $67 - 32 = \boxed{} + \boxed{} = \boxed{}$ 4. $89 - 45 = \boxed{} + \boxed{} = \boxed{}$

5. $26 - 12 = \boxed{} + \boxed{} = \boxed{}$ 6. $35 - 23 = \boxed{} + \boxed{} = \boxed{}$

7. $47 - 15 = \boxed{} + \boxed{} = \boxed{}$ 8. $58 - 34 = \boxed{} + \boxed{} = \boxed{}$

Take It Further: Now try all the steps in your head!

9. $36 - 22 = \boxed{}$ 10. $98 - 31 = \boxed{}$

Reading and Writing Math

The table below shows how many stamps Robbie has. How many more beetle stamps than butterfly stamps does he have?

Kind of Stamp	Number of Stamps
Beetle	35
Butterfly	28

Word Bank
difference
regroup
subtract
ten

Choose a word from the word bank for each blank.

1. To solve the problem, you _____ 35 − 28.

2. When you _____ in subtraction, you are trading 1 _____ for 10 ones.

3. The result of a subtraction problem is called the _____.

4. **Writing Math** Write a subtraction problem and tell which way you used to solve it. Explain why you chose that way.

_____

_____

_____

KEY NS 2.2 Find the sum or difference of two whole numbers up to three digits long.
Also **AF 1.2, MR 1.1**

Name _____

Concepts and Skills

Complete the subtraction sentences.
Use quick pictures or a basic fact to help. KEY NS 2.2

1. 9 tens − 4 tens = _____ tens

   _____ − _____ = _____

Use the hundred chart or Workmat 5.
Subtract. KEY NS 2.2

1	2	3	4	5	6	7	8	9	10
11	12	13	14	15	16	17	18	19	20
21	22	23	24	25	26	27	28	29	30
31	32	33	34	35	36	37	38	39	40
41	42	43	44	45	46	47	48	49	50
51	52	53	54	55	56	57	58	59	60
61	62	63	64	65	66	67	68	69	70
71	72	73	74	75	76	77	78	79	80
81	82	83	84	85	86	87	88	89	90
91	92	93	94	95	96	97	98	99	100

2. 64 − 20 = _____

3. 85 − 40 = _____

Record the subtraction. KEY NS 2.2

4.

Tens	Ones
☐	☐
7	6
−	9

5.

Tens	Ones
☐	☐
4	0
−	8

Subtract. Regroup if you need to. KEY NS 2.2

6. 52
  − 6
  ____

7. 75
  − 38
  ____

8. 64
  − 16
  ____

Subtract. Explain how you found the difference.   KEY **NS 2.2**, MR 2.1

9. 66 − 4 = _____

   How I solved: _____

Round each number to the nearest ten.
Estimate the difference.   NS 6.0

10. 98 − 30

   _____ − _____ = _____

   98 − 30 is about _____.

11. 57 − 32

   _____ − _____ = _____

   57 − 32 is about _____.

Add or subtract.   KEY **NS 2.2**

12.   76¢
    + 19¢

13.   68¢
    − 39¢

Subtract. Then add to check.   KEY **NS 2.1**

14.   64
    − 27

Problem Solving

Solve.   MR 2.0, KEY **NS 2.2**

15. Lee-Ann and Paul both have stickers.
    Paul has **33** stickers. Together they
    have **70** stickers in all. How many
    stickers does Lee-Ann have?

    _____

Draw or write to explain.

Unit 6

Geometry and Fractions

Houghton Mifflin California Math

BIG IDEAS!

- You can name, describe, and compare shapes and combine or separate them to make other shapes.

- A fraction is a number that tells about part of a group, part of a whole, or a whole.

Songs and Games

Math Music Track 6
We Will Share It Now!

eGames
www.eduplace.com/camap/

Literature

Read Aloud Big Book
- A Triangle for Adaora

Math Readers

Square Fair
by Francisco Garcia
illustrated by Jane McCreary

Taking Shape
by Ricardo Ramos
illustrated by Juan Garcia

The Pizza Puzzle
by William Jeffreys
illustrated by Bob Monahan

The Missing Muffins
by Bronwyn Morgan
illustrated by Nicole Rutten

Fun with Fractions

How to Play

1. Mix the cards. Place them face down. Take turns picking one card.

2. Match the card with a picture on the game board that shows the shading on the card.

3. The first player to get 4 matches in a row in any direction wins.

What You Need

2 or 3 players

$\frac{1}{2}$	$\frac{1}{2}$	$\frac{1}{2}$	$\frac{1}{2}$	$\frac{1}{2}$
$\frac{1}{3}$	$\frac{1}{3}$	$\frac{1}{3}$	$\frac{1}{3}$	$\frac{1}{3}$
$\frac{1}{4}$	$\frac{1}{4}$	$\frac{1}{4}$	$\frac{1}{4}$	$\frac{1}{4}$	$\frac{1}{4}$

KEY NS 4.2 Recognize fractions of a whole and parts of a group (e.g., one-fourth of a pie, two-thirds of 15 balls).
Also **KEY** NS 4.1, NS 4.0, MR 1.2

Education Place
Visit **www.eduplace.com/camap/** for eGames and Brain Teasers.

Math at Home

Dear Family,

My class is starting Unit 6, **Geometry and Fractions.** I will be learning how to name, sort, and combine flat and solid shapes. I will also learn how to model, write, and compare fractions. You can help me learn these vocabulary words, and we can do the Math Activity together.

From,

_____

Vocabulary

plane shape A flat figure

solid shape A figure that is not flat

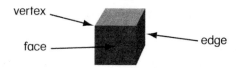

vertex/vertices Where two faces or sides meet

face The flat surface of a solid figure

edge Where two faces of a solid figure meet

fraction A fraction names equal parts of a whole or group.

 Education Place
Visit **www.eduplace.com/camaf/** for
• eGames and Brain Teasers
• Math at Home in other languages

Family Math Activity

Draw a square, triangle, rectangle, and circle on pieces of paper. Fold them up and put them in a bowl. Players take turns taking a piece of paper from the bowl and then giving clues to the other player about the shape.

Literature

These books link to the math in this unit. Look for them at the library.

• **Eating Fractions**
by Bruce McMillan
(Scholastic, 1991)

• **Fraction Fun**
by David A. Adler
Illustrated by Nancy Tobin

• **Polar Bear Math**
by Ann Whitehead Nagda
and Cindy Bickel

Matemáticas en casa

Estimada familia:

Mi clase está comenzando la Unidad 6, **Geometría y fracciones**. Aprenderé a nombrar, clasificar y combinar figuras planas y cuerpos geométricos. También aprenderé a representar, escribir y comparar fracciones. Me pueden ayudar a aprender estas palabras de vocabulario y podemos hacer juntos la Actividad de matemáticas para la familia.

De:

_____

Vocabulario

figura plana Figura que es llana.

cuerpo geométrico Figura que no es llana.

vértice

cara

arista

vértice/vértices Punto en el que dos caras o lados se encuentran.

cara Superficie plana de un cuerpo geométrico.

arista Lugar en que se encuentran dos caras de un cuerpo geométrico.

fracción Una fracción nombra partes iguales de un entero o un grupo.

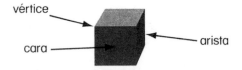

Education Place
Visite **www.eduplace.com/camaf/** para
• Juegos en línea y acertijos
• Matemáticas en casa en otros idiomas

Actividad de matemáticas para la familia

Dibuje figuras como cuadrados, triángulos, rectángulos y círculos en pedazos de papel. Dóblelos y póngalos en un tazón. Los jugadores se turnan para sacar un pedazo de papel y luego dan pistas a los otros jugadores sobre la figura que tienen.

Literatura

Estos libros hablan sobre las matemáticas de esta unidad. Búscalos en la biblioteca.

• **La feria musical de matemáticas** por Sue Kassirer
(Kane Press, 2005)

• **Mi primer libro de formas** por Toni Rann

Shape Up at Pizza Palace

written by Chloe Weasley

illustrated by Wallace Keller

This Take-Home Book belongs to

_____

Reading and Writing Math

This take-home book will help you preview shapes and fractions.

Draw a square pizza. Divide it in half.

Draw a triangular pizza. Divide it in half.

Draw a rectangular pizza. Divide it into thirds.

Draw a circular pizza. Divide it into fourths.

KEY **NS 4.1** Recognize, name, and compare unit fractions from $\frac{1}{12}$ to $\frac{1}{2}$.

8

All night long she rolls out dough.

Nona's pizza pies are good, you know.

What shape is this pizza?

Draw lines to show how Nona could cut each of these pizzas into four equal parts.

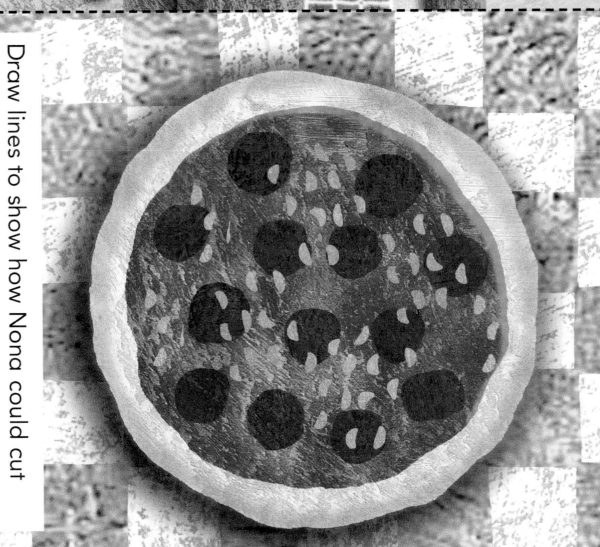

Nona makes her pies in many shapes,
and folks enjoy the shapes she bakes.

What shapes are these pizzas?

If a pizza cut in two is
too much food for you,
Nona will divide one into four.
You can buy a slice or more!

When Nona's pies are baked, she starts to cut the pizzas into parts.

Draw a line to show how Nona could cut each of the four pizzas into two equal parts.

Shapes

Vocabulary

Here are some vocabulary words you will learn in the chapter.

plane shape A flat shape

triangle   pentagon   square   rectangle

circle   hexagon

side A line that is part of a shape

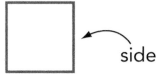
side

A square has 4 sides.

vertex (vertices) A point where two sides meet

vertex

See English-Spanish Glossary pages 573–589.

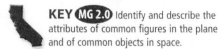 **KEY MG 2.0** Identify and describe the attributes of common figures in the plane and of common objects in space.

Education Place
Visit www.eduplace.com/camap/ for the eGlossary and eGames.

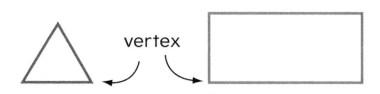

Check What You Know

Circle the one that is the same shape.

1.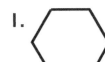

2.

3.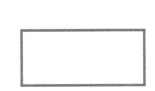

Circle the shape that doesn't belong.

4.

5.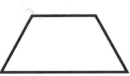

Use this page to review important skills needed for this chapter.

Name _____

Sort Shapes

 **Explore**

Hands On

Objective
Describe the number of vertices and sides of plane shapes.

Vocabulary
side
angle
vertex/vertices

Geometric shapes may have **sides, angles** and **vertices.**

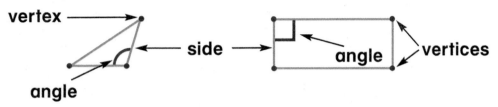

3 sides and 3 vertices   4 sides and 4 vertices

1. Cut out the shapes. Sort them.

2. Draw your sorted shapes.
   Tell your sorting rule.

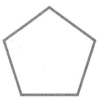
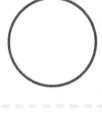

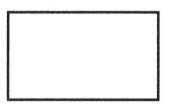

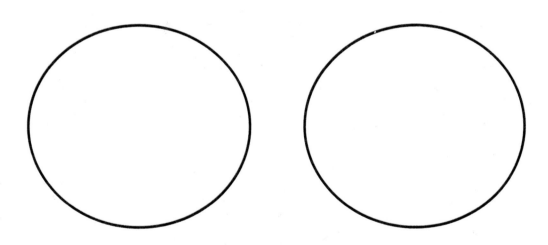

3. Sort the shapes a different way.

4. **123** **Math Talk** What do you notice about the number of sides and vertices?

KEY MG 2.1 Describe and classify plane and solid geometric shapes (e.g., circle, triangle, square, rectangle, sphere, pyramid, cube, rectangular prism) according to the number and shape of faces, edges, and vertices.
Also **KEY** MG 2.0, MR 1.2, MR 3.0

Use the shapes you cut out.
Count the sides and vertices.
Match the shape to the clues.

Remember!
Count the number of sides and vertices on each shape.

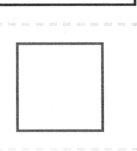

5. 0 sides, 0 vertices

6. 3 sides, 3 vertices

7. 4 sides, 4 vertices

8. 4 sides, 4 vertices

9. 5 sides, 5 vertices

10. 6 sides, 6 vertices

11. If you draw a shape with 7 sides, how many vertices will it have? _____

 At Home Ask your child to describe some of the figures on this page.

En casa Pida a su niño que describa algunas de las figuras de esta página.

Name _____

Plane Shapes

▶ **Learn**

Geometric shapes have names.
Flat shapes are called **plane shapes.**
Describe each shape.

triangle   square   rectangle

pentagon   hexagon   circle

Objective
Identify and describe
a variety of plane
shapes.

Vocabulary
plane shape
triangle
square
rectangle
pentagon
hexagon
circle

▶ **Guided Practice**

Draw 2 plane shapes.
Describe them and write their names.

1. _____

2. _____

3. **(123)** **Math Talk** Describe the sides and vertices
of a piece of notebook paper.

KEY **MG 2.1** Describe and classify plane and
solid geometric shapes (e.g., circle, triangle, square,
rectangle, sphere, pyramid, cube, rectangular prism)
according to the number and shape of faces, edges,
and vertices.
Also **KEY** **MG 2.0**, MR 2.0, MR 1.2

two hundred seventy-three **273**

Circle each shape that matches the name.

4. rectangle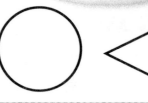

5. circle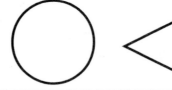

6. triangle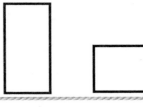

7. square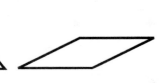

8. pentagon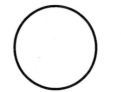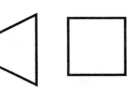

9. How many vertices will a 6-sided shape have? Why?

_____

_____

Problem Solving: Logical Reasoning

10. There is something alike in all three shapes. What is it?

_____

_____

Name _____

Chapter 14 Lesson 3

Compare Plane Shapes

► Learn

Some shapes have the same number of vertices.
Some shapes have sides that are the same length.

► Guided Practice

Compare the shapes.

Think!
I know both shapes have the same number of sides and vertices.

1.

Alike because _____

Different because _____

2.

Alike because _____

Different because _____

3.

Alike because _____

Different because _____

4. (123) **Math Talk** How is a circle different from all the other shapes on this page?

 **KEY MG 2.1** Describe and classify plane and solid geometric shapes (e.g., circle, triangle, square, rectangle, sphere, pyramid, cube, rectangular prism) according to the number and shape of faces, edges, and vertices.
Also **KEY MG 2.0**, MR 2.0, MR 1.2

two hundred seventy-five **275**

Compare the shapes.

Remember!
Look at the angles
and the sides.

5.

Alike because _____

Different because _____

6.

Alike because _____

Different because _____

7. Describe the difference between a circle and a triangle.

_____

_____

Problem Solving: Visual Thinking

8. Draw two shapes. Tell how
they are alike and different.

_____

_____

_____

_____

At Home Find objects that suggest
geometric figures. Compare them.

En casa Busque objetos que parezcan figuras
geométricas. Compárelos.

▶ **Practice**

9. Circle each triangle.

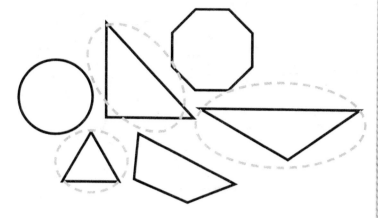

10. Circle each circle.

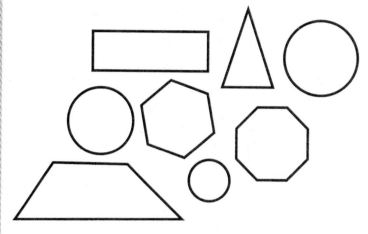

11. Circle each hexagon.

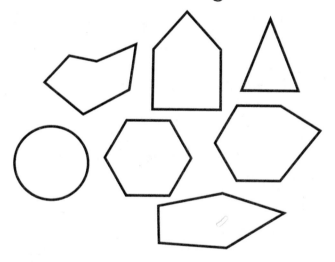

12. Circle each rectangle.

13. Circle each square.

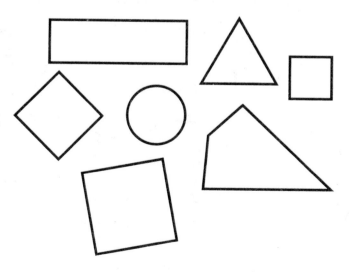

14. Circle each pentagon.

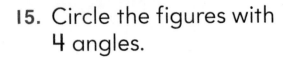

15. Circle the figures with 4 angles.

16. Circle the figures that have all angles the same size.

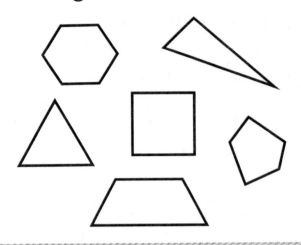

17. Circle all the 5-sided figures.

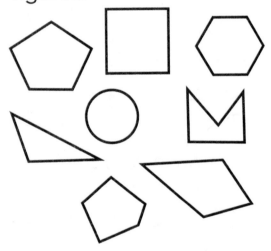

18. Circle all the 4-sided figures.

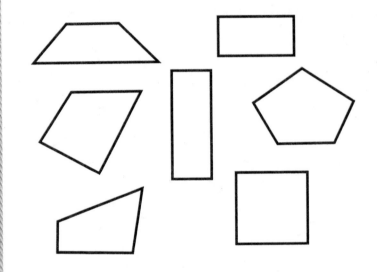

19. Circle all the figures with 4 or more vertices.

20. Circle all the figures that have sides the same length.

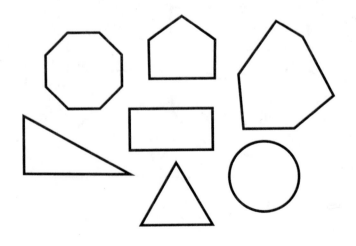

At Home Look for objects in your house and ask your child to name the shape of the objects.

En casa Busque objetos en su casa y pida a su niño que diga el nombre de la forma o objetos.

Name _____

Combine and Separate Shapes

 **Explore**

You can cut shapes apart to make other shapes.

Use pattern blocks.

1. Use blocks to make this shape. Draw the blocks.

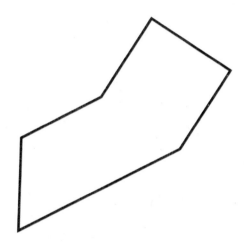

2. Draw 2 shapes 2 different ways to make this shape.

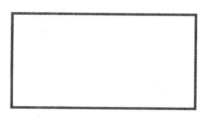  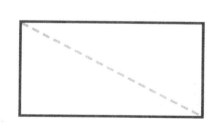

3. **Math Talk** What shapes could you use to make a pentagon?

KEY MG 2.2 Put shapes together and take them apart to form other shapes (e.g., two congruent right triangles can be arranged to form a rectangle). Also **KEY MG 2.0**, **KEY MG 2.1**

MR 1.2 Use tools, such as manipulatives or sketches, to model problems.

▶ Extend

Use pattern blocks.
Make the shape
with **2** blocks.
Draw the blocks.

Remember!
Many shapes are
made of smaller
shapes.

4.

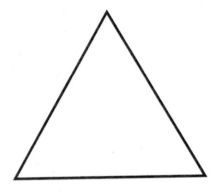

5.

Draw lines to show how these shapes
are made from other shapes.

6.

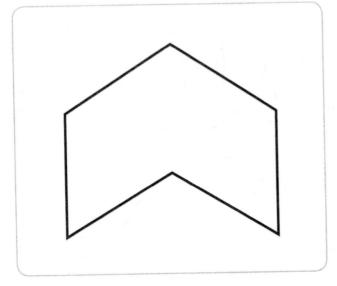

7.

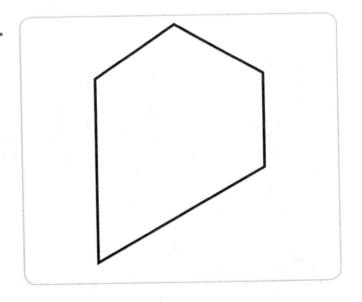

At Home Fold a card or paper into
equal parts and cut it apart. Then ask
your child to make a different shape
using all of the parts.

En casa Doble una tarjeta o una hoja en
partes iguales y recórtela. Luego pida a su
niño que forme una figura diferente usando
todas las partes.

Name _____

Use Models: Make New Shapes

 **Learn**

Objective
Use models to solve problems by combining and separating shapes.

John wants to make a sign.
It is the size of **2** pieces of paper.
How can he make it?

Understand
What do you know?
• John wants to make a sign.
• John will make it in two sections.

Plan
You can use models to act out the problem.
What shape is the sign?

  hexagon
_____

Which pattern block can you place twice on the sign?

  the red pattern block
_____

Solve
Place the pattern blocks on the shape.

Look Back
Does your model work?
What helped you decide which **2** shapes John used to make the sign?

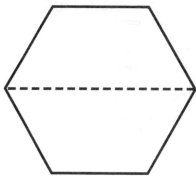

KEY MG 2.2 Put shapes together and take them apart to form other shapes (e.g., two congruent right triangles can be arranged to form a rectangle).

MR 2.0 Solve problems and justify reasoning.
Also **KEY MG 2.0**, MR 1.2, MR 1.1, MR 2.1, MR 1.0

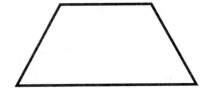

Think!
I can move the triangles to make this shape.

1. Jean has these 3 triangles. She wants to make this shape. How can she do it?

   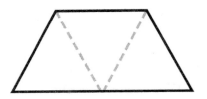

Tell what you know.

Tell what you need to know.

Choose pattern blocks and place them over the plane shape.

Draw lines showing how the triangles were placed.

2. (123) **Math Talk** Look at the shape you made in Exercise 1. Is there another combination of pattern blocks you can use to make that shape? If so, what blocks?

▶ **Problem Solving Practice**

3. Use pattern blocks to make Shape A. Draw lines to show how you placed the blocks. Then move the blocks to make a different shape. Trace the blocks.

Shape A

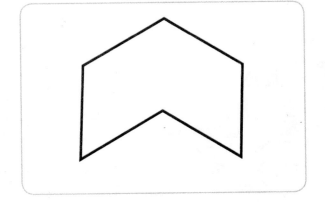

New Shape

At Home Cut out some paper shapes. Ask your child to use them to make pictures of objects such as houses and boats.

En casa Recorte algunas figuras de papel. Pida a su niño que las use para hacer dibujos de objetos como casas y barcos.

Name _____

California Field Trip

At the Vineyard Farmer's Market in Fresno

History-Social Science

The Vineyard Farmer's Market

You can buy different kinds of fruits and vegetables. You can also buy flowers. You can even buy artwork and crafts that people are selling.

Choose a way to solve. Show your work.

1. Bridget sees a sign on a fruit stand with **3** sides and **3** vertices. What shape is the sign?

fruit stand

_____

2. Robbie puts together **2** crates. I is a triangle and I is a square. What shape can he make if he puts them together?

crate

_____

3. Kendra uses some vegetable boxes to make a new shape. She uses I rectangle and **2** triangles. Draw her shape. How many sides does the shape have?

vegetable

_____

KEY MG 2.2 Put shapes together and take them apart to form other shapes (e.g., two congruent right triangles can be arranged to form a rectangle).

Also **KEY MG 2.1**, **KEY MG 2.0**, MR 1.0, MR 1.1, History-Social Science 4.1

Problem Solving on Tests
Listening Skills

Listen to your teacher read the problem.
Choose the correct answer.

Select a Strategy
Use a Table
Guess and Check
Write a Number
    Sentence
Act It Out

1. Jackie buys 62 marbles.
   Which two jars does she buy?

   Jar 1: 13   Jar 2: 33   Jar 3: 35   Jar 4: 29

   Jar 1 and 2   Jar 2 and 3   Jar 1 and 4   Jar 2 and 4
      ○   ○   ○   ○

   KEY NS 2.2

2. Cam buys a kite for 52¢ and a ball for 38¢.
   How much does Cam spend?

   80¢   90¢   95¢ $1.00
   ○   ○   ○   ○

   NS 5.0

3.

   65   53   29   17

   ○   ○   ○   ○

   Amy's Buttons

Color	Number
Red	35
Yellow	47
Blue	

   KEY NS 2.2

4.

   15   25   30   35

   ○   ○   ○   ○

   KEY NS 2.2

MR 1.0 Make decisions about how to set up a
problem.
MR 1.1 Determine the approach, materials, and
strategies to be used.

Education Place
Visit www.eduplace.com/camap/ for
Test-Taking Tips and Extra Practice.

Name _____

 # Key Standards Review

```
+--+--+--+--+--+--+--+--+--+--+--+--+--+--+--+--+--+--+--+--+
30 31 32 33 34 35 36 37 38 39 40 41 42 43 44 45 46 47 48 49 50
```

Round each number to the nearest ten.
Estimate the difference.

1. 45 – 38

   _____ – _____ = _____

2. 42 – 32

   _____ – _____ = _____

3. 48 – 33

   _____ – _____ = _____

4. 47 – 31

   _____ – _____ = _____

Subtract.

5. 93¢ – 26¢ = _____

6. 82¢ – 45¢ = _____

7. 64¢ – 58¢ = _____

8. 55¢ – 27¢ = _____

Challenge   Algebra

Sandy's cat knocked a glass of juice all over her homework. Can you help Sandy find what numbers go in the spill spots?

a. _____   b. _____   c. _____

a. 47 + 45 = ⬤

b. 36 + ⬤ = 94

c. ⬤ + 29 = 93

KEY NS 2.2 Find the sum or difference of two whole numbers up to three digits long.
Also **KEY NS 2.1**

two hundred eighty-five **285**

The Tangram Puzzle

A tangram is a Chinese puzzle. The seven pieces form a square. You can use all seven pieces to make a picture. You can make pictures of animals with the pieces.

Examples:

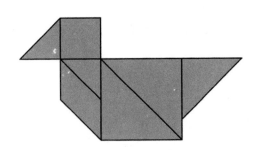

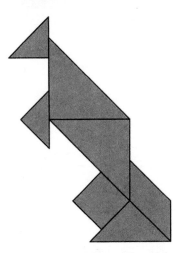

Your teacher will give you a copy of the tangram puzzle.

Name the shape of the puzzle. _____

Cut out the shapes in the puzzle.

How many pieces are triangles? _____ triangles

Try to make pictures of animals, plants, or people. Use all the pieces.

KEY **MG 2.2** Put shapes together and take them apart to form other shapes (e.g., two congruent right triangles can be arranged to form a rectangle).
Also **KEY MG 2.1**, **KEY MG 2.0**, MR 1.2

Name _____

Concepts and Skills

Draw a picture of the shape described. Name the shape. KEY **MG 2.1**

1. 3 sides, 3 vertices _____

Circle each shape that matches the name. KEY **MG 2.1**

2. pentagon

Compare the shapes. KEY **MG 2.1**

3.

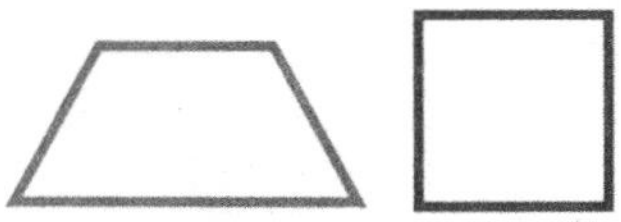

Alike because _____

Different because _____

4. Draw lines to show how the shape is made from other shapes. KEY **MG 2.2**

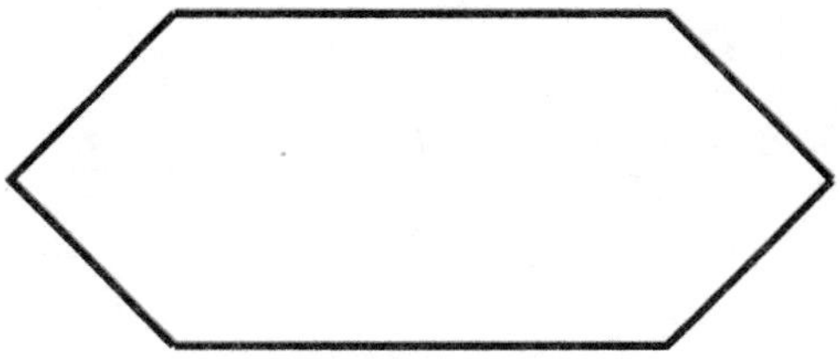

Problem Solving KEY **MG 2.1**

5. Ivan drew a closed shape that had 6 sides. How many vertices does Ivan's shape have?

_____ vertices

Spiral Review and Test Practice

1. Which is another way to show 89?

   ○ 8 ones and 9 tens   ○ 8 tens and 9 tens

   ○ 8 ones and 9 ones   ○ 8 tens and 9 ones

NS 1.2, NS 1.0 Page 55

---

2. What is the sum?   35¢ + 18¢ = _____

   43¢   48¢   53¢   54¢
   ○   ○   ○   ○

NS 5.0, KEY NS 5.2, KEY NS 2.2, NS 2.0 Page 195

---

3. Subtract. Which is the difference?

   $$\begin{array}{r} 72 \\ -\ \ 7 \\ \hline \end{array}$$

   55   65   75   79
   ○   ○   ○   ○

KEY NS 2.2 Page 233

---

4. Which addition problem can be used to check 87 − 29?

   $$\begin{array}{r} 28 \\ +29 \\ \hline \end{array}$$ $$\begin{array}{r} 38 \\ +29 \\ \hline \end{array}$$ $$\begin{array}{r} 48 \\ +29 \\ \hline \end{array}$$ $$\begin{array}{r} 58 \\ +29 \\ \hline \end{array}$$

   ○   ○   ○   ○

KEY NS 2.1 Page 255

---

5. Which is a pentagon?

        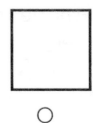   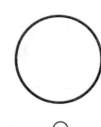

   ○   ○   ○   ○

KEY MG 2.1, KEY MG 2.0 Page 273

Education Place
Visit www.eduplace.com/camap/ for
Test-Taking Tips and Extra Practice.

Spiral Review

More About Shapes

Vocabulary

Here are some vocabulary words you will learn in the chapter.

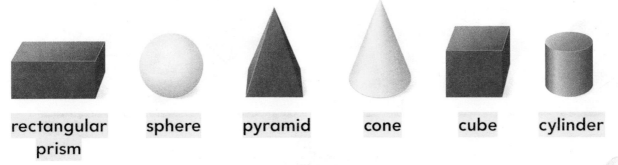

solid shape A shape that is not flat

rectangular prism   sphere   pyramid   cone   cube   cylinder

face A flat surface on a solid shape

edge Where two faces of a solid shape meet

vertex (vertices) A point where 3 or more edges meet

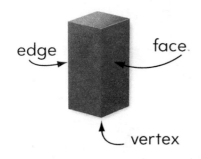

edge →   face

↓ vertex

See English-Spanish Glossary pages 573–589.

KEY MG 2.1 Describe and classify plane and solid geometric shapes (e.g., circle, triangle, square, rectangle, sphere, pyramid, cube, rectangular prism) according to the number and shape of faces, edges, and vertices.

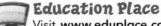
Education Place
Visit **www.eduplace.com/camap/** for the eGlossary and eGames.   two hundred eighty-nine **289**

Name _____

✓ Check What You Know

Circle the shapes that are the same.

1.

2.

3.

Circle the shape that doesn't belong.

4.

5.

Use this page to review important skills needed for this chapter.

Name _____

Chapter 15 Lesson 1
Solid Shapes

▶ **Learn**

Tina is building in the sand. Help her name the shapes she is using.

Use your classroom models. Match the model with the picture.

Objective
Identify solid shapes.

Vocabulary
rectangular prism
sphere
pyramid
cone
cube
cylinder

 cone

 cube

 cylinder

 rectangular prism

 sphere

pyramid

▶ **Guided Practice**

Use the models. Write the name of the shape. Circle the objects that are the same as your model.

Think!
I can see that 2 of the objects are pyramids.

1.

_____

2.

_____

3. **123** **Math Talk** Name some objects that are the same shape as a sphere.

KEY MG 2.0 Identify and describe the attributes of common figures in the plane and of common objects in space.

MR 1.2 Use tools, such as manipulatives or sketches, to model problems.
Also **KEY MG 2.1**, **KEY MG 2.2**, MR 3.0, MR 2.0

▶ Practice

Write the names of the two solid shapes in each picture. Use models to help.

Remember!
Think about the shapes below to name each part.

cube

sphere

rectangular prism

cylinder

pyramid

cone

4.

sphere
_____

cone
_____

5.

_____

_____

6.

_____

_____

7.
JUICE

_____

_____

Problem Solving: Visual Thinking

8. Which one is not a rectangular prism? How do you know?

At Home Ask your child to use shapes to create his or her own picture of an object.

En casa Pida a su niño que use figuras para crear un dibujo de un objeto.

Name _____

Faces, Edges, and Vertices

 **Learn**

You can describe solid shapes by the number of **faces**, **edges**, and **vertices**.

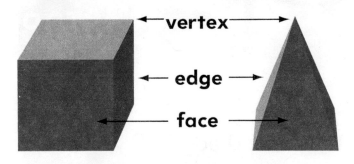

A **face** is a flat surface.
An **edge** is where 2 faces meet.
A **vertex** is the point where edges meet.

Hands On 🖐

Objective
Describe the faces, edges, and vertices of solid shapes.

Vocabulary
edge
face
vertex/vertices

▶ **Guided Practice**

Use solid shapes to count the faces, edges, and vertices.

Think!
I count 6 faces on the cube.

		Faces	Edges	Vertices
1.	cube	6	12	8
2.	sphere	___	___	___
3.	pyramid	___	___	___
4.	cylinder	___	___	___
5.	rectangular prism	___	___	___
6.	cone	___	___	___

7. (123) **Math Talk** How can you sort the solid shapes in Exercises 1–6 into two different groups?

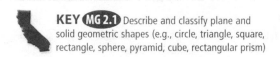

KEY MG 2.1 Describe and classify plane and solid geometric shapes (e.g., circle, triangle, square, rectangle, sphere, pyramid, cube, rectangular prism)

according to the number and shape of faces, edges, and vertices.
Also **KEY MG 2.0**, MR 1.2, MR 2.0

▶ Practice

Circle the shapes that
match the description.
Use models to help.

8. 2 faces, 0 edges, 0 vertices

9. 6 faces, 12 edges, 8 vertices

10. 5 faces, 8 edges, 5 vertices

11. 1 face, 0 edges, 0 vertices

12. 0 faces, 0 edges, 0 vertices

13. Draw a shape with 6 faces,
12 edges, and 8 vertices.

Problem Solving: Reasoning

14. Circle the solids that roll. Put an
X on the solids that slide. Put a
line under the solids that stack
on top of each other.

15. Explain how you know which
solids will slide.

🏠 **At Home** Find objects in your home
that slide, roll, or stack. Ask your child
to show how they are alike and different.

En casa Busque objetos en casa que se
deslicen, rueden o se apilen. Pida a su niño
que le muestre en qué se parecen y en qué
se diferencian.

Chapter 15 Lesson 3

Identify Faces

 **Explore**

Objective
Make plane shapes from faces of solid shapes.

Some solid shapes have faces. You can trace around a face to make a plane shape.

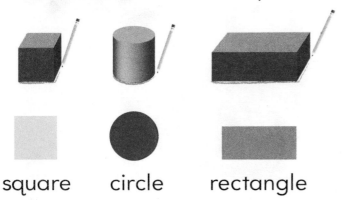

square   circle   rectangle

Trace all the faces of the solid on a separate sheet of paper. Circle the plane shape that matches what you traced. Write the name of the face.

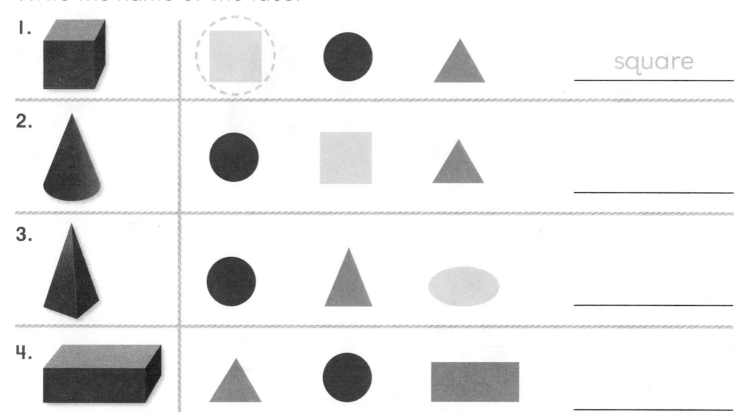

1. _____ square _____

2. _____

3. _____

4. _____

5. **Math Talk** What solid shapes have more than one face?

KEY MG 2.1 Describe and classify plane and solid geometric shapes (e.g., circle, triangle, square, rectangle, sphere, pyramid, cube, rectangular prism) according to the number and shape of faces, edges, and vertices.
Also **KEY MG 2.0**, MR 1.2

▶ **Extend**

Draw the plane shapes you would make if you traced the faces of the object. Use models to help.

Remember!
Some solid shapes have differently shaped faces.

6.

7.

8.

9.

10. What solid shapes could you trace to make this picture?

_____

_____

Objective
Classify and compare solid shapes.

Compare Plane and Solid Shapes

▶  **Learn**

Many shapes have faces, edges, and vertices.
Some shapes have the same faces.

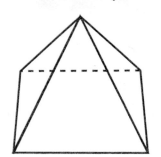

This is a pyramid. It has __5__ faces.

Four of the faces are __triangles__.

The other face is a __rectangle__.

A pyramid has __5__ vertices.

A pyramid has __8__ edges.

▶ **Guided Practice**

Name the shape.
Write three reasons for your answer.

1.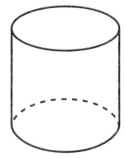

   Think!
   This shape has two faces that are circles.

   This is a _____.

   It has _____

   _____

2.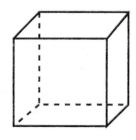

   This is a _____.

   It has _____

   _____

3. **(123) Math Talk** How is a cylinder like a cone?

 KEY MG 2.1 Describe and classify plane and solid geometric shapes (e.g., circle, triangle, square, rectangle, sphere, pyramid, cube, rectangular prism)

according to the number and shape of faces, edges, and vertices.
Also **KEY MG 2.0**, MR 2.0

Write how the shapes are alike and different. Count the faces, edges, and vertices.

Remember!
A sphere has no face, edge, or vertex.

4.

Alike

Both shapes roll.

_____

_____

Different

A sphere has 0 faces.

A cone has 1 face.

5.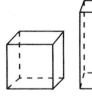

_____

_____

_____

_____

_____

_____

6.

_____

_____

_____

_____

_____

_____

Problem Solving: Visual Thinking

7. Sort the shapes into two groups. Color one group red, the other blue.

Tell how you sorted them.

_____

_____

At Home Take your child on a shape walk to find examples of the shapes included in the lesson.

En casa Lleve a su niño a un paseo en busca de figuras para encontrar ejemplos de las figuras incluidas en la lección.

Name _____

Chapter 15 Lesson 5

Geometric Patterns

▶ **Learn**

Problem Solving
Plan

Objective
Use patterns to solve problems.

Gia makes a pattern with her sand toys.
What is likely to be the next shape?

What do you know about this pattern?

- This pattern is made with rectangular prisms and cylinders.
- This pattern repeats.

Circle the pattern unit.

The shape Gia is likely to make next is a <u>rectangular prism</u> .

Ramon makes this pattern.
What is likely to come next?

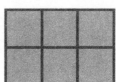

What do you know about this pattern?

- This pattern is made with squares.
- This is a growing pattern.
- It increases by 2 squares each time.

Draw what comes next in the pattern.

KEY SDAP 2.0 Demonstrate an understanding of patterns and how patterns grow and describe them in general ways.
Also **KEY MG 2.0, KEY MG 2.1**, MR 2.0

SDAP 2.1 Recognize, describe, and extend patterns and determine a next term in linear patterns (e.g., 4, 8, 12…; the number of ears on one horse, two horses, three horses, four horses).

Think!
What part of the
pattern repeats?

1. This pattern is on Gabe's beach towel.
   What shape is likely to come next?

Draw the pattern unit.

Draw the shape that is
likely to come next.

The _____ is likely to come next.

2. (123) **Math Talk** How can you tell the difference
   between repeating and growing patterns?

► **Problem Solving Practice**

3. Taylor made this pattern.

   Abby draws the next shape.
   What shape does Abby draw? _____

4. Max made this pattern.

   What is missing? _____

At Home Place a mixed handful
of coins on the table. Ask your child
to make a repeating pattern with
pennies, nickels, and dimes.

En casa Coloque un puñado de monedas
variadas en la mesa. Pida a su niño que haga
un patrón que se repite con monedas de un
centavo, cinco centavos y diez centavos.

Name _____

Chapter 15 Lesson 5

Create and Solve

The math club members make shapes out of cardboard. The table shows the number of shapes they make.

Shape	Number of Shapes
Triangle	4
Square	6
Hexagon	8
Pentagon	7

1. How many triangles and squares does the math club make?

    _____ + _____ = _____

2. Write an addition problem about the shapes in the table.

    _____

    _____

    _____

    _____

3. Write an addition sentence to solve your problem.

    _____ + _____ = _____

Share your addition problem with a classmate.

SDAP 1.4 Ask and answer simple questions related to data representations.
Also **KEY NS 2.2**, MR 1.0, AF 1.0, AF 1.2

AF 1.3 Solve addition and subtraction problems by using data from simple charts, picture graphs, and number sentences.

three hundred one **301**

The math club members voted for their favorite solid shape. The table shows the results of the vote.

Favorite Shape	Number of Votes
Cone	3
Cylinder	6
Rectangular Prism	9
Cube	4

4. How many more members voted for cylinder than for cube?

_____ – _____ = _____

5. Write a subtraction problem about the shapes in the table.

_____

_____

_____

_____

_____

6. Write a subtraction sentence to solve your problem.

_____ – _____ = _____

Share your subtraction problem with a classmate.

Key Standards Review

Complete the table.

Shape drawing	Name of shape	Number of sides	Number of vertices
1.	rectangle	_____	_____
2.	_____	_____	3
3.	_____	_____	_____

4. Draw lines to show which shapes could make up a pentagon.

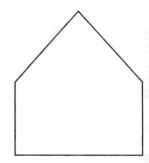

**Challenge**   Geometry

Rachel wants to make a star cake. She only has a triangle cake pan.

How many times does she need to use her triangular pan to make the star cake?

_____ times

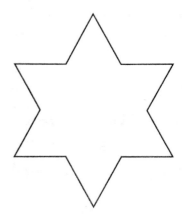

KEY MG 2.2 Put shapes together and take them apart to form other shapes (e.g., two congruent right triangles can be arranged to form a rectangle). Also **KEY** MG 2.1, **KEY** MG 2.0

US Bank Tower

The US Bank Tower in Los Angeles was built in 1989. It has **73** stories and is the tallest building in the United States west of the Mississippi River. The tower is made of granite and glass, and it can support the force of an earthquake.

Circle the correct shape.
Write the name of the shape.

1. Maya wants to make a model of the US Bank Tower. Which shape should she start with?

_____

2. Kayla sits on a  outside the US Bank Tower. Which shape does the bench look most like?

_____

3. Brad sees a  in a nearby shop. Which shape does it look most like?

_____

KEY **MG 2.1** Describe and classify plane and solid geometric shapes (e.g., circle, triangle, square, rectangle, sphere, pyramid, cube, rectangular prism) according to the number and shape of faces, edges, and vertices.
Science ES 3.e

Name _____

Concepts and Skills

1. Write the name of the two solid shapes in each picture. Use models to help. **KEY MG 2.0**

_____

_____

2. Circle the shapes that match the description. **KEY MG 2.1**

   0 edges

Draw the shapes you would make if you traced the faces of the object. Use models to help. **KEY MG 2.1**

3.

4.

Write how the pair is alike and different. Count the faces, edges, and vertices. **KEY MG 2.1**

5.

_____

_____

Problem Solving **KEY SDAP 2.0**

6. Will is building stairs out of blocks. Draw the cubes to complete Will's stairs.

Spiral Review and Test Practice

1. What is the sum?

$$\begin{array}{r} 28 \\ +58 \\ \hline \end{array}$$

76	78	86	88
○	○	○	○

---

2. What is the sum?

$$\begin{array}{r} 25 \\ 3 \\ +48 \\ \hline \end{array}$$

28	51	66	76
○	○	○	○

---

3. What is the sum?

$$\begin{array}{r} 59¢ \\ +19¢ \\ \hline \end{array}$$

69¢	78¢	79¢	88¢
○	○	○	○

---

4. Which shape has 4 sides?

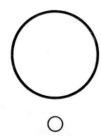  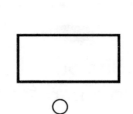 

○	○	○	○

 Education Place
Visit www.eduplace.com/camap/ for
Test-Taking Tips and Extra Practice.

Spiral Review

Fractions

Vocabulary

Here are some vocabulary words you will learn in the chapter.

whole All parts; one whole is equal to 1

$\frac{4}{4}$ are shaded.　$\frac{4}{4}$ = 1

equal parts Parts of a whole that are the same size

Two equal parts are shaded.

fraction Part of a whole

unit fraction One of the equal parts of a whole

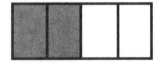

$\frac{1}{2}$　$\frac{1}{3}$　$\frac{1}{4}$

See English-Spanish Glossary pages 573–589.

KEY NS 4.1 Recognize, name, and compare unit fractions from $\frac{1}{12}$ to $\frac{1}{2}$.
Also **KEY** NS 4.2, **KEY** NS 4.3

Education Place
Visit www.eduplace.com/camap/ for the eGlossary and eGames.

three hundred seven **307**

Name _____

✓ Check What You Know

Write how many parts are shaded.
Then write how many parts there are in all.

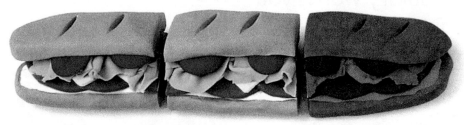

1. _____ part shaded

2. _____ parts in all

3. _____ parts shaded

4. _____ parts in all

Write how many parts there are in all.
Color **5** parts.

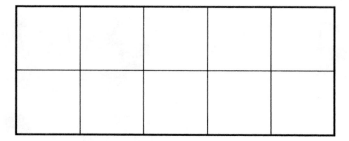

5. _____ parts

Use this page to review important skills needed for this chapter.

308

Chapter 16 Lesson 1

Halves and Fourths

▶ **Explore**

Fractions divide a **whole** into equal **parts.**
Together, all the parts make a whole.

Objective
Model halves and
fourths of a whole.

Vocabulary
fraction
part
whole
one half
one fourth

Step 1		
Start with a piece of paper.	 This is a whole.	

Step 2		
Fold the paper over.	 The paper is folded into 2 equal parts. Each equal part is called **one half**.	Write the fraction this way: $\frac{1}{2}$

Step 3		
Fold the paper over again.	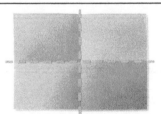 The paper is folded into 4 equal parts. Each equal part is called **one fourth**.	Write the fraction this way: $\frac{1}{4}$

In a fraction, the number on the top tells
how many parts of the whole you have. The
number on the bottom tells how many equal
parts are in the whole.

1. **(123) Math Talk** What does $\frac{1}{2}$ mean?

KEY NS 4.1 Recognize, name, and compare unit
fractions from $\frac{1}{12}$ to $\frac{1}{2}$.
Also **NS 4.0, KEY NS 4.3, MR 1.2**

KEY NS 4.2 Recognize fractions of a whole and
parts of a group (e.g., one-fourth of a pie, two-thirds
of 15 balls).

Draw to show how many equal parts.
Then fill in one part.
Write the fraction.

2. 2 equal parts

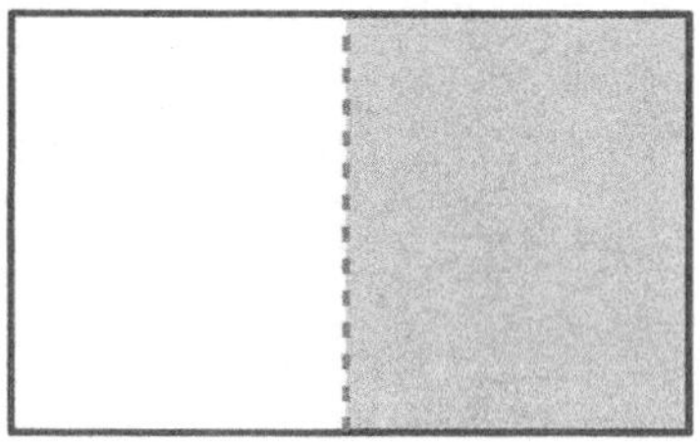

$\dfrac{1}{2}$

3. 4 equal parts

4. 4 equal parts

5. one whole

Color in the fraction strip to show the fraction.

6. $\dfrac{1}{2}$

7. $\dfrac{1}{4}$

Draw lines to show 4 equal parts.
Color in one part. Write the fraction.

8.

Name _____

Unit Fractions

 **Learn**

A fraction names equal parts of a whole.
A **unit fraction** names one of the equal parts.

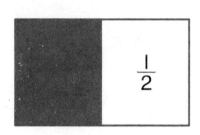

one half

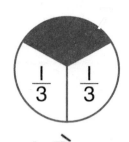

one third

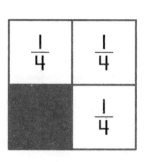

one fourth

▶ **Guided Practice**

Write the fraction for the shaded part.

1.  _____

Think!
There are 3 equal parts.
Each part is one third.

2.  _____

3.  _____

4.  _____

5.  _____

Color to show the fraction.

6. $\frac{1}{8}$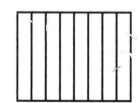

7. $\frac{1}{10}$

8. $\frac{1}{6}$

9. **123** **Math Talk** What does the bottom number
mean in the fraction $\frac{1}{8}$?

 KEY NS 4.1 Recognize, name, and compare unit
fractions from $\frac{1}{12}$ to $\frac{1}{2}$.
Also NS 4.0, MR 1.2

KEY NS 4.2 Recognize fractions of a whole and
parts of a group (e.g., one-fourth of a pie, two-thirds
of 15 balls).

three hundred eleven **311**

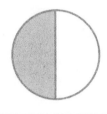

► **Practice**

Write the fraction for
the shaded part.

Remember!
The bottom number of a fraction
tells how many equal parts in all.
The top number tells how many
parts are shaded.

10. 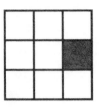 $\frac{1}{2}$ _____

11.  _____

12.  _____

13. 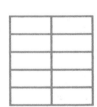 _____

14.  _____

15.  _____

Color one part.
Write the fraction.

16.  _____

17. 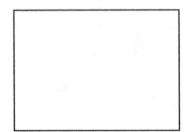 _____

18.  _____

Problem Solving: Reasoning

Draw lines and color to show the
fraction. Write the fraction.

19. Divide into sixths.
Color one sixth.

_____

20. Divide into fourths.
Color one fourth.

_____

21. Divide into thirds.
Color one third.

_____

At Home Ask your child to fold
towels or papers to show thirds and
sixths. Have him or her write the
fraction for one of the equal parts.

En casa Pida a su niño que doble toallas
o papeles para mostrar tercios y sextos.
Pídale que escriba la fracción de una de las
partes iguales.

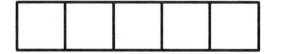 ▶ **Practice**

Color. Write the fraction that you colored.

16. Color **2** parts.

_____

17. Color **8** parts.

_____

18. Color **4** parts.

_____

19. Sam has a pizza with **8** equal slices. **3** slices have mushrooms. **2** slices have peppers. The other slices have extra cheese. What fraction of the pizza has extra cheese?

_____

Practice Game

Fraction Match

How to Play

1. Place the cards face down. Take turns. Pick one Fraction Card at a time.

2. Try to match the fraction on the card to a picture on the game board. Put a counter on the picture.

3. The first player to get 4 counters in a row or column wins.

What You Need

2 players

16 ● for each player

Fraction Cards (LT 19 and 20)

 KEY NS 4.2 Recognize fractions of a whole and parts of a group (e.g., one-fourth of a pie, two-thirds of 15 balls).

Education Place
Visit www.eduplace.com/camap/ for more games.

Wholes and Parts

 **Learn**

Objective
Identify fractions that name one whole, more than one whole, and less than one whole.

A fraction can name one whole or more than one whole.

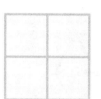

The whole square is purple.

$\frac{4}{4} = 1$

$\frac{4}{4}$ are purple.

Four fourths are purple.

6 parts are yellow.

$\frac{6}{4}$ are yellow.

Six fourths are yellow.

 **Guided Practice**

Circle the fraction that names the shaded parts.

1.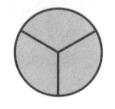

$\frac{1}{4}$ $\frac{3}{3}$ $\frac{4}{3}$

Think!
I know each shaded part is one third.

2.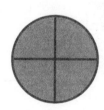

$\frac{3}{4}$ $\frac{4}{4}$ $\frac{2}{3}$

3.

$\frac{3}{2}$ $\frac{1}{2}$ $\frac{2}{3}$

4.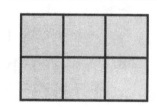

$\frac{3}{4}$ $\frac{6}{6}$ $\frac{5}{5}$

5. **Math Talk** How do you know that $\frac{5}{5}$ is equal to one whole?

 KEY NS 4.3 Know that when all fractional parts are included, such as four-fourths, the result is equal to the whole and to one.
Also NS 4.0, MR 2.0, MR 2.1

KEY NS 4.2 Recognize fractions of a whole and parts of a group (e.g., one-fourth of a pie, two-thirds of 15 balls).

► **Practice**

Write the fraction for the shaded parts.

6.
_____

7.
_____

8.
_____

9.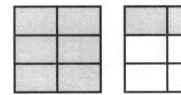
_____

10.
_____

11.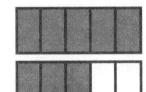
_____

12.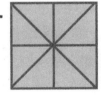
_____

13.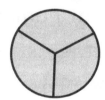
_____

Problem Solving: Reasoning

14. These fractions fell off the chart. Where do they belong? Write each fraction on the chart. Tell how you solved.

$\frac{3}{2}$ $\frac{5}{5}$ $\frac{1}{4}$ $\frac{7}{5}$ $\frac{2}{6}$ $\frac{9}{9}$

Less than I whole	One whole	More than I whole

 At Home Ask your child to name each fraction and explain if it is less than, equal to, or more than one whole.

En casa Pida a su niño que nombre cada fracción y que explique si es menor, mayor o igual a un entero.

Use a Picture

 **Learn**

Use a picture to solve a problem.
The sandwich is cut into **8** equal pieces.

You can use a picture to find a fraction.

Chan eats **3** pieces of the sandwich.
What fraction of the sandwich does he eat?
Color the picture to show the fraction.

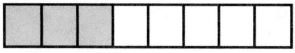

| 3 | number of pieces Chan eats |
| 8 | pieces in the whole sandwich |

Think!
How many pieces
are in the whole sandwich?
How many pieces
does he eat?

Chan eats $\frac{3}{8}$ _____
of the sandwich.

You can use a picture to compare two fractions.

Sabrina and Ty eat $\frac{5}{6}$ of a sandwich.

Is that amount closer to all of the sandwich,
closer to $\frac{1}{2}$ of the sandwich or closer to none of the sandwich?

Color the picture to show the fraction.

Think!
Use the number line
to help you decide.

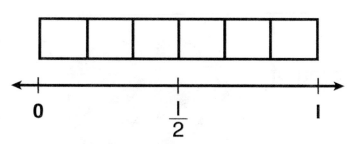

Sabrina and Ty have eaten almost all of the sandwich.

 **KEY NS 4.2** Recognize fractions of a whole and
parts of a group (e.g., one-fourth of a pie, two-thirds
of 15 balls).
Also **SDAP 1.4, KEY NS 4.1**, NS 4.0, MR 2.1

MR 1.2 Use tools, such as manipulatives or sketches,
to model problems.

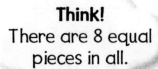

Think!
There are 8 equal
pieces in all.

1. Misha eats 5 parts of this large cracker.
What fraction of the cracker does
Misha eat?

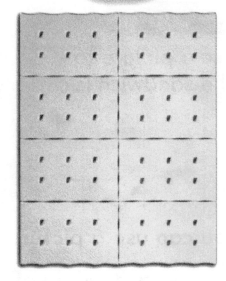

You can use a picture to solve the problem.
Color the picture to show how many
pieces he eats.

Write the fraction.

Misha eats _____ of the cracker.

2. (123) **Math Talk** How can it help to use a
picture to solve fraction problems?

▶ **Problem Solving Practice**

Use the picture to solve.

3. Anya cuts an apple into 5 equal
pieces. She eats 4 pieces.
Does she eat about all, about $\frac{1}{2}$,
or about none of the apple?

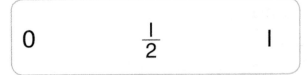

0       $\frac{1}{2}$ 1

4. Brian cuts a pie into 4 pieces.
Liza eats 1 piece. What fraction of
the pie does Liza eat?

_____

At Home Share a snack, such as a
sandwich, with your child. Have him
or her write the fraction for each part.

En casa Comparta una merienda, como un
sándwich, con su niño. Pídale que escriba la
fracción de cada parte.

Name _____

Complete the table.

Shape	Name of shape	Number of faces	Number of vertices	Number of edges
1. 	_____	_____	_____	_____
2.	_____	_____	_____	_____
3.	_____	_____	_____	_____

Challenge   Geometry

Use the clues to find which shapes Kim and Steve are thinking of.

Kim	Steve
My mystery shape has no vertices. My mystery shape has two faces. It can roll, slide, and stack.	My mystery shape has one face. My mystery shape has no edges. It can roll and slide.

1. Kim's mystery shape is a _____.

2. Steve's mystery shape is a _____.

KEY MG 2.1 Describe and classify plane and solid geometric shapes (e.g., circle, triangle, square, rectangle, sphere, pyramid, cube, rectangular prism) according to the number and shape of faces, edges, and vertices.

Also **KEY** MG 2.0

three hundred twenty-one **321**

Chef Julia Child

Julia Child was a famous chef. She was born in Pasadena, California. She really enjoyed cooking French food. She also cooked many other kinds of food. People watched Julia cook on her television shows.

Solve.

1. Tova has this much chocolate. Does she have closer to $\frac{1}{2}$ of a bar or 1 whole bar?

_____

2. Sunil has the raisins shown. Does he have closer to $\frac{1}{2}$ or 1 cup of raisins?

_____

Anna baked this cake. She cut it into 6 equal slices.

3. Sam and Lara eat 1 slice each. Tell what fraction of the cake has been eaten. _____

4. What fraction of the cake has not been eaten? _____

KEY NS 4.2 Recognize fractions of a whole and parts of a group (e.g., one-fourth of a pie, two-thirds of 15 balls).
Also **KEY NS 4.1**, NS 4.0, NS 6.1
History-Social Science 5.0

Name _____

Concepts and Skills

Fill the fraction strip to show the fraction. KEY **NS 4.1**

1. $\dfrac{1}{3}$

2. $\dfrac{1}{4}$

Write the fraction for the shaded part. KEY **NS 4.1**, KEY **NS 4.2**

3.  _____

4. 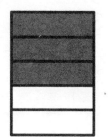 _____

Circle the fraction that names the shaded part. KEY **NS 4.3**

5.

$\dfrac{3}{3}$ $\dfrac{3}{2}$ $\dfrac{3}{5}$

6.

$\dfrac{3}{3}$ $\dfrac{6}{6}$ $\dfrac{4}{3}$

Problem Solving KEY **NS 4.2**

7. Ariel cuts her carrot into **8** equal pieces. She eats **5** of them. What fraction of the carrot does Ariel eat?

_____

Draw or write to explain.

Spiral Review and Test Practice

1. Follow the pattern. Which are the two missing numbers?

10, 15, 20, 25, _____, _____, 40, 45

23, 24   26, 27   28, 33   30, 35
  ○   ○   ○   ○

---

2. Which addition problem can be used to check the subtraction?

$$\begin{array}{r} 94 \\ -37 \\ \hline \end{array}$$

$$\begin{array}{r} 94 \\ +94 \\ \hline \end{array}$$ $$\begin{array}{r} 37 \\ +37 \\ \hline \end{array}$$ $$\begin{array}{r} 37 \\ +57 \\ \hline \end{array}$$ $$\begin{array}{r} 57 \\ +57 \\ \hline \end{array}$$

  ○   ○   ○   ○

---

3. What shape is the blue face?

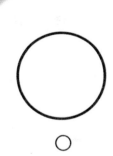

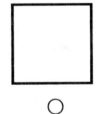 

  ○   ○   ○   ○

---

4. What fraction does the shaded part show?

6          $\dfrac{1}{3}$ $\dfrac{1}{5}$ $\dfrac{1}{6}$

  ○   ○   ○   ○

Education Place
Visit www.eduplace.com/camap/ for
Test-Taking Tips and Extra Practice.

Spiral Review

More About Fractions

Vocabulary

Here are some vocabulary words you will learn in the chapter.

fraction Part of a whole or a group

2 parts of the group are red.

$\frac{2}{3}$ of the apples are red.

1 part of the group is yellow.

$\frac{1}{3}$ of the apples are yellow.

See English-Spanish Glossary pages 573–589.

 KEY NS 4.2 Recognize fractions of a whole and parts of a group (e.g., one-fourth of a pie, two-thirds of 15 balls). Also **KEY** NS 4.1

 **Education Place** Visit **www.eduplace.com/camap/** for the eGlossary and eGames.

three hundred twenty-five **325**

Name _____

 Check What You Know

1. Draw a group of 7 apples.

2. Write how many parts are apples.

_____ parts are apples

3. Write how many parts are in the group.

_____ parts in the group

4. Write how many parts are oranges.

_____ parts are oranges

5. Write how many parts are in the group.

_____ parts in the group

Use this page to review important skills needed for this chapter.

Chapter 17 Lesson 1

Compare Fractions

 **Explore**

Hands On ✋

Objective
Make a model to
compare fractions.

You can use fraction strips to compare fractions.

Compare $\frac{1}{2}$ and $\frac{1}{3}$.

Step 1

When you make halves, how many parts make the whole?

_2_

Find the fraction strip on Learning Tool 21 that has the same number of parts in the whole.

Color one part to show $\frac{1}{2}$.

Step 2

When you make thirds, how many parts make the whole?

_3_

Find the fraction strip that has the same number of parts in the whole.

Color one part to show $\frac{1}{3}$.

Step 3

Compare the colored parts of the fraction strips to compare the fractions.

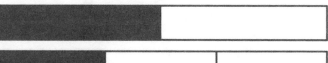

$\frac{1}{2}$ ⊙> $\frac{1}{3}$

1. **123** **Math Talk** How do fraction strips help you compare fractions?

 **KEY NS 4.1** Recognize, name, and compare unit fractions from $\frac{1}{12}$ to $\frac{1}{2}$.
Also **KEY NS 4.2**, NS 4.0

MR 1.2 Use tools, such as manipulatives or sketches, to model problems.

▶ Extend

Use Learning Tool 21 to compare the fractions. Then write >, <, or =.

2. $\frac{1}{2}$ ◯< $\frac{2}{3}$

3. $\frac{1}{3}$ ◯ $\frac{1}{4}$

4. $\frac{1}{2}$ ◯ $\frac{1}{12}$

5. $\frac{1}{4}$ ◯ $\frac{1}{9}$

6. $\frac{1}{8}$ ◯ $\frac{1}{3}$

7. $\frac{1}{2}$ ◯ $\frac{4}{8}$

8. $\frac{1}{4}$ ◯ $\frac{1}{2}$

9. $\frac{2}{12}$ ◯ $\frac{1}{4}$

10. $\frac{5}{8}$ ◯ $\frac{1}{2}$

11. $\frac{3}{4}$ ◯ $\frac{3}{9}$

12. $\frac{4}{6}$ ◯ $\frac{2}{4}$

13. $\frac{8}{9}$ ◯ $\frac{4}{4}$

14. $\frac{2}{2}$ ◯ $\frac{7}{8}$

15. $\frac{3}{5}$ ◯ $\frac{3}{4}$

16. $\frac{3}{12}$ ◯ $\frac{1}{4}$

 **At Home** Ask your child to use fraction strips to compare $\frac{1}{2}$ and $\frac{2}{3}$.

En casa Pida a su niño que use barras de fracción para explicar cómo comparar $\frac{1}{2}$ y $\frac{2}{3}$.

Chapter 17 Lesson 2

Fractions of a Group

Hands On 🖐

Objective
Recognize and name
fractions of a group.

▶ Learn

Use 🔲 to model. What fraction
of the trucks are blue?

$\frac{6}{8}$ of the trucks are blue.

What fraction of the trucks are green?

$\frac{2}{8}$ of the trucks are green.

$\dfrac{6 \text{ blue trucks}}{8 \text{ trucks in all}}$

$\dfrac{2 \text{ green trucks}}{8 \text{ trucks in all}}$

▶ Guided Practice

Use cubes to model.
Write a fraction for each part.

Think!
I know 2 out of the
7 plums are purple.

1.

What fraction of the
plums are purple?   ___ are purple

What fraction of the
plums are red?   ___ are red

2.

What fraction of the
baskets are brown?   ___ are brown

What fraction of the
baskets are yellow?   ___ are yellow

3. (123) **Math Talk** In Exercise 2, what fraction would
you write to show all of the baskets? Why?

 KEY NS 4.2 Recognize fractions of a whole and
parts of a group (e.g., one-fourth of a pie, two-thirds
of 15 balls).
Also **MR 1.2, KEY NS 4.3, MR 2.0**

NS 4.0 Understand that fractions and decimals may
refer to parts of a set and parts of a whole.

three hundred twenty-nine **329**

▶ Practice

Use cubes to model.
Write a fraction for each color.

4.

What fraction of the
peppers are orange? $\dfrac{5}{8}$ orange peppers

What fraction of the
peppers are green?   ___   green peppers

5.

What fraction of the
flowers are yellow?   ___   yellow flowers

What fraction of the
flowers are blue?   ___   blue flowers

6.

What fraction of the
apples are red?   ___   red apples

What fraction of the
apples are yellow?   ___   yellow apples

7.

What fraction of the
flowers are yellow
and red?   ___   red and yellow flowers

What fraction of the
flowers are blue?   ___   blue flowers

Problem Solving: Visual Thinking

8. Draw and color to
show the flowers.

$\dfrac{2}{3}$ are red. $\dfrac{1}{3}$ are blue.

330

 At Home Show 3 cups. Mark 2 of
them and leave the last one alone.
Help your child to make up a fraction to
show the marked and unmarked cups.

En casa Muestre 3 vasos. Marque 2 de ellos
y deje el último sin marcar. Ayude a su niño a
inventar una fracción que muestre los vasos
marcados y sin marcar.

 **Practice**

Trinh buys **1** rose and **2** daisies.
What fraction of the flowers is the rose?
What fraction are the daisies?

Fractions can name parts of a group.
Use cubes to model the flowers.

1 red cube
3 cubes in all
$\frac{1}{3}$ of the cubes are red.

The rose is $\frac{1}{3}$ of the flowers.

2 blue cubes
3 cubes in all
$\frac{2}{3}$ of the cubes are blue.

The daisies are $\frac{2}{3}$ of the flowers.

Write a fraction for the
parts of the group.

Think!
There are 4 flowers in
the group. What part is purple?
What part is yellow?

9.

$\frac{1}{4}$

$\frac{3}{4}$

_____ purple flowers _____ yellow flowers

10.

_____ yellow apples   _____ red apples

11.

_____ red peppers   _____ green peppers

Write a fraction for each color.

12.

_____ green   _____ yellow

13.

_____ pink   _____ yellow

14.

_____ red   _____ yellow

15.

_____ orange   _____ green

16.

_____ yellow   _____ blue

17.

_____ yellow   _____ red

18.

_____ yellow   _____ white

19.

_____ red   _____ yellow

At Home Place 6 to 10 pennies on the table. Ask your child to write a fraction for the pennies that are heads up and those that are tails up.

En casa Coloque de 6 a 10 monedas de un centavo en la mesa. Pida a su niño que escriba una fracción para las monedas de un centavo que tienen la cara y la cruz hacia arriba.

Fractional Parts of a Group

Objective
Identify fractional parts of a group.

 **Learn**

Tasha has 2 red flowers and 4 blue flowers.
What fraction of the flowers is red?
What fraction is blue?

$\frac{1}{3}$ is red. $\frac{1}{3}$ of 6 is ____2____

$\frac{2}{3}$ is blue. $\frac{2}{3}$ of 6 is ____4____

▶ **Guided Practice**

Think!
I need to color 4 out of 8 cubes.

Color to show the fraction.

1.
$\frac{4}{8}$

$\frac{4}{8}$ of 8 is _____

2.
$\frac{1}{4}$

$\frac{1}{4}$ of 8 is _____

3.
$\frac{2}{4}$

$\frac{2}{4}$ of 8 is _____

4.
$\frac{4}{10}$

$\frac{4}{10}$ of 10 is _____

5. **(123) Math Talk** How can you find an equal part of a group?

KEY NS 4.2 Recognize fractions of a whole and
parts of a group (e.g., one-fourth of a pie, two-thirds
of 15 balls).
Also NS 4.0, MR 2.1

Practice

Remember!
The answer will be a whole number. It stands for a fraction of that set.

Color to show each fraction.
Write the number.

6. $\frac{2}{3}$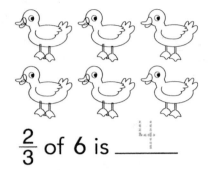

$\frac{2}{3}$ of 6 is _____

7. $\frac{7}{8}$

$\frac{7}{8}$ of 8 is _____

8. $\frac{1}{10}$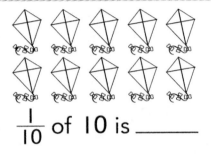

$\frac{1}{10}$ of 10 is _____

9. $\frac{4}{6}$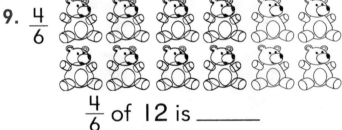

$\frac{4}{6}$ of 12 is _____

10. $\frac{1}{2}$

$\frac{1}{2}$ of 8 is _____

11. $\frac{2}{3}$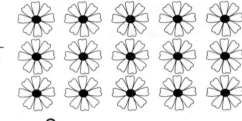

$\frac{2}{3}$ of 15 is _____

Problem Solving: Reasoning

12. Color the balls. Write how many.

Color $\frac{2}{3}$ of the balls blue.

Color $\frac{1}{5}$ of the balls red.

Color $\frac{2}{15}$ of the balls yellow.

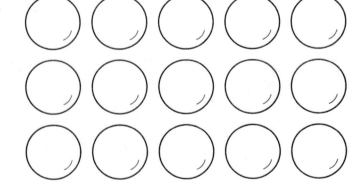

_____ blue balls   _____ red balls   _____ yellow balls

$\frac{2}{3}$ of 15 is _____ $\frac{1}{5}$ of 15 is _____ $\frac{2}{15}$ of 15 is _____

At Home Ask your child to explain how he or she decided to color each fraction in the exercises on the page.

En casa Pida a su niño que explique cómo decidió colorear cada fracción en los ejercicios de la página.

334

Chapter 17 Lesson 4

Draw a Picture

▶ **Learn**

You can draw a picture to solve a problem. Marc picks 12 peaches from a tree in his yard.

You can draw a picture to find a fraction.

Marc uses 6 peaches to make a pie. What fraction of the peaches does he use for the pie?

Think!
How many peaches does Marc pick in all? How many peaches does he use in the pie?

☐ peaches in the pie
──────────
☐ total number of peaches

Marc uses $\dfrac{6}{12}$ of the peaches for the pie.

You can draw a picture to compare two fractions.

There are 12 peaches in a basket.

Paul eats $\dfrac{3}{12}$ of the peaches.

Leah eats $\dfrac{2}{12}$ of the peaches.

Who eats more peaches, Paul or Leah?

$$\dfrac{3}{12} \bigcirc \dfrac{2}{12}$$

_____ eats more peaches.

Think!
Draw a picture to find $\dfrac{3}{12}$.

Draw a picture to find $\dfrac{2}{12}$. Which is greater?

KEY **NS 4.2** Recognize fractions of a whole and parts of a group (e.g., one-fourth of a pie, two-thirds of 15 balls).
Also KEY **NS 4.3**, NS 4.0, MR 2.0

MR 1.2 Use tools, such as manipulatives or sketches, to model problems.

Think!
How many equal parts
are there in all?

Solve.

1. Dad puts **8** strawberries on a plate. Miri eats **2** of them. What fraction of the strawberries does Miri eat?

Tell what you know.

Tell what you need to know.

Draw to model the problem.

Circle the part showing what Miri eats.

Write the fraction.

Miri eats —— of the strawberries.

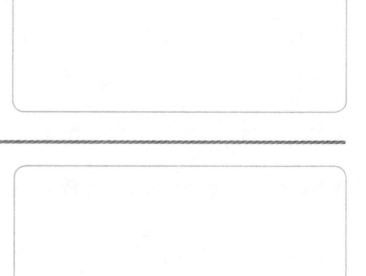

2. (123) **Math Talk** What fraction tells about all of the strawberries together?

► **Problem Solving Practice**

Draw a picture to solve.

3. Carla has **5** cherries. She gives Don **3** cherries. What fraction of the cherries does Don have?

_____ of the cherries

4. What fraction of the cherries does Carla have?

_____ of the cherries

At Home Make up a word problem for your child about blueberries.

En casa Invente un problema para su niño sobre arándanos.

Name _____

California Field Trip

At the Hidden Villa Farm

You can see plants and animals. You can see where peppers, tomatoes, and carrots grow in the garden. You can see cows that give milk and chickens that lay eggs. You can even pet a sheep.

History-Social Science

Feeding birds on the farm

Choose a way to solve. Show your work.

1. Jared picks 10 peppers. $\frac{4}{5}$ of the peppers are red. How many peppers are red?

_____ peppers

pepper

2. Cora cuts a cucumber into 4 equal parts. She uses 3 parts to make sandwiches. What fraction of the cucumber does Cora use for sandwiches?

_____

cucumber

3. Mr. and Mrs. Shim dig up 15 potatoes. Mr. Shim digs up $\frac{1}{3}$ of the potatoes. Mrs. Shim digs up $\frac{2}{3}$ of the potatoes. How many more potatoes does Mrs. Shim dig up than Mr. Shim?

_____ more potatoes

potato

KEY **NS 4.2** Recognize fractions of a whole and parts of a group (e.g., one-fourth of a pie, two-thirds of 15 balls). **History-Social Science 4.1**

Also **NS 4.0, MR 1.0, MR 1.1**

Problem Solving on Tests
Listening Skills

Listen to your teacher read the problem.
Choose the correct answer.

Select a Strategy
Draw a Picture
Act It Out

1. Emma has **8** eggs. She uses $\frac{1}{4}$ of the eggs to bake a cake. How many eggs does Emma use to bake the cake?

1	2	4	6
○	○	○	○

KEY **NS 4.2**

2. There are **12** tomatoes in all.

   Joey picks $\frac{2}{6}$ of the tomatoes.

   Ricardo picks $\frac{3}{6}$ of the tomatoes.

   How many tomatoes are left over?

2	3	5	6
○	○	○	○

KEY **NS 4.2**

3.

12	9	6	3
○	○	○	○

KEY **NS 4.2**

4.

$\frac{1}{5}$	$\frac{1}{6}$	$\frac{2}{6}$	$\frac{5}{6}$
○	○	○	○

KEY **NS 4.2**

MR 1.0 Make decisions about how to set up a problem.
MR 1.1 Determine the approach, materials, and strategies to be used.

Education Place
Visit **www.eduplace.com/camap/** for Test-Taking Tips and Extra Practice.

Name _____

Concepts and Skills

Use Learning Tool 21 to compare the fractions.
Then write >, <, or =.   KEY **NS 4.1**

1. $\frac{1}{5}$ ◯ $\frac{1}{4}$

2. $\frac{1}{7}$ ◯ $\frac{1}{9}$

3. $\frac{1}{8}$ ◯ $\frac{1}{3}$

Write a fraction for each color.   KEY **NS 4.2**

4.

What fraction of the flowers are red? _____

What fraction of the flowers are yellow? _____

Color to show each fraction. Write the number.   KEY **NS 4.2**

5. $\frac{3}{5}$

$\frac{3}{5}$ of 10 is _____.

6. $\frac{2}{3}$

$\frac{2}{3}$ of 12 is _____.

Problem Solving   KEY **NS 4.2**, NS 4.0

7. Color to show the fractions.

$\frac{4}{6}$ of the cars are red.

$\frac{2}{6}$ of the cars are green.

Spiral Review and Test Practice

1. Round each number to the nearest ten.
Which is an estimate of the difference? $82 - 24$

80	70	60	50
○	○	○	○

NS 6.0, NS 2.0 Page 249

2. Which shape is a rectangle?

      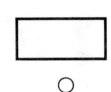   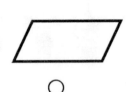

○	○	○	○

KEY MG 2.1, KEY MG 2.0 Page 273

3. Which best describes these two shapes?

○ They both have flat faces.   ○ They both have square faces.

○ They both have triangular faces.   ○ They both have 4 faces.

KEY MG 2.1 Page 297

4. Write the fraction for the shaded part.

$\frac{1}{2}$	$\frac{1}{3}$	$\frac{1}{4}$	$\frac{2}{2}$
○	○	○	○

KEY NS 4.2, KEY NS 4.1, NS 4.0 Page 313

 Education Place
Visit www.eduplace.com/camap/ for
Test-Taking Tips and Extra Practice.

Greg Tang's **Go Fast, Go Far**

Unit 6 **Mental Math Strategies**

Add 9

Adding 9 is fast and fun.
First add 10, then take away 1!

1. $16 + 9 =$ **25**

    10 − **1**

Start with $16 + 10 = 26$.
Since I've added 1 too
many, I take away
1 from 26 and get 25.

2. $37 + 9 = \boxed{}$

    $\boxed{}$ − $\boxed{}$

3. $45 + 9 = \boxed{}$

    $\boxed{}$ − $\boxed{}$

Keep It Up !

4. $18 + 9 = \boxed{}$

    $\boxed{}$ − $\boxed{}$

5. $23 + 9 = \boxed{}$

    $\boxed{}$ − $\boxed{}$

Take It Further: Now try all the steps in
your head!

6. $79 + 9 = \boxed{}$

7. $86 + 9 = \boxed{}$

Reading and Writing Math

Choose a word from the word bank for each blank.

Word Bank
circle
cube
equal parts
fraction
rectangle
rectangular
  prism
sphere
square
unit fractions
whole

1. Parts of a _____ that are the same

   size are called _____.

2. $\frac{1}{2}$, $\frac{1}{6}$, and $\frac{1}{12}$ are all _____.

3. A _____ names part of a group or a whole.

Plane Shapes	Solid Shapes
4. _____	5. _____
6. _____	7. _____
8. _____	9. _____

10. **Writing Math** Choose a plane shape.

    Show $\frac{3}{5}$ of a whole. Then show $\frac{3}{5}$ of a group.

$\frac{3}{5}$ of a whole	$\frac{3}{5}$ of a group

KEY MG 2.1 Describe and classify plane and solid geometric shapes (e.g., circle, triangle, square, rectangle, sphere, pyramid, cube, rectangular prism) according to the number and shape of faces, edges, and vertices.   Also **KEY NS 4.2**

Name _____

Concepts and Skills

Circle the shape that matches the name. KEY **MG 2.1**

1. rectangle

_____

Compare the shapes. KEY **MG 2.1**

2.

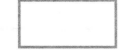

Alike because _____

Different because _____

_____

Write the name of the two solid shapes. KEY **MG 2.1**

3.

_____   _____

_____

Circle the shape that matches. KEY **MG 2.1**

4. Has 12 edges

_____

Draw the shapes you would make if
you traced the faces of the object.
Use a model to help. KEY **MG 2.1**

5.

Write the fraction for the shaded part. KEY **NS 4.2**

6. 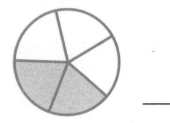 _____

7.  _____

Compare the fractions with >, <, or =. KEY **NS 4.1**

8. $\frac{1}{6}$ ◯ $\frac{1}{3}$

9. $\frac{1}{5}$ ◯ $\frac{1}{8}$

Write the fraction. KEY **NS 4.2**

10.

What fraction of the roses are red? _____

Color to show each fraction.
Write the number. KEY **NS 4.2**

11. $\frac{4}{5}$

$\frac{4}{5}$ of 10 is _____.

12. $\frac{4}{6}$

$\frac{4}{6}$ of 12 is _____.

Problem Solving

Solve. MR 2.0, KEY **MG 2.1**

Draw or write to explain.

13. Ivan drew a closed shape with 5 sides. How many vertices does Ivan's shape have?

_____

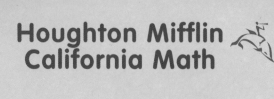
Unit

7

Measurement

BIG IDEAS!

- You can measure length with different kinds of units.

- Minutes, hours, days, weeks, months, and years are units used to measure time.

- You can say the time on a clock by counting minutes or using fractions such as a "quarter-hour."

Songs and Games

Math Music Track 7
Show and Tell

eGames
www.eduplace.com/camap/

Literature

Read Aloud Big Book
- Measuring Penny

Math Readers

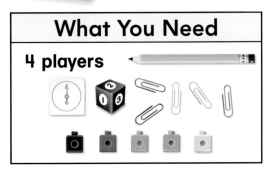

Get Ready Game

Measurement Hunt

How to Play

1. Work in a team.

2. Spin the spinner. Measure with 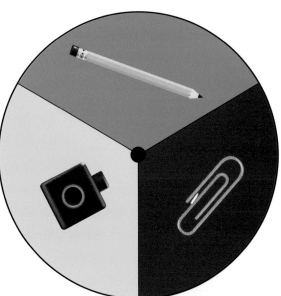, or ◄━━━━━■.

3. Roll the number cube. Use that many , , or ◄━━━━━■ to measure.

4. Find an object that tall or that long. Write it in the chart.

5. The first team to fill the chart wins.

What You Need

4 players ◄━━━━━■

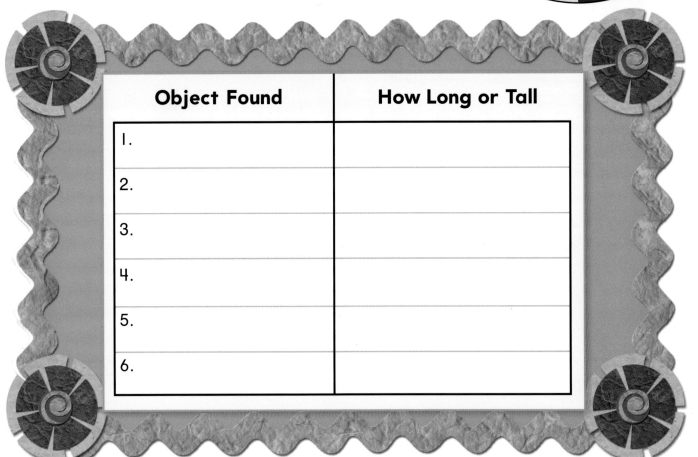

Object Found	How Long or Tall
1.	
2.	
3.	
4.	
5.	
6.	

MG 1.1 Measure the length of objects by iterating (repeating) a nonstandard or standard unit. Also **MG 1.0, MR 1.2**

Education Place
Visit **www.eduplace.com/camap/** for eGames and Brain Teasers.

Math at Home

Dear Family,

My class is starting Unit 7, **Measurement.** I will be learning how to measure length with inches, centimeters, and classroom objects. I will also learn how to make and read clocks and calendars. You can help me learn these vocabulary words, and we can do the Math Activity together.

From,

_____

Vocabulary

inch A customary unit used to measure length

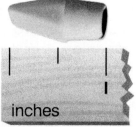

inches

centimeter A metric unit used to measure length

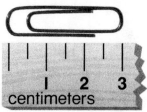

centimeters

minute A unit of time
There are 60 minutes in an hour.

hour A unit of time
There are 24 hours in a day.

Education Place
Visit **www.eduplace.com/camaf/** for
• eGames and Brain Teasers
• Math at Home in other languages

Family Math Activity

Play a game called "Catch the Clock". When the clock at home shows the time to the hour, such as 6:00, call out to the members of your family, "I caught the clock on 6 o'clock!" You can also play this game to the half-hour, such as 6:30, and quarter-hour, such as 6:15 or 6:45.

Literature

These books link to the math in this unit. Look for them at the library.

• **How Tall How Short How Far Away**
by David A. Adler
Illustrated by Nancy Tobin
(Holiday House, 1999)

• **Keep Your Distance!**
by Gail Herman
Illustrated by Jerry Smath

• **Lulu's Lemonade**
by Barbara deRubertis
Illustrated by Paige Billin-Frye

Matemáticas en casa

Estimada familia:

Mi clase está comenzando la Unidad 7, **Medición**. Aprenderé a medir longitud en pulgadas, centímetros y con objetos de la clase. También aprenderé a hacer y leer relojes y calendarios. Me pueden ayudar a aprender estas palabras de vocabulario y podemos hacer juntos la Actividad de matemáticas para la familia.

De:

_____

Vocabulario

pulgada Unidad del sistema inglés (usual) para medir longitud.

pulgadas

centímetro Unidad métrica para medir longitud.

centímetros

minuto Unidad de tiempo; en una hora hay 60 minutos.

hora Unidad de tiempo; en un día hay 24 horas.

 Education Place
Visite **www.eduplace.com/camaf/** para
• Juegos en línea y acertijos
• Matemáticas en casa en otros idiomas

Actividad de matemáticas para la familia

Jueguen a "Sorprender al reloj". Cuando el reloj de la casa muestre la hora en punto, como las **6:00**, háganlo saber a los miembros de la familia: "¡Sorprendí al reloj en las **6** en punto!" También pueden jugarlo para cada media hora, como las **6:30**, y cada cuarto de hora, como las **6:15** ó las **6:45**.

Literatura

Estos libros hablan sobre las matemáticas de esta unidad. Búscalos en la biblioteca.

• **¡Mantén tu distancia!**
  por Gail Herman
  (Kane Press, 2006)

• **Carrie está a la altura**
  por Linda Williams Aber

A New School for Paul Bunyan

written by Timothy Johnson

illustrated by Alexandra Colombo

This Take-Home Book belongs to

Reading and Writing Math

This take-home book will help you review measurement.

Look inside this brand-new school. Don't you think it's just so cool?

MG 1.0 Understand that measurement is accomplished by identifying a unit of measure, iterating (repeating) that unit, and comparing it to the item to be measured.

At age 5, Paul began his schooling.
He was HUGE, and I'm not fooling.
He hardly fit through the school door.
Then he kept on growing MORE!

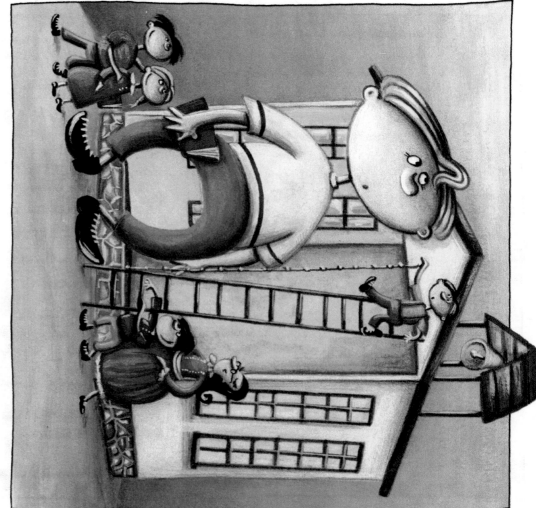

The new school was huge, but just right
For someone with Paul's big size and height.
The class measured Paul once more,
So they could build a Paul-sized door.
What was used to measure Paul's height?

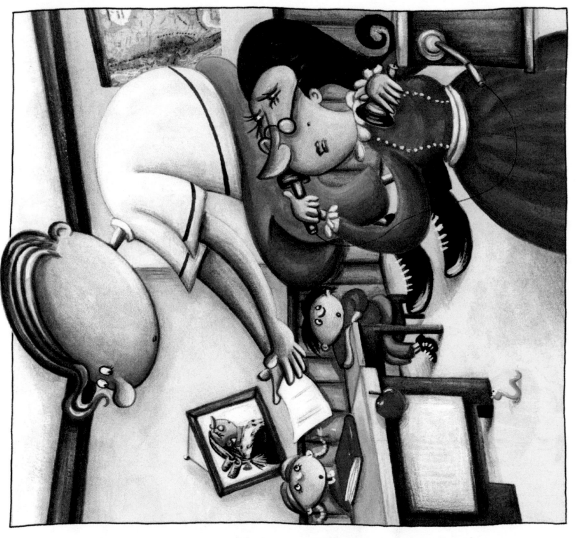

When Paul walked in, the floor would shake.
The teacher said, "For goodness' sake!
Paul's so big, this school's too small.
Soon he won't fit in here at all!"

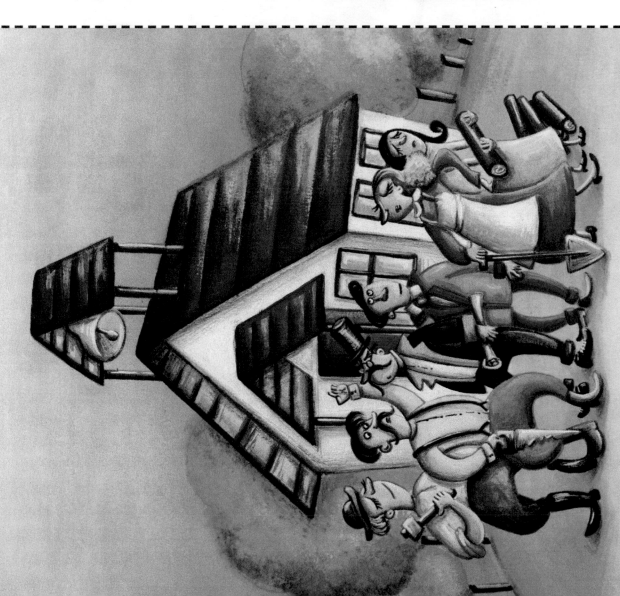

The school board met and they decided
A bigger school should be provided.
So everyone picked up a tool.
Together, the town built a new school.

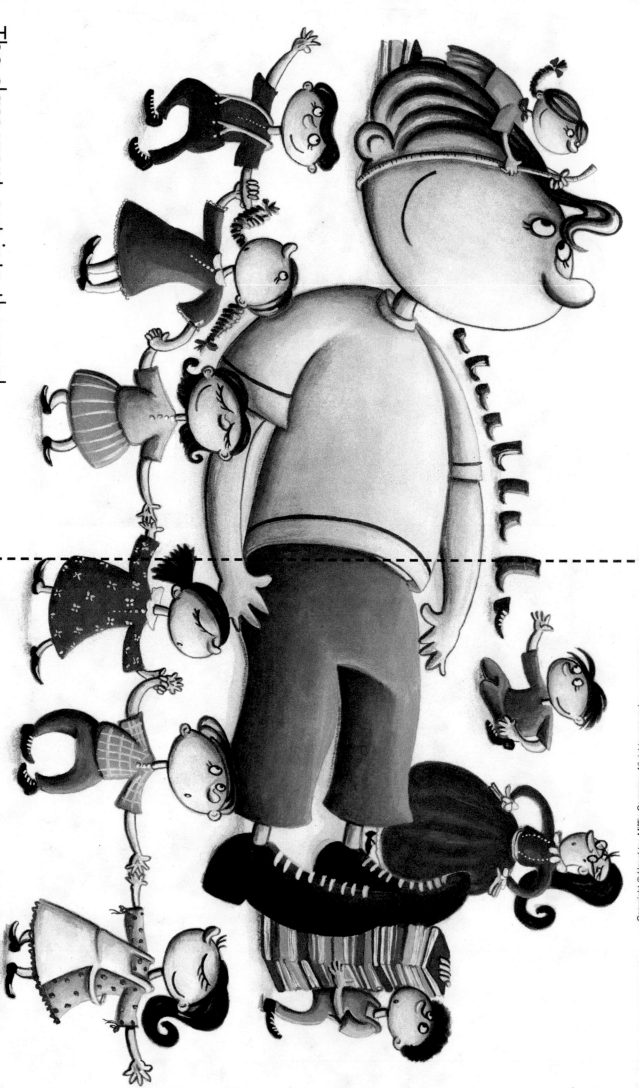

The class went out into the yard,
And measured Paul, though it was hard.
The teacher shouted, "My, my, Paul,
You are 22 feet tall!"

4

What things are the children using to measure Paul?

5

Vocabulary

Here are some vocabulary words you will learn in the chapter.

length The distance from one end to the other end of an object

longer, shorter Words that compare the length of two objects

longer

shorter

inch (in.), centimeter (cm) Units used to measure length

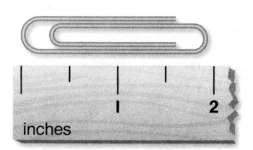

inches

This paper clip is about **2** inches long.

This eraser is about **4** centimeters long.

See English-Spanish Glossary pages 573–589.

KEY MG 1.3 Measure the length of an object to the nearest inch and/or centimeter. Also **MG 1.0, MG 1.1**

Education Place
Visit **www.eduplace.com/camap/** for the eGlossary and eGames.

three hundred forty-nine **349**

Name _____

 Check What You Know

1. Circle the shorter piece of rope.

2. Circle the longer piece of rope.

3. Circle the longest unit of measure.

4. About how many paper clips long is the pencil?

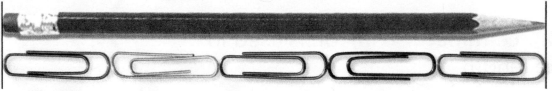

   about _____ paper clips

5. About how many inches long is the crayon?

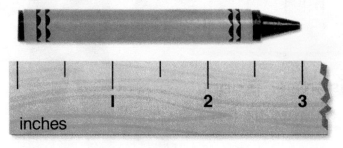

   about _____ inches

Use this page to review important skills needed for this chapter.

Chapter 18 Lesson 1

Nonstandard Units

 **Explore**

You can measure **length** by using your finger. How many fingers long is this pencil? How long is the crayon?

Objective
Measure the length of objects with nonstandard units.

Vocabulary
length

1.

about _____ 👆

2.

about _____ 👆

Measure the object with your finger.

3.

about _____ 👆

4.

about _____ 👆

5. **123** **Math Talk** How did you measure the objects on this page with your finger?

MG 1.1 Measure the length of objects by iterating (repeating) a nonstandard or standard unit. Also **MG 1.0, NS 6.1, MR 2.0, MR 2.1**

MR 1.2 Use tools, such as manipulatives or sketches, to model problems.

three hundred fifty-one **351**

Use your finger to measure.
Write about how many.

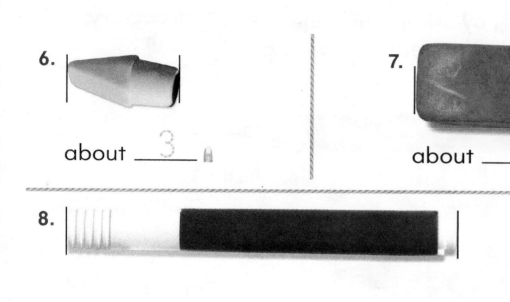

6. about ___3___ 🖑

7. about _____ 🖑

8. about _____ 🖑

9. about _____ 🖑

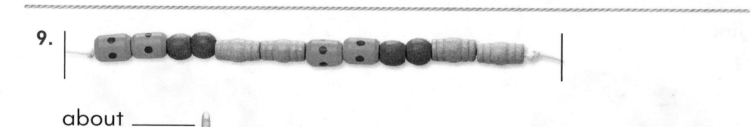

Work with a partner. Compare your measurements.

10. Are your measurements the same or different? Why do you think
this is so?

_____

_____

_____

🏠 **At Home** Measure 3 items with
something small, such as a dried bean
or a toothpick. Compare the measures.

En casa Mida 3 objetos con algo pequeño,
como un frijol o un palillo de dientes.
Compare las medidas.

Name _____

Chapter 18 Lesson 2

Compare Nonstandard Units

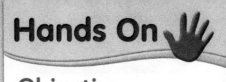

 **Learn**

You can use different units to measure the same object.

Use paper clips and your finger to measure each object. Start at one end and line up the units along the object. Count the units used.

The crayon is about ____3____ ⬭ long.

The crayon is about ____10____ 🖐 long.

Think!
Line up the units end to end.

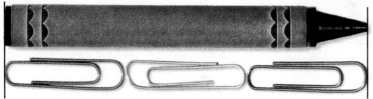 **Guided Practice**

Use ⬭ and your finger to measure the length.

1.

about _____ ⬭   about _____ 🖐

2.

about _____ ⬭   about _____ 🖐

3. **(123)** **Math Talk** Which is a longer unit of measure, a paper clip or a finger width? How do you know?

 MG 1.2 Use different units to measure the same object and predict whether the measure will be greater or smaller when a different unit is used. Also **MR 1.2, MG 1.0, MR 2.0, MR 1.0, MR 1.1**

MG 1.1 Measure the length of objects by iterating (repeating) a nonstandard or standard unit.

▶ Practice

Find the length of each real object.
Use  and your finger to
measure.

Object	Measurement
4. My Math	about _____ 🖇 about _____ 👆
5. (shoe)	about _____ 🖇 about _____ 👆
6. (eraser)	about _____ 🖇 about _____ 👆

> **Remember!**
> The smaller the unit of measure, the more of them you will need.

Problem Solving: Measurement Sense

7. Lily wants to measure the length of her classroom.
   Circle the best unit to use. Explain why.

   🖇

_____

_____

🏠 **At Home** Have your child measure the length of a room by counting the steps. You do the same. Have your child explain the difference in the measures.

En casa Pida a su niño que mida la longitud de una habitación contando los pasos. Haga usted lo mismo. Pida a su niño que explique la diferencia en las medidas.

Name _____

Inches

▶ **Learn**

You can estimate and measure length using **inches.** An **inch ruler** can help measure length in inches.

First estimate.
About how long is the acorn?

The acorn is about _____ inch long.

Line up the end of the object with the first mark on the left end of the ruler. Then measure.

The acorn is about _____ inch long.

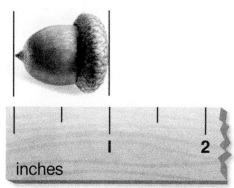

inches

▶ **Guided Practice**

Estimate. Then measure with a ruler.

Think!
My pinky finger is about 2 inches long. I can use it to estimate.

1.
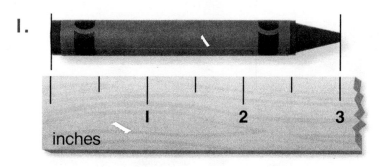
inches

Estimate: about _____ in.

Measure: about _____ in.

2.
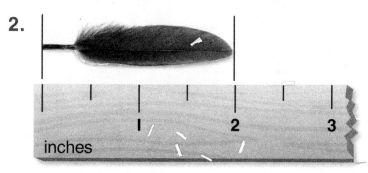
inches

Estimate: about _____ in.

Measure: about _____ in.

3. **(123) Math Talk** How do you know when your estimate is reasonable?

 KEY MG 1.3 Measure the length of an object to the nearest inch and/or centimeter. Also **MG 1.0, MR 1.2, MR 2.0**

NS 6.1 Recognize when an estimate is reasonable in measurements (e.g., closest inch).

Objective
Measure objects to the nearest inch.

Vocabulary
inch (in.)
inch ruler

Hands On 🖐

► Practice

Estimate.
Then measure with a ruler.

4.

Estimate: about _____ in.   Measure: about _____ in.

5.

Estimate: about _____ in.   Measure: about _____ in.

6.

Estimate: about _____ in.   Measure: about _____ in.

7. Circle the best measurement.

5 inches $4\frac{1}{2}$ inches   4 inches

Problem Solving: Reasoning

8. Lee estimates that his chalk is about 6 inches long. Is he correct? How do you know?

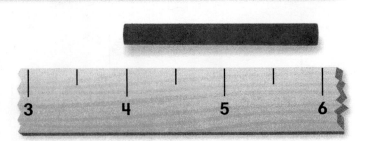

_____

_____

At Home Have your child estimate the length of three items, then measure each. Compare the measurements to the estimates.

En casa Pida a su niño que estime la longitud de tres objetos y que luego mida cada uno. Compare las medidas con las estimaciones.

Chapter 18 Lesson 4

Centimeters

 **Learn**

Centimeters are another way to measure length. You can use a **centimeter ruler** to measure length in centimeters.

Objective
Measure objects to the nearest centimeter.

Vocabulary
centimeter ruler
centimeter (cm)

First estimate.
About how long is the leaf?

A ones block is about 1 cm long.

The leaf is about _____ centimeters long.

Line up the end of the object with the first mark on the left end of the ruler. Then measure.

The leaf is about _____ centimeters long.

▶ **Guided Practice**

Estimate.
Then use a ruler to measure to the nearest centimeter.

Think!
My finger is about 1 centimeter wide. I can use it to estimate.

1.

A rope with a centimeter ruler showing marks 1 through 17.

Estimate: about _____ cm   Measure: about _____ cm

2. **(123) Math Talk** Is your math book more centimeters long or more inches long? Why?

KEY **MG 1.3** Measure the length of an object to the nearest inch and/or centimeter.
Also **MG 1.0, MG 1.1, MR 1.2, MG 1.2, MR 3.0**

NS 6.1 Recognize when an estimate is reasonable in measurements (e.g., closest inch).

three hundred fifty-seven **357**

Find the real object.
Estimate.
Then use a ruler to measure.

Remember!
You can round the length to the nearest centimeter.

	Object	Estimate	Measure
3.		about _____ cm	about _____ cm
4.		about _____ cm	about _____ cm
5.		about _____ cm	about _____ cm
6.		about _____ cm	about _____ cm
7.		about _____ cm about _____ in.	about _____ cm about _____ in.

Problem Solving: Measurement Sense

About how long is the real object?
Circle the better estimate.

8.

about **3** centimeters long

about **3** inches long

9.

about **45** centimeters long

about **45** inches long

At Home Help your child find and measure something at home that is about 10 centimeters (approximately 4 inches) long. Use a ruler to help.

En casa Ayude a su niño a encontrar y medir algo que mida aproximadamente 10 centímetros (4 pulgadas) de largo. Use una regla como ayuda.

Chapter 18 Lesson 5

Use Measurement

 **Learn**

You can use measurement to solve a problem.

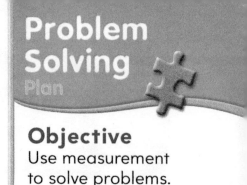

Objective
Use measurement
to solve problems.

Camila wants to add a piece of ribbon to her bookmark. She wants the total length to be 8 inches. How long should her ribbon be?

Understand
What do you know?

• The total length should be **8** inches.

Plan
What do you need
to measure?

• I need to measure the bookmark.

Will you add
or subtract?

• I can subtract to find the length
of the ribbon.

Solve
Measure.

length of bookmark: ___5___ inches

Subtract.

total length − length of bookmark
= length of ribbon

___8___ inches − ___5___ inches = ___3___ inches

The ribbon should be ___3___ inches long.

Look Back
Did you answer the question?
Does your answer make sense?

KEY MG 1.3 Measure the length of an object to
the nearest inch and/or centimeter.
Also **MG 1.0, MG 1.2, MR 2.2**

MR 2.0 Solve problems and justify reasoning.

Remember!
Understand
Plan
Solve
Look Back

Use measurement to solve.

1. Christina measures these hair clips to the nearest cm. How much longer is the pink clip than the blue clip?

Think!
What do I need to measure before I can subtract?

_____ cm − _____ cm = _____ cm

The pink clip is _____ cm longer than the blue clip.

2.  **Math Talk** How would your answers in Exercise 1 change if you measured in inches?

▶ **Problem Solving Practice**

3. Kevin measures these ribbons to the nearest centimeter. How much longer is the yellow ribbon than the blue ribbon?

_____ cm longer

4. Talar wants to add beads to her bracelet. She wants the total length to be 6 inches. How many inches should she add?

_____ inches

 At Home Ask your child to make up a word problem that uses measurement. Have your child solve the problem.

En casa Pida a su niño que invente un problema que requiera tomar medidas. Pídale que resuelva el problema.

Name _____

California Field Trip

At the Santa Monica Pier

You can learn about the ocean. You can touch sea stars and crabs in a tank. You can see sharks, rays, and eels. You can also take a walk on the sandy beach.

Science

Aquarium on the pier

Choose a way to solve. Show your work.

1. Rachel measures two pieces of seaweed to the nearest centimeter. One is 6 cm and the other is 4 cm. How much longer is the bigger piece?

   seaweed

   _____ cm longer

2. A sea cucumber is about as long as your hand. About how many inches long is a sea cucumber? Choose a reasonable answer.

   sea cucumber

   10 in.   4 in.   1 in.

3. One piece of kelp is 14 inches long. Another piece of kelp is 5 inches longer than the first. Lia put the pieces of kelp end-to-end to measure them. How long are the two pieces of kelp together?

   kelp

   _____ inches

KEY **NS 2.2** Find the sum or difference of two whole numbers up to three digits long. Also **NS 6.1, MG 1.0, MR 1.0, MR 1.1**

Problem Solving on Tests
Listening Skills

Listen to your teacher read the problem.
Choose the correct answer.

1. Beth buys a pencil that costs 73¢.
   She pays with a one-dollar bill.
   How much change does she get?

   17¢   27¢   73¢ $1.00
   ○   ○   ○   ○

   KEY NS 5.2

2. Round each number to the nearest ten.
   What is the best estimate?

   $$45 - 18 = \boxed{}$$

   10   20   30   40
   ○   ○   ○   ○

   NS 6.0

3.

   triangle   rectangle   hexagon   pentagon
   ○   ○   ○   ○

   KEY MG 2.1

4.
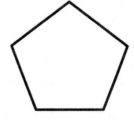

   $\dfrac{2}{3}$ $\dfrac{1}{2}$ $\dfrac{3}{4}$ $\dfrac{4}{4}$
   ○   ○   ○   ○

   KEY NS 4.1

MR 1.0 Make decisions about how to set up a problem.
MR 1.1 Determine the approach, materials, and
strategies to be used.

Education Place
Visit **www.eduplace.com/camap/** for
Test-Taking Tips and Extra Practice.

Key Standards Review

Write a fraction for each part.

1.

What fraction of the crayons are blue? _____

What fraction of the crayons are red? _____

2.

What fraction of the pets are cats? _____

What fraction of the pets are dogs? _____

3.

What fraction of the books are science books? _____

What fraction of the books are math books? _____

Challenge   Fractions

Reema made 10 muffins.

Her parents ate $\frac{1}{2}$ of the muffins.

Her brother ate $\frac{1}{5}$ of the muffins.

Her sister ate $\frac{1}{10}$ of the muffins.

How many are left for Reema?

_____ muffins

You can color the muffins to help you find how many muffins Reema's family ate.

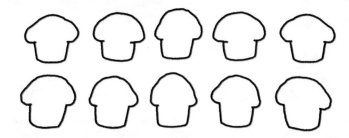

KEY NS 4.2 Recognize fractions of a whole and parts of a group (e.g., one-fourth of a pie, two-thirds of 15 balls). Also **KEY NS 4.1**

California Frogs and Toads

Frogs and toads have some differences that help them survive in their environments. Frogs live near or in the water and usually have smooth, wet skin. Toads live mostly on land and have rough, dry skin.

Measure in inches.

1. You can find the California Treefrog near desert and canyon streams. It uses its sticky tongue to catch food, such as bugs and spiders.

_____ in.

2. You can find the California Toad in woodlands and forests. Like the California Treefrog, it also uses its sticky tongue to catch food.

_____ in.

3. The toad is _____ inches longer than the frog.

KEY **MG 1.3** Measure the length of an object to the nearest inch and/or centimeter.
Also **MG 1.0, MR 1.2**
Science LS 2.c

Name _____

Concepts and Skills

Use ⬭ and your finger to measure. MG 1.2

1.

about _____ ✏

about _____ ⬭

2.

about _____ ✏

about _____ ⬭

Estimate. Then use a ruler to measure in inches. KEY MG 1.3

3.

Estimate: about _____ inches   Measure: _____ inches

Estimate. Then use a ruler to measure in centimeters. KEY MG 1.3

4.

Estimate: about _____ cm   Measure: _____ cm

Problem Solving KEY MG 1.3, MG 1.0

Use your ruler.

5. How many centimeters longer
is the marker than the crayon?

_____ centimeters

Spiral Review and Test Practice

1. What is the sum?

$$\begin{array}{r} 56 \\ 23 \\ +\ 6 \\ \hline \end{array}$$

   29   75   79   85

○   ○   ○   ○

KEY **AF 1.1**, AF 1.0, NS 2.0 Page 197

---

2. Which solid shape has no faces?

○   ○   ○   ○

KEY **MG 2.1** Page 293

---

3. Which fraction does the shaded part show?

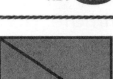

  $\dfrac{1}{4}$ $\dfrac{2}{4}$ $\dfrac{3}{4}$ $\dfrac{4}{2}$

○   ○   ○   ○

KEY **NS 4.3**, KEY **NS 4.2**, NS 4.0 Page 317

---

4. What is $\dfrac{2}{5}$ of 10?

   1   4   5   10

○   ○   ○   ○

KEY **NS 4.2**, NS 4.0 Page 333

Education Place
Visit **www.eduplace.com/camap/** for
Test-Taking Tips and Extra Practice.

Spiral Review

Time and Calendar

Vocabulary

Here are some vocabulary words you will learn in the chapter.

second A small unit of time
It takes about one second to raise your hand.

minute A unit of time that equals **60** seconds

hour A unit of time equal to **60** minutes

quarter hour A unit of time equal to **15** minutes

half-hour A unit of time equal to **30** minutes

calendar A table that shows a year as days, weeks, and months

Sunday	Monday	Tuesday	Wednesday	Thursday	Friday	Saturday
			1	2	3	4
5	6	7	8	9	10	11
12	13	14	15	16	17	18
19	20	21	22	23	24	25
26	27	28	29	30	31	

week — [

day — (12)

month —

See English-Spanish Glossary pages 573–589.

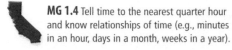

MG 1.4 Tell time to the nearest quarter hour and know relationships of time (e.g., minutes in an hour, days in a month, weeks in a year).

Education Place
Visit **www.eduplace.com/camap/** for the eGlossary and eGames.

Name _____

 # Check What You Know

1. Circle the activity that takes longer.

2. Circle the digital clock that matches.

$$12{:}00 \qquad 4{:}00 \qquad 5{:}00$$

3. Count by 5s. Start with **30.**

30, _____, _____, _____, _____, _____, _____

Use the calendar.

4. How many days are in the month of May?

29   30   31

5. What day of the week is May 20th?

Monday   Friday   Sunday

May						
Sunday	Monday	Tuesday	Wednesday	Thursday	Friday	Saturday
			1	2	3	4
5	6	7	8	9	10	11
12	13	14	15	16	17	18
19	20	21	22	23	24	25
26	27	28	29	30	31	

Use this page to review important skills needed for this chapter.

368

Chapter 19 Lesson 1

Make a Clock and Show Time to the Hour

▶ **Explore**

There are 60 **seconds** in one **minute**.
There are 60 minutes in one **hour**.
The **hour hand** on a clock points to
the hour. The **minute hand** points to
the minutes past the hour.

In one hour, the
minute hand moves
all the way around
the clock.

1. Write the hours inside the
   clock below. Count by 1s.

2. Write the minutes outside the
   clock. Skip count by 5s.

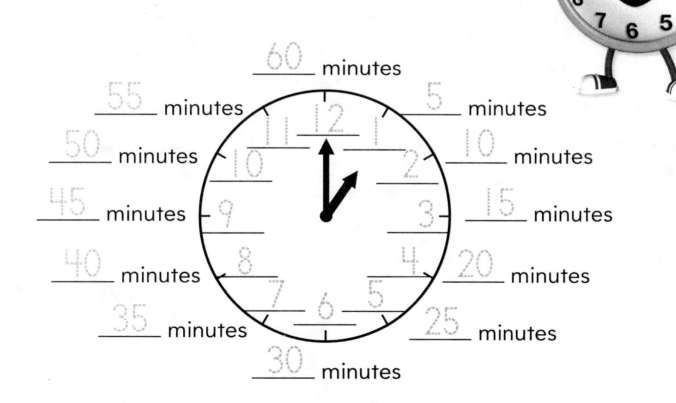

3. **123** **Math Talk** Where would the hour hand point
   at 5:00? How do you know?

MG 1.4 Tell time to the nearest quarter hour and
know relationships of time (e.g., minutes in an hour,
days in a month, weeks in a year).
Also MG 1.0, MR 1.2, MR 2.0

At each hour, the minute hand points to the 12.

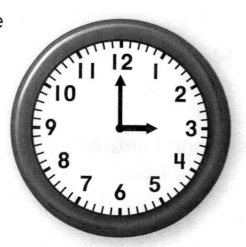

Read three o'clock.

Draw the hands on the clock to show the time.
Then write the time in the digital clock.

4. six o'clock

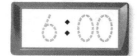

5. eight o'clock

6. four o'clock

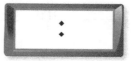

7. seven o'clock

8. nine o'clock

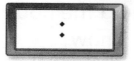

9. eleven o'clock

At Home Point to the numbers on a clock. Ask your child to name the hours as you point to each number.

En casa Señale a los números en un reloj. Pida a su niño que nombre las horas mientras usted señala cada número.

Time Before and After the Hour

▶ **Learn**

Time After the Hour

30 minutes after 2

hour ⟶ 2 : 30 ⟵ minutes after the hour

Time Before the Hour

30 minutes before 3 is how many minutes after 2?

_30_ minutes after 2

▶ **Guided Practice**

Draw the minute hand to show the time.
Write the time.

1. 30 minutes before 6

: ___

Think!
I start at the 12.
Then I count back 5, 10, 15, 20, 25, 30.

2. 30 minutes before 2

: ___

3. 30 minutes after 8

: ___

4. **123** **Math Talk** Why do you think 2:30 is sometimes called **half past** 2?

MG 1.4 Tell time to the nearest quarter hour and know relationships of time (e.g., minutes in an hour, days in a month, weeks in a year).
Also **MG 1.0, MR 2.0**

► **Practice**

Draw the hands on the clock.
Write the time.

5. five o'clock

5 : 00

6. 30 minutes
after 5

____ : ____

7. 30 minutes
after 10

____ : ____

8. 30 minutes
before 8

____ : ____

9. one o'clock

____ : ____

10. 30 minutes
before 1

____ : ____

11. four o'clock

____ : ____

12. 30 minutes
after 3

____ : ____

13. 30 minutes
after 9

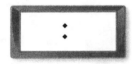

14. 30 minutes
before 2

15. twelve o'clock

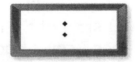

16. 30 minutes
after 6

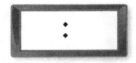

Problem Solving: Reasoning

17. Sometimes people estimate
time and use the word *about*.
Estimate these times to the
nearest hour. Then draw a
line to match.

about
6:00

about
7:00

about
5:00

Copyright © Houghton Mifflin Company. All rights reserved.

Time to 15 Minutes

 **Learn**

There are 15 minutes in a **quarter hour.**

   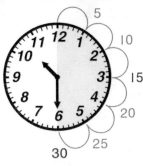   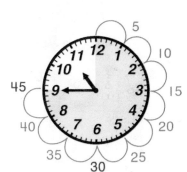

15 minutes after 10   30 minutes after 10   45 minutes after 10

10:15   10:30   10:45

quarter past ten   half past ten   quarter to eleven

In a quarter hour, the minute hand moves around one-fourth of the clock.

▶ **Guided Practice**

Write the time.

1.

Think!
I can tell the minute hand is one quarter of the way around the clock.

____ : ____

2.

____ : ____

3.

____ : ____

4. **(123)** **Math Talk** How many quarter hours are in 1 hour? Tell or show how you know.

MG 1.4 Tell time to the nearest quarter hour and know relationships of time (e.g., minutes in an hour, days in a month, weeks in a year).
Also **MG 1.0, MR 2.0**

three hundred seventy-three **373**

▶ Practice

Draw the hour and minute hands to show the time. Write the time.

5. half past 11

11:30

6. quarter past 1

____:____

7. quarter to 3

____:____

8. quarter past 8

____:____

9. quarter past 5

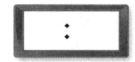

10. quarter to 4

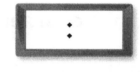

11. half past 7

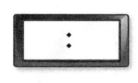

12. quarter to 10

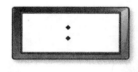

Reading Math: Vocabulary

Draw a line to the word that completes the sentence.

13. An _____ is 60 minutes.

14. There are 15 minutes in a _____.

quarter hour

hour

At Home Discuss things you do every day that take about 15 minutes, such as making lunch.

En casa Hable de las cosas que usted hace todos los días que toman más o menos 15 minutos, como preparar el almuerzo.

Name _____

Elapsed Time

 **Learn**

Objective
Determine how much time has passed.

Vocabulary
A.M.
P.M.

You can count on a clock to find elapsed time.

School supplies are on sale from 11:00 A.M. to 2:00 P.M. How long does the sale last?

P.M. is used for the time from 12 noon to 12 midnight.

A.M. is used for the time from 12 midnight to 12 noon.

Step 1

Begin at the start time.

11:00 A.M.

Step 2

Count on to the end time.

2:00 P.M.

The sale lasts for ___3___ hours.

 Guided Practice

Think!
4:00 to 5:00 is 1 hour. 5:00 to 6:00 is another hour.

Write the times. Then write how much time has passed.

1.

Start   End

_____ P.M.   _____ P.M.

_____ hours passed.

2.

Start   End

_____ A.M.   _____ A.M.

_____ hours passed.

3.  **Math Talk** How much time passes from 8:00 A.M. to 8:00 P.M.?

 MG 1.5 Determine the duration of intervals of time in hours (e.g., 11:00 A.M. to 4:00 P.M.).
Also **MG 1.4, MG 1.0, MR 2.0**

three hundred seventy-five **375**

Write the times.
Then write how much
time has passed.

Remember!
Begin counting at
the start time.

	On Sale	Start Time	End Time	How long does the sale last?
4.		8:00 A.M.	9:00 A.M.	_____ hour
5.	FRESH FRUIT	_____ A.M.	_____ P.M.	_____ hours
6.		_____ A.M.	_____ P.M.	_____ hours

Problem Solving: Reasoning

7. Rianna starts class at **8** A.M. She eats
   lunch from 12:00 P.M. to 1 P.M.
   Then she has more classes until
   3 P.M. How many total hours does
   Rianna spend in class?

   _____ hours

Draw or write to explain.

 At Home Have your child write the
times he or she eats dinner and goes
to sleep. Discuss how many hours
pass between those times.

En casa Pida a su niño que escriba la hora a
la que cena y a la que va a la cama. Comente
cuánto tiempo trascurre entre esas horas.

Name _____

Calendar

▶ **Learn**

A **calendar** shows **days**, **weeks**, and **months** in a **year**. This calendar shows one month.

April

Sunday	Monday	Tuesday	Wednesday	Thursday	Friday	Saturday
			1	2	3	4
5	6	7	8	9	10	11
12	13	14	15	16	17	18
19	20	21	22	23	24	25
26	27	28	29	30		

Objective
Understand information in a calendar and relationships of time.

Vocabulary
calendar
day
week
month
year

Think!
I need to find April 5 on the calendar and see which day of the week it is.

▶ **Guided Practice**

Use the calendar to answer the questions.

1. What day of the week is April 5? _____

2. What is the date of the first Monday? _____

3. On what day of the week will the next month begin? _____

4. What is the date of the third Tuesday? _____

5. How many months are in a year? _____

6. **123** **Math Talk** Is 2 weeks longer than 15 days? How do you know?

 MG 1.4 Tell time to the nearest quarter hour and know relationships of time (e.g., minutes in an hour, days in a month, weeks in a year).
Also **MG 1.0, MR 2.0**

three hundred seventy-seven **377**

SUN	MON	TUES	WED	THURS	FRI	SAT
1	2	3	4	5	6	7
8	9	10	11	12	13	14

24 hours = 1 day
7 days = 1 week
about 52 weeks = 1 year
12 months = 1 year

Circle the longer amount of time.

7. (2 weeks)   10 days

8. 30 hours   1 day

9. 1 year   6 months

10. 45 weeks   1 year

Circle the shorter amount of time.

11. 1 week   10 days

12. 15 hours   1 day

13. 2 hours   60 minutes

14. 1 year   57 weeks

Reading Math: Vocabulary

Use the words in the box. Write the best estimate for the length of the activity.

hours   days   weeks   months

15. Swimming

_____

16. Camping trip

_____

At Home Have your child explain which is longer, 10 days or 2 weeks. Repeat with similar examples.

En casa Pida a su niño que explique qué dura más: 10 días ó 2 semanas. Repita con ejemplos similares.

Use a Table

Objective
Use a table to solve problems.

▶ **Learn**

Every Monday, Lisa helps out at an animal shelter. How long does it take her to walk the dogs?

Understand

Circle what you need to find.

What time does Lisa start walking the dogs?

(How long does it take Lisa to walk the dogs?)

Plan

Find information in the table.

Dog walking starts at __4:00__.

Dog walking ends at __6:00__.

Helper's Activities

Activity	Start Time	End Time
Feed Cats	3:30	4:00
Walk Dogs	4:00	6:00
Sweep Floors	6:00	7:00

Think!
I have to find out how much time passes between 4:00 and 6:00.

Solve

Find how long the activity lasts.

Dog walking lasts __2__ hours.

Look Back

Did you answer the question?
Does your answer make sense?

MG 1.5 Determine the duration of intervals of time in hours (e.g., 11:00 A.M. to 4:00 P.M.).
Also **MG 1.4, MG 1.0, SDAP 1.4, MR 2.0, MR 2.2**

Remember!
Understand
Plan
Solve
Look Back

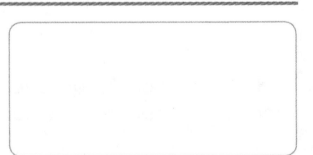

Use the table and a clock to help you solve.

1. Dana leaves for the library at 8:00. She arrives on time to start work. How long does it take her to get there?

   Circle the information you need in the table.

   Dana leaves for the library at _____.

   Dana's help time starts at _____.

   It takes Dana _____ hour to get to the library.

Library Helpers		
Helper	Start Time	End Time
Dana	9:00	10:00
Phillip	9:00	10:00
Marco	10:00	12:00
Elena	11:00	12:00

2. (123) **Math Talk** How did you use the table to solve the problem?

Use the table to solve.

Draw or write to explain.

3. How long does Philip help at the library?

   _____ hour

4. Marco returns books to shelves during his help time. How long does Marco return books to shelves?

   _____ hours

At Home Have your child tell how much time passes between 4:00 and 5:30.

En casa Pida a su niño que le diga cuánto tiempo pasa entre las 4:00 y las 5:30.

Name _____

Create and Solve

Problem Solving

Objective
Write problems and use strategies to solve them.

The clocks show some of Daniela's activities on Saturday.

Morning	Afternoon	Evening	Night
start time end time	start time end time	start time end time	start time end time
eat breakfast	ride bike	read a book	sleep

1. How much time does Daniela spend eating breakfast?

   Daniela spends _____ minutes eating breakfast.

2. Write a problem about Daniela's activities. Use the clocks above.

   _____

   _____

   _____

   _____

3. Solve your problem.

   _____

   Share your time problem with a classmate.

MG 1.5 Determine the duration of intervals of time in hours (e.g., 11:00 A.M. to 4:00 P.M.).
Also **MG 1.4, MG 1.0, MR 1.0, MR 1.1**

three hundred eighty-one **381**

The calendar shows the month of September.

September

Sunday	Monday	Tuesday	Wednesday	Thursday	Friday	Saturday
	1	2	3	4	5	6
7	8	9	10	11	12	13
14	15	16	17	18	19	20
21	22	23	24	25	26	27
28	29	30				

4. Mrs. Tang leaves on a trip on September 12.
   She comes back on September 18.
   How many days does Mrs. Tang's trip last?

   Mrs. Tang's trip lasts _____ days.

5. Write a problem about the calendar above.

   _____

   _____

   _____

   _____

6. Solve your problem.

   _____

   Share your calendar problem with a classmate.

Key Standards Review

Measure to the nearest centimeter.

1.

about _____ cm

2.

about _____ cm

3.

about _____ cm

Challenge   Measurement

Measure each line path in inches.

Path A   Path B

1. How many inches long is Path A? _____ inches

2. How many inches long is Path B? _____ inches

3. Which path is longer? _____

How much longer? _____

KEY MG 1.3 Measure the length of an object to the nearest inch and/or centimeter.

three hundred eighty-three **383**

Math Music

Show and Tell

Math Music, Track 7
Tune: "I've Been Working on the Railroad"

My cat, Fluffy, has a long tail—
Longer than this string.
Ben's cat, Pepper, has a short tail.
She's a tiny little thing.
Look at Carla's collie, Lucky—
His tail's the longest of all three.
Look at Lucky's tail. It's wagging.
Don't you all agree?

Pepper's tail is short. Fluffy's tail is long—
Longer than this string, you see, you see.
Lucky's tail is long. Lucky's tail is long—
The longest tail of all three!

384

MG 1.0 Understand that measurement is accomplished
by identifying a unit of measure, iterating (repeating)
that unit, and comparing it to the item to be measured.

Name _____

Concepts and Skills

Draw the hands on the clock to show the time.
Then write the time in the digital clock. MG 1.4

1. 15 minutes after 4

2. quarter to 6

Write the times.
Then write how much time has passed. MG 1.5

3.

_____ A.M.   _____ P.M.   _____ hours

Problem Solving   MG 1.5, MR 2.0

Use the table.

4. How long will the class be reading?

_____

5. How do you know?

_____

_____

Today's Schedule	
Reading	9:00
Writing	11:00
Math	12:00

1. Which set shows the fewest coins with this value?

 75¢

○   ○   ○   ○

KEY **NS 5.1**, NS 5.0 Page 125

2. What shape is the blue face?

square   triangle   rectangle   circle

○   ○   ○   ○

KEY **MG 2.1** Page 295

3. What fraction does the shaded part show?

$\frac{1}{5}$ $\frac{1}{7}$ $\frac{1}{8}$ $\frac{1}{9}$

○   ○   ○   ○

KEY **NS 4.1**, NS 4.0 Page 311

4. Which clock shows **30** minutes before 5?

○   ○   ○   ○

MG 1.4, MG 1.0 Page 371

Education Place
Visit www.eduplace.com/camap/ for
Test-Taking Tips and Extra Practice.

Greg Tang's  **Go Fast, Go Far**

Unit 7 Mental Math Strategies

Look for Tens

Don't just add them left to right.
Thinking tens is really bright!

I make tens to add $12 + 17 + 18$. I start with $12 + 18 = 30$ and then I add 17 to make 47. Numbers can be added in any order!

1. $12 + 17 + 18 =$ ☐ 47

  ☐ 30 $+$ ☐ 17 $=$ ☐ 47

2. $31 + 16 + 39 =$ ☐

  ☐ 70 $+$ ☐ $=$ ☐

3. $53 + 18 + 27 =$ ☐

  ☐ $+$ ☐ $=$ ☐

4. $13 + 16 + 17 =$ ☐

  ☐ $+$ ☐ $=$ ☐

5. $25 + 38 + 22 =$ ☐

  ☐ $+$ ☐ $=$ ☐

Take It Further: Now try doing all the steps in your head!

Doing Great!

6. $23 + 37 + 24 =$ ☐

7. $37 + 26 + 34 =$ ☐

Reading and Writing Math

Show what you know about measuring length, telling time, and reading a calendar. Write each vocabulary word in the section of the circle where it belongs.

Word Bank
centimeters
days
hour hand
inches
minute
months
quarter hour
ruler
second
weeks
year

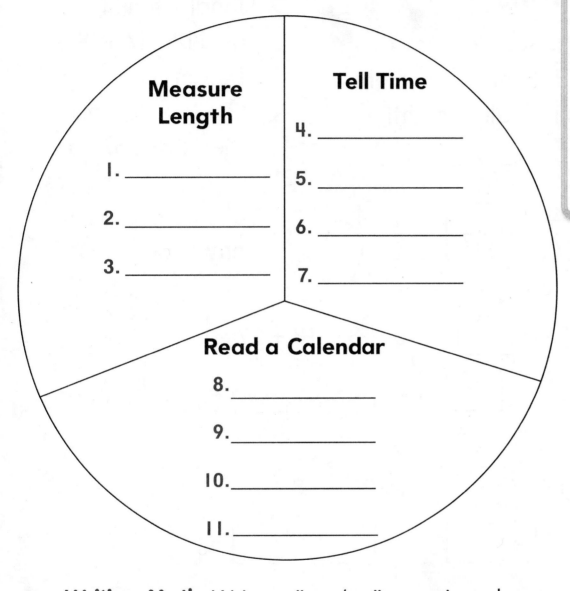

Measure Length

1. _____

2. _____

3. _____

Tell Time

4. _____

5. _____

6. _____

7. _____

Read a Calendar

8. _____

9. _____

10. _____

11. _____

12. **Writing Math** Write a "yes/no" question about one of the vocabulary words. For example, "Is 15 minutes a quarter hour? Yes or no?" Ask a classmate to answer the question.

_____

_____

MG 1.0 Understand that measurement is accomplished by identifying a unit of measure, iterating (repeating) that unit, and comparing it to the item to be measured. Also **MG 1.4**

Name _____

Concepts and Skills

Use  and your finger to measure. MG 1.2

1. about _____ 📏

   about _____

2. about _____ 📏

   about _____

Estimate. Then use a ruler to measure in inches. KEY MG 1.3

3.

Estimate: about _____ inches   Measure: _____ inches

4.

Estimate: about _____ inches   Measure: _____ inches

Estimate. Then use a ruler to measure in centimeters. KEY MG 1.3

5.

Estimate: about _____ cm   Measure: _____ cm

Draw the hands on the clock to show the time.
Write the time. MG 1.4

6. 15 minutes before 7

_____

7. 15 minutes after 10

_____

8. 30 minutes before 3

_____

9. 15 minutes before 11

_____

Draw the hands on the clock to show the time.
Then write the time in the digital clock. MG 1.4

10. quarter past 6

11. half past noon

Answer the question. MG 1.4

12. How many hours are there in a day? _____

Problem Solving

Use the schedule at the right. MG 1.5

13. How much time is there between the end of the sequoia tour and the start of the beach tour?

_____

Park Tours		
	Start of Tour	**End of Tour**
Sequoia	9:00	10:00
Beach	12:00	1:00

☐☐☐|||||||||

Unit

8

Multiplication and Division

BIG IDEAS!

- When you multiply, you join equal groups.

- When you divide, you separate equal groups.

- When you divide, there are sometimes remainders that do not make an equal group.

Songs and Games

Math Music Track 8
Groups of Bugs
eGames
www.eduplace.com/camap/

Literature

Read Aloud Big Book
- Amanda Bean's Amazing Dream

Math Readers

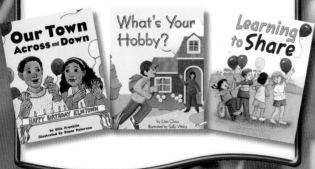

Get Ready Game

Multiplication Toss

How to Play

1. Put counters on Start.
2. Take turns spinning the spinner. Count on by 2s that many times.
3. The first player to reach the end of the game board wins.

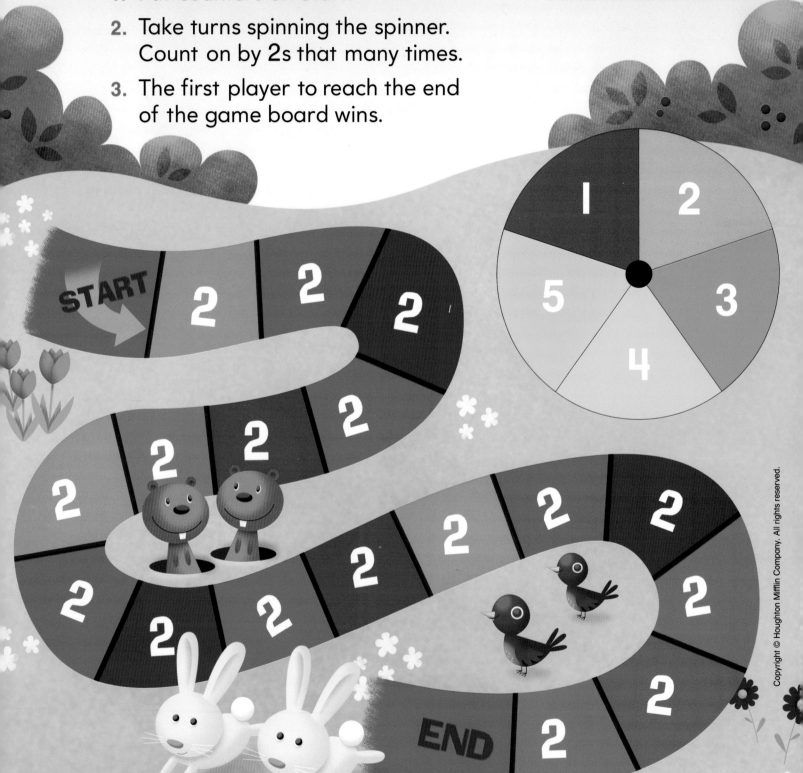

KEY NS 3.1 Use repeated addition, arrays, and counting by multiples to do multiplication.
Also **KEY NS 3.0** , **KEY NS 3.3** , MR 1.2

Education Place
Visit **www.eduplace.com/camap/** for eGames and Brain Teasers.

Math at Home

Dear Family,

My class is starting Unit 8, **Multiplication and Division.** I will be learning how to use arrays, tables, and skip counting to multiply. I will also learn how to use equal groups and repeated subtraction to divide. You can help me learn these vocabulary words, and we can do the Math Activity together.

From,

_____

Vocabulary

equal groups Groups with the same amount

The grapes are in 4 equal groups of 6.

multiply Join equal groups and find the total number

product The result of multiplication

$$3 \times 2 = 6 \longleftarrow \text{product}$$

divide Separate a group of items into smaller equal groups

remainder The number left over in a division problem

$$15 \div 2 = 7 \text{ remainder } 1$$

Education Place
Visit **www.eduplace.com/camaf/** for
- eGames and Brain Teasers
- Math at Home in other languages

Family Math Activity

Collect some objects at home, such as pairs of socks or shoes. Ask your child to set them out in equal groups. Then, skip count together and multiply to find the total amount.

Literature

These books link to the math in this unit. Look for them at the library.

- **Amanda Bean's Amazing Dream**
  by Cindy Neuschwander
  Illustrated by Liza Woodruff
  Math Activities by
  Marilyn Burns
  (*Scholastic*, 1998)

- **The Doorbell Rang**
  by Pat Hutchins

- **A Remainder of One**
  by Elinor J. Pinczes
  Illustrated by Bonnie MacKain

Matemáticas en casa

Estimada familia:

Mi clase está comenzando la Unidad 8, **La multiplicación y la división.** Aprenderé a usar matrices y tablas, y a contar salteado para multiplicar. También aprenderé a usar grupos iguales y resta repetida para dividir. Me pueden ayudar a aprender estas palabras de vocabulario y podemos hacer juntos la Actividad de matemáticas para la familia.

De:

_____

Vocabulario

grupos iguales Grupos que tienen la misma cantidad.

Las uvas están en 4 grupos iguales de 6.

multiplicar Unir grupos iguales y hallar el número total.

producto El resultado de la multiplicación.

$3 \times 2 = 6$ ← producto

dividir Separar un grupo de objetos en grupos iguales más pequeños.

residuo Número que sobra en un problema de división.

$15 \div 2 = 7$ residuo 1

Education Place
Visite **www.eduplace.com/camaf/** para
• Juegos en línea y acertijos
• Matemáticas en casa en otros idiomas

Actividad de matemáticas para la familia

Reúnan algunos objetos en casa, como pares de calcetines o zapatos. Pida a su niño que los organice en grupos iguales. Decidan cuán grande es cada grupo. Luego cuenten salteado juntos y multipliquen para hallar la cantidad total.

Literatura

Estos libros hablan sobre las matemáticas de esta unidad. Búscalos en la biblioteca.

• **Tú puedes dividir**
  por Danielle Carroll
  (*Yellow Umbrella Books*, 2006)

• **¡Todos ganan!**
  por Sheila Bruce

• **Duplicar y Multiplicar**
  por Richard Leffingwell

Flowers for Gram

written by Elvira Tippin

This Take-Home Book belongs to

_____

Reading and Writing Math

This take-home book will help you review equal groups.

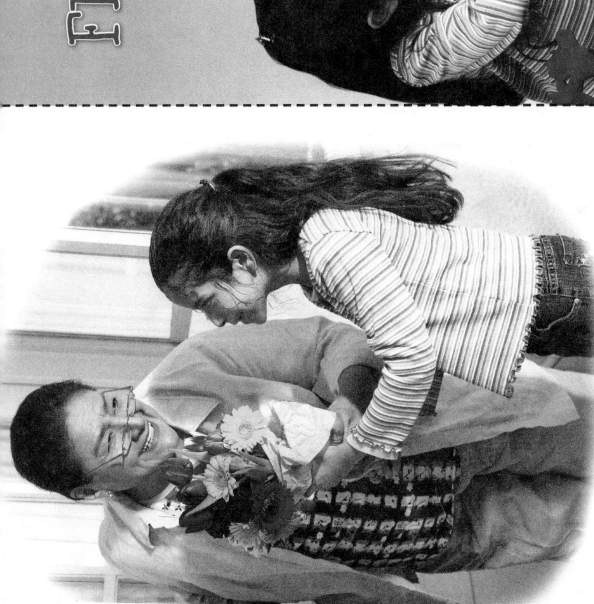

I'll sing "Happy Birthday," then give her a hug.

Oh, my Gram's the best one in town!

KEY NS3.1 Use repeated addition, arrays, and counting by multiples to do multiplication.

8

Today is Gram's birthday, I'll buy her a gift.
Today my Gram turns 82.
Since she loves flowers, all colors, all kinds,
I've decided to give her a few!

2

Won't Gram be surprised when
she opens her door
And sees all the flowers I found?

7

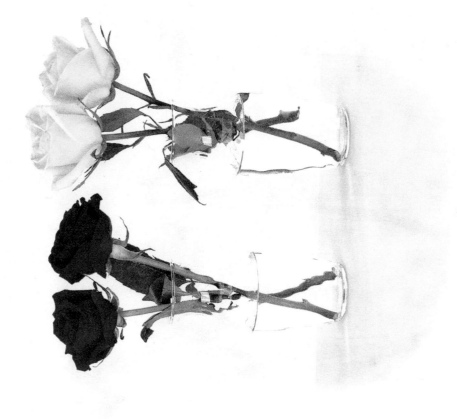

☐ + ☐ + ☐ = ☐

I'll start with some roses because they
smell nice, 2 yellow, 2 pink and 2 red.
But 3 sets of 2 just might be too many.
I'll buy her just 4 roses instead.

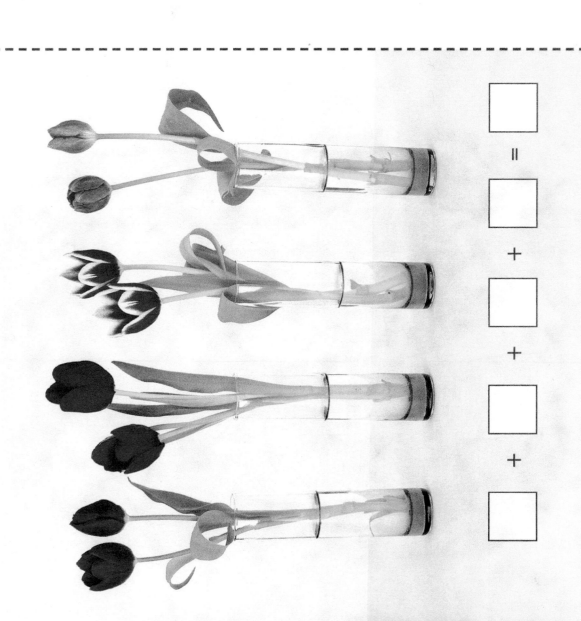

☐ + ☐ + ☐ + ☐ = ☐

Gram also loves tulips, especially pink.
I will get 4 sets of 2!
Roses with daisies and tulips, how nice!
But I think that's plenty, don't you?

Oh, how about some daisies?
Should I buy 3, 6 or 9?

☐ + ☐ + ☐ = ☐

Roses and daisies, all placed in a vase
Will look perfectly fine!

Multiplication

Vocabulary

Here are some vocabulary words you will learn in the chapter.

equal groups Numbers or objects with the same amount in each group

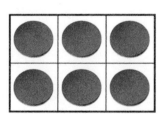

3 equal groups of 4 flowers

multiply Join equal groups to find how many in all

array A way to show objects in equal rows to multiply

 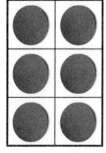

2 rows of 3 = 6 in all   3 rows of 2 = 6 in all

If you turn the array, you get the same total number.

See English-Spanish Glossary pages 573–589.

 **KEY NS 3.1** Use repeated addition, arrays, and counting by multiples to do multiplication.
Also **KEY NS 3.0**

 **Education Place**
Visit **www.eduplace.com/camap/**
for the eGlossary and eGames.

Name _____

 Check What You Know

Follow the pattern.
Write the missing numbers.

1. 2, 4, 6, _____, _____,

   12, 14, _____, _____, 20

2. 45, 50, 55, _____, 65, _____, _____,

   _____, 85, _____, 95, _____

3. How many flowers are in each group?

   _____

4. How many groups are there?

   _____

5. How many flowers are there in all?

   _____

Use this page to review important skills needed for this chapter.

394 □□□||||||||||○○○○

Name _____

Equal Groups

Hands On

Objective
Relate equal groups, repeated addition, and skip counting to multiplication.

Vocabulary
equal groups

 **Learn**

When all groups have the same number they are **equal groups.**

Ayita is putting 2 plants on each step up to her porch. She has 4 steps. How many plants does she need?

There are 4 equal groups. There are 2 in each group. Add to find how many in all.

  __2__ + __2__ + __2__ + __2__ = __8__

Ayita needs __8__ plants.

▶ **Guided Practice**

Use ⬭ .
Make equal groups.
Complete the addition sentence.

Think!
I can skip count by 3s:
3, 6, 9, 12.

	Number of Equal Groups	Number in Each Group	How Many in All?
1.	4	3	_____ + _____ + _____ + _____ = _____
2.	2	5	_____ + _____ = _____
3.	3	4	_____ + _____ + _____ = _____

4.  **Math Talk** How can you use addition to find 5 groups of 4?

KEY NS 3.1 Use repeated addition, arrays, and counting by multiples to do multiplication.
Also **KEY NS 3.0**

MR 1.2 Use tools, such as manipulatives or sketches, to model problems.

► **Practice**

Use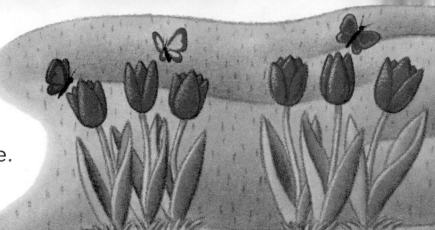
Make equal groups.
Complete the addition sentence.

	Number of Equal Groups	Number in Each Group	How Many in All?
5.	2	3	_3_ + _3_ = _6_
6.	3	5	____ + ____ + ____ = ____
7.	4	4	____ + ____ + ____ + ____ = ____
8.	4	5	____ + ____ + ____ + ____ = ____
9.	5	7	____ + ____ + ____ + ____ + ____ = ____

Problem Solving: Number Sense

Use the number line to skip count or add equal groups. Write the answer.

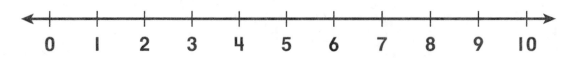

10. There are 3 flower pots. There are 2 flowers in each flower pot. How many flowers are there in all?

_____ flowers

11. There are 2 plants. There are 4 leaves on each plant. How many leaves are there in all?

_____ leaves

At Home Use dry cereal or pasta to make equal groups of 5. Ask your child to find the total number of items.

En casa Use cereal o pasta para formar grupos iguales de 5. Pida a su niño que halle el número total de objetos.

Chapter 20 Lesson 2

Arrays

 **Learn**

An **array** shows objects in equal rows.
You can use arrays to help you **multiply.**

You can use an array to find the total
number of stickers. When you multiply,
the total is called the **product.**

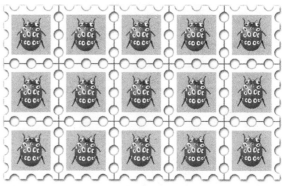

3   ×   5   =   15
↑   ↑   ↑

rows   number in   product
          each row

If you turn the array of stickers, the
total number of stickers does not
change. The order of the numbers in
the multiplication sentence changes,
but the product stays the same.

5   ×   3   =   15
↑   ↑   ↑

rows   stickers in   total
          each row   stickers

▶ **Guided Practice**

Draw the array two ways.
Write the multiplication sentences.

1. 4 rows of 1

Think!
If I turn the array,
the number of rows
changes, but the
product is still the
same.

1 row of 4

_____ × _____ = _____

_____ × _____ = _____

2. 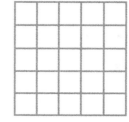 **Math Talk** In Exercise 1, how are the arrays different?
How are they the same?

 **KEY NS 3.1** Use repeated addition, arrays, and
counting by multiples to do multiplication.
Also **KEY NS 3.3**, **KEY AF 1.1**, **MR 2.0**

KEY NS 3.0 Model and solve simple problems
involving multiplication and division.

Show each array two ways.
Write the multiplication sentences.

3. 2 rows of 3

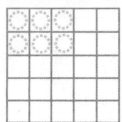

_2_ × _3_ = _6_

3 rows of 2

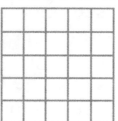

_____ × _____ = _____

4. 4 rows of 5

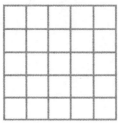

_____ × _____ = _____

5 rows of 4

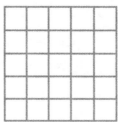

_____ × _____ = _____

5. 5 rows of 2

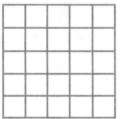

_____ × _____ = _____

2 rows of 5

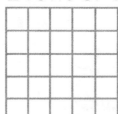

_____ × _____ = _____

Algebra Readiness: Number Sentences

6. There are five benches in a park.
There are three people sitting on
each bench. How many people are
on all five benches?

Draw or write to explain.

There are _____ people in all.

At Home Have your child solve
multiplication problems such as 4 x 2
and 2 x 4. Ask him or her to explain
why the product is the same.

En casa Pida a su niño que resuelva
problemas de multiplicación como 4 x 2 y 2 x
4. Pídale que explique por qué el producto es
el mismo.

Name _____

Chapter 20 Lesson 3

Skip Counting to Multiply

Hands On

Objective
Use skip counting to multiply equal groups.

▶ Learn

There are 10 cubes in each cube train.
How many cubes are in 5 trains?

$5 \times 10 = \underline{50}$

<u>10</u>, <u>20</u>, <u>30</u>, <u>40</u>, <u>50</u>   There are <u>50</u> cubes in 5 trains.

▶ Guided Practice

Use cubes to make equal groups.
Skip count. Then find the product.

Think!
I can skip count by 4s:
4, 8, 12, 16.

1. Make 4 groups of 4.

_____, _____, _____, _____ $4 \times 4 = $ _____

2. Make 5 groups of 2.

_____, _____, _____, _____, _____

$5 \times 2 = $ _____

3. Make 4 groups of 3.

_____, _____, _____, _____

$4 \times 3 = $ _____

4. Make 5 groups of 3.

_____, _____, _____, _____, _____

$5 \times 3 = $ _____

5. Make 4 groups of 5.

_____, _____, _____, _____

$4 \times 5 = $ _____

6. **123** **Math Talk** How can you use multiplication to find the value of 8 dimes?

KEY NS 3.1 Use repeated addition, arrays, and counting by multiples to do multiplication.
Also **KEY NS 3.3**, MR 1.2

KEY NS 3.0 Model and solve simple problems involving multiplication and division.

► Practice

Draw petals on the flowers.
Skip count.
Then find the product.

7. 2 groups of 3 petals

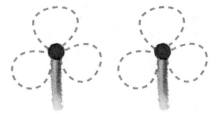

_3_, _6_

2 × 3 = _6_ petals

8. 4 groups of 5 petals

_____, _____, _____, _____

4 × 5 = _____ petals

9. 2 groups of 10 petals

_____, _____

2 × 10 = _____ petals

10. 4 groups of 4 petals

_____, _____, _____, _____

4 × 4 = _____ petals

Problem Solving: Number Sense

11. Dora bought red, blue, yellow and green flower pots. She bought **2** of each color. How many flower pots did she buy?

_____ × _____ = _____ flower pots

At Home Practice multiplying numbers 1 through 5 with your child.

En casa Practique con su niño cómo multiplicar números del 1 al 5.

Name _____

Use Tables to Multiply

▶ **Learn**

You can use a table to help solve a multiplication problem.

Mr. Vega has 3 flower pots.
He plants 3 flowers in each pot.
How many flowers are there?

You can skip count by 3s.
The counting pattern
is 3, 6, 9....

There are _____ flowers.

Pots	1	2	3
Flowers	3	6	9

___3___ × ___3___ = ___9___

▶ **Guided Practice**

Find a pattern to complete the table.
Write the multiplication sentence to solve.

Think!
I can count
by 2: 2, 4, 6, 8.

1. Mr. Vega sells 4 flower pots.
   Each pot has 2 flowers.
   How many flowers
   are there in all?

Flower pots	1	2	3	4
Flowers	2			

_____ × _____ = _____ flowers

2. Jill has 5 plants. Each plant has 4 flowers.
   How many flowers does she have?

Plants	1	2	3	4	5
Flowers	4				

_____ × _____ = _____ flowers

3. **123** **Math Talk** How can a table help you
   multiply?

KEY NS 3.1 Use repeated addition, arrays, and counting by multiples to do multiplication.
Also **KEY NS 3.0**, **KEY NS 3.3**, **KEY SDAP 2.0**, MR 2.2

SDAP 2.1 Recognize, describe, and extend patterns and determine a next term in linear patterns (e.g., 4, 8, 12...; the number of ears on one horse, two horses, three horses, four horses).

Find a pattern to complete the table.
Write the multiplication sentence to solve.

4. Bev buys 3 packages of planting tools.
Each package has 5 tools.
How many tools does she buy?

Packages	1	2	3
Tools	5	10	15

___3___ × ___5___ = ___15___ tools

5. Yoni's uncle has 4 rows of pecan trees in
his orchard. There are 10 trees in each row.
How many pecan trees does he have?

Rows	1	2	3	4
Trees	10			

_____ × _____ = _____ trees

6. Alex has 6 garden carts. Each cart has 3 wheels.
How many wheels are on the carts?

Carts	1	2	3	4	5	6
Wheels	3					

_____ × _____ = _____ wheels

Reading Math: Vocabulary

7. Two numbers have a **product**
of 6 and a **sum** of 5.
What are the numbers?   _____ and _____

 At Home Give your child a
multiplication problem to solve using
a table.

En casa Dé a su niño un problema de
multiplicación. Pida a su niño que lo resuelva
usando una tabla.

Problem Solving

California Field Trip

At the Mining and Mineral Museum

You can learn about gold mining in California. As you walk through an old mine tunnel, you can learn about the California gold rush. You can also see many kinds of rocks.

Choose a way to solve. Show your work.

Science

An old mine shaft

1. At the museum, Bessie sees 5 display cases. Each case has 3 gold nuggets. How many gold nuggets does Bessie see?

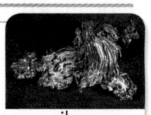

gold nugget

_____ gold nuggets

2. Teresa sees 4 display cases. Each case has 10 pieces of silver. How many pieces of silver does Teresa see?

silver

_____ pieces of silver

3. 6 first-graders and 7 second-graders visit the museum. Each student buys 2 mineral samples at the museum store. How many mineral samples do the students buy in all?

minerals

_____ mineral samples

KEY **NS 3.1** Use repeated addition, arrays, and counting by multiples to do multiplication.
Science ES 3.a

KEY **NS 3.0** Model and solve simple problems involving multiplication and division.
Also **MR 1.0, MR 1.1**

four hundred three **403**

4. Jason sees 6 miner's pails. Each pail has 2 hammers. How many hammers does Jason see in all?

miner's tools

_____ hammers

5. 20 people have a ticket for the first tour. 35 people have a ticket for the second tour. 17 people have a ticket for the last tour. How many people have tickets for a tour?

ticket

_____ people

6. Ms. Brown wants to buy some postcards. Each postcard costs 50¢. How much do 5 postcards cost?

postcard

_____

7. Jana has 3 quarters, 2 dimes, and 2 nickels. She buys 2 postcards. How much money does Jana have left?

California
EXPLORE
postcards

Jana has _____ left.

Name _____

 # Key Standards Review

Use a pattern to complete the table.
Write the multiplication sentence.

1. There are 4 flowers.
   There are 2 butterflies near
   each flower. How many
   butterflies are there in all?

Flowers	1	2	3	4
Butterflies	2			

   _____ × _____ = _____ butterflies in all

2. There are 3 ladybugs.
   Each ladybug has 6 legs.
   How many legs are there in all?

Ladybugs	1	2	3
Legs			

   _____ × _____ = _____ legs in all

Challenge   Number Sense

Roger loves to play bingo.
Here is what an empty bingo card looks like.

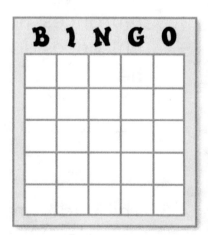

1. Write a multiplication sentence to show
   the number of spaces in a bingo card.

   _____ × _____ = _____

2. If Roger has 10 spaces filled, what fraction
   of the total board is covered?

   _____

3. If Roger has $\frac{3}{5}$ of the card filled, how
   many spaces are covered?

   _____ spaces

KEY NS 3.1 Use repeated addition, arrays, and
counting by multiples to do multiplication.
Also KEY NS 4.2, KEY NS 3.0

Science Link

Ants Alive!

The life cycle of the leaf cutter ant starts with an egg. Then, it grows to look like a worm. Next, the ant wraps itself in a cocoon. It comes out as an adult!

Use a table to solve.

1. Leaf cutter ants have 6 legs. How many legs do 5 ants have?

   _____ legs

Number of ants	1	2	3	4	5
Legs	6				

2. Leaf cutter ants live in colonies. The entrances are near mounds of sand. If a colony has 5 entrances, how many entrances do 4 colonies have?

   _____ entrances

Number of colonies	1	2	3	4
Entrances				

3. The underground nests are connected by tunnels. If each ant digs for 10 inches, how far do 6 ants dig?

   _____ inches

Number of ants	1	2	3	4	5	6
Inches dug						

406 ☐☐☐☐ ⦿○○○○

KEY NS 3.1 Use repeated addition, arrays, and counting by multiples to do multiplication.
Also **KEY NS 3.0**, SDAP 2.1, **KEY SDAP 2.0**, SDAP 2.2, Science LS 2.b

Name _____

Concepts and Skills

Complete the addition sentence. KEY **NS 3.1**

Number of groups	Number in each group	How many in all?
I. 3	4	_____ + _____ + _____ = _____

Show the array.
Write the multiplication sentence. KEY **NS 3.1**

2. 2 rows of 3

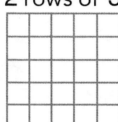

_____ × _____ = _____

3. 3 rows of 2

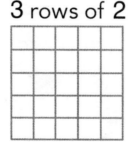

_____ × _____ = _____

Use a pattern to complete the table. Write the multiplication sentence to solve. KEY **NS 3.1**

4.

Dollars	I	2	3	4	5
Quarters	4	8			

_____ × _____ = _____

Problem Solving KEY **NS 3.1**, MR 2.0

5. There are 3 rows of chairs.
There are 10 chairs in each row.
How many chairs are there in all?

Draw or write to explain.

_____ chairs

Spiral Review and Test Practice

1. Which set shows these numbers ordered from least to greatest?

8   95   45   22

22, 45, 8, 95   8, 45, 95, 22   95, 45, 22, 8   8, 22, 45, 95
    ○   ○   ○   ○

2. What is the sum?   54¢ + 17¢ = _____

61¢   71¢   81¢   91¢
 ○   ○   ○   ○

3. Which clock shows quarter to 4?

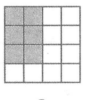   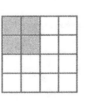

    ○   ○   ○   ○

4. Which array shows 2 rows of 3 shaded?

    ○   ○   ○   ○

5. Which fraction names the shaded part?

$\frac{1}{8}$ $\frac{7}{4}$ $\frac{7}{7}$ $\frac{3}{4}$
 ○   ○   ○   ○

 Education Place
Visit **www.eduplace.com/camap/** for
Test-Taking Tips and Extra Practice.

Spiral Review

Multiply by 2, 5, or 10

Vocabulary

Here are some vocabulary words you will learn in the chapter.

multiply Join equal groups to find how many in all

$$3 \times 2 = 6$$

3 equal groups of 2 flowers = 6 flowers in all

multiplication sentence A number sentence using multiplication

$$3 \times 5 = 15$$
↑
multiplication symbol

product The answer in a multiplication problem

$$7 \times 2 = 14$$
↑
product

See English-Spanish Glossary pages 573–589.

KEY NS 3.1 Use repeated addition, arrays, and counting by multiples to do multiplication.
Also **KEY NS 3.0**, **KEY NS 3.3**

Education Place
Visit **www.eduplace.com/camap/** for the eGlossary and eGames.

Name _____

 # Check What You Know

1. How many flowers are in each vase? _____

   How many vases are there? _____

2. Use the picture to complete the table.

Vases	1				
Flowers	3				

3. Write an addition sentence to show how
   many flowers in all.

   _____ + _____ + _____ + _____ + _____ = _____

4. Write a multiplication sentence to show
   how many flowers in all.

   _____ × _____ = _____

5. Follow the pattern.
   Write the missing numbers.

   10, 20, _____, _____, 50, _____, _____, 80, 90, _____

Use this page to review important skills needed for this chapter.

Name _____

Multiply in Any Order

 **Explore**

You can multiply in any order
and get the same product.

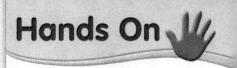

Objective
Understand that
multiplying in any
order gives the
same product.

Vocabulary
array

Make an **array** with 4 rows of 2.

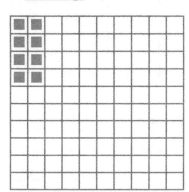

Now show 2 rows of 4.

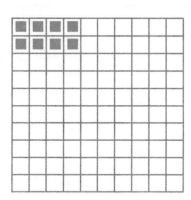

Write the multiplication sentence.

__4__ × __2__ = __8__

Write the multiplication sentence.

__2__ × __4__ = __8__

Use Learning Tool 23 and 🔲 to make the arrays.
Color to show your work. Find each product.

1. 5 rows of 3

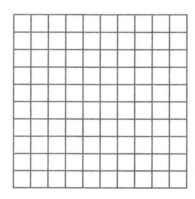

3 rows of 5

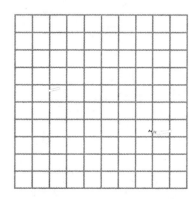

When I turn the
array, the answer
is the same.

5 × 3 = _____

_____ × _____ = _____

2. (123) **Math Talk** Is 5 × 4 the same as 4 × 5? How
do you know? Multiply to check.

KEY **AF 1.1** Use the commutative and associative
rules to simplify mental calculations and to check
results.

KEY **NS 3.1** Use repeated addition, arrays, and
counting by multiples to do multiplication.
Also **MR 1.2, KEY NS 3.0, KEY NS 3.3,
MR 3.0**

four hundred eleven **411**

Use Learning Tool 23 and  to make the arrays.
Color to show your work. Find each product.

3. 4 rows of 5   5 rows of 4   **4.** 5 rows of 6   6 rows of 5

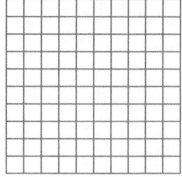

$4 \times 5 =$ _____ $5 \times 4 =$ _____ $5 \times 6 =$ _____ $6 \times 5 =$ _____

5. 6 rows of 4   4 rows of 6   **6.** 7 rows of 5   5 rows of 7

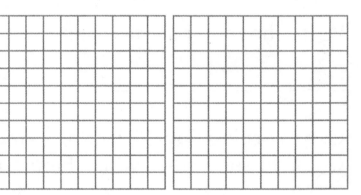

$6 \times 4 =$ _____ $4 \times 6 =$ _____ $7 \times 5 =$ _____ $5 \times 7 =$ _____

Multiply.

Use Learning Tool 23 and  to help.

7. $6 \times 2 =$ _____ $2 \times 6 =$ _____   **8.** $2 \times 9 =$ _____ $9 \times 2 =$ _____

9. $2 \times 7 =$ _____ $7 \times 2 =$ _____   **10.** $3 \times 5 =$ _____ $5 \times 3 =$ _____

11. $8 \times 2 =$ _____ $2 \times 8 =$ _____   **12.** $8 \times 5 =$ _____ $5 \times 8 =$ _____

13. $7 \times 3 =$ _____ $3 \times 7 =$ _____   **14.** $2 \times 5 =$ _____ $5 \times 2 =$ _____

At Home Have your child solve multiplication problems such as 4 x 2 and 2 x 4. Ask him or her to explain why the products are the same.

En casa Pida a su niño que resuelva problemas de multiplicación como 4 x 2 y 2 x 4. Pídale que explique por qué los productos son iguales.

Name _____

Multiply by 2

Objective
Know multiplication facts for 2.

 **Learn**

You can add equal groups to find the sum.
You can multiply equal groups to find the product.

3 groups of 2

Add.

$2 + 2 + 2 =$ _____6_____
↑
sum

Multiply.

3   ×   2   =   _____6_____
↑   ↑   ↑
number   number in   product
of groups   each group

$3 × 2 = 6$ is a multiplication sentence.

▶ **Guided Practice**

Find the sum. Then find the product.

1. 4 groups of 2

$2 + 2 + 2 + 2 =$ _____

$4 × 2 =$ _____

Think!
2 + 2 + 2 + 2 is
the same as
4 × 2.

2. 2 groups of 2

$2 + 2 =$ _____

$2 × 2 =$ _____

3. 5 groups of 2

$2 + 2 + 2 + 2 + 2 =$ _____

$5 × 2 =$ _____

4.  **Math Talk** How is 3 × 2 the same as 2 + 2 + 2?

KEY NS 3.3 Know the multiplication tables of 2s, 5s, and 10s (to "times 10") and commit them to memory. Also **KEY** NS 3.0, MR 3.0, MR 2.0

KEY NS 3.1 Use repeated addition, arrays, and counting by multiples to do multiplication.

Find the sum. Then find the product.

5. 3 groups of 2

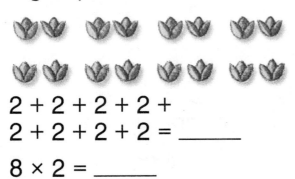

$2 + 2 + 2 =$ ___6___

$3 \times 2 =$ ___6___

6. 4 groups of 2

$2 + 2 + 2 + 2 =$ _____

$4 \times 2 =$ _____

7. 8 groups of 2

$2 + 2 + 2 + 2 +$
$2 + 2 + 2 + 2 =$ _____

$8 \times 2 =$ _____

8. 6 groups of 2

$2 + 2 + 2 + 2 + 2 + 2 =$ _____

$6 \times 2 =$ _____

9. $7 \times 2 =$ _____

10. $9 \times 2 =$ _____

11. $10 \times 2 =$ _____

12. $5 \times 2 =$ _____

13. $1 \times 2 =$ _____

14. $0 \times 2 =$ _____

Problem Solving: Number Sense

15. Each plant has two blossoms. How many blossoms do 6 plants have?

Draw or write to explain.

_____ blossoms

 At Home Use small objects to make groups of 2. Ask your child to write multiplication sentences to show how many in all.

En casa Use objetos pequeños para formar grupos de 2. Pida a su niño que escriba enunciados de multiplicación para mostrar cuántos hay en total.

Chapter 21 Lesson 3

Multiply by 5

 **Learn**

There are 5 flowers in each group.
How many flowers are there in all?

You can skip count by 5s to add.

 +  = _____

You can write a multiplication sentence to show how many in all.

____ × ____ = ____

$2 \times 5 = 10$

There are ____ flowers in all.

▶ **Guided Practice**

Write the sum.
Then write the multiplication sentence.

Think!
I can skip count
by 5s: 5, 10, 15,....

1. 6 groups of 5

$5 + 5 + 5 + 5 + 5 + 5 =$ _____

_____ × _____ = _____

2. 4 groups of 5

$5 + 5 + 5 + 5 =$ _____

_____ × _____ = _____

3. 3 groups of 5

$5 + 5 + 5 =$ _____

_____ × _____ = _____

4. 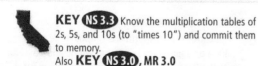 **Math Talk** How can skip counting by 5s help you multiply by 5?

KEY NS 3.3 Know the multiplication tables of 2s, 5s, and 10s (to "times 10") and commit them to memory.
Also **KEY** NS 3.0, MR 3.0

KEY NS 3.1 Use repeated addition, arrays, and counting by multiples to do multiplication.

four hundred fifteen **415**

▶ **Practice**

Write how many in all.
Then write the multiplication sentence.

> **Remember!**
> Multiplication is
> a quick way to add
> equal groups.

5.

7 groups of 5 = ___35___

___7___ × ___5___ = ___35___

6.

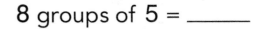

6 groups of 5 = _____

_____ × _____ = _____

7.

8 groups of 5 = _____

_____ × _____ = _____

8.

5 groups of 5 = _____

_____ × _____ = _____

Multiply.

9. 2 × 5 = _____   **10.** 4 × 5 = _____   **11.** 1 × 5 = _____

12. 10 × 5 = _____   **13.** 9 × 5 = _____   **14.** 0 × 5 = _____

Problem Solving: Reasoning

15. How many pennies can you trade
for the nickels in the table?
Multiply to complete the table.

Nickels		Pennies
1		
2	⊗ × 5	
3		
4		
5		

At Home Use small objects like
macaroni to make 3 groups of 5. Ask
your child to write a multiplication
sentence to show how many in all.

En casa Use objetos pequeños, como
macarrones, para formar 3 grupos de 5.
Pida a su niño que escriba un enunciado de
multiplicación para mostrar cuánto hay en total.

416

Name _____

Multiply by 10

▶ **Learn**

You can skip count to help multiply by 10.

There are 10 flowers in each vase. How many flowers are in 5 vases?

You can skip count by 10s: 10, 20, 30, 40, 50.

10, 20, 30, 40, 50

_5_ tens

$5 \times 10 =$ _50_

▶ **Guided Practice**

Skip count by 10s.
Write how many tens. Multiply.

Think!
I can skip count by 10s: 10, 20.

1.

_____, _____

_____ tens

$2 \times 10 =$ _____

2.

_____, _____, _____, _____

_____ tens

$4 \times 10 =$ _____

3. **123** **Math Talk** How can skip counting by 10s help you multiply by 10?

 **KEY NS 3.3** Know the multiplication tables of 2s, 5s, and 10s (to "times 10") and commit them to memory.
Also **KEY NS 3.0**, MR 3.0

KEY NS 3.1 Use repeated addition, arrays, and counting by multiples to do multiplication.

Write how many tens.
Multiply.

Remember!
You can skip count
by 10s to multiply
by 10.

4.

_3_ tens

$3 \times 10 =$ _30_

5.

_____ tens

$6 \times 10 =$ _____

6.

_____ tens

$5 \times 10 =$ _____

7.

_____ tens

$7 \times 10 =$ _____

8.

_____ tens

$10 \times 10 =$ _____

Problem Solving: Reasoning

9. How many pennies can you trade
for the dimes in the table?
Multiply to complete the table.

Dimes		Pennies
1		
2	×10	
3		
4		
5		

418

At Home Give your child several
dimes and point out that a dime is
worth 10¢. Have your child multiply
by 10 to find the value of the dimes.

En casa Dé a su niño varias monedas de diez
centavos y dígale que vale 10¢. Pida a su niño
que multiplique por 10 para hallar el valor de
las monedas.

Write a Number Sentence

 **Learn**

Problem Solving
Plan

Objective
Write number sentences to solve problems.

Kayla, Mateo, and Angela bring seeds for the class planting project. Each child brings 5 seeds. How many seeds do the children bring in all?

Understand

What do you know?
• 3 children bring seeds to school.
• Each child brings 5 seeds.

Plan

Circle the operation you will use.

addition   subtraction

(multiplication)   division

Think!
I have equal groups.
I need to find the total,
so I multiply.

Solve

Write a number sentence.
Then solve.

__3__ ⊗ __5__ = __15__

__15__

The children bring __15__ seeds in all.

Look Back

Did you answer the question?
How can you check your answer?

KEY **NS 3.0** Model and solve simple problems involving multiplication and division.
Also **MR 2.0, MR 2.2, KEY NS 3.1**

KEY **NS 3.3** Know the multiplication tables of 2s, 5s, and 10s (to "times 10") and commit them to memory.

four hundred nineteen **419**

► Guided Problem Solving

1. There are **20** children in Mr. Lee's class.
   Each child gets **5** seeds.
   How many seeds are there in all?

   What do you know?

   There are _____ children in the class.

   Each child gets _____ seeds.

   What do you need to find?

   _____

   Write a number sentence. Then solve.

   _____ ◯ _____ = _____

   There are _____ seeds in all.

2. **Math Talk** How did you choose
   which operation to use?

seeds

Remember!
Understand
Plan
Solve
Look Back

Think!
There are equal
groups, so I can
multiply 20 x 5 to find
the total.

► Problem Solving Practice

Write a number sentence to solve.   Draw or write to explain.

3. The class orders ants for their ant
   farm. There are **8** ants in each group.
   The class orders **2** groups. How many
   ants does the class order in all?

   _____ ◯ _____ ◯ _____ ants

4. The children work in groups of
   3 to talk about the class ants.
   There are **10** groups. How many
   children are there in all?

   _____ ◯ _____ ◯ _____ children

At Home Have your child explain
how he or she knew to multiply to
solve Exercise 3.

En casa Pida a su niño que explique cómo
supo que debía multiplicar para resolver el
Ejercicio 3.

420 ☐☐☐☐‖

Create and Solve

Problem Solving

Objective
Write problems and
use strategies to solve.

The bar graph shows
the number of seeds
in each seed pack.

1. Mrs. Caraway's
   class orders 5
   packs of pumpkin
   seeds. How many
   pumpkin seeds do
   they order in all?

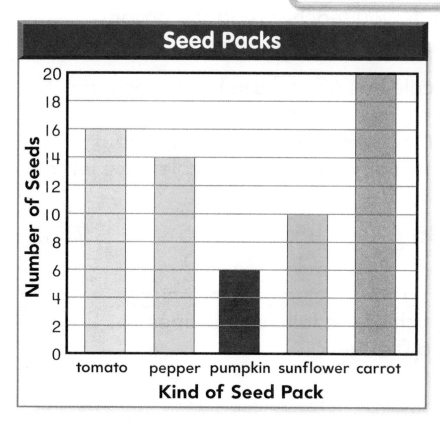

_____ ◯ _____ = _____

The class orders _____ pumpkin seeds.

2. Write a multiplication problem about
   the seeds in the graph.

   _____

   _____

   _____

3. Solve your problem. _____ ◯ _____ ◯ _____

   Share your problem with a classmate.

SDAP 1.4 Ask and answer simple questions related
to data representations.
Also **KEY NS 3.3**, **KEY SDAP 1.0**, MR 1.0,
MR 1.1

KEY NS 3.0 Model and solve simple problems
involving multiplication and division.

Problem Solving on Tests
Listening Skills

Listen to you teacher read the problem. Choose the correct answer.

1. Nicole has 65 rocks in her collection. She gives 26 rocks to one friend and some more rocks to another. About how many rocks could Nicole have left?

   35   45   65   75
   ○   ○   ○   ○

   KEY NS 2.2

2. Which of the following shapes has 2 faces and 0 edges?

   rectangular
     prism   sphere   cylinder   cube
      ○   ○   ○   ○

   KEY MG 2.1

3.

   $\frac{3}{5}$ $\frac{3}{8}$ $\frac{5}{8}$ $\frac{1}{2}$
    ○   ○   ○   ○

   KEY NS 4.2

4.

   2:30   2:45   3:15   3:30
    ○   ○   ○   ○

   MG 1.4

MR 1.0 Make decisions about how to set up a problem.
MR 1.1 Determine the approach, materials, and strategies to be used.

Education Place
Visit www.eduplace.com/camap/ for Test-Taking Tips and Extra Practice.

Key Standards Review

Find the product.

1. $2 \times 3 =$ _____   2. $5 \times 6 =$ _____   3. $10 \times 7 =$ _____

4. $5 \times 7 =$ _____   5. $10 \times 4 =$ _____   6. $2 \times 9 =$ _____

7. $10 \times 5 =$ _____   8. $2 \times 7 =$ _____   9. $5 \times 8 =$ _____

10. $2 \times 8 =$ _____   11. $5 \times 9 =$ _____   12. $10 \times 10 =$ _____

Challenge Number Sense

Solve.

1. Robbie works in a pet store. He counts 3 cats in each group. There are 5 groups. How many cats are there in all?

   _____ cats

2. Some of the cats are sold. Now there are 4 cats in each group. There are 3 groups. How many cats were sold?

   _____ cats

KEY NS 3.3 Know the multiplication tables of 2s, 5s, and 10s (to "times 10") and commit them to memory.
Also **KEY NS 3.0**

four hundred twenty-three **423**

Recycle!

Recycling is a way to help keep the Earth clean. Here are some ways you can recycle things instead of throwing them away.

Write a multiplication sentence to solve.

1. Dora and Max each fill 10 empty soda bottles with colored sand. How many bottles do they fill in all?

_____ × _____ = _____ bottles in all

2. Allie and Pete use an egg carton to collect rocks. They put 4 rocks in each section. How many rocks do they collect?

_____ × _____ = _____ rocks

3. Patrick makes wrapping paper from an old bag. He prints 4 rows. There are 5 stars in each row. How many stars are there in all?

_____ × _____ = _____ stars

4. 6 children make bird feeders from old juice boxes. They make 5 bird feeders each. How many feeders do they make in all?

_____ × _____ = _____ bird feeders

KEY NS 3.3 Know the multiplication tables of 2s, 5s, and 10s (to "times 10") and commit them to memory.
History-Social Science 4.3

Name _____

Concepts and Skills

Fill in the arrays.
Find each product. **KEY NS 3.1**

1. 3 rows of 5   5 rows of 3

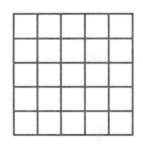 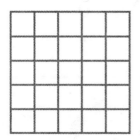

3 × 5 = _____   5 × 3 = _____

Find the sum.
Then find the product. **KEY NS 3.1**

2. 7 groups of 2

7 + 7 = _____

7 × 2 = _____

Write how many in all.
Then write the multiplication sentence. **KEY NS 3.1**

3.

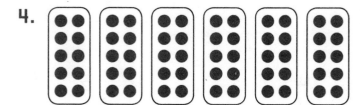

8 groups of 5 = _____

_____ × _____ = _____

Write how many tens. Multiply. **KEY NS 3.0, KEY NS 3.1**

4.

_____ tens

6 × 10 = _____

Problem Solving **KEY NS 3.1, KEY NS 3.3, KEY NS 3.0, MR 2.0**

5. The ceiling is made up of 6 rows of 5 tiles each. How many tiles are in the ceiling?

Draw or write to explain.

_____ tiles

Spiral Review and Test Practice

1. What is $\frac{1}{5}$ of 10?

   ○ $\frac{1}{5}$ of 10 is 1.   ○ $\frac{1}{5}$ of 10 is 5.

   ○ $\frac{1}{5}$ of 10 is 2.   ○ $\frac{1}{5}$ of 10 is 10.

KEY **NS 4.2**, NS 4.0 Page 333

2. How many hours have passed between the two times?

   3 hours   4 hours   7 hours   10 hours
     ○   ○   ○   ○

MG 1.5, MG 1.4, MG 1.0 Page 375

3. Which multiplication fact do the cubes show?

   2 × 5   3 × 5   4 × 5   5 × 5
     ○   ○   ○   ○

KEY **NS 3.1** Page 399

4. Which addition sentence has the same sum as the product of this multiplication sentence? $4 \times 2 =$ _____

   ○ 2 + 2 + 2 + 2 = 8   ○ 4 + 2 = 6

   ○ 4 + 4 + 4 + 4 = 16   ○ 4 + 2 + 4 + 2 = 12

KEY **NS 3.1** Page 413

Education Place
Visit **www.eduplace.com/camap/** for
Test-Taking Tips and Extra Practice.

Spiral Review

Division

Vocabulary

Here are some vocabulary words you will learn in the chapter.

divide Separate a group into smaller, equal groups

You can divide **8** ants into equal groups of **2**.

division sentence A number sentence using division

$$10 \div 2 = 5$$

↑
division symbol

remainder The number left over in a division problem

You can divide **9** into **4** groups of **2**
with one left over.
$$9 \div 2 = 4 \text{ remainder } 1$$

See English-Spanish Glossary pages 573–589.

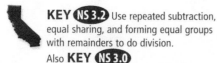 **KEY NS 3.2** Use repeated subtraction, equal sharing, and forming equal groups with remainders to do division.
Also **KEY NS 3.0**

Education Place
Visit **www.eduplace.com/camap/** for the eGlossary and eGames.

four hundred twenty-seven **427**

Name _____

 # Check What You Know

Count back. Follow the pattern.
Write the missing numbers.

1. 100, 90, 80, _____, 60,

   _____, _____, 30, 20, _____

2. 100, 95, _____, 85, 80, _____, 70,

   _____, 60, _____, _____

3. 40, 38, 36, _____, _____, 30,

   28, _____, _____, 22, 20

Circle groups of 2 butterflies.
4. How many butterflies in all?

   _____

5. How many groups are there?

   _____ groups of 2

Use this page to review important skills needed for this chapter.

Name _____

Chapter 22 Lesson 1

Equal Groups

▶ **Explore**

Objective
Relate equal sharing and equal groups to division.

Michelle has 15 nature stamps. She wants to give an equal number to each of her 5 friends. How many stamps will each friend get?

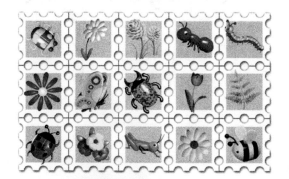

Step 1	**Step 2**	**Step 3**
Show 15 counters.	Make 5 groups. Put a counter in each group to share.	Keep sharing until all counters are placed.
	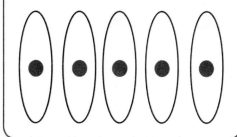	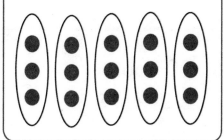

15 divided into 5 groups is 3. $15 \div 5 = 3$

Each friend gets ___3___ stamps.

Use counters. Draw dots to show the number in each group. Write how many are in each group.

1. 20 counters
   2 groups

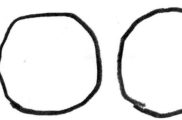

$20 \div 2 =$ _____ in each group

2.  **Math Talk** How could 4 children share 20 counters equally?

KEY NS 3.2 Use repeated subtraction, equal sharing, and forming equal groups with remainders to do division. Also **MR 1.2**

KEY NS 3.0 Model and solve simple problems involving multiplication and division.

▶ **Extend**

Use counters.
Draw dots to show the
number in each group.
Write how many are in each group.

Remember!
Put the same number
of counters in
each group.

3. 12 counters
   4 groups

$12 \div 4 =$ ___3___

___3___ in each group

4. 16 counters
   8 groups

$16 \div 8 =$ _____

_____ in each group

5. 20 counters
   5 groups

$20 \div 5 =$ _____

_____ in each group

6. 18 counters
   6 groups

$18 \div 6 =$ _____

_____ in each group

7. 10 counters
   5 groups

$10 \div 5 =$ _____

_____ in each group

 At Home Have your child arrange
10 pennies into 5 equal groups.

En casa Pida a su niño que distribuya 10
monedas de un centavo en 5 grupos iguales.

Name _____

Equal Groups

> ▶ **Learn**

When you make equal groups, you **divide**.

A **division sentence** tells how many equal groups there are.

Ms. Perez has **8** bird pictures. She gives them away in groups of **2**. How many groups can she give away?

Objective
Use repeated subtraction to make equal groups.

Vocabulary
divide
division sentence

Step 1

Start with **8**.

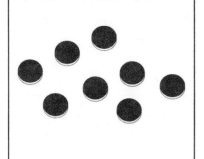

Step 2

Subtract groups of **2** until none are left.

$8 - 2 - 2 - 2 - 2 = 0$

Step 3

Write how many groups.

divided by
↓
$8 ÷ 2 =$ _____ groups

8 divided by **2** equals **4**.

She makes _____ groups.

> ▶ **Guided Practice**

Complete the table.
You can use counters to model.

Think!
I take away equal groups until I have none.

	Start with this many.	Number in each group	Divide. How many groups?
1.	4	2	$4 ÷ 2 =$ __2__ groups
2.	6	2	$6 ÷ 2 =$ _____ groups
3.	8	2	$8 ÷ 2 =$ _____ groups

4. **(123) Math Talk** Think about $8 + 8$. Think about $2 × 8$. How are they the same?

KEY NS 3.2 Use repeated subtraction, equal sharing, and forming equal groups with remainders to do division.
Also **SDAP 1.4, MR 3.0, SDAP 1.3**

KEY NS 3.0 Model and solve simple problems involving multiplication and division.

Circle equal groups of 2.
Divide. Write the number of groups.

Remember!
Take away equal groups until there are none left.

5.

$14 \div 2 =$ _____ groups

6.

$18 \div 2 =$ _____ groups

7.

$16 \div 2 =$ _____ groups

8.

$20 \div 2 =$ _____ groups

Complete the division sentence.

	Start with this many.	Number in each group	Divide. How many groups?
9.	10	2	_____ ÷ _____ = _____ groups
10.	22	2	_____ ÷ _____ = _____ groups

Problem Solving: Data Sense

11. What is the range? Write a number sentence.

   _____ – _____ = _____

12. What is the mode of the data?

   _____ butterflies

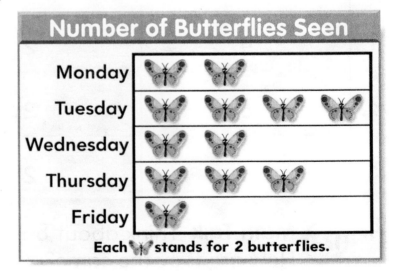

Number of Butterflies Seen

Monday	
Tuesday	
Wednesday	
Thursday	
Friday	

Each 🦋 stands for 2 butterflies.

At Home Ask your child to divide 12 objects into equal groups of 2.

En casa Pida a su niño que divida 12 objetos en grupos iguales de 2.

Repeated Subtraction

Objective
Use repeated subtraction to divide.

 **Learn**

You can use repeated subtraction to divide.

Divide $15 \div 5$.

Step 1	**Step 2**	**Step 3**
Start at 15.	Subtract 5s until you have 0.	Count how many times you subtracted 5.

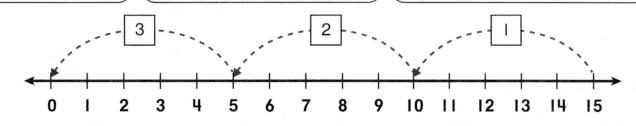

I subtracted 5 three times. $15 \div 5 = \underline{}$

▶ **Guided Practice**

Subtract by 5s to divide by 5.
Use the number lines on Workmat 4 to help.

1. $10 \div 5 = \underline{}$

Think!
I subtract 5 two times.

2. $25 \div 5 = \underline{}$

3. $30 \div 5 = \underline{}$

4. $5 \div 5 = \underline{}$

Subtract by 2s to divide by 2.

5. $4 \div 2 = \underline{}$

6. $10 \div 2 = \underline{}$

7. $12 \div 2 = \underline{}$

8. $8 \div 2 = \underline{}$

9. $14 \div 2 = \underline{}$

10. $18 \div 2 = \underline{}$

11. **123** **Math Talk** How is subtracting by 5s like making groups of 5?

KEY **NS 3.2** Use repeated subtraction, equal sharing, and forming equal groups with remainders to do division. Also **MR 2.0**

KEY **NS 3.0** Model and solve simple problems involving multiplication and division.

▶ Practice

Remember!
You are finding the number of equal groups.

Subtract by 5s to divide by 5.
Use the number lines on Workmat 4 to help.

12. $30 \div 5 = \underline{6}$

13. $15 \div 5 = \underline{}$

14. $45 \div 5 = \underline{}$

15. $35 \div 5 = \underline{}$

16. $20 \div 5 = \underline{}$

17. $25 \div 5 = \underline{}$

18. $5 \div 5 = \underline{}$

19. $10 \div 5 = \underline{}$

Subtract by 2s to divide by 2.

20. $14 \div 2 = \underline{}$

21. $16 \div 2 = \underline{}$

22. $18 \div 2 = \underline{}$

23. $8 \div 2 = \underline{}$

24. $10 \div 2 = \underline{}$

25. $22 \div 2 = \underline{}$

Problem Solving: Reasoning

26. Chantal has 15 jars of honey. She wants to share them equally among 5 people. Circle the picture that shows how she should divide.

At Home Ask your child to write a division sentence about 20 children sitting in 4 equal groups.

En casa Pida a su niño que escriba un enunciado de división acerca de 20 niños sentados en 4 grupos iguales.

434

Name _____

Equal Groups with Remainders

 **Learn**

Objective
Divide with remainders.

Vocabulary
remainder

When you divide, the number left over is called the **remainder.**

Jonathan sees 9 ladybugs on a leaf. He divides them into 4 equal groups. How many ladybugs are in each group? How many are left over?

Step 1

Start with 9.

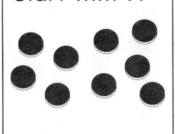

Step 2

Make 4 equal groups.

Step 3

There are 2 ladybugs in each group. One is left over.

$9 \div 4 \rightarrow$ ___2___ remainder ___

| number in all | number of groups | number in each group | left over |

 Guided Practice

Start with 10. Make equal groups. Draw a model. Write the division sentence and the remainder.

Think!
If I divide 10 into 2 equal groups, are there any left over?

	Number of equal groups	Draw your model.	Complete the division sentence.
1.	2		____ ÷ ____ → ____ remainder ____
2.	3		____ ÷ ____ → ____ remainder ____

3. **(123) Math Talk** Can 3 children divide 14 pencils equally with none left over? How do you know?

KEY NS 3.2 Use repeated subtraction, equal sharing, and forming equal groups with remainders to do division.
Also **MR 1.2, MR 2.0**

KEY NS 3.0 Model and solve simple problems involving multiplication and division.

Practice

Start with 12. Make equal groups.
Draw a model. Write the division sentence
and the remainder.

Remember!
The number left over
after you divide is called
the remainder.

	Number of equal groups	Draw your model.	Complete the division sentence.
4.	5		12 ÷ 5 → 2 remainder 2
5.	7		_____ ÷ _____ → _____ remainder _____

Write the division sentence and the remainder.

	Start with this many.	Number of equal groups	Complete the division sentence.
6.	9	2	_____ ÷ _____ → _____ remainder _____
7.	11	3	_____ ÷ _____ → _____ remainder _____
8.	11	4	_____ ÷ _____ → _____ remainder _____
9.	20	9	_____ ÷ _____ → _____ remainder _____

Problem Solving: Reasoning

10. Carolyn has a pack of 25 balloons.
She gives an equal number of
balloons to each of her seven
friends. How many balloons will
be left over?

_____ balloons

Draw or write to explain.

At Home Ask your child to explain
why some division sentences have
remainders.

En casa Pida a su niño que explique por
qué algunos enunciados de división tienen
residuos.

Name _____

Choose a Method

 **Learn**

Objective
Choose a method
to solve problems.

Lila picks **30** roses from her garden.
She gives an equal number of roses to
each of her **5** friends. How many roses
does each friend get?

Understand
What do you know?
- Lila picks **30** roses.
- She gives roses to **5** friends.
- She gives an equal number of
  roses to each friend.

What operation will you
use to solve?

Think!
I have to find the
number of roses in
each equal group, so
I'll divide.

__division__

Plan
Choose a way to solve the problem.

| model equal | use repeated | write a number |
| groups | subtraction | sentence |

Solve
Use the method you chose and solve.

Each friend gets __6__ roses.

Look Back
Did you answer the question?
How can you check your answer?

KEY **NS 3.2** Use repeated subtraction, equal
sharing, and forming equal groups with remainders
to do division.
Also **MR 1.1, MR 2.1, MR 2.2**

KEY **NS 3.0** Model and solve simple problems
involving multiplication and division.

Guided Problem Solving

Remember!
Understand
Plan
Solve
Look Back

1. Drew has **20** flowers.
   He plants **4** flowers in each pot.
   How many flower pots does he use?

   What do you know?

   Drew has _____ flowers.

   He plants _____ flowers in each pot.

   What do you need to find?

   _____

   Choose a method to solve the problem.

   Division Methods
   • use repeated subtraction
   • draw equal groups
   • write a number sentence

   Drew uses _____ flower pots in all.

   Think!
   I can draw 20 flowers in groups of 4.

2. **123** **Math Talk** How did you solve the problem?

Problem Solving Practice

Choose a method. Solve.

Draw or write to explain.

3. Emma has **18** plants. She divides them into **2** equal groups. How many plants are in each group?

   _____ plants

4. Eli has **70** tulips. He plants them in rows of **10**. How many rows does Eli plant?

   _____ rows

At Home Have your child explain at least two ways to solve one of the problems above.

En casa Pida a su niño que explique al menos dos maneras de resolver uno de los problemas de arriba.

Name _____

 Key Standards Review

Draw the groups.
Then write the multiplication sentence.

1. 3 groups of 2

[ ]

_____ × _____ = _____

2. 5 groups of 3

[ ]

_____ × _____ = _____

3. 4 groups of 6

[ ]

_____ × _____ = _____

4. 2 groups of 10

[ ]

_____ × _____ = _____

 **Number Sense**

This chart shows points you can earn for doing tasks in a computer game.

Jaime finds 3 towns and builds 4 roads. His sister Lea finds 2 towns and builds 6 roads.

Game Task	Points
Build a road	2
Find a town	5

1. How many points does Jaime get?

_____ points

2. How many points does Lea get?

_____ points

KEY **NS 3.1** Use repeated addition, arrays, and counting by multiples to do multiplication.
Also KEY **NS 3.0**, KEY **NS 3.3**

four hundred thirty-nine **439**

Math Music

Groups of Bugs

Math Music, Track 8
Tune: "This Old Man"

There are 2 groups of 2—
Moving toward this bowl of stew.
Can you count the ants you see?
Skip count carefully—
2, 4—counting ants I see!

There are 3 groups of 2—
Crawling up this bowl of stew.
Can you count the ants you see?
Skip count carefully—
2, 4, 6—count ants I see!

There are 4 groups of 2—
Munching on this bowl of stew.
Can you count the ants you see?
Skip count carefully—
2, 4, 6, 8—ants I see!

There are 5 groups of 2—
Cleaning up this bowl of stew.
Can you count the ants you see?
Skip count carefully—
2, 4, 6, 8, 10—I see!

KEY **NS 3.1** Use repeated addition, arrays, and counting by multiples to do multiplication.
Also **KEY** **NS 3.0**

Name _____

Concepts and Skills

Draw to show the number in each group. Divide. KEY **NS 3.2**

Circle equal groups of 2. Divide. KEY **NS 3.2**

1. 12 dots
   3 groups

   $12 \div 3 =$ _____

   _____ in each group

2.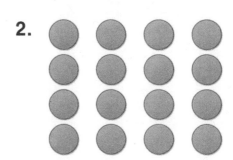

   $16 \div 2 =$ _____ groups

Subtract by 5 to divide by 5. Use the number line. KEY **NS 3.2**

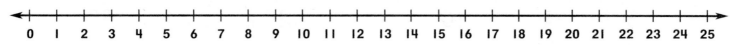

3. $20 \div 5 =$ _____

4. $15 \div 5 =$ _____

5. Complete the division sentence. Write the remainder. KEY **NS 3.2**

   $20 \div 6 =$ _____

   remainder _____

Problem Solving   KEY **NS 3.2**, MR 2.0

6. Tina has packed 50 apples. She packed them 5 to a gift box. How many gift boxes did Tina pack?

   _____ gift boxes

   Explain how you know.

   _____

   _____

Spiral Review and Test Practice

1. Which fraction names the shaded part?

$\frac{1}{6}$ ○

$\frac{1}{3}$ ○

$\frac{4}{3}$ ○

$\frac{4}{6}$ ○

KEY **NS 4.3**, KEY **NS 4.2**, NS 4.0 Page 317

---

2. Use a pattern to complete the table. What is the product of 5 x 5?

Gloves	1	2	3	4	5
Fingers	5	10			

5 ○

10 ○

25 ○

55 ○

KEY **NS 3.3**, KEY **NS 3.0**, KEY **SDAP 2.0**, SDAP 2.1 Page 401

---

3. What multiplication sentence does the model show?

6 + 5 = 11 ○

6 × 5 = 30 ○

5 × 5 = 25 ○

6 × 6 = 36 ○

KEY **NS 3.0**, KEY **NS 3.1** Page 415

---

4. What is the answer to the division problem?

$12 \div 2 = $ _____

2 ○

5 ○

6 ○

7 ○

KEY **NS 3.0**, KEY **NS 3.2** Page 431

Education Place
Visit www.eduplace.com/camap/ for
Test-Taking Tips and Extra Practice.

Spiral Review

Greg Tang's Go Fast, Go Far

Unit 8 Mental Math Strategies

Multiply by 2

A group of 2? It's no trouble. Just make sure you always double!

I have a fast way to multiply 2 x 4. Since it's just 2 groups of 4, or 4 + 4, I double 4 to get 8.

1. $2 \times 4 = \boxed{4} + \boxed{4} = \boxed{8}$

2. $2 \times 6 = \boxed{} + \boxed{} = \boxed{}$ 3. $2 \times 7 = \boxed{} + \boxed{} = \boxed{}$

Take It Further: Now try doing all the steps in your head!

4. $2 \times 8 = \boxed{}$ 5. $2 \times 9 = \boxed{}$

6. $2 \times 5 = \boxed{}$ 7. $2 \times 10 = \boxed{}$

8. $2 \times 12 = \boxed{}$ 9. $2 \times 15 = \boxed{}$

Doing Great!

10. $2 \times 24 = \boxed{}$ 11. $2 \times 36 = \boxed{}$

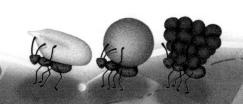

Reading and Writing Math

Choose a word from the word bank for each blank.

<table>
<tr><td>Word Bank</td></tr>
<tr><td>array</td></tr>
<tr><td>divide</td></tr>
<tr><td>division
  sentence</td></tr>
<tr><td>equal groups</td></tr>
<tr><td>multiplication
  sentence</td></tr>
<tr><td>multiply</td></tr>
<tr><td>product</td></tr>
<tr><td>remainder</td></tr>
</table>

1. A way to show objects in equal rows to help you multiply is called an _____.

2. The number you have left over after you divide is called a _____.

3. When you multiply 2 × 2, the _____ is 4.

Read the problem. Then answer the questions.

Josh has 8 tulips. He wants to plant them in groups of 2. How many groups of tulips does Josh plant?

4. Draw a picture to solve.

5. The picture shows how to divide _____ into equal groups of _____.

6. Write a division sentence and solve.

_____ ÷ _____ = _____

Josh plants _____ groups.

7. **Writing Math** What is another way to solve the problem above?

_____

444 ☐☐☐☐☐||||°°°°

KEY NS 3.2 Use repeated subtraction, equal sharing, and forming equal groups with remainders to do division.
Also **KEY** NS 3.0, MR 1.1, MR 1.2

Name _____

Concepts and Skills

Make equal groups with counters.
Use repeated addition to solve. KEY NS3.1

	Number of groups	Number in each group	How many in all?
1.	4	5	_____ + _____ + _____ + _____ = _____
2.	3	6	_____ + _____ + _____ = _____

Draw to show the array.
Write the multiplication sentence. KEY NS3.1

3. 3 rows of 3

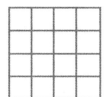

_____ × _____ = _____

4. 4 rows of 3

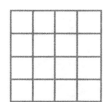

_____ × _____ = _____

Find the pattern to complete the table.
Multiply to solve. KEY NS3.1

5.

Hands	1	2	3	4	5	6
Fingers	5	10				

6 × 5 = _____

Find the sum. Then find the product. KEY **NS 3.1**

6. 5 groups of 2

$2 + 2 + 2 + 2 + 2 =$ _____

$5 \times 2 =$ _____

7. 2 groups of 9

$9 + 9 =$ _____

$2 \times 9 =$ _____

Circle equal groups of 2.
Divide. Write the number of groups. KEY **NS 3.2**

8.

$14 \div 2 =$ _____ groups

Complete the division sentence.
Write the remainder. KEY **NS 3.2**

Start with this many.	Number of groups	Complete the division sentence.
9. 19	6	_____ ÷ _____ = _____ remainder _____

Problem Solving

Solve. MR 2.0, KEY **NS 3.2**

Draw or write to explain.

10. Charles has packed **60** pineapples.
He packed **5** in each box.
How many boxes did Charles pack?

_____

446 □□□□□||||⁰°°°°

Houghton Mifflin
California Math

Unit

9

Numbers and Patterns to 1,000

BIG IDEAS!

- You can show how many ones, tens, and hundreds are in a number.

- You can use symbols such as +, =, <, and > to tell about numbers.

- You can use a decimal point and a dollar sign to show dollars and cents.

Songs and Games

 Math Music Track 9
Count by 100s

eGames
www.eduplace.com/camap/

Literature

Read Aloud Big Book
- From the Tallest to the Heaviest

Math Readers

Spin Six

How to Play

1. Each player chooses a counter.

2. Players take turns spinning the spinner. Color in one space on the graph to show the place value of the 2 in the number you spin.

3. Continue taking turns and coloring in the graph until one of the bars reaches 6.

What You Need

2–3 players

1 ⬤ per player

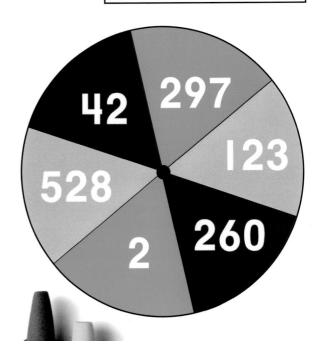

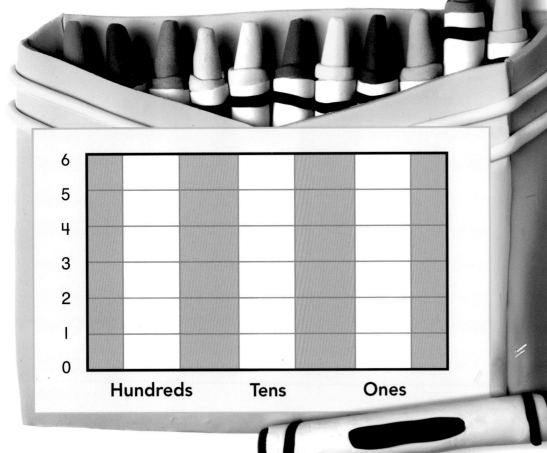

KEY NS 1.1 Count, read, and write whole numbers to 1,000 and identify the place value for each digit.
Also **NS 1.0, MR 1.2**

Education Place
Visit www.eduplace.com/camap/
for eGames and Brain Teasers.

Dear Family,

My class is starting Unit 9, **Numbers and Patterns to 1,000.** I will be learning how to count by hundreds, identify place value, and compare and order 3-digit numbers. You can help me learn these vocabulary words, and we can do the Math Activity together.

From,

_____

Vocabulary

thousand 10 hundreds or 1,000

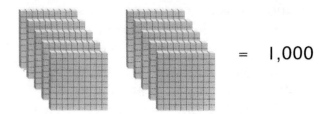

= 1,000

regroup With 3-digit numbers, you may need to trade 10 tens for 1 hundred.

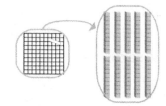

 Education Place
Visit **www.eduplace.com/camaf/** for
• eGames and Brain Teasers
• Math at Home in other languages

Family Math Activity

You and your child each write a **3**-digit number. Have your child say both numbers aloud and then tell which number is greater. Then write a third **3**-digit number. Have your child put all three numbers in order from least to greatest using the words *before*, *after*, and *between*.

Literature

These books link to the math in this unit. Look for them at the library.

• **The Wildlife ABC & 123** by Jan Thornhill *(Maple Tree Press, 2004)*

Matemáticas en casa

Estimada familia:

Mi clase está comenzando la Unidad 9, **Números y patrones hasta 1,000**. Aprenderé a contar de cien en cien, a identificar valor de posición y a comparar y ordenar números de 3 dígitos. Me pueden ayudar a aprender estas palabras de vocabulario y podemos hacer juntos la Actividad de matemáticas para la familia.

De:

_____

Vocabulario

millar 10 centenas ó 1,000.

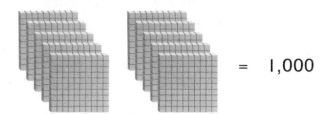

= 1,000

reagrupar Con números de 3 dígitos, algunas veces se pueden cambiar 10 decenas por 1 centena.

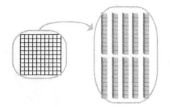

 Education Place
Visite **www.eduplace.com/camaf/** para
• Juegos en línea y acertijos
• Matemáticas en casa en otros idiomas

Actividad de matemáticas para la familia

Con su niño, escriban cada uno un número de 3 dígitos. Pida a su niño que diga en voz alta ambos números y luego que diga qué número es mayor. Luego escriba un tercer número de 3 dígitos. Pida a su niño que ordene los tres números de menor a mayor usando las palabras *antes*, *después* y *entre*.

Literatura

Estos libros hablan sobre las matemáticas de esta unidad. Búscalos en la biblioteca.

• **Los 500 sombreros de Bartolomé Cubbins** de Dr. Suess (*Lectorum Publications*, 1999)

448

Auto Factory

written by Mike Tippin

illustrated by Rafael Mendoza

This Take-Home Book belongs to _____

Reading and Writing Math

This take-home book will help you review number patterns.

Be a car designer! What kind of car would you design? Draw it here.

SDAP 2.2 Solve problems involving simple number patterns.

8

Welcome to our auto factory.

How many headlights are on the belt?

Count by twos.

_____ headlights

Cars are driven to auto dealers by truck.

How many cars are on each truck? _____

How many cars are being carried in all?

_____ cars

Each of our cars will need five tires.
One of the five is a spare tire kept
in the trunk.

How many tires are ready to be used?
Count by fives.

_____ tires

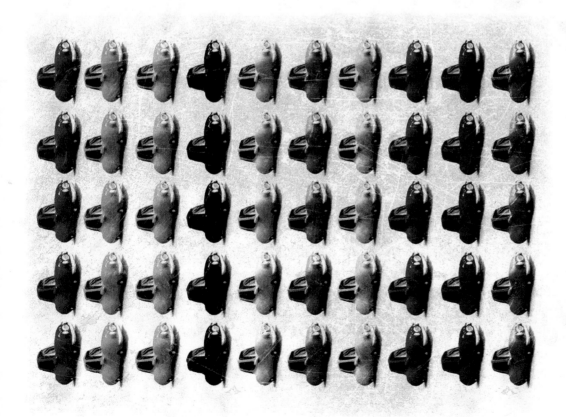

Look at the shiny new cars.
How many are there in all?
Count by fives.

_____ cars

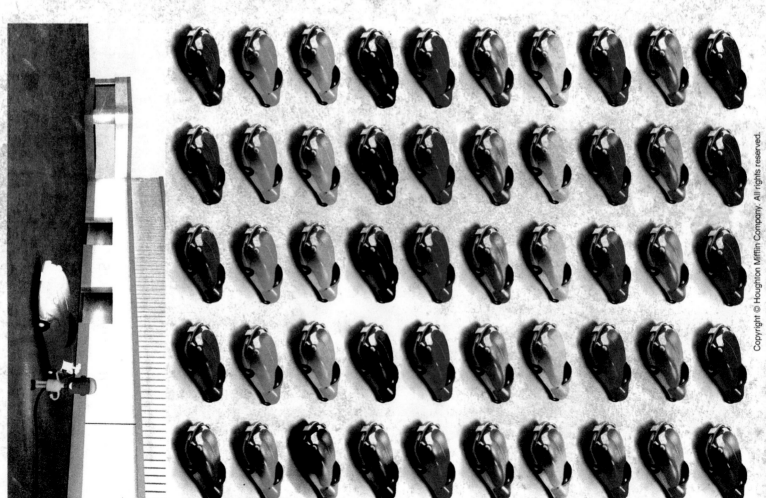

The cars are painted ten at a time.
How many cars have been painted in all?
Count by tens.

_____ cars

4

5

Numbers to 1,000

Vocabulary

Here are some vocabulary words you will learn in the chapter.

hundred 10 tens

= 100

1 hundred

thousand 10 hundreds

= 1,000

one thousand

place value The value of the place where a digit is

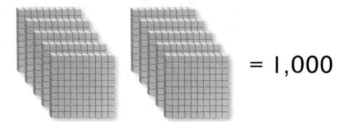

Hundreds	Tens	Ones
7	8	4

700 + 80 + 4

See English-Spanish Glossary pages 573–589.

 KEY NS 1.1 Count, read, and write whole numbers to 1,000 and identify the place value for each digit.
Also **NS 1.2, NS 1.0**

Education Place
Visit www.eduplace.com/camap/ for the eGlossary and eGames.

four hundred forty-nine **449**

Name _____

✓ Check What You Know

1. Which number has more tens, 357 or 375?

   _____ has more tens.

2. Circle the value of the 6 in the number 162.

   6   60   600

3. Circle the value of the 3 in the number 370.

   3   30   300

4. Show the number 198 as hundreds, tens, and ones.

Hundreds	Tens	Ones

5. Show the number 304 as hundreds, tens, and ones.

Hundreds	Tens	Ones

Use this page to review important skills needed for this chapter.

Chapter 23 Lesson 1

Count by 100s

▶ **Explore**

Hands On 🤚

Objective
Count by hundreds to one thousand.

Vocabulary
thousand
hundred

You can count up to one **thousand** by **hundreds.**

10 tens   = one hundred   100

10 hundreds   =   one thousand   1,000

Show 2 hundreds with ▢ .

Count by hundreds: 100, 200.
Draw your model with quick pictures.
One hundred is one square.

Write the number.   _200_

Model the number with Learning Tool 24.
Draw your model with quick pictures. Write the number.

1. 3 hundreds

_____

2. 4 hundreds

_____

3. (123) **Math Talk** What pattern do you see in the numbers you have written?

KEY NS 1.1 Count, read, and write whole numbers to 1,000 and identify the place value for each digit.
Also **NS 1.2, KEY SDAP 2.0**, MR 1.2, SDAP 2.2

NS 1.0 Understand the relationship between numbers, quantities, and place value in whole numbers up to 1,000.

four hundred fifty-one **451**

▶ **Extend**

Model the number with Learning Tool 24.
Draw your model with quick pictures.
Write the number.

Remember!
One hundred is the same as 10 tens.

4. 5 hundreds

_500_

5. 6 hundreds

_____

6. 7 hundreds

_____

7. 8 hundreds

_____

8. 9 hundreds

_____

9. 10 hundreds

_____

Write the missing numbers.

10. 100, 200, _____, 400, _____,

_____, 700, _____, 900, 1,000

☐☐☐☐☐|||||°°

At Home Have your child count forward by hundreds from 100 to 1,000.

En casa Pida a su niño que cuente hacia adelante de cien en cien, desde 100 hasta 1,000.

Chapter 23 Lesson 2

Hundreds, Tens, Ones

Hands On

Objective
Use models to show and count by hundreds, tens, and ones.

▶ **Learn**

There are 134 apartments in Kevin's building. Show 134 two other ways.

You can show a number as hundreds, tens, and ones.

Workmat 6		
Hundreds	**Tens**	**Ones**

Hundreds	Tens	Ones
1	3	4

_134_

one hundred thirty-four

▶ **Guided Practice**

Use Learning Tool 24. Show the number.
Write how many.

1. Show 6 🟦, 4 ▭, and 7 ▪.

Hundreds	Tens	Ones

_____

Think!
I count 6 hundreds,
4 tens, and 7 ones.

2. Show 3 🟦 and 2 ▭.

Hundreds	Tens	Ones

_____

3. Show 5 🟦 and 6 ▪.

Hundreds	Tens	Ones

_____

4. **(123) Math Talk** Explain why 1 does not have the same value in the numbers 361 and 163.

KEY NS 1.1 Count, read, and write whole numbers to 1,000 and identify the place value for each digit.
Also **NS 1.0, NS 6.0, MR 1.2**

NS 1.2 Use words, models, and expanded forms (e.g., 45 = 4 tens + 5) to represent numbers (to 1,000).

Use Learning Tool 24.
Show the numbers. Write how many.

Remember!
Count hundreds first, then tens, and then ones.

	Show this many.	Write how many hundreds, tens, and ones.	Write the number.
5.		Hundreds: 2, Tens: 4, Ones: 2	242
6.		Hundreds / Tens / Ones	_____
7.		Hundreds / Tens / Ones	_____
8.		Hundreds / Tens / Ones	_____

9. Draw a picture to show 827.

Problem Solving: Reasoning

Circle the best answer.

10. I go to school about _____ days each year.   2   20   200

11. My class has about _____ children.   2   20   200

At Home Have your child collect 100 objects, such as buttons or beans, and count them in groups of 10.

En casa Pida a su niño que reúna 100 objetos, como botones o frijoles, y que los cuente en grupos de 10.

Chapter 23 Lesson 3

Numbers Through 1,000

▶ Learn

You can read and write numbers with words or symbols.
Show **235** in three different ways.

Remember!
Put a hyphen between the tens and ones if the tens digit is 2 or more.

Example 1

You can write out the number in word form.

two hundred thirty-five
↑
hyphen

Example 2

You can use expanded form.

_200_ + _30_ + _5_

Example 3

You can write the hundreds, tens, and ones.

_2_ hundreds

_3_ tens

_5_ ones

▶ Guided Practice

Write the missing numbers to complete the table.

Think!
I see a 3 in the hundreds place, a zero in the tens place, and a seven in the ones place.

	Number	Word Form	Expanded Form	Place Value
1.	307	three hundred seven	_____ + _____	_____ hundreds _____ tens _____ ones
2.	586	five hundred eighty-six	_____ + _____ + _____	_____ hundreds _____ tens _____ ones

3. **(123) Math Talk** What is the place value of each of the digits in **841**?

KEY NS 1.1 Count, read, and write whole numbers to 1,000 and identify the place value for each digit.
Also NS 1.0, SDAP 1.4

NS 1.2 Use words, models, and expanded forms (e.g., 45 = 4 tens + 5) to represent numbers (to 1,000).

▶ Practice

Circle the word name for the number.

4. 643   seven hundred thirty-four   (six hundred forty-three)

5. 906   nine hundred six   nine hundred sixteen

6. 513   five hundred thirteen   five hundred thirty-one

7. 748   seven hundred eighty-four   seven hundred forty-eight

Complete the table.

	Number	Word Form	Expanded Form	Place Value
8.	924	_____	____ + ____ + ____	____ hundreds ____ tens ____ ones
9.	____	_____	800 + 70 + 6	____ hundreds ____ tens ____ ones

Problem Solving: Data Sense

10. How many people were at the fair on Friday and Saturday?

    _____ people

11. How many more people were at the fair on Saturday than on Sunday?

    _____ more people

People at the Fair

Friday	🧍🧍
Saturday	🧍🧍🧍🧍🧍
Sunday	🧍🧍🧍🧍

Key: Each 🧍 stands for 100 people.

Identify Place Value

Objective
Identify place value to 1,000.

Vocabulary
digit

▶ **Learn**

To find the value of a **digit**, find the value of its place. Find the value of the digits in 257.

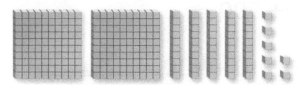

Hundreds	Tens	Ones
2	5	7

200 + 50 + 7

257

The 2 is in the hundreds place. Its value is 200.

The 5 is in the tens place. Its value is 50.

The 7 is in the ones place. Its value is 7.

▶ **Guided Practice**

Write the number.

Think!
I write 9 in the hundreds place, 6 in the tens place, and 1 in the ones place.

1. $900 + 60 + 1 =$ _____

2. $600 + 50 + 2 =$ _____

3. $800 + 50 + 3 =$ _____   4. $300 + 4 =$ _____

5. $8 + 60 + 300 =$ _____   6. $7 + 100 =$ _____

Circle the value of the red digit.

7.
| 849 |
800   80   8

8.
| 962 |
600   60   6

9.
| 294 |
400   40   4

10. **Math Talk** What does the digit 0 in 704 mean?

 KEY NS 1.1 Count, read, and write whole numbers to 1,000 and identify the place value for each digit.
Also NS 1.0, MR 1.0

NS 1.2 Use words, models, and expanded forms (e.g., 45 = 4 tens + 5) to represent numbers (to 1,000).

four hundred fifty-seven **457**

▶ Practice

Write the number.

Remember!
To find the value of a digit, find the value of its place.

11. $1 + 20 + 300 =$ _321_

12. $4 + 80 + 200 =$ _____   13. $6 + 800 =$ _____

14. $7 + 60 =$ _____   15. $3 + 10 + 400 =$ _____

16. $600 + 30 + 2 =$ _____   17. $7 + 50 + 800 =$ _____

Circle the value of the red digit.

18.	492	400	40	4	19.	781	800	80	8

20.	352	300	30	3	21.	527	200	20	2

22.	637	700	70	7	23.	576	500	50	5

24. Write a **3**-digit number with a **5** in the tens place. _____

Problem Solving: Number Sense

Solve.

25. Mavis has **2** tens rods, **2** ones blocks and **4** hundreds flats. What number can she show?

_____

26. Nam shows **657** using quick pictures. Show **657** another way.

_____

At Home Write a three-digit number, such as 465 or 891. Have your child name the value of the digit in the tens place.

En casa Escriba un número de tres dígitos, como 465 u 891. Pida a su niño que diga el valor del dígito en la posición de las decenas.

Name _____

Make a Table

▶ **Learn**

Problem Solving
Strategy

Objective
Solve problems using a table.

Sometimes you can make a table to help solve a problem.

Toby's family is planning a block party. They asked 5 neighbors to bring paper plates. They each bring 100 paper plates. How many plates do they have for the party?

Understand

Circle what you need to find out.

How many paper plates did each neighbor bring?

(How many paper plates did all 5 neighbors bring?)

Plan

Make a table and look for a pattern. What information will be in your table?

_____ neighbors

_____ paper plates from each neighbor

Solve

Make a table.

Neighbors	1	2	3	4	5
Paper plates	100	200	300	400	500

The neighbors brought ___500___ paper plates in all.

Look Back

How did the table help you find the answer?
Did you find a pattern in the table?

SDAP 2.1 Recognize, describe, and extend patterns and determine a next term in linear patterns (e.g., 4, 8, 12. . .; the number of ears on one horse, two horses, three horses, four horses).

SDAP 2.2 Solve problems involving simple number patterns.
Also **KEY SDAP 2.0**, MR 2.0

1. 4 of Toby's neighbors brought balloons.
   Each person brought 8 balloons.
   How many balloons were brought in all?

   Make a table.

   How many people brought balloons? _____

   How many balloons did each person bring? _____

People	1			
Balloons	8			

   _____ balloons

2. **123 Math Talk** How would you find the number
   of balloons that 2 people brought?

   Remember!
   Understand,
   Plan, Solve,
   Look Back

▶ **Problem Solving Practice**

Solve. Complete the table.

3. Some people are playing football on the grass.
   Each team has 6 people. If 30 people are playing,
   how many teams are there?

Teams	1				
People	6				

   _____ teams

4. A few children caught fireflies. They caught 10 fireflies
   in each jar. How many fireflies are in 4 jars?

Jars	1			
Fireflies	10			

   _____ fireflies

At Home Have your child explain
how he or she completed the tables to
help solve the problems.

En casa Pida a su niño que explique cómo
completó las tablas como ayuda para resolver
los problemas.

California Field Trip

At the Route 66 Museum

You can learn about the history of cars and highways. You can see neon signs, colorful posters, and an old gas pump. The museum also has displays about pioneers and trains.

History-Social Science

Signs at the museum

Choose a way to solve.

1. 100 people visit the Route 66 exhibit each day. How many visitors does the museum have in 4 days?

Days	1			
Visitors	100			

_____ visitors

Route 66 exhibit

2. The museum has some neon signs. The number of signs has a 1 in the hundreds place, a 0 in the tens place and an 8 in the ones place. What is the number?

_____ neon signs

neon sign

3. Jesse counts 200 stop signs. Patty counts 70 stop signs. Ollie counts 5 stop signs. How many do they count in all?

_____ stop signs

stop sign

KEY NS 1.1 Count, read, and write whole numbers to 1,000 and identify the place value for each digit.
History-Social Science 1.3

Also **NS 1.0, SDAP 2.2, MR 1.0, MR 1.1**

four hundred sixty-one **461**

Problem Solving on Tests
Listening Skills

Listen to your teacher read the problem.
Choose the correct answer.

> **Select a Strategy**
> **Write a Number**
>   **Sentence**
> **Act It Out**
> **Draw a Picture**
> **Use a Model**

1. How many faces of a pyramid are triangles?

   2   3   4   5
   ○   ○   ○   ○

   KEY **MG 2.1**

2. Abdul reads 3 books each month. How many
   books does he read in 4 months?

   6   9   12   15
   ○   ○   ○   ○

   KEY **NS 3.1**

3.
   12   35   57   75
   ○   ○   ○   ○

   KEY **NS 3.3**

4.
   5   4   3   2
   ○   ○   ○   ○

   KEY **NS 3.2**

MR 1.0 Make decisions about how to set up a
problem.
MR 1.1 Determine the approach, materials, and
strategies to be used.

Education Place
Visit **www.eduplace.com/camap/** for
Test-Taking Tips and Extra Practice.

Name _____

 # Key Standards Review

Use repeated subtraction
or equal groups to divide.

1. 8 ÷ 2 = _____

2. 9 ÷ 3 = _____

3. 16 ÷ 2 = _____

4. 10 ÷ 5 = _____

5. 25 ÷ 5 = _____

6. 12 ÷ 3 = _____

7. 18 ÷ 3 = _____

8. 20 ÷ 4 = _____

9. 21 ÷ 7 = _____

10. 30 ÷ 10 = _____

11. 16 ÷ 4 = _____

12. 14 ÷ 2 = _____

Challenge   Number Sense

1. There are **28** children in Andy's class.
4 children sit in each row. Andy is in
the last row. What row is he in?

Row _____

2. There are **24** children in Kendra's class.
4 children sit in each row. Kendra is
in the last row. What row is she in?

Row _____

KEY NS 3.2 Use repeated subtraction, equal
sharing, and forming equal groups with remainders
to do division.
Also **KEY NS 3.0**

California Trains

Back in 1869, trains used steam engines to create enough energy to move their wheels. You can see a steam engine at the California State Railroad Museum.

Solve.

Draw or write to explain.

1. Harry is reading a book about trains. He tells his brother that the page number he is on has 3 hundreds, 0 tens, and 6 ones. What page is he on?

   _____

2. Robbie visits a train museum. He counts 400 photographs, 70 posters, and 8 trains. How many items does he see at the museum in all?

   _____ items

3. Karen is thinking of a number between 500 and 700. It has a 3 in the tens place. The number in the hundreds place is equal to 3 × 2. The number in the ones place is equal to 8 ÷ 2. What is Karen's number?

   _____

KEY **NS 1.1** Count, read, and write whole numbers to 1,000 and identify the place value for each digit.
Also **NS 1.2, NS 1.0**
Science PS 1.d

Name _____

Concepts and Skills

Draw a quick picture. Write the number. **KEY** NS 1.1

1. 6 hundreds

_____

Write the numbers two ways. **KEY** NS 1.1

Show this many	Write how many hundreds, tens, and ones	Write the number
2. 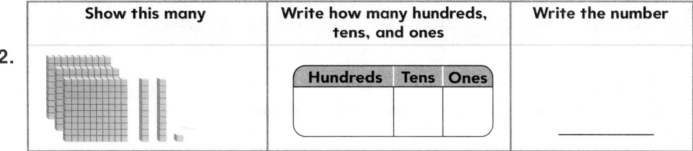	Hundreds | Tens | Ones	_____

Circle the word name for the number. **KEY** NS 1.1

3. 836   eight hundred sixty-three   eight hundred thirty-six

4. 903   nine hundred thirty   nine hundred three

Circle the value of the red digit. **KEY** NS 1.1

5.
527

five hundred   two tens   two

6.
907

900   100   9

Problem Solving **KEY** NS 1.1

7. Tania gets 10 rolls of pennies. Each roll holds 100 pennies. How many pennies does Tania get?

_____

Spiral Review and Test Practice

1. Which solid figure has the most vertices?

○   ○   ○   ○

KEY **MG 2.1** Page 297

---

2. What is the product? $3 \times 10 =$ _____

310   30   13   7

○   ○   ○   ○

KEY **NS 3.0**, KEY **NS 3.3**, KEY **NS 3.1** Page 417

---

3. Divide.
Use the number line help.

$20 \div 5 =$ _____

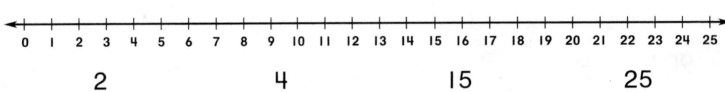

2   4   15   25

○   ○   ○   ○

KEY **NS 3.0**, KEY **NS 3.2** Page 433

---

4. Which is the word name for this number?   826

○ eight hundred sixty-two   ○ eighty-two

○ eight hundred twenty-six   ○ twenty-six

KEY **NS 1.1**, NS 1.2 Page 455

Education Place
Visit **www.eduplace.com/camap/** for
Test-Taking Tips and Extra Practice.

Spiral Review

Use Numbers to 1,000

Vocabulary

Here are some vocabulary words you will learn in the chapter.

regroup
With 3-digit numbers, sometimes you need to trade 10 tens for 1 hundred.

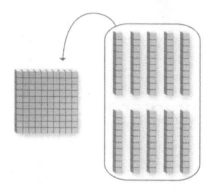

greatest, least Words used to compare three or more numbers

 345   445   454

Hundreds	Tens	Ones
3	4	5

Hundreds	Tens	Ones
4	5	4

345 comes before 445.   454 comes after 445.
345 is the least number.   454 is the greatest number.

See English-Spanish Glossary pages 573–589.

KEY NS 1.3 Order and compare whole numbers to 1,000 by using the symbols <, =, >.
Also **KEY NS 1.1**

Education Place
Visit **www.eduplace.com/camap/** for the eGlossary and eGames.

four hundred sixty-seven **467**

Name _____

Use the mailbox numbers to solve.

1. Which mailbox numbers are greater than **350**?

   _____ and _____

2. Which mailbox numbers are greater than **250** but less than **350**?

   _____ and _____

3. Rewrite the mailbox numbers in order from least to greatest.

   _____, _____, _____, _____, _____

Write >, <, or = to compare the numbers.

4. 684 ◯ 648

5. 375 ◯ 573

Use this page to review important skills needed for this chapter.

Name _____

Chapter 24 Lesson 1

Regroup Tens as Hundreds

▶ **Explore**

Use Workmat 6 with Learning Tool 24.

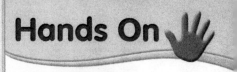
Objective
Regroup tens to
make hundreds.

Vocabulary
regroup

Step 1

Show 216 with 1 ,
11 ⬛⬛⬛, and 6 ◾.

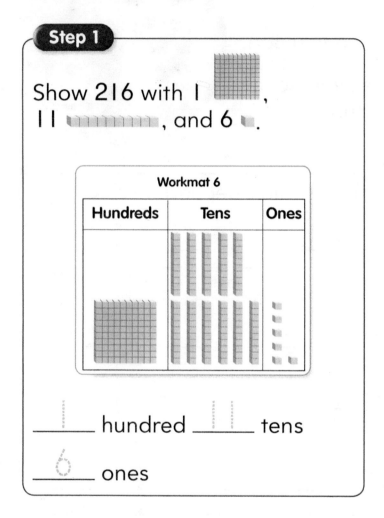

_____1_____ hundred _____11_____ tens

_____6_____ ones

Step 2

Now show 216 with the fewest
blocks. You can **regroup**
10 tens as 1 hundred.

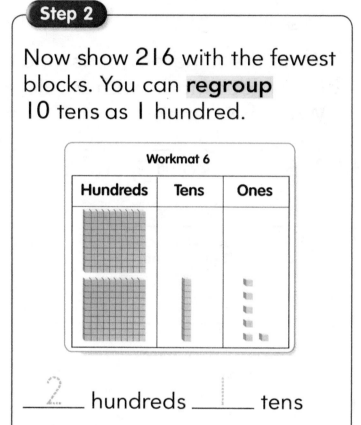

_____2_____ hundreds _____1_____ tens

_____6_____ ones

Use Workmat 6 with Learning Tool 24.

	Show this many.	Regroup 10 tens as 1 hundred.
1.	2 hundreds 16 tens 5 ones	_____ hundreds _____ tens _____ ones
2.	4 hundreds 17 tens 3 ones	_____ hundreds _____ tens _____ ones

3. **(123) Math Talk** Why can you regroup 1 hundred 15 tens as
2 hundreds 5 tens?

KEY NS 1.1 Count, read, and write whole
numbers to 1,000 and identify the place value for
each digit.
Also **NS 1.2, MR 1.2**

NS 1.0 Understand the relationship between
numbers, quantities, and place value in whole
numbers up to 1,000.

four hundred sixty-nine **469**

▶ Extend

Use Workmat 6 with Learning Tool 24.
Work with a partner.

1. Spin the spinner two times. Write both
   numbers. Find the sum. Take that many tens.
   Show them on Workmat 6.

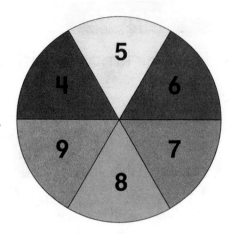

2. Regroup 10 tens as 1 hundred when you can.

3. Write the hundreds, tens, and ones you have.
   Draw your model with a quick picture.
   Write the number.

First Spin	Second Spin	Sum
_____	_____	_____

Hundreds	Tens	Ones

First Spin	Second Spin	Sum
_____	_____	_____

Hundreds	Tens	Ones

First Spin	Second Spin	Sum
_____	_____	_____

Hundreds	Tens	Ones

First Spin	Second Spin	Sum
_____	_____	_____

Hundreds	Tens	Ones

Compare Three-Digit Numbers

Objective
Use place value to compare three-digit numbers.

Vocabulary
place value
least
greatest

 **Learn**

Use **place value** to compare numbers. You can find which number is the **least** and which number is the **greatest**.

Compare 225 and 234.

First compare hundreds. The hundreds are the same. Then, compare the tens.

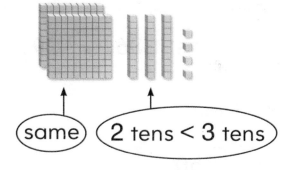

Hundreds	Tens	Ones
2	2	5

Hundreds	Tens	Ones
2	3	4

(same) (2 tens < 3 tens) 225 is less than 234
225 < 234

Think!
The hundreds and the tens are the same, so I compare the ones.

▶ **Guided Practice**

Compare the numbers. Write >, <, or = in the ◯.
Use place-value blocks if you wish.

1. 523 ◯ 529

2. 783 ◯ 792

3. 542 ◯ 542

4. 430 ◯ 425

5. 801 ◯ 719

6. 305 ◯ 350

7. (123) **Math Talk** How does knowing about place value help you compare numbers?

KEY NS 1.3 Order and compare whole numbers to 1,000 by using the symbols <, =, >. Also NS 1.0, MR 2.0

KEY NS 1.1 Count, read, and write whole numbers to 1,000 and identify the place value for each digit.

four hundred seventy-one **471**

Remember!
Compare the hundreds
first, then the tens,
then the ones.

Compare the numbers.
Write >, <, or = in the ◯.

8. 425 ◯< 503

9. 343 ◯ 351

10. 519 ◯ 287

11. 852 ◯ 851

12. 416 ◯ 372

13. 476 ◯ 476

14. 255 ◯ 401

15. 785 ◯ 779

16. 625 ◯ 498

17. 20 ◯ 220

18. 803 ◯ 803

19. 236 ◯ 240

20. 247 ◯ 198

21. 531 ◯ 508

22. 10 ◯ 100

23. 713 ◯ 713

24. 921 ◯ 912

25. 336 ◯ 299

26. Fill in the number that makes the exercise true.

354 < _____ | 340 | | 345 | | 355 | | 350 |

Problem Solving: Reasoning

27. Joe has seat number 632 at the concert. Ling has seat number 487. Carlos has seat number 556. Whose seat number has the greatest number? Tell how you know.

_____

664 665 667
653 654
642 643 4
631 632 533
620 622

At Home Write 2 three-digit numbers. Ask your child which number is greater.
En casa Escriba 2 números de tres dígitos. Pregunte a su niño qué número es mayor.

Chapter 24 Lesson 3

Before, After, and Between

 **Explore**

Objective
Identify three-digit numbers to determine what comes before, after, and between.

Mario and Sue have several tickets to the school concert. The tickets are blue.

A number line can help you find a number that is just before, just after, or between other numbers.

Cut out the tickets on the side of this page. Use the number line to help put the tickets in order.

```
←——+——+——+——+——+——+——+——+——+——+——→
  185  186  187  188  189  190  191  192  193  194  195
```

1. What ticket number comes before 188? _____

2. What ticket number comes after 189? _____

3. What ticket number comes before 194? _____

4. What ticket number comes between 189 and 191? _____

5. (123) **Math Talk** Is there a ticket number between 188 and 189? Explain.

KEY NS 1.3 Order and compare whole numbers to 1,000 by using the symbols <, =, >.
Also **KEY NS 1.1**, NS 1.0, MR 2.0

MR 1.2 Use tools, such as manipulatives or sketches, to model problems.

four hundred seventy-three **473**

Use the pink tickets.
Put the tickets in order.
You can use the number line.

Remember!
You can also count
to find a number.

527
523
526
522
528
525
524

← 520 521 522 523 524 525 526 527 528 529 530 →

6. What ticket number
comes before 526? _____

7. What ticket number comes
between 527 and 529? _____

8. What ticket number
comes after 522? _____

9. You had ticket number 531.
What ticket number comes next? _____

What ticket number comes before? _____

10. Jason has 4 tickets.
Write the numbers in
order on the number line.

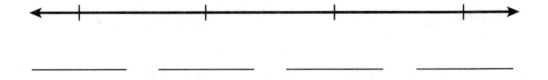

← | | | →

_____ _____ _____ _____

11. What number should come next? _____

12. What number should come just
before these tickets? _____

At Home Write a three-digit number.
Ask your child to write the numbers
that come just before and just after it.

En casa Escriba un número de tres dígitos.
Pida a su niño que escriba los números
que vienen justo antes y justo después del
número.

Order Three-Digit Numbers

▶  **Learn**

Use place value to order numbers.
Order the numbers from least to greatest.

212	159	215

Step 1 Compare the hundreds. 1 < 2.

_159__ < _____ < _____

Hundreds	Tens	Ones
2	1	2

Step 2 Compare the tens. 1 ten = 1 ten.

Hundreds	Tens	Ones
1	5	9

Step 3 So, compare the ones. 2 < 5.

_159_ < _212_ < _215_

Hundreds	Tens	Ones
2	1	5

159 comes before 212.
212 comes between 159 and 215.
215 comes after 212.

Think!
640 and 635 both have 6 hundreds, so I compare the tens.

▶ **Guided Practice**

Write the numbers in order from least to greatest.

1. 640   175   635   _____ < _____ < _____   640

2. 781   718   308   _____ < _____ < _____

Write the numbers in order from greatest to least.

3. 125   561   526   _____ > _____ > _____

4. 343   333   434   _____ > _____ > _____

5. (123) **Math Talk** How does knowing about place value help you order numbers?

KEY NS 1.3 Order and compare whole numbers to 1,000 by using the symbols <, =, >. Also NS 1.0, MR 2.0

KEY NS 1.1 Count, read, and write whole numbers to 1,000 and identify the place value for each digit.

four hundred seventy-five **475**

Remember!
Use place value to
order numbers.

Write the numbers in order
from least to greatest.

6. 199 154 291 192   154 < 192 < 199 < 291

7. 430 434 345 344   _____ < _____ < _____ < _____

8. 795 800 999 759   _____ < _____ < _____ < _____

Write the numbers in order from greatest to least.

9. 175 180 158 178   _____ > _____ > _____ > _____

10. 922 892 927 999   _____ > _____ > _____ > _____

11. 723 774 747 727   _____ > _____ > _____ > _____

12. Circle the numbers that do not
come between 830 and 842.

840   837   852   882

Problem Solving: Reasoning

Solve.

Draw or write to explain.

13. Which number is out of order if Paul
is ordering numbers from least to
greatest? How do you know?

715   775   735   762

_____ is out of order.

_____

At Home Write 3 three-digit numbers.
Have your child put the numbers in
order from greatest to least.

En casa Escriba 3 números de tres dígitos.
Pida a su niño que ponga los números en
orden de mayor a menor.

Count Dollars and Cents

Objective
Count dollars and cents and write the amount.

Vocabulary
dollar sign
decimal point
one-dollar bill
five-dollar bill
ten-dollar bill

▶ **Learn**

Use a **dollar sign** and a **decimal point** when you write amounts greater than one dollar.

one-dollar bill
$1.00

five-dollar bill
$5.00

ten-dollar bill
$10.00

Eric has the amount shown.
He wants to buy a ball for **$5.50**.
Can he buy the ball?

Count the dollars. Then count the coins.

$5.00, $6.00, $6.05, $6.06, $6.07

Eric can buy the ball because he has __$6.07__.

$5.50

▶ **Guided Practice**

Write the total value of the bills and coins.

1.

Think!
I count the bills first and then the cents.

$ _____

2. **123** **Math Talk** Why do you count the dollar bills first and then the coins?

 **KEY NS 5.1** Solve problems using combinations of coins and bills.
Also NS 5.0, MR 2.0

KEY NS 5.2 Know and use the decimal notation and the dollar and cent symbols for money.

four hundred seventy-seven **477**

▶ **Practice**

Count and write the total value
of the bills and coins.

3.  $ _$7.71_

4.  $ _____

Draw bills and coins to show the amount.

5. $9.88

6. 11 dollars and thirty-five cents

Problem Solving: Reasoning

Circle the correct way to write
each amount.

7.
$2.06 $2.60 $2.16

8.
$0.06 $0.60 $6.00

 At Home Ask your child to show you
how he or she counted the money on
this page.

En casa Pida a su niño que le muestre cómo
contó el dinero que aparece en esta página.

Name _____

Comparison Problems

 **Learn**

Objective
Use comparison to solve problems.

The table below shows the prices of boat pictures. How much more does the rowboat picture cost than the canoe picture?

Understand
What do you know?
• The rowboat picture costs $1.67.
• The canoe picture costs $0.52.

Kind of Picture	Price
Canoe	$0.52
Raft	$1.33
Rowboat	$1.67
Sailboat	$0.89

Plan
Choose the operation you need to solve.

Think!
I need to find the difference, so I subtract.

addition   (subtraction)

Use comparison bars.
Write the parts you know.

Rowboat	$1.67	
Canoe	$0.52	?

Solve
Write a number sentence.
Then solve.

Think!
$1.67 is the larger amount. $0.52 is the smaller amount.

$1.67 (−) $0.52 = $1.15

The rowboat picture costs $1.15 more.

Look Back
Did you answer the question?
How can you check your answer?

NS 5.0 Model and solve problems by representing, adding, and subtracting amounts of money. Also **KEY NS 5.2**, **KEY NS 2.2**, NS 2.0, MR 2.0, MR 2.2

AF 1.3 Solve addition and subtraction problems by using data from simple charts, picture graphs, and number sentences.

1. Kelsey buys an airplane postcard and another postcard that costs $0.14 more. Which other postcard does Kelsey buy?

Kind of Postcard	Price
Airplane	$0.74
Bicycle	$0.93
Bus	$0.88
Car	$0.65

Remember!
Understand, Plan, Solve, Look Back

Write the parts you know in the comparison bars.

Write a number sentence. Then solve.

Airplane Postcard		
Other Postcard	?	

_____ ◯ _____ = _____

Think!
I know two parts. I need to add to find the total.

The _____ postcard costs $0.88.

Kelsey buys an airplane postcard

and a _____ postcard.

2. (123) **Math Talk** How did you use comparison bars to solve the problem?

Use comparison bars. Solve.

Draw or write to explain.

3. How much more does the bicycle postcard cost than the bus postcard?

_____

4. Hena buys a bus postcard and another postcard that costs $0.23 less. Which other postcard does Hena buy?

the _____ postcard

At Home Ask your child to find which postcard costs $0.19 more than the airplane postcard.

En casa Pida a su niño que halle qué postal cuesta $0.19 más que la postal del aeroplano.

Create and Solve

Objective
Write problems and use strategies to solve them.

The table shows some toy prices.

Toy Prices	
Toy	**Price**
toy car	$0.75
toy train	$0.91
toy truck	$0.84
toy plane	$0.89

1. How much more does the toy train cost than the toy truck?

   _____ ◯ _____ = _____

   The toy train costs _____ more.

2. Write a comparison problem about the toys in the table.

   _____

   _____

   _____

   _____

   _____

3. Write a number sentence. Solve your problem.

   _____ −◯ _____ ◯ _____

   Share your comparison problem with a classmate.

AF 1.0 Model, represent, and interpret number relationships to create and solve problems involving addition and subtraction.
NS 5.0 Model and solve problems by representing,

adding, and subtracting amounts of money.
Also NS 2.0, KEY NS 5.2, KEY NS 2.2,
AF 1.2, AF 1.3, MR 1.0, MR 1.1, SDAP 1.4

four hundred eighty-one **481**

The table shows the prices of some stickers.

Sticker Prices	
Kind	Price
boat	$0.65
bicycle	$0.94
helicopter	$0.42
motorcycle	$0.51

4. Colin buys a helicopter sticker and another sticker that costs $0.23 more. Which other sticker does Colin buy?

_____ ◯ _____ = _____

The _____ sticker costs $0.23 more than the helicopter sticker.

Colin buys a helicopter sticker and a _____ sticker.

5. Write a comparison problem about the stickers in the table.

_____

_____

_____

_____

_____

6. Write a number sentence. Solve your problem.

_____ ◯ _____ ◯ _____

Share your comparison problem with a classmate.

Name _____

 # Key Standards Review

Complete the chart.

	Word Form	Expanded Form	Number
1.	three hundred sixty-two	_____ + _____ + _____	_____
2.	_____	400 + 70 + 8	_____
3.	_____	800 + 90 + 3	_____
4.	_____	_____ + _____ + _____	561
5.	_____	_____ + _____ + _____	715

Challenge   Number Sense

1. Javier lives on Maple Street. His house number is between 230 and 250. The sum of its tens and ones digits is 13. What is his house number?

_____

2. Joy lives on Green Street. Her house number is between 140 and 170. The product of the tens and ones digits is 20. The tens digit is less than the ones digit. What is her house number?

_____

KEY **NS 1.1** Count, read, and write whole numbers to 1,000 and identify the place value for each digit.
Also **KEY NS 2.2**, **KEY NS 3.0**

four hundred eighty-three **483**

Math Music

Count By 100s

Math Music, Track 9
Tune: "Down in the Valley"

100 children walk quickly each day.
200 children will ride the subway.

300 children ride cars everywhere.
400 children ride jets in the air.

500 children ride boats in the sea.
600 children ride buses past me.

700 children ride trains to and fro.
800 children ride horses, you know.

900 children ride bikes just like you.
1000 children ride tricycles, too.

Count by 100s. Can you do it now?
If you can do it, then please take a bow!

KEY NS 1.1 Count, read, and write whole numbers to
1,000 and identify the place value for each digit.

Name _____

Concepts and Skills

Write the numbers. Add. KEY **NS 1.1**

1. 7 tens _____   7 tens + 6 tens = _____ tens

   6 tens _____   13 tens = _____ hundred, _____ tens

Compare the numbers.
Write >, <, or = in the ◯. KEY **NS 1.3**

2. 905 ◯ 950   3. 106 ◯ 99   4. 840 ◯ 480

Write the number that comes before
and the number that comes after. KEY **NS 1.1**

5. _____, 679, _____   6. _____, 530, _____

Write the numbers in order from least to greatest. KEY **NS 1.3**

7. 105, 99, 650, 569   _____ < _____ < _____ < _____

Count and write the total value of
the bills and coins. KEY **NS 5.1**

8.

_____

Problem Solving   NS 5.0, KEY **NS 2.2**, MR 1.0

Write the number sentence.

9. A birthday card costs $1.95.
   Candles cost $2.45. How much
   more do the candles cost?

   _____ ◯ _____ ◯ _____

🐻 Spiral Review and Test Practice

1. Which is the fraction that names the shaded part?

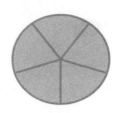 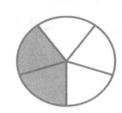

$\frac{7}{10}$ ○ $\frac{7}{5}$ ○ $\frac{5}{10}$ ○ $\frac{7}{7}$ ○

KEY **NS 4.3**, KEY **NS 4.2**, NS 4.0 Page 317

---

2. What is the remainder? $23 \div 5$

3 ○   4 ○   5 ○   6 ○

KEY **NS 3.0**, KEY **NS 3.2** Page 435

---

3. Which is the value of the red digit?   703

7 ○   70 ○   100 ○   700 ○

KEY **NS 1.1**, NS 1.0, NS 1.2 Page 457

---

4. Which symbol makes this comparison true?   705 ◯ 750

> ○   < ○   = ○   − ○

KEY **NS 1.3**, NS 1.0 Page 471

□□□□□|||||||°°°°°

Education Place
Visit **www.eduplace.com/camap/** for
Test-Taking Tips and Extra Practice.

Spiral Review

Name _____

Greg Tang's Go Fast, Go Far

Multiply by 4

A group of 4 is fast to do, if you think in groups of 2!

I add 2 groups of 5 to another 2 groups of 5. I get 10 + 10 = 20.

1. $4 \times 5 =$ ☐10☐ + ☐10☐ = ☐20☐
   5 + 5   5 + 5

2. $4 \times 7 =$ ☐14☐ + ☐ ☐ = ☐ ☐
   7 + 7   7 + 7

3. $4 \times 8 =$ ☐ ☐ + ☐ ☐ = ☐ ☐
   8 + 8   8 + 8

Take It Further: Now try doing all the steps in your head!

4. $4 \times 9 =$ ☐ ☐

5. $4 \times 10 =$ ☐ ☐

6. $4 \times 4 =$ ☐ ☐

7. $4 \times 6 =$ ☐ ☐

8. $4 \times 12 =$ ☐ ☐

9. $4 \times 15 =$ ☐ ☐

Great Job!

Reading and Writing Math

There are **365** days in a year. Complete the word web to show the number **365** in different ways.

Word Bank
digit
greatest
hundred
least
place value

Ways to Show 365

1. Draw a quick picture.

3. Show the number in expanded form.

_____ + _____ + _____

2. Write the place value of the number.

_____ hundreds

_____ tens

_____ ones

4. **Writing Math** Write three different numbers using the digits 3, 6, and 5.

[_____]   [_____]   [_____]

Now write the numbers in order from least to greatest. Explain your thinking.

_____   _____   _____

_____

_____

KEY **NS 1.1** Count, read, and write whole numbers to 1,000 and identify the place value for each digit.
Also **NS 1.0, NS 1.2, KEY NS 1.3**

Name _____

Concepts and Skills

Complete the table. KEY NS1.1

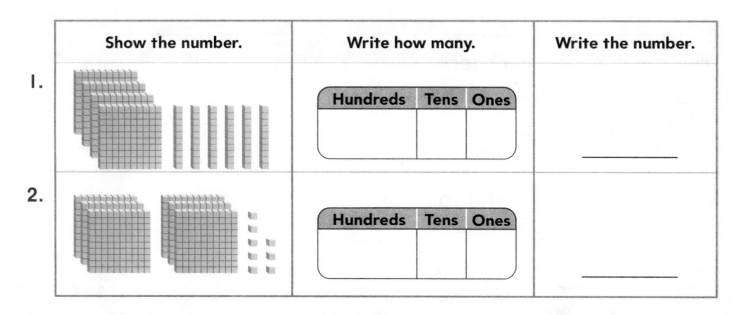

Show the number.	Write how many.	Write the number.
1.	Hundreds / Tens / Ones	_____
2.	Hundreds / Tens / Ones	_____

Circle the word name for the number. KEY NS1.1

3. 790   seven hundred nine   seven hundred ninety

4. 116   one hundred sixteen   one hundred sixty

Circle the value of the red digit. KEY NS1.1

5. 489   **6.** 320

four hundred   forty   four   200   20   2

Compare the numbers.
Write >, <, or = in the . KEY NS1.3

7. 508 ◯ 850   **8.** 783 ◯ 789   **9.** 910 ◯ 900 + 10

Write the number that comes before
and the number that comes after. KEY **NS 1.1**

10. _____, 405, _____   11. _____, 320, _____

Write the numbers in order
from least to greatest. KEY **NS 1.3**

12. 295, 88, 450, 379   _____ < _____ < _____ < _____

Count and write the total value of
the bills and coins. KEY **NS 5.1**

13.

_____

Problem Solving

Complete the table to solve. SDAP 2.2

14. Lina bought 7 boxes of envelopes.
    Each box holds 100 envelopes.

Box	1	2	3	4	5	6	7
Envelopes	100						

How many envelopes did Lina buy? _____

Unit 10

Add and Subtract 3-Digit Numbers

Houghton Mifflin
California Math

★ BIG IDEAS!

- When you add a three-digit number, you may have to regroup the ones, tens, or hundreds.

- When you subtract from a three-digit number, you may have to regroup the tens or hundreds.

- You can show a number sentence that relates to an addition or subtraction situation.

Songs and Games

 Math Music Track 10
Check What You Subtract

eGames
www.eduplace.com/camap/

Literature

Read Aloud Big Book
- Flight of the Monarchs

Math Readers

The IF Game

The Bug Boys
by Calla Salerno
Illustrated by Chi Chung

Fish Arithmetic
by Lionel Washington
Illustrated by Shirley V. Beckes

Sum Difference
by Matt Harts
Illustrated by Laura Ovresat

Spin a Number

How to Play

1. Spin the spinner two times. Write both numbers.

2. Find the sum. Take that many tens.

3. Regroup 10 tens for 1 hundred if you can.

4. Write the hundreds and tens. Write the number.

5. The player with the highest number after 3 turns wins.

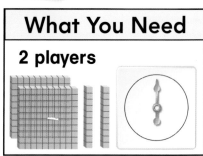

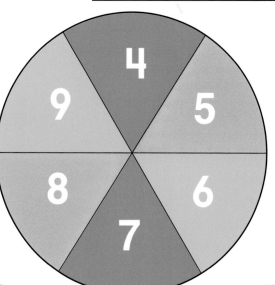

First spin	Second spin	Sum

_____ Hundreds _____ Tens _____

First spin	Second spin	Sum

_____ Hundreds _____ Tens _____

First spin	Second spin	Sum

_____ Hundreds _____ Tens _____

First spin	Second spin	Sum

_____ Hundreds _____ Tens _____

First spin	Second spin	Sum

_____ Hundreds _____ Tens _____

First spin	Second spin	Sum

_____ Hundreds _____ Tens _____

KEY NS 2.2 Find the sum or difference of two whole numbers up to three digits long. Also NS 2.0, MR 1.2, MR 2.2

Education Place
Visit www.eduplace.com/camap/ for eGames and Brain Teasers.

Math at Home

Dear Family,

My class is starting Unit 10, **Add and Subtract 3-Digit Numbers.** I will be learning about how to regroup with 3-digit numbers, how to use addition to check subtraction, and how to write in vertical form. You can help me learn these vocabulary words, and we can do the Math Activity together.

From,

_____

Vocabulary

inverse operation Addition and subtraction are inverse operations.

$$
\begin{array}{r} 567 \\ -239 \\ \hline 328 \end{array}
\qquad
\begin{array}{r} 328 \\ +239 \\ \hline 567 \end{array}
$$

You can use addition to check subtraction.

vertical form Rewriting the problem by lining up the digits to solve

$1.35 + $0.78 $\xrightarrow[\text{to solve}]{\text{rewrite}}$ $\begin{array}{r} \$1.35 \\ +\$0.78 \\ \hline \$2.13 \end{array}$

Education Place
Visit **www.eduplace.com/camaf/** for
• eGames and Brain Teasers
• Math at Home in other languages

Family Math Activity

At the grocery store, find two items that each cost less than **$2.00**. Have your child add up the two prices to find the total cost. Then have your child subtract to find how much change he or she should get from a **$5** bill.

Literature

These books link to the math in this unit. Look for them at the library.

• **Earth Day—Hooray!** by Stuart J. Murphy Illustrated by Renée Andriani (HarperCollins, 2004)

• **The Tour de France** by Joseph A. Saviola

Matemáticas en casa

Estimada familia:

Mi clase está comenzando la Unidad 10, **Suma y resta de números de 3 dígitos**. Aprenderé a reagrupar con números de 3 dígitos, a usar la suma para comprobar la resta y a escribir en forma vertical. Me pueden ayudar a aprender estas palabras de vocabulario y podemos hacer juntos la Actividad de matemáticas para la familia.

De:

_____

Vocabulario

operación inversa La suma y la resta son operaciones inversas. Se puede usar la suma para comprobar la resta.

$$
\begin{array}{r} 567 \\ -239 \\ \hline 328 \end{array}
\qquad
\begin{array}{r} 328 \\ +239 \\ \hline 567 \end{array}
$$

forma vertical Escribir de nuevo el problema, alineando los dígitos para resolverlo.

$1.35 + $0.78 → escribir de nuevo para resolver →
$$
\begin{array}{r} \$1.35 \\ +\$0.78 \\ \hline \$2.13 \end{array}
$$

Education Place

Visite **www.eduplace.com/camaf/** para
• Juegos en línea y acertijos
• Matemáticas en casa en otros idiomas

Actividad de matemáticas para la familia

En el supermercado, busque dos artículos que cuesten menos de $2.00 cada uno. Pida a su niño que sume los dos precios para hallar el costo total. Luego, imagine que pagaría los artículos con un billete de $5. Pida a su niño que reste para hallar el cambio que debe recibir.

Literatura

Estos libros hablan sobre las matemáticas de esta unidad. Búscalos en la biblioteca.

• **Diseños: Para aprender matemáticas jugando**
por Ivan Bulloch
(*Turtleback Books, 2000*)

492

You Can Be a Winner!

written by Tim Johnson

illustrated by Lance Lekander

This Take-Home Book belongs to

Hey Kids!
Are you good at math?
If so, you could win
a week to

SPACE CITY
a new camp for kids!
TAKE ONE

Reading and Writing Math

This take-home book will help you review adding and subtracting two-digit numbers.

What do you think will happen? Write a few sentences to tell how this story will end.

NS 2.0 Students estimate, calculate, and solve problems involving addition and subtraction of two- and three-digit numbers.

Solve these math problems.
Show how you got each answer.
Correct answers will help you
to win! Good luck!

One Moon day is about 28 Earth
days long. How many Earth days
are the same as 2 Moon days?

___ + ___ = ___ Earth days

Lucy is 8 years old now.
She becomes an astronaut
when she is 35 years old.
How many years until she
becomes an astronaut?

___ − ___ = ___ years

2

7

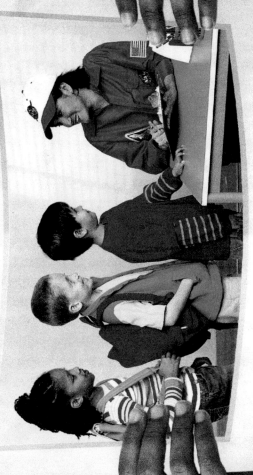

Last year 94 boys and 97 girls attended Space City camp. How many children attended in all?

_____ + _____ = _____ children

It takes Uranus about 84 years to orbit the sun.
It takes Saturn about 29 years to orbit the sun.
What is the difference in years?

_____ − _____ = _____ years

47 small meteors hit the moon's surface in one hour.
65 hit the moon's surface during the next hour.
How many meteors hit the moon's surface in those two hours?

_____ + _____ = _____ meteors

SPACE CITY

Only four more math problems to solve and you could be here! Imagine!

ROCKET BUILDING CENTER

WEIGHTLESS BUBBLE

INTERPLANETARY ADVENTURE RIDE

Add 3-Digit Numbers

Vocabulary

Here are some vocabulary words you will learn in the chapter.

add hundreds You can use hundreds flats to model three-digit addition.

$$400 + 200$$

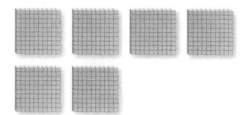

4 hundreds		400
+2 hundreds		+200
6 hundreds		600

regroup You can regroup tens or ones to find the sum of two 3-digit numbers.

H	T	O
1		
1	3	5
+3	8	0
5	1	5

You can regroup 10 tens as 1 hundred.

H	T	O
	1	
2	1	9
+4	6	3
6	8	2

You can regroup 10 ones as 1 ten.

See English-Spanish Glossary pages 573–589.

KEY NS 2.2 Find the sum or difference of two whole numbers up to three digits long.

Education Place
Visit www.eduplace.com/camap/ for the eGlossary and eGames.

four hundred ninety-three **493**

Name _____

 # Check What You Know

Space Books in the Library	
Stars	320
Comets	200
Planets	290
Astronauts	300

1. How many books does the library have about comets and astronauts?

   _____ + _____ = _____ books

2. How many books does the library have about astronauts and stars?

   _____ + _____ = _____ books

3. How many books does the library have about planets and stars?

   _____ + _____ = _____ books

4. How many books does the library have about stars, comets, and astronauts?

   _____ + _____ + _____ = _____ books

5. How many books does the library have on comets and planets?

   _____ + _____ = _____ books

Use this page to review important skills needed for this chapter.

□□□□□||||||||||○○○○

Chapter 25 Lesson 1

Add Hundreds

 **Learn**

To add hundreds, think of an addition fact.

Find $300 + 200$.
Use Workmat 6 and Learning Tool 24.

Step 1
Model the hundreds.
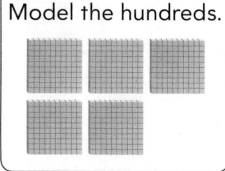

Step 2
Draw your model with a quick picture.

Step 3
Use the addition fact $3 + 2$ to help solve.

$$
\begin{array}{r}
3 \text{ hundreds} \\
+2 \text{ hundreds} \\
\hline
5 \text{ hundreds}
\end{array}
\qquad
\begin{array}{r}
300 \\
+200 \\
\hline
500
\end{array}
$$

▶ Guided Practice

Use Learning Tool 24.
Draw your model with a quick picture.
Add.

Think!
I can use $4 + 3$ to help me find $400 + 300$.

1.
$$
\begin{array}{r} 4 \\ +3 \\ \hline \end{array}
\qquad
\begin{array}{r} 4 \text{ hundreds} \\ +3 \text{ hundreds} \\ \hline \text{hundreds} \end{array}
\qquad
\begin{array}{r} 400 \\ +300 \\ \hline \end{array}
$$

2.
$$
\begin{array}{r} 2 \\ +6 \\ \hline \end{array}
\qquad
\begin{array}{r} 2 \text{ hundreds} \\ +6 \text{ hundreds} \\ \hline \text{hundreds} \end{array}
\qquad
\begin{array}{r} 200 \\ +600 \\ \hline \end{array}
$$

3.
$$
\begin{array}{r} 5 \\ +2 \\ \hline \end{array}
\qquad
\begin{array}{r} 5 \text{ hundreds} \\ +2 \text{ hundreds} \\ \hline \text{hundreds} \end{array}
\qquad
\begin{array}{r} 500 \\ +200 \\ \hline \end{array}
$$

4. **(123) Math Talk** How does $3 + 4 = 7$ help you solve $300 + 400$?

KEY NS 2.2 Find the sum or difference of two whole numbers up to three digits long.
Also **NS 2.3, SDAP 2.2, NS 2.0, KEY SDAP 2.0, MR 3.0**

MR 1.2 Use tools, such as manipulatives or sketches, to model problems.

Use Learning Tool 24. Add.
Draw your model with a quick picture.

Remember!
Use a basic fact to help add hundreds.

5. 3 hundreds   300
   + 5 hundreds   + 500
    8 hundreds   800

6. 4 hundreds   400
   + 4 hundreds   + 400
      hundreds

7. 3 hundreds   300
   + 6 hundreds   + 600
      hundreds

8. 2 hundreds   200
   + 7 hundreds   + 700
      hundreds

9. 3 hundreds   300
    2 hundreds   200
   + 4 hundreds   + 400
      hundreds

Problem Solving: Number Sense

Follow each rule.

10.

Add 100	
200	
300	
400	

11.

Add 300	
100	
200	
300	

12.

Add 500	
100	
200	
300	

At Home Ask your child to tell you how knowing 3 + 2 = 5 helps him or her solve 300 + 200.

En casa Pida a su niño que le explique cómo saber que 3 + 2 = 5 lo ayuda a resolver 300 + 200.

Chapter 25 Lesson 2

Regroup Ones

 **Learn**

Hands On

Objective
Regroup ones to find
the sum of two three-
digit numbers.

Find 227 + 146.

Use Workmat 6 and Learning Tool 24.

Step 1

Show 227 and 146.
Add the ones.
Regroup 10 ones
as 1 ten.

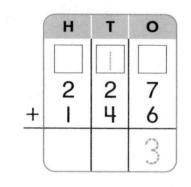

H	T	O
	1	
2	2	7
+ 1	4	6
		3

Step 2

Add the tens.

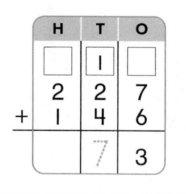

H	T	O
	1	
2	2	7
+ 1	4	6
	7	3

Step 3

Add the hundreds.

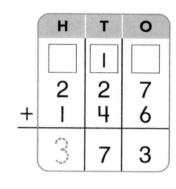

H	T	O
	1	
2	2	7
+ 1	4	6
3	7	3

▶ **Guided Practice**

Use Workmat 6 and Learning Tool 24.
Add.

1.

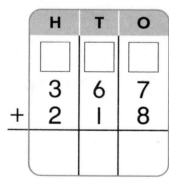

H	T	O
3	6	7
+ 2	1	8

Think!
7 + 8 = 15. I need to
regroup 15 ones as 1 ten
and 5 ones.

2.

H	T	O
8	6	8
+		8

3. **(123)** **Math Talk** How does knowing that
10 ones = 1 ten help you add?

 KEY NS 2.2 Find the sum or difference of two
whole numbers up to three digits long.
Also NS 2.0, MR 2.0

MR 1.2 Use tools, such as manipulatives or
sketches, to model problems.

four hundred ninety-seven **497**

Use Workmat 6 and Learning Tool 24.
Add.

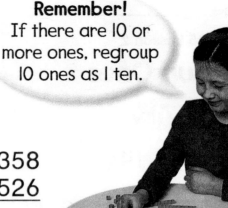

4. 617
   + 45
   ‾‾‾‾
    662

5. 143
   +524

6. 358
   +526

7. 318
   + 35

8. 123
   +359

9. 237
   +428

10. 468
    + 7

11. 723
    +147

12. 305
    +327

13. 223
    +619

14. 570
    + 29

15. 189
    +307

16. 848
    + 38

17. 567
    +226

18. 362
    + 38

Problem Solving: Number Sense

19. Liz has 147 stamps from Mexico
    and 49 stamps from Japan.
    How many does she have in all?

Draw or write to explain.

_____ stamps

At Home Ask your child to circle the
exercises on this page that require
regrouping, and then explain why
regrouping is necessary.

En casa Pida a su niño que rodee con un
círculo los ejercicios de esta página en los que
tiene que reagrupar, y que explique por qué
reagrupar es necesario.

Name _____

Regroup Tens

 **Learn**

Hands On

Objective
Regroup tens to find the sum of two three-digit numbers.

Find 152 + 265.

Use Workmat 6 and Learning Tool 24.

Step 1

Show 152 and 265.
Add the ones.

H	T	O
1	5	2
+ 2	6	5
		7

Step 2

Add the tens.
Regroup 10 tens
as 1 hundred.

H	T	O
1		
1	5	2
+ 2	6	5
		7

Step 3

Add the hundreds.

H	T	O
1		
1	5	2
+ 2	6	5
	1	7

▶ Guided Practice

Use Workmat 6 and Learning Tool 24.
Add.

1.

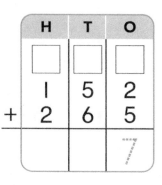

H	T	O
4	6	2
+ 4	6	7

Think!
6 tens + 6 tens =
12 tens. I need to
regroup the tens.

2.

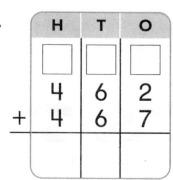

H	T	O
2	5	3
+	7	5

3. **(123) Math Talk** How do you know if you
need to regroup tens?

KEY NS 2.2 Find the sum or difference of two
whole numbers up to three digits long.
Also **NS 2.0, AF 1.3, MR 2.1, SDAP 1.4**

MR 1.2 Use tools, such as manipulatives or
sketches, to model problems.

▶ **Practice**

Use Workmat 6 and Learning Tool 24.
Add.

Remember!
Regroup 10 tens
to make 100.

4. 183
   +516
   ‾‾‾‾
    699

5. 357
   + 14
   ‾‾‾‾

6. 431
   +294
   ‾‾‾‾

7. 335
   +171
   ‾‾‾‾

8. 136
   +792
   ‾‾‾‾

9. 636
   + 83
   ‾‾‾‾

10. 762
    + 67
    ‾‾‾‾

11. 624
    +182
    ‾‾‾‾

12. 342
    +264
    ‾‾‾‾

13. 653
    +293
    ‾‾‾‾

14. 548
    + 71
    ‾‾‾‾

15. 459
    + 90
    ‾‾‾‾

16. 260
    +179
    ‾‾‾‾

17. 633
    +282
    ‾‾‾‾

18. 256
    +367
    ‾‾‾‾

Problem Solving: Data Sense

19. Susan and Juan put their postcards
together. How many do they have
in all? How do you know?

_____ postcards

Postcards Collected	
Susan	214
Kyle	178
Juan	146

At Home Have your child explain how he or she knows when to regroup tens.

🏠 **At Home** Have your child explain
how he or she knows when to
regroup tens.

En casa Pida a su niño que explique cómo
sabe cuándo debe reagrupar las decenas.

Chapter 25 Lesson 4

Practice Adding Three-Digit Numbers

 **Learn**

When you add three-digit numbers, decide whether you need to regroup.

Find $300 + 125$.   Find $127 + 35$.   Find $245 + 93$.

I'll add with mental math.

$$\begin{array}{r} 300 \\ + 125 \end{array}$$

I need to regroup 10 ones as 1 ten.

$$\begin{array}{r} 127 \\ + 35 \end{array}$$

I need to regroup 10 tens as 1 hundred.

$$\begin{array}{r} 245 \\ + 93 \end{array}$$

▶ Guided Practice

Add.
Decide whether you need to regroup.

Think!
I have 13 ones so I need to regroup ones. I have fewer than 10 tens so I don't need to regroup tens.

1. $$\begin{array}{r} 135 \\ +\ 58 \\ \hline \end{array}$$

2. $$\begin{array}{r} 641 \\ +167 \\ \hline \end{array}$$

3. $$\begin{array}{r} 573 \\ +\ 41 \\ \hline \end{array}$$

4. $$\begin{array}{r} 253 \\ +\ 75 \\ \hline \end{array}$$

5. $$\begin{array}{r} 371 \\ +284 \\ \hline \end{array}$$

6. **(123) Math Talk** How can you use mental math to solve $700 + 150$?

KEY NS 2.2 Find the sum or difference of two whole numbers up to three digits long.
Also **AF 1.3, MR 2.0**

NS 2.0 Estimate, calculate, and solve problems involving addition and subtraction of two- and three-digit numbers.

five hundred one **501**

Add. Decide whether you need to regroup.

7. 874
    + 52
    _____
    926

8. 147
    +191

9. 333
    + 57

10. 385
    + 81

11. 491
    + 15

12. 172
    +114

13. 755
    + 44

14. 937
    + 39

15. 558
    +181

16. 629
    +246

17. 258
    +471

18. 806
    +157

19. 234
    +250

20. 500
    +225

21. 701
    +139

22. 789
    +111

Problem Solving: Data Sense

Mrs. Blanco's class counts stars at the planetarium. The table shows some of their results. Use the table to answer the questions.

23. How many stars did Rob and Taci count together?

    _____ stars

24. How many stars did Kento and Beth count together?

    _____ stars

Stars Counted	
Beth	162
Rob	183
Taci	241
Kento	217

At Home Ask your child to choose an exercise on this page and explain how he or she solved it.

En casa Pida a su niño que elija un ejercicio de esta página y que explique cómo lo resolvió.

Multi-Step Problems

▶ **Learn**

Objective
Solve multi-step problems.

Each pack has 125 planet stickers. Diana has 3 packs. Tracy has 2 packs. How many planet stickers do they have all together?

Understand

Circle what you need to find out.
Underline the final step.

Think!
I need to circle more than one question.

How many stickers does Tracy have in all?

How many more stickers does Diana have than Tracy?

How many stickers does Diana have in all?

How many stickers do Diana and Tracy have together?

Plan

Solve the first steps.

Diana's stickers: __125__ + __125__ + __125__ = __375__ stickers

Tracy's stickers: __125__ + __125__ = __250__ stickers

Solve

Solve the final step.

__375__ + __250__ = __625__ stickers

Diana and Tracy have __625__ stickers in all.

Look Back

Is your answer reasonable?
Did you answer the question?

KEY **NS 2.2** Find the sum or difference of two whole numbers up to three digits long.
Also **MR 2.0, MR 2.2**

NS 2.0 Estimate, calculate, and solve problems involving addition and subtraction of two- and three-digit numbers.

five hundred three **503**

Remember!
Understand
Plan
Solve
Look Back

1. Rosa and Connor count stars for 3 nights. Rosa counts 55 stars each night. Connor counts 75 stars each night. How many stars do Rosa and Connor count in all?

Solve the first steps.

Rosa: _____ + _____ + _____ = _____ stars.

Rosa counts _____ stars.

Connor: _____ + _____ + _____ = _____ stars.

Connor counts _____ stars.

Solve the final step.

_____ + _____ = _____

Think!
I need to add the answers from the first steps.

Rosa and Connor count _____ stars in all.

2. (123) **Math Talk** What steps did you follow to solve Exercise 1?

► **Problem Solving Practice**

3. Each star stamp book has 100 stamps. Jerome has 6 stamp books. Henry has 2 stamp books. How many stamps do they have in all?

Draw or write to explain.

_____ star stamps

4. Katie has 150 sun stickers on one sheet and 148 sun stickers on another sheet. Her sister has 136 moon stickers. How many stickers do they have in all?

_____ stickers

At Home Ask your child to explain the steps he or she followed to solve Exercise 4.

En casa Pida a su niño que explique los pasos que siguió para resolver el Ejercicio 4.

California Field Trip

Science

At the Chabot Space Center

You can learn about outer space. You can see stars and planets at the planetarium. At the solar system exhibit, you can design your own planets and sun. You can even plan a mission to Mars.

Chabot Space Center

Choose a way to solve. Show your work.

1. On Monday, 325 children look through the telescope. On Tuesday, 276 children look through the telescope. How many children look through the telescope in all?

   _____ children

telescope

2. In the morning, 150 children launch rockets. In the afternoon, 180 children launch rockets. How many children launch rockets in all?

   _____ children

rocket

3. On Wednesday, 126 children try on a space suit. On Thursday, 187 children try on a space suit. How many children try on a space suit in all?

   _____ children

space suit

KEY NS 2.2 Find the sum or difference of two whole numbers up to three digits long. **Science ES 3.a**

Also **NS 2.0, MR 1.0, MR 1.1**

Problem Solving on Tests
Listening Skills

Listen to your teacher read the problem.
Choose the correct answer.

Select a Strategy
Make a Table
Write a Number
   Sentence
Act It Out
Draw a Picture

1. 5 groups of 30 people visit the space
   museum on Wednesday. 4 groups of
   20 people visit the museum on Thursday.
   How many people visit the museum in all?

   80   130   230   330
   ○   ○   ○   ○   KEY NS 2.2

2. Andrea has 13 planet erasers. She gives
   an equal number to each of her 6 friends.
   How many erasers does Andrea have left?

   1   2   3   4
   ○   ○   ○   ○   KEY NS 3.2

3.
   100   130   200   300
   ○   ○   ○   ○

                                                             KEY SDAP 2.0

4.

   □□   □ □   □ △   △ △
   ○   ○   ○   ○   KEY MG 2.1

MR 1.0 Make decisions about how to set up a problem.
MR 1.1 Determine the approach, materials, and
strategies to be used.

Education Place
Visit www.eduplace.com/camap/ for
Test-Taking Tips and Extra Practice.

Key Standards Review

Use >, <, or = to compare the numbers.

1. 234 ◯ 324   2. 746 ◯ 476   3. 285 ◯ 528

4. 651 ◯ 561   5. 368 ◯ 638   6. 408 ◯ 418

7. 514 ◯ 415   8. 784 ◯ 700 + 40 + 8

Challenge   Data

Solve. Use the bar graph.
This graph shows how many times
Tomiko did each of her chores this week.

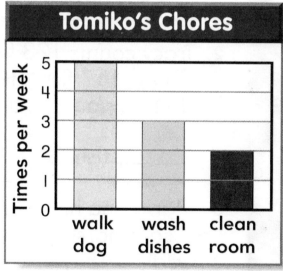

Tomiko's Chores

1. If Tomiko earns 10¢ each time she
   does a chore, how much does she
   earn in one week?

   Tomiko earns $_____.

2. Tomiko gets a raise in her allowance.
   She now gets paid 25¢ each time she
   does a chore. How much money does
   she make in one week?

   Tomiko makes $_____.

KEY **NS 1.3** Order and compare whole numbers
to 1,000 by using the symbols <, =, >.
Also **NS 5.0, KEY SDAP 1.0**

five hundred seven **507**

Science Link

Coastal Wetlands in California

Many different kinds of plants and animals live in the salt marshes of California's coastal wetlands. They have adapted to the wet soil and salty water. Some of the animals you can find there are striped bass, flounder, mallards, and sandpipers.

Solve.

Draw or write to explain.

1. Jackson and Ella go bird watching for a week. Jackson sees **227** birds. Ella sees **246** birds. How many do they see in all?

   _____ birds

2. Tracy counts **123** fish. Eddie counts **157** fish. How many do they count in all?

   _____ fish

3. Mario and his family drive to a salt marsh to see the wildlife. They drive **267** miles one day and **159** miles the next day. How many miles do they drive in all?

   _____ miles

KEY **NS 2.2** Find the sum or difference of two whole numbers up to three digits long.
Also **NS 2.0**
Science LS 2.e, LS 2.c

Name _____

Concepts and Skills

Draw a quick picture. Write the sum. KEY NS 2.2

1. 7 hundreds   700
   +2 hundreds   +200
   _____ hundreds

2. 3 hundreds   300
   +5 hundreds   +500
   _____ hundreds

Add. Decide if you need to regroup. KEY NS 2.2

3. 309
   +137

4. 884
   +107

5. 286
   +308

6. 208
   +306

7. 340
   +167

8. 654
   +195

9. 566
   +243

10. 546
   +163

Problem Solving   KEY NS 2.2, MR 2.0

11. On her vacation, Barb drove 52 miles, flew 659 miles, and biked 112 miles. How many miles is that in all?

   _____ miles

12. How did you solve the problem?

Draw or write to explain

_____

_____

Spiral Review and Test Practice

1. Which two shapes have 4 vertices?

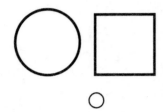 ○
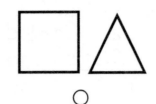 ○
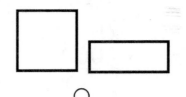 ○
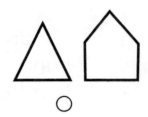 ○

KEY **MG 2.1**, MG 2.0 Page 275

2. What is $\frac{2}{3}$ of 9?

| 2 | 3 | 6 | 9 |
| ○ | ○ | ○ | ○ |

KEY **NS 4.2**, NS 4.0 Page 333

3. What time does the clock show?

○ a quarter to 10

○ a quarter to 11

○ a quarter past 10

○ 11:15

MG 1.4, MG 1.0 Page 373

4. What is the product of 5 × 10?

| 15 | 20 | 40 | 50 |
| ○ | ○ | ○ | ○ |

KEY **NS 3.1**, KEY **NS 3.0**, KEY **NS 3.3** Page 417

Education Place
Visit **www.eduplace.com/camap/** for
Test-Taking Tips and Extra Practice.

Subtract 3-Digit Numbers

Vocabulary

Here are some vocabulary words you will learn in the chapter.

subtract hundreds You can use hundreds flats to model three-digit subtraction.

$$300 - 100$$

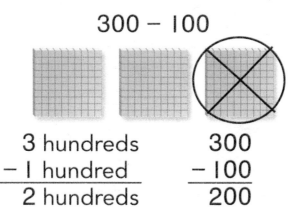

$$
\begin{array}{r}
3 \text{ hundreds} \\
-\ 1 \text{ hundred} \\
\hline
2 \text{ hundreds}
\end{array}
\qquad
\begin{array}{r}
300 \\
-\ 100 \\
\hline
200
\end{array}
$$

regroup You can regroup hundreds or tens to find the difference of two 3-digit numbers.

H	T	O
5	13	
6	3	8
− 4	7	5
1	6	3

You can regroup 1 hundred as 10 tens.

H	T	O
	8	12
4	9	2
− 2	6	6
2	2	6

You can regroup 1 ten as 10 ones.

See English-Spanish Glossary pages 573–589.

 **KEY NS 2.2** Find the sum or difference of two whole numbers up to three digits long.

 **Education Place** Visit www.eduplace.com/camap/ for the eGlossary and eGames.

five hundred eleven **511**

Name _____

 # Check What You Know

Stars Our Class Counted	
Pam	400
Zack	450
Claire	200
John	370

1. How many more stars does Pam count than Claire?

   _____ – _____ = _____ more stars

2. How many more stars does Zack see than Claire?

   _____ – _____ = _____ more stars

3. How many more stars does Zack see than John?

   _____ – _____ = _____ more stars

4. How many stars do Zack and Pam see in all?

   _____ + _____ = _____ stars

5. How many stars do John and Claire see in all?

   _____ + _____ = _____ stars

Use this page to review important skills needed for this chapter.

Chapter 26 Lesson 1

Subtract Hundreds

 Learn

Objective
Subtract hundreds using models, pictures, and mental math.

To subtract hundreds, think of a subtraction fact.

Find 500 − 200.
Use Workmat 6 with the from Learning Tool 24.

Step 1	**Step 2**	**Step 3**
Model the hundreds. 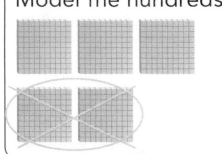	Draw your model with a quick picture. 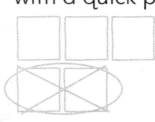	Use the subtraction fact 5 − 2 to solve. 5 hundreds 500 −2 hundreds −200 _____ 3 hundreds 300

▶ **Guided Practice**

Use Learning Tool 24 to model.
Draw your model with a quick picture.
Subtract.

Think!
I can use 7 − 2 to help me find 70 − 20 and 700 − 200.

1.   7   7 hundreds   700
   −2   −2 hundreds   −200
              hundreds

2.   8   8 hundreds   800
   −3   −3 hundreds   −300
              hundreds

3. **(123)** **Math Talk** How does 6 − 2 = 4 help you solve 600 − 200?

KEY NS 2.2 Find the sum or difference of two whole numbers up to three digits long. Also **NS 2.3, NS 2.0, MR 3.0**

MR 1.2 Use tools, such as manipulatives or sketches, to model problems.

five hundred thirteen **513**

Remember!
Use a basic fact to help
subtract hundreds.

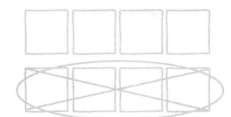

Use Learning Tool 24 to model.
Draw your model with a quick picture.
Subtract.

4. 8 hundreds   800
   −4 hundreds   −400
    4 hundreds   400

5. 8 hundreds   800
   −5 hundreds   −500
    hundreds

6. 7 hundreds   700
   −3 hundreds   −300
    hundreds

7. 9 hundreds   900
   − 1 hundred   − 100
    hundreds

8.   1 thousand   1000
   −5 hundreds   − 500
    hundreds

Problem Solving: Reasoning

9. The Johnsons fly **900** miles on
   Monday. They fly **600** miles on
   Tuesday. How many more miles
   do they fly on Monday than
   on Tuesday?

   Draw or write to explain.

_____ miles

At Home Ask your child to tell you
how knowing 4 − 2 = 2 helps him or
her solve 400 − 200.

En casa . Pida a su niño que le explique cómo
saber que 4 − 2 = 2 lo ayuda
a resolver 400 − 200.

Chapter 26 Lesson 2

Regroup Tens

 **Learn**

Objective
Regroup tens to find the difference between two three-digit numbers.

Find 253 – 137.

Use Workmat 6 with the ▨ , ▥▥▥▥▥▥▥ , and ▨ from Learning Tool 24.

Step 1

Show 253. Regroup 1 ten as 10 ones. Subtract the ones.

H	T	O
	4	13
2	5	3
– 1	3	7
		6

Step 2

Subtract the tens.

H	T	O
	4	13
2	5̶	3̶
– 1	3	7
		6

Step 3

Subtract the hundreds.

H	T	O
	4	13
2	5̶	3̶
– 1	3	7
	1	6

▶ Guided Practice

Use Learning Tool 24 to model. Subtract.

Think!
I need to regroup 9 tens and 4 ones as 8 tens and 14 ones.

1.

H	T	O
6	9	4
– 3	8	9

2.

H	T	O
3	8	0
– 1	2	6

3.

H	T	O
2	2	6
–		9

4. (123) **Math Talk** How does regrouping tens and ones help you subtract?

KEY NS 2.2 Find the sum or difference of two whole numbers up to three digits long. Also **NS 2.0**

MR 1.2 Use tools, such as manipulatives or sketches, to model problems.

Use Learning Tool 24 to model.
Subtract.

5.

H	T	O
	8	13
3	9	3
− 1	6	5
2	2	8

6.

H	T	O
1	5	9
− 1	0	7

7.

H	T	O
6	3	0
− 1	2	8

8.

H	T	O
5	6	0
− 2	2	8

9.
```
□ □ □
  1 9 3
−   4 6
```

10.
```
□ □ □
  3 8 8
−   7 9
```

11.
```
□ □ □
  5 7 2
−   3 5
```

12.
```
□ □ □
  9 5 2
− 5 1 7
```

13.
```
  432
− 329
```

14.
```
  899
− 632
```

15.
```
  751
− 218
```

16.
```
  577
− 468
```

Problem Solving: Visual Thinking

17. Mr. and Mrs. Ant are climbing a hill.
The hill is 691 feet high.
They have climbed 75 feet so far.
How many more feet do they
have to climb?

_____ feet

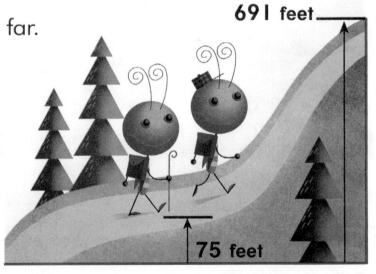

691 feet

75 feet

Regroup Hundreds

▶ **Learn**

If there are not enough tens to subtract, regroup I hundred as 10 tens.

Objective
Regroup hundreds to find the difference between two three-digit numbers.

Find 336 – 172.

Use Workmat 6 with the , ▬▬▬▬▬▬, and ▪ from Learning Tool 24.

Step 1

Show 336.
Subtract the ones.

H	T	O
☐	☐	☐
3	3	6
− 1	7	2
		4

Step 2

Regroup I hundred as 10 tens.
Subtract the tens.

H	T	O
2	13	☐
3	3	6
− 1	7	2
	6	4

Step 3

Subtract the hundreds.

H	T	O
2	13	☐
3̸	3̸	6
− 1	7	2
1	6	4

▶ **Guided Practice**

Think!
I need to regroup 4 hundreds I ten as 3 hundreds II tens.

Use Workmat 6 with Learning Tool 24.
Subtract.

1.

H	T	O
☐	☐	☐
4	1	7
− 2	6	3

2.

H	T	O
☐	☐	☐
8	2	6
−	9	3

3.

H	T	O
☐	☐	☐
3	8	2
− 1	2	6

4. **(123) Math Talk** When do you need to regroup I hundred as 10 tens?

 KEY NS 2.2 Find the sum or difference of two whole numbers up to three digits long. Also **NS 2.0, AF 1.3**

MR 1.2 Use tools, such as manipulatives or sketches, to model problems.

five hundred seventeen **517**

► **Practice**

Use Workmat 6 with
Learning Tool 24. Subtract.

Remember!
If there are not enough
tens to subtract, regroup
1 hundred as 10 tens.

5.
```
  4 12
  528
 -233
  295
```

6.
```
  537
 -257
```

7.
```
  831
 -440
```

8.
```
  943
 -471
```

9.
```
  917
 -736
```

10.
```
  308
 -177
```

11.
```
  479
 - 99
```

12.
```
  708
 - 64
```

13.
```
  816
 -542
```

14.
```
  418
 -193
```

15.
```
  607
 - 26
```

16.
```
  981
 -690
```

17.
```
  245
 -151
```

18.
```
  417
 -344
```

19.
```
  358
 -194
```

20.
```
  875
 - 99
```

Problem Solving: Data Sense

21. How many more rooms does
the Market Hotel have than
the Castle Hotel?

Hotel Name	Number of Rooms
Castle Hotel	280
Sandy Hotel	560
Market Hotel	710

_____ rooms

At Home Ask your child how he or
she knows if it is necessary to regroup
in the subtraction problem 325 – 160.

En casa Pregunte a su niño cómo sabe si es
necesario reagrupar en el problema de resta
325 – 160.

518

Objective
Subtract numbers up
to three digits long.

Practice Subtracting 3-Digit Numbers

 **Learn**

When you subtract three-digit numbers,
decide whether you need to regroup.

Find 800 – 200.

Find 473 – 46.

Find 318 – 252.

I don't need to
regroup. I'll subtract
with mental math.

I need
to regroup 1 ten
as 10 ones.

I need to
regroup 1 hundred
as 10 tens.

$$\begin{array}{r} 800 \\ -200 \\ \hline \end{array}$$

$$\begin{array}{r} 473 \\ -\ 46 \\ \hline \end{array}$$

$$\begin{array}{r} 318 \\ -252 \\ \hline \end{array}$$

▶ **Guided Practice**

Subtract.
Decide whether you need to regroup.

1. $\begin{array}{r} 900 \\ -400 \\ \hline \end{array}$

Think!
I can use the basic
fact 9 – 4 = 5 to help
me subtract.

2. $\begin{array}{r} 754 \\ -139 \\ \hline \end{array}$

3. $\begin{array}{r} 338 \\ -291 \\ \hline \end{array}$

4. $\begin{array}{r} 535 \\ -162 \\ \hline \end{array}$

5. $\begin{array}{r} 874 \\ -657 \\ \hline \end{array}$

6. (123) **Math Talk** How can you use regrouping
to solve 325 – 8?

 KEY NS 2.2 Find the sum or difference of two
whole numbers up to three digits long.
Also **NS 2.0, MR 2.0**

► Practice

Subtract. Decide whether you need to regroup.

Remember!
Check to see whether you have enough tens and ones to subtract.

7. $\overset{8\ 12}{927}$
    -652
     275

8.   174
    $-\ 49$

9.   600
    -400

10.   663
    -238

11.   727
    -253

12.   516
    -312

13.   983
    -259

14.   758
    -577

15.   244
    -182

16.   395
    -267

17.   535
    -293

18.   984
    -556

19.   772
    -156

20.   408
    -233

21.   776
    -193

22.   622
    -455

Problem Solving: Reasoning

23. Rita and Ted make model spaceships. Rita's spaceship weighs 476 grams. Ted's spaceship weighs 532 grams. How much more does Ted's spaceship weigh than Rita's?

_____ grams

Draw or write to explain.

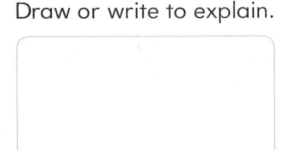

 At Home Ask your child to choose an exercise on this page and explain how he or she solved it.

En casa Pida a su niño que elija un ejercicio de esta página y que explique cómo lo resolvió.

Write a Number Sentence

 **Learn**

Objective
Write number sentences to solve problems.

Mrs. Carlton drives 425 miles to the NASA Exploration Center in Mountain View, California. She drives 280 miles on Friday and the rest of the way on Saturday. How many miles does she drive on Saturday?

Understand

What do you know?
• Mrs. Carlton drives 425 miles in all.
• She drives 280 miles on Friday.

Think!
I need to subtract the miles she drives on Friday from the total number of miles.

Plan

Circle the operation you will use.

addition   (subtraction)

Solve

Write a number sentence.
Then solve.

425 ◯ 280 = 145

Mrs. Carlton drives ____145____ miles on Saturday.

Look Back

Did you answer the question?
How can you check your answer?

KEY **NS 2.2** Find the sum or difference of two whole numbers up to three digits long.
Also NS 2.0, AF 1.2, MR 2.2, AF 1.0

MR 2.0 Solve problems and justify reasoning.

Guided Problem Solving

1. Mike's family takes a trip from San Diego to Mountain View. They drive 470 miles in all. They drive 280 miles on the first day and the rest on the second day. How far does Mike's family drive on the second day?

   What operation will you use?

   _____

   Write the number sentence.
   Then solve.

   _____ ◯ _____ = _____

   Mike's family drives _____ miles on the second day.

Think!
I need to subtract the miles Mike's family drives on the first day from the total number of miles.

2. **123 Math Talk** How did you write your number sentence?

Problem Solving Practice

Write a number sentence. Then solve.

3. The NASA Exploration Center has 527 visitors on Friday and 473 visitors on Monday. How many more visitors are there on Friday?

   _____ ◯ _____ = _____

   _____ more visitors

4. Miguel counts 193 exhibits at the center. Alana counts 146 exhibits. How many more exhibits does Miguel count?

   _____ ◯ _____ = _____

   _____ exhibits

At Home Have your child find 525 –180 and then make up a story to go with the number sentence.

En casa Pida a su niño que halle 525–180 y que luego invente un cuento que vaya con el enunciado numérico.

Name _____

Chapter 26 Lesson 5

Create and Solve

Objective
Write problems an
use strategies to
solve them.

The bar graph shows the number of
visitors at the NASA Exploration Center
in one week.

1. How many
   people visited
   the center on
   Tuesday and
   Wednesday?

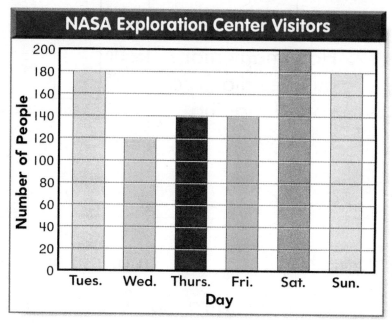

_____ ◯ _____ = _____

_____ people visited the center on Tuesday and
Wednesday.

2. Write an addition problem about the data in the
   graph above.

_____

_____

3. Write a number sentence. Solve your problem.

_____ ◯ _____ ◯ _____

Share your addition problem with a classmate.

KEY NS 2.2 Find the sum or difference of two
whole numbers up to three digits long.
Also **NS 2.0, AF 1.3, MR 1.0, MR 1.1**

SDAP 1.4 Ask and answer simple questions related
to data representations.

five hundred twenty-three

The bar graph shows the number of minutes some children spent reading about space last month.

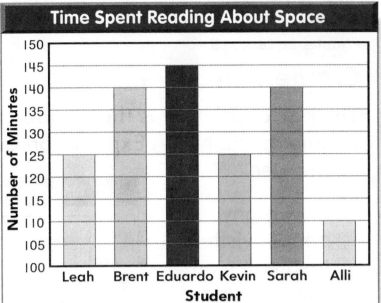

Time Spent Reading About Space

4. How many more minutes did Sarah spend reading than Kevin?

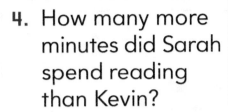

_____ ◯ _____ = _____

Sarah spent _____ more minutes reading.

5. Write a subtraction problem about the data in the graph above.

_____

_____

_____

_____

_____

6. Write a number sentence. Solve your problem.

_____ ◯ _____ ◯ _____

Share your subtraction problem with a classmate.

□□□□□‖°°°°

Name _____

 # Key Standards Review

Add.
Decide whether you need to regroup.

1. 238
   +170

2. 392
   +436

3. 568
   +323

4. 150
   +193

5. 615
   +245

6. 593
   +256

7. 345
   +282

8. 333
   +337

9. 446
   +282

10. 181
    +171

11. 348
    +546

12. 734
    +129

Challenge   **Number Sense**

1. The page numbers on facing pages
   of a book have a sum of 325.
   What are the numbers?

   _____ and _____

2. Jake is on a page that is between 330
   and 345. The tens digit is double the
   ones digit. What page is Jake reading?

   page _____

KEY NS 2.2 Find the sum or difference of two
whole numbers up to three digits long.
Also NS 1.0

five hundred twenty-five **525**

California Sea Lions

California sea lions are social animals. They eat squid, octopus, and fish. Their babies, or pups, are born in the summer and weigh about 13–20 pounds. A full grown male sea lion can weigh 1,000 pounds!

Solve.

Draw or write to explain.

1. One female sea lion weighs 468 pounds. One male sea lion weighs 792 pounds. How much more does the male sea lion weigh?

   _____ pounds

2. There are 327 sea lions in one group. There are 294 sea lions in another group. How many more sea lions are in the first group?

   _____ more sea lions

3. At the zoo, Don sees a mountain lion that weighs 168 pounds. He also sees a sea lion that weighs 838 pounds. How much more does the sea lion weigh?

   _____ pounds

 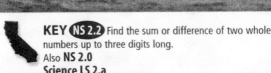
KEY NS 2.2 Find the sum or difference of two whole numbers up to three digits long.
Also **NS 2.0**
Science LS 2.a

Name _____

Concepts and Skills

Subtract. KEY **NS 2.2**

1. 7 hundreds   700
    − 2 hundreds   − 200
       hundreds

2. 3 hundreds   300
    − 3 hundreds   − 300
       hundreds

Subtract. KEY **NS 2.2**

3.
H	T	O
□	□	□
7	5	5
− 3	4	8

4.
H	T	O
□	□	□
9	1	8
− 4	0	9

5.
H	T	O
□	□	□
8	0	9
− 7	9	7

Subtract. Decide if you need to regroup. KEY **NS 2.2**

6.   333
   − 160

7.   655
   − 194

8.   566
   − 243

9.   546
   − 163

Problem Solving KEY **NS 2.2**

Write a number sentence to solve.

10. 525 people were at the movie theater.
    119 had popcorn. How many did not
    have popcorn?

_____ ◯ _____ ◯ _____

Spiral Review and Test Practice

1. $\frac{4}{5}$ of 10 is _____.

4	8	10	45
○	○	○	○

KEY **NS 4.2**, NS 4.0 Page 333

---

2. Which multiplication sentence is shown by the shaded area of this array?

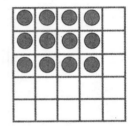

$3 \times 3 = 9$	$3 \times 4 = 12$	$4 \times 4 = 16$	$5 \times 5 = 25$
○	○	○	○

KEY **NS 3.1**, KEY **NS 3.0** Page 397

---

3. Divide. What is the remainder? $19 \div 6$

1	3	6	13
○	○	○	○

KEY **NS 3.2**, KEY **NS 3.0** Page 435

---

4. Which of these is true?

- ○ $189 > 205 > 656 > 740$
- ○ $189 < 656 < 205 < 740$
- ○ $189 < 205 < 740 < 656$
- ○ $189 < 205 < 656 < 740$

KEY **NS 1.3**, NS 1.0 Page 475

Education Place
Visit www.eduplace.com/camap/ for
Test-Taking Tips and Extra Practice.

Spiral Review

More Addition and Subtraction

Vocabulary

Here are some vocabulary words you will learn in the chapter.

regroup Trade 1 hundred for 10 tens, or trade 1 ten for 10 ones

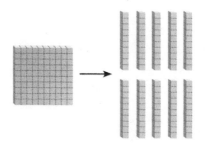

You can regroup 1 hundred as 10 tens.

You can regroup 1 ten as 10 ones.

vertical form Rewriting the problem by lining up the digits to solve

$$367 + 282 \xrightarrow[\text{to solve}]{\text{rewrite}} \begin{array}{r} 367 \\ +282 \\ \hline 649 \end{array}$$

See English-Spanish Glossary pages 573–589.

 **KEY NS 2.2** Find the sum or difference of two whole numbers up to three digits long.

 **Education Place**
Visit www.eduplace.com/camap/
for the eGlossary and eGames.

five hundred twenty-nine **529**

Name _____

☑️ Check What You Know

1. Venus takes about **225** days to go around the Sun once. The Earth takes about **365** days to go around the Sun once. How much longer does the Earth take to go around the Sun than Venus?

   _____ − _____ = _____ more days

2. How many days does it take Venus to go around the Sun twice?

   _____ + _____ = _____ days

3. How many days does it take the Earth to go around the Sun twice?

   _____ + _____ = _____ days

4. Pluto takes about **248** years to go around the Sun once. Neptune takes about **165** years to go around the Sun once. How much longer does it take Pluto to go around the Sun than Neptune?

   _____ − _____ = _____ more years

5. How many years does it take Pluto to go around the sun twice?

   _____ + _____ = _____ years

Use this page to review important skills needed for this chapter.

Name _____

Subtract with 2 Regroupings

 **Learn**

Sometimes you need to regroup twice.

Find 324 − 158.

Step 1

Show 324.

H	T	O
3	2	4
− 1	5	8

Step 2

Regroup 1 ten as 10 ones. Subtract the ones.

H	T	O
	1	14
3	2	4
− 1	5	8
		6

Step 3

Regroup 1 hundred as 10 tens. Subtract the tens. Subtract the hundreds.

H	T	O
2	1	14
3	2	4
− 1	5	8
1	6	6

▶ **Guided Practice**

Use Workmat 6 and Learning Tool 24. Subtract.

Think!
I can regroup 4 tens 7 ones as 3 tens 17 ones. Then I can regroup 7 hundreds 3 tens as 6 hundreds 13 tens.

1.

H	T	O
7	4	7
− 2	6	8

2.

H	T	O
5	3	2
−	5	9

3.

H	T	O
6	1	4
− 3	7	7

4. **123 Math Talk** When do you need to regroup twice?

 KEY NS 2.2 Find the sum or difference of two whole numbers up to three digits long. Also **NS 2.0, AF 1.3, AF 1.0**

MR 1.2 Use tools, such as manipulatives or sketches, to model problems.

Use Workmat 6 and Learning Tool 24.
Subtract.

Remember!
Regroup 1 ten as 10 ones.
Regroup 1 hundred
as 10 tens.

5.

H	T	O
⁶7̶	¹⁴5̶	¹⁴4̶
− 3	8	6
3	6	8

6.

H	T	O
4	4	7
− 1	5	8

7.

H	T	O
2	3	1
−	3	5

8.
```
  862
− 354
```

9.
```
  233
−  76
```

10.
```
  725
−  68
```

11.
```
  921
− 746
```

12.
```
  634
− 188
```

13.
```
  563
−  95
```

14.
```
  442
− 187
```

15.
```
  364
−  99
```

16.
```
  783
−  97
```

17.
```
  535
− 146
```

18.
```
  954
− 379
```

19.
```
  871
− 488
```

Problem Solving: Data Sense

20. How many more visitors came to the planetarium on Monday than on Thursday?

_____ more visitors

21. How many more visitors came to the planetarium on Tuesday than on Wednesday?

_____ more visitors

Visitors at the Planetarium	
Monday	517
Tuesday	489
Wednesday	421
Thursday	398

At Home Ask your child if he or she has to regroup twice to find 856 − 673.

En casa Pregunte a su niño si tiene que reagrupar dos veces para resolver 856 − 673.

Chapter 27 Lesson 2

Subtract with 2 Regroupings

▶ **Learn**

When you subtract, you have to decide whether you need to regroup.

Adita spends 242 minutes reading books about Jupiter. She spends 179 minutes reading books about Mercury.
How much more time does Adita spend reading about Jupiter than about Mercury?

JUPITER

Mercury

Step 1

Regroup 1 ten as 10 ones.

□	3	12
2	4	2
− 1	7	9
		3

Step 2

Regroup 1 hundred as 10 tens.

1	13	12
2	4	2
− 1	7	9
	6	3

Step 3

Subtract.

1	13	12
2	4	2
− 1	7	9
	6	3

Adita spends ___63___ more minutes reading about Jupiter.

▶ **Guided Practice**

Think!
I need to regroup 1 ten as 10 ones.

Subtract.

1.
□	□	□
3	6	2
− 1	6	7

2.
□	□	□
4	8	3
− 1	4	9

3.
□	□	□
5	1	1
−	5	4

4. **(123)** **Math Talk** To solve 818 − 472, do you have to regroup 1 ten as 10 ones? Why not?

KEY NS 2.2 Find the sum or difference of two whole numbers up to three digits long. Also **MR 2.2, MR 2.1, MR 2.0, MR 1.1, MR 1.0**

NS 2.0 Estimate, calculate, and solve problems involving addition and subtraction of two- and three-digit numbers.

five hundred thirty-three **533**

Subtract.

Remember!
Decide whether you need to regroup to subtract.

5.
```
    □  6  12
    6  7̶  2
 -  1  5  9
    5  1  3
```

6.
```
    □  □  □
    4  4  4
 -  2  8  6
```

7.
```
    □  □  □
    7  1  5
 -     8  8
```

8.
```
   523
 - 377
```

9.
```
   825
 -  91
```

10.
```
   641
 - 586
```

11.
```
   933
 -  75
```

12.
```
   853
 - 458
```

13.
```
   517
 - 136
```

14.
```
   425
 - 276
```

15.
```
   344
 -  67
```

16.
```
   937
 -  79
```

17.
```
   284
 - 175
```

18.
```
   553
 - 139
```

19.
```
   922
 -  77
```

Problem Solving: Reasoning

20. Jenny wrote $845 - 339 = 516$.
Explain Jenny's mistake. Write the correct difference.

Draw a picture to explain.

_____

_____

At Home Ask your child to solve 743 – 561 and explain whether he or she needs to regroup tens or hundreds.

En casa Pida a su niño que resuelva 743 – 561 y que explique si necesita reagrupar decenas o centenas.

Subtract Across Zeros

 **Learn**

When there are zeros in the tens and ones places, you need to regroup hundreds before tens.

Find 300 − 132.

Step 1

Regroup 1 hundred as 10 tens.

	H	T	O
	2	10	
	3	0	0
−	1	3	2

Step 2

Regroup 1 ten as 10 ones.

	H	T	O
	2	10	10
	3	0	0
−	1	3	2

Step 3

You have enough tens and ones to subtract.

	H	T	O
	2	9̶10̶	10
	3	0	0
−	1	3	2
	1	6	8

▶ Guided Practice

Think!
There are 0 tens. I need to regroup 1 hundred as 10 tens.

Subtract. Use models if you wish.

1.

H	T	O
3	0	6
−	7	5

2.

H	T	O
3	6	0
−	1	2	4

3.

H	T	O
2	0	0
−	1	5	8

4. (123) **Math Talk** When you find 200 − 158, why do you regroup hundreds first?

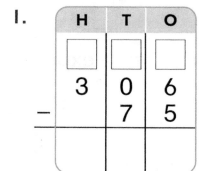

► **Practice**

Subtract.
Use models if you wish.

Remember!
When you have 0 tens
and 0 ones, you need to
regroup hundreds
before tens.

5.

H	T	O
0̶	1̶6̶	1̶0̶
1̶	7̶	0̶
−	8	8
	8	2

6.

H	T	O
2	0	4
− 1	3	2

7.

H	T	O
4	0	0
− 2	7	6

8.   300
         − 118

9.   190
         − 36

10.   305
         − 23

11.   230
         − 126

12.   200
         − 54

13.   207
         − 144

14.   450
         − 217

15.   400
         − 382

16.   408
         − 92

17.   500
         − 261

18.   370
         − 180

19.   700
         − 323

Problem Solving: Reasoning

20. A toy store has 4 boxes of
100 spaceship models. Andrew
buys 31 spaceship models. How
many spaceship models does
the store have left?

Draw or write to explain.

_____ spaceship models

At Home Have your child explain
why he or she must regroup hundreds
first to find 400 − 235.

En casa Pida a su niño que explique por qué
debe reagrupar las centenas primero para
resolver 400 − 235.

536

► **Practice**

21. 700
    − 24

22. 506
    − 83

23. 909
    −273

24. 236
    −159

25. 952
    −438

26. 400
    − 44

27. 800
    −394

28. 680
    −383

29. 390
    −251

30. 240
    − 73

31. 604
    −286

32. 470
    −362

33. 800
    − 54

34. 703
    −622

35. 400
    −387

36. 801
    −493

37. 500
    −176

38. 309
    − 83

39. 540
    −385

40. 430
    −129

41. 500
    −288

42. 201
    − 53

43. 650
    −261

44. 820
    − 37

45. 300
    − 49

KEY NS 2.2 Find the sum or difference of two
whole numbers up to three digits long.
Also **NS 2.0**

What You Need

2 players

Subtract to Win

How to Play

1. Place your counter on START. Write 999 on your paper.

2. Take turns tossing the number cube. Move that many spaces.

3. Follow the directions on the space. On each turn, add or subtract that number on your paper.

4. Continue until you reach the end. The player with the greater final number wins.

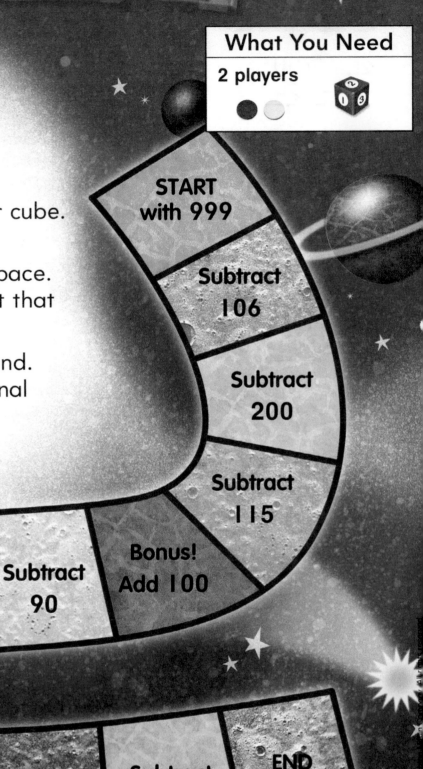

START with 999

Subtract 106

Subtract 200

Subtract 115

Bonus! Add 100

Subtract 90

Subtract 210

Subtract 19

Subtract 75

Bonus! Add 200

Subtract 108

Subtract 39

Subtract 18

END

KEY NS 2.2 Find the sum or difference of two whole numbers up to three digits long.

Education Place
Visit **www.eduplace.com/camap/** for more games.

Write in Vertical Form

► Learn

Rewrite the numbers to help you add or subtract.

Find **346 + 235**.

First line up the ones. Then line up the tens. Add.

```
    1
  3 | 4 | 6
+ 2 | 3 | 5
  5 | 8 | 1
```

Find **549 − 367**.

Line up the digits. Then subtract.

```
  4  14
  5 | 4 | 9
− 3 | 6 | 7
  1 | 8 | 2
```

► Guided Practice

Add or subtract.

1. 428 + 62

```
  4 | 2 | 8
+   | 6 | 2
```

Think!
I must make sure that the ones, tens, and hundreds are lined up before I add.

2. 654 − 82

```
  6 | 5 | 4
−   | 8 | 2
```

3. 327 − 174

```
  3 | 2 | 7
− 1 | 7 | 4
```

4. 229 + 6

```
  2 | 2 | 9
+   |   | 6
```

5. 596 − 39

```
  5 | 9 | 6
−   | 3 | 9
```

6. **123** **Math Talk** When you rewrite an exercise in vertical form, which place value should you start with? Why?

KEY NS 2.2 Find the sum or difference of two whole numbers up to three digits long.
Also **NS 2.0**, **KEY NS 1.1**, **MR 2.1**

five hundred thirty-nine **539**

▶ **Practice**

Rewrite the numbers.
Add or subtract.

Remember!
Line up the ones.
Then line up the tens,
then hundreds.

7. 364 + 64

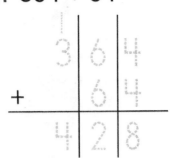

```
   3 6 4
+    6 4
   4 2 8
```

8. 454 − 182

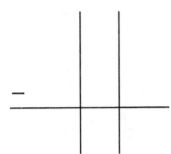

9. 237 + 8

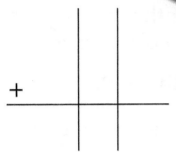

10. 745 − 182

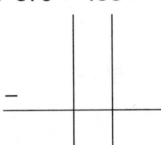

11. 408 + 263

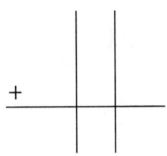

12. 473 − 58

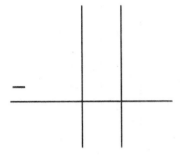

13. 876 − 433

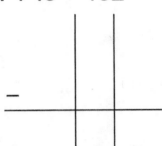

14. 392 − 43

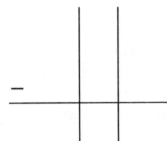

15. 647 + 25

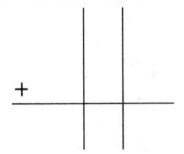

Problem Solving: Reasoning

16. Betsy counts 187 stars in the sky.
    Devon counts 48 stars.
    How many stars do they see in all?

    _____ stars

Draw or write to explain.

17. How many more stars does Betsy
    count than Devon?

    _____ more stars

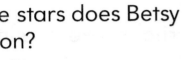

At Home Have your child show
you how to rewrite and then solve
267 + 18.

En casa Pida a su niño que le muestre cómo
escribir de otra manera los números para
luego resolver 267 + 18.

Name _____

Write a Number Sentence

 **Learn**

Mrs. Tran's class counts stars at the planetarium. The table shows some of their results. How many more stars did Anna count than Imran?

Name	Stars Counted
Anna	200
Brad	136
Imran	184
Zara	220

Think!
I can find out how many stars Anna and Imran count by looking at the table.

Understand
What do you know?

• Anna counts ___200___ stars.

• Imran counts ___184___ stars.

Plan
Choose an operation.

addition   (subtraction)

multiplication   division

Solve
Write a number sentence.
Then solve.

___200___ ⊖ ___184___ = ___16___

Anna counts ___16___ more stars than Imran.

Look Back
Did you answer the question?
How can you check your answer?

 AF 1.3 Solve addition and subtraction problems by using data from simple charts, picture graphs, and number sentences.

KEY NS 2.2 Find the sum or difference of two whole numbers up to three digits long.
Also **AF 1.0, AF 1.2, NS 2.0, MR 2.0, MR 2.2, SDAP 1.4**

Kind of Poster	Posters Sold
Jupiter	170
Mars	200
Mercury	300
Saturn	250
Venus	180

1. The Space Club is selling posters to raise money for a field trip. The table shows how many of each poster they sell. How many more Mars posters than Jupiter posters does the club sell?

Write what you know.

The Space Club sells _____ Mars posters.

They sell _____ Jupiter posters.

Will you add or subtract? _____

Write a number sentence. Then solve.

_____ ◯ _____ = _____

The club members sell _____ more Mars posters.

Think!
I have to find the number of Mars and Jupiter posters sold.

2. **(123) Math Talk** How did you use the table to solve the problem?

Write a number sentence. Then solve.

3. How many more Mercury posters than Venus posters does the club sell?

_____ ◯ _____ = _____

_____ more posters

4. How many more Mercury posters than Saturn posters does the class sell?

_____ ◯ _____ = _____

_____ more posters

 At Home Have your child write and solve a number sentence to find out how many Saturn and Mars posters the club sells in all.

En casa Pida a su niño que escriba y resuelva un enunciado numérico para hallar cuántos posters de Saturno y Marte vende en total el club.

Key Standards Review

Subtract.
Decide whether you need to regroup.

1. 564
    −346

2. 782
    −691

3. 936
    −273

4. 681
    −355

5. 364
    −182

6. 527
    −453

7. 493
    −174

8. 844
    −636

9. 271
    −152

10. 354
    −283

11. 763
    −671

12. 676
    −567

Challenge — Number Sense

Write the missing digits.

1. 8 ☐ 5
    − ☐ 4 7
    ─────
    3 2 ☐

2. ☐ 5 8
    + 4 ☐ 5
    ─────
    6 8 ☐

3. 3 ☐ 9
    + 1 8 ☐
    ─────
    ☐ 9 4

KEY NS 2.2 Find the sum or difference of two whole numbers up to three digits long. Also KEY NS 2.1

five hundred forty-three **543**

History-Social Science Link

Red

Map of California

California is the third largest state in the United States. The capital of California is Sacramento. This map shows the distances between Sacramento and a few other cities in California.

88 Miles — Sacramento
San Francisco
286 Miles
384 Miles
505 Miles
Bakersfield
Los Angeles
San Diego

Use the map to solve.
Write or draw to show your work.

1. How much longer is the distance between Sacramento and Los Angeles than between Sacramento and Bakersfield?

   _____ miles

2. How much longer is the distance between Sacramento and San Diego than between Sacramento and Los Angeles?

   _____ miles

3. Cassie and her family live in San Diego. They want to take a trip to Sacramento and then continue on to San Francisco. How many miles will they travel in all?

   _____ miles

Ukiah

nta Rosa

REYES
SHORE
San Rafae
Mill Valley
San Francisco Ba
San Francis

Pal
Su
L
Sar

El

White River

Calie
93
93

an Springs

Vegas
Henderson

Ne

TREE
NAL
ENT

Brawley
El Cen

KEY NS 2.2 Find the sum or difference of two whole numbers up to three digits long.
Also **NS 2.0**
History-Social Science 2.2

Name _____

Concepts and Skills

Subtract. **KEY NS 2.2**

1.

H	T	O
☐	☐	☐
6	1	7
− 3	4	8

2.

H	T	O
☐	☐	☐
7	2	8
− 5	6	9

3.

H	T	O
☐	☐	☐
7	5	0
− 3	9	8

Subtract. **KEY NS 2.2**

4.   745
    −387

5.   423
    − 74

6.   846
    −759

7.   673
    −195

Rewrite to add or subtract. **KEY NS 2.2**

8. 598 − 423   9. 312 + 787   10. 605 − 346   11. 504 − 236

Problem Solving   **KEY NS 2.2**

Write a number sentence to solve.

12. Jefferson Elementary School has
    605 students. Today 78 students
    are absent. How many students are
    at Jefferson school today?

    _____ ◯ _____ ◯ _____

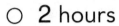 **Spiral Review and Test Practice**

1. How many hours passed between the two times?

○ 2 hours

○ 3 hours

○ 9 hours

○ 13 hours

MG 1.5, MG 1.4, MG 1.0 Page 375

2. Which is the value of the red digit?   839

3	10	30	300
○	○	○	○

KEY NS 1.1, NS 1.0 Page 457

3. What is the total value of the money shown?

$4.90	$4.75	$4.70	$1.75
○	○	○	○

KEY NS 5.1, KEY NS 5.2 Page 477

4. What is the difference?

$$\begin{array}{r} 423 \\ -\ 165 \\ \hline \end{array}$$

258	358	342	588
○	○	○	○

KEY NS 2.2, NS 2.0 Page 519

Education Place
Visit www.eduplace.com/camap/ for
Test-Taking Tips and Extra Practice.

Spiral Review

Relate 3-Digit Addition and Subtraction

Vocabulary

Here are some vocabulary words you will learn in the chapter.

regroup

You can regroup money in the same way that you regroup other numbers.

```
        1                    2 12
     $4.38                 $3.26
   +  2.15               -  2.50
   ───────               ───────
     $6.53                 $0.76
```

inverse operation Addition and subtraction are inverse operations.

You can use addition to check subtraction.

```
    733  ←               251
   -482                 +482
   ─────                ─────
    251  ←──────────     733
```

See English-Spanish Glossary pages 573–589.

KEY NS 2.1 Understand and use the inverse relationship between addition and subtraction (e.g., an opposite number sentence for 8 + 6 = 14 is 14 − 6 = 8) to solve problems and check solutions.

Education Place
Visit **www.eduplace.com/camap/** for the eGlossary and eGames.

Name _____

 # Check What You Know

1. Ann buys a toy telescope for 39¢.
   Charlie buys a space magazine for 52¢.
   How much money do Ann and Charlie
   spend in all?

   _____¢ + _____¢ = _____¢

2. How much more does the magazine cost
   than the telescope?

   _____¢ − _____¢ = _____¢

3. Rafael has 2 one-dollar bills, 2 quarters, and
   4 nickels. How much money does he have? $_____

4. Find the nearest hundred.
   Is 363 closer to 300 or 400?

   363 is closer to _____

   Is 532 closer to 400 or 500?

   532 is closer to _____

5. Find the difference of 532 − 363.

   _____ − _____ = _____

   Use addition to check your answer.

   _____ + _____ = _____

Use this page to review important skills needed for this chapter.

Add and Subtract Money

Hands On

Objective
Add and subtract
with coins and bills.

▶ **Explore**

You can use bills and coins to help
add and subtract money. Use the
table to solve. Model the amounts
with coins and bills.

Hannah buys a Mercury model
and star stickers. How much
does she spend in all?

Museum Store Prices	
Galaxy Notepad	$1.55
Mercury Model	$3.18
Star Stickers	$1.85
Star Chart	$4.07
Planet Stamps	$3.79

Step 1

Show both amounts
with coins and bills.

Step 2

Add the amounts.
Regroup 100 cents
as a dollar if you can.

Hannah spends $5.03 in all.

1. 123 **Math Talk** If you bought a star chart and paid
with a $5 bill, how could you subtract to find your
change?

KEY NS 5.1 Solve problems using combinations
of coins and bills.
Also **NS 5.0, MR 1.2, AF 1.3, AF 1.0, MR 2.1**

KEY NS 5.2 Know and use decimal notation and
the dollar and cent symbols for money.

five hundred forty-nine **549**

► Extend

Use the table to solve.
Model the amounts with coins and bills.
Write the sum or difference.

Remember!
Write a dollar sign and a decimal point in your answer.

More Museum Store Prices	
Jupiter Mug	$4.80
Space Shuttle Model	$3.25
Planet Book	$5.19
Astronaut Pen	$0.75
Moon Eraser	$1.13

2. Marita buys a space shuttle model and a planet book. How much does she spend in all?

$8.44

3. Philip buys a moon eraser. He pays with a $5 bill. How much change does Philip get back?

_____

4. Chan Hee buys a planet book. He pays with a $10 bill. How much change does Chan Hee get back?

_____

5. Rosa buys a Jupiter mug and an astronaut pen. How much does she spend in all?

_____

6. Curtis buys a space shuttle model and a moon eraser. How much money does he spend in all?

_____

7. Becca buys two astronaut pens. She pays with a $5 bill. How much change does she get back?

_____

At Home Ask your child to add the prices of two objects that you see at the store or in an advertisement.

En casa Pida a su niño que sume los precios de dos objetos que haya en la tienda o en un anuncio.

Chapter 28 Lesson 2

Add and Subtract Money

▶ **Learn**

When you add and subtract money, check whether you need to regroup. You can regroup in the same way that you regroup other numbers.

$1.25
$0.65

Sally has $4.75. She buys a flashlight and a star notepad. How much money does she spend? How much does she have left?

Step 1

Add to find the amount that Sally spends.

Write the amounts and line up the digits.	Regroup ones to make another ten to add.

$1.25
+ $0.65

$1.25
+ $0.65
$1.90

Sally spends $1.90 .

Step 2

Subtract to find how much Sally has left.

Write the amounts and line up the digits.	Regroup hundreds to have enough tens to subtract.

$4.75
− $1.90

3 17
$4.75
− $1.90
$2.85

Sally has $2.85 left.

▶ **Guided Practice**

Add or subtract.

1. $3.17
+ $4.65

Think!
I can add the same way I add 317 and 465. I have to regroup.

2. $7.65
− $0.92

3. $2.62
+ $3.28

4. **(123) Math Talk** How does knowing how to find 575 − 268 help you find $5.75 − $2.68?

KEY NS 5.2 Know and use the decimal notation and dollar and cent symbols for money.
Also NS 5.0, MR 3.0

Solve.

Remember!
Check whether you
have to regroup.

5. 7 12
   $8.22
   −$4.61
   ――――
   $3.61

6. $4.38
   +$2.26

7. $3.54
   −$2.38

8. $6.72
   +$0.81

9. $3.56
   +$4.35

10. $7.34
    −$4.42

11. $4.37
    +$1.48

12. $5.03
    +$0.82

13. $6.52
    −$0.48

14. $4.72
    −$2.81

15. $4.27
    +$4.91

16. $4.11
    −$2.07

17. $3.29
    +$2.64

18. $6.08
    −$2.93

19. $1.52
    +$3.76

20. $7.00
    −$5.64

Problem Solving: Reasoning

21. Nan buys a pen and a keychain.
    How much does she spend?

    ――――――

22. If Nan pays $6.50, how much
    change does she get back?

    ――――――

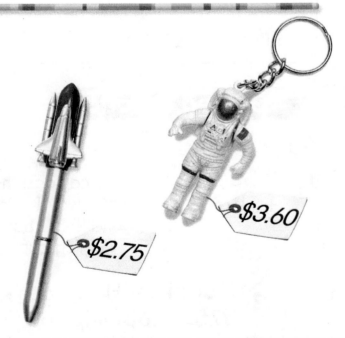

$3.60

$2.75

At Home Have your child tell you
which bills and coins he or she could
use to buy the pen and keychain
above.

En casa Pida a su niño que le diga qué
billetes y monedas podría usar para comprar
el bolígrafo y el llavero de arriba.

▶ **Practice**

This table shows the amount of money that Allen and Carmen have. Use the table to answer the questions below.

Allen	Carmen

23. How much money does   Show your work.
    Allen have?

    _____

24. How much money does
    Carmen have?

    _____

25. Who has more money?

    _____ has more money.

26. How much more? Write the
    amount in two ways.

    _____¢ $_____

KEY NS 5.2 Know and use the decimal notation and dollar and cent symbols for money. Also **NS 5.0**

KEY NS 5.1 Solve problems using combinations of coins and bills.

This table shows the amount of money that Sarah and Matt have. Use the table to answer the questions below.

Matt	Sarah
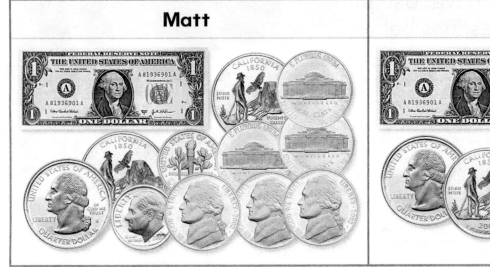	

27. How much money does Sarah have?

Show your work.

_____

~~~~~~

28. How much money does Matt have?

_____

~~~~~~

29. Who has more money?

_____ has more money.

~~~~~~

30. How much more? Write the amount in two ways.

_____¢ $_____

~~~~~~

Rewrite the amount using decimal notation.

31. 78¢ _____   **32.** 22¢ _____

33. 63¢ _____   **34.** 94¢ _____

Check Subtraction

 **Learn**

Objective
Check subtraction by using the inverse operation, addition.

Vocabulary
inverse operation

You can use addition to check subtraction.
Addition and subtraction are **inverse operations.**

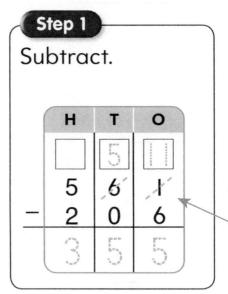

Step 1				Step 2			

Step 1
Subtract.

H	T	O
5	5	1
5	6	1
− 2	0	6
3	5	5

Step 2
Start with the difference you found.
Add the number you subtracted.

H	T	O
	1	
3	5	5
+ 2	0	6
5	6	1

The sum should equal the number
you subtracted from.

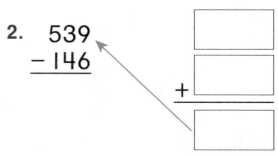 **Guided Practice**

Subtract. Check by adding.

1. 573
   −239
   + _____

Think!
I add 239 to the
difference to see if
the sum is 573.

2. 539
   −146
   + _____

3. 455
   − 37
   + _____

4. **Math Talk** What does it mean if the sum does
   not equal the number you subtracted from?

KEY NS 2.1 Understand and use the inverse
relationship between addition and subtraction
(e.g., an opposite number sentence for 8 + 6 = 14
is 14 − 6 = 8) to solve problems and check solutions.

Also **KEY NS 2.2**, NS 2.0, MR 2.2, MR 3.0,
MR 2.0, AF 1.2, AF 1.0

▶ **Practice**

Remember!
Add the difference to the
number you subtracted to
check your subtraction.

Find the difference.
Check by using addition.

5.   372
  −109
  263
       263
      + 109
       372

6.   484
  − 26
       + _____

7.   652
  −161
       + _____

8.   777
  −269
       + _____

9.   428
  −238
       + _____

10.   382
  −145
       + _____

11.   691
  −345
       + _____

12.   596
  −189
       + _____

Problem Solving: Number Sense

13. Connor subtracts $311 - 230$
and gets a difference of 81.
Which addition problem
checks to show that he
has the right answer? Circle.

a.   311
  +230
    81

b.   81
  +311
   230

c.   81
  +230
   311

d.   81
   +81
   311

At Home Ask your child to show
you how to use addition to check the
answer to 453 – 127.

En casa Pida a su niño que le muestre cómo
usar la suma para comprobar la respuesta de
453 – 127.

Chapter 28 Lesson 4

Estimate Sums and Differences

Objective
Estimate reasonable sums and differences.

 **Learn**

You can estimate a sum or difference.

Find the nearest hundred for each number in the problem.
Then add or subtract.

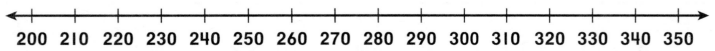

| 200 | 210 | 220 | 230 | 240 | 250 | 260 | 270 | 280 | 290 | 300 | 310 | 320 | 330 | 340 | 350 |

$$\begin{array}{r} 220 \\ +290 \end{array}$$ nearest hundred → 200
nearest hundred → 300
+

500

$$\begin{array}{r} 320 \\ -210 \end{array}$$ nearest hundred → 300
nearest hundred → 200
−

100

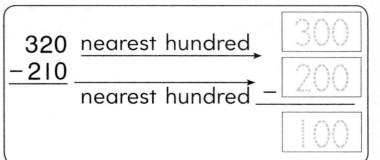

▶ **Guided Practice**

Think!
520 is closer to 500 than to 600.

Find the nearest hundred.
Add or subtract.

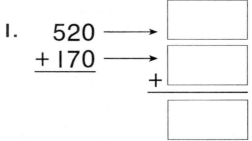

1.
$$\begin{array}{r} 520 \longrightarrow \\ +170 \longrightarrow \\ + \end{array}$$

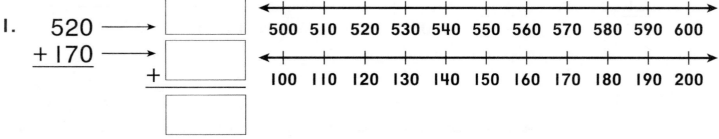

| 500 | 510 | 520 | 530 | 540 | 550 | 560 | 570 | 580 | 590 | 600 |

| 100 | 110 | 120 | 130 | 140 | 150 | 160 | 170 | 180 | 190 | 200 |

2.
$$\begin{array}{r} 610 \longrightarrow \\ -280 \longrightarrow \\ - \end{array}$$

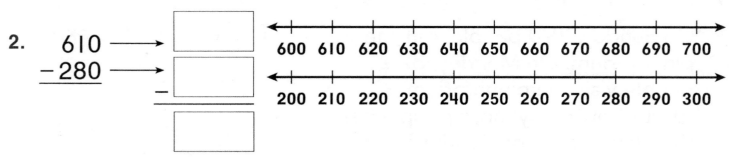

| 600 | 610 | 620 | 630 | 640 | 650 | 660 | 670 | 680 | 690 | 700 |

| 200 | 210 | 220 | 230 | 240 | 250 | 260 | 270 | 280 | 290 | 300 |

3. **(123) Math Talk** How did you find the nearest
hundred for each number in Exercises 1 and 2?

 NS 6.0 Use estimation strategies in computation
and problem solving that involve numbers that use
the ones, tens, hundreds, and thousands places.

NS 2.0 Estimate, calculate, and solve problems
involving addition and subtraction of two- and
three-digit numbers.
Also **KEY NS 2.2**, MR 2.0, MR 2.1

Find the nearest hundred.
Add or subtract.

Remember!
Use the number line
to find the nearest
hundred.

4.

$$520 \longrightarrow \boxed{500}$$
$$+370 \longrightarrow \boxed{400}$$
$$+$$
$$\boxed{900}$$

500 510 520 530 540 550 560 570 580 590 600

300 310 320 330 340 350 360 370 380 390 400

5.

$$490 \longrightarrow \boxed{}$$
$$-210 \longrightarrow \boxed{}$$
$$-$$
$$\boxed{}$$

400 410 420 430 440 450 460 470 480 490 500

200 210 220 230 240 250 260 270 280 290 300

6.

$$742 \longrightarrow \boxed{}$$
$$-121 \longrightarrow \boxed{}$$
$$-$$
$$\boxed{}$$

700 710 720 730 740 750 760 770 780 790 800

100 110 120 130 140 150 160 170 180 190 200

Problem Solving: Reasoning

7. On Sunday, 490 people visit the
planetarium. On Monday, 320
people visit the planetarium.
About how many more people visit
the planetarium on Sunday?

about _____ more people

Draw or write to explain.

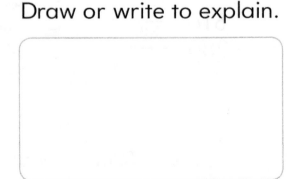

At Home Have your child explain
to you when it would be helpful to
estimate an amount rather than find
an exact amount.

En casa Pida a su niño que le explique
cuándo sería de ayuda estimar una cantidad,
en vez de hallar una cantidad exacta.

Name _____

Work Backward

 **Learn**

On Tuesday and Wednesday, Bryan draws **200** stars on a poster for his space project. He draws **87** of the stars on Tuesday. How many stars does Bryan draw on Wednesday?

Problem Solving
Strategy

Objective
Work backward to solve problems.

Understand

What do you know?
- Brian draws **200** stars on Tuesday and Wednesday.
- Brian draws **87** stars on Tuesday.

Plan

Write a number sentence.
Show the missing addend.

Think!
I know the sum. I know one part. I need to find the other part.

stars on Tuesday + stars on Wednesday = total stars

$$\underline{87} + \boxed{?} = \underline{200}$$

Think!
I can find the missing part by subtracting.

Solve

Work backward.

$$\underline{200} - \underline{87} = \underline{113}$$

Subtract.

Brian draws ___113___ stars on Wednesday.

Look Back

Is your answer reasonable?
Does it answer the question?

KEY NS 2.1 Understand and use the inverse relationship between addition and subtraction (e.g., an opposite number sentence for 8 + 6 = 14 is 14 − 6 = 8) to solve problems and check solutions.

AF 1.2 Relate problem situations to number sentences involving addition and subtraction.
Also **AF 1.0, KEY NS 2.2, NS 2.0, MR 2.0, MR 2.2**

1. On Monday and Tuesday, Linda works for 100 minutes on her Jupiter report. She works for 58 minutes on Monday. How many minutes does Linda work on Tuesday?

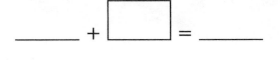

What do you know?

• Linda works for _____ minutes in all.

• She works on _____ and _____.

• She works for _____ minutes on Monday.

Write a number sentence.

Think!
I know the sum.
I can work backward to find the missing addend.

_____ + ⬚ = _____

_____ − _____ = _____

Linda works for _____ minutes on Tuesday.

2. **Math Talk** How can you check your answer?

► **Problem Solving Practice**

Work backward to solve.

Draw or write to explain.

3. 300 children visit the space museum.
   182 of the children are girls.
   How many boys visit the museum?

   _____ boys

4. Mrs. Endo has 200 stickers to give as prizes. 145 of the stickers are stars. How many stickers are not stars?

   _____ stickers

 At Home Ask your child to explain how he or she worked backward to solve Exercise 4.

En casa Pida a su niño que explique cómo comenzó con el final para resolver el Ejercicio 4.

Name _____

Problem Solving

California Field Trip

At the Tessman Planetarium

You can see a big model of the night sky. You can learn about the planets in our solar system. You can take a tour of the Milky Way and see pictures of stars.

Choose a way to solve. Show your work.

Science

Tessman Planetarium

1. 100 children draw a constellation. 67 children draw with crayons. The rest use pencils. How many children draw with pencils?

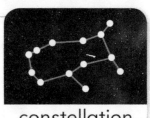

constellation

_____ children

2. 200 children see a show about the Milky Way galaxy. 84 of the children are boys. How many girls see the show?

galaxy

_____ girls

3. Mrs. Jefferson's class drives 300 miles to see a show about Saturn. They drive 123 miles before lunch. How many miles do they drive after lunch?

Saturn

_____ miles

KEY NS 2.2 Find the sum or difference of two whole numbers up to three digits long.

Also **AF 1.0, NS 2.0, MR 1.0, MR 1.1**

five hundred sixty-one **561**

Problem Solving on Tests
Listening Skills

Listen to your teacher read the problem.
Choose the correct answer.

Select a Strategy
Reasonable
   Answers
Write a Number
   Sentence
Work Backward
Use a Model

1. 239 people see the star show on Saturday. 125 people see the show on Sunday. How many people see the show on both days?

114	264	364	464
○	○	○	○

KEY **NS 2.2**

2. Estimate the difference of 823–594.

100	200	300	400
○	○	○	○

NS 6.0

3.

$3.71	$3.91	$4.51	$4.71
○	○	○	○

NS 5.0

4.

102	122	132	142
○	○	○	○

KEY **NS 2.2**

MR 1.0 Make decisions about how to set up a problem.
MR 1.1 Determine the approach, materials, and strategies to be used.

Education Place
Visit **www.eduplace.com/camap/** for Test-Taking Tips and Extra Practice.

Key Standards Review

Subtract.

1.   300
  −150
	2. 400
	  −203
		3. 500
		  −387
			4. 600
			  −455

5.   600
  −328
	6. 700
	  −562
		7. 800
		  −173
			8. 900
			  −666

9.   523
  −378
	10. 741
	  −694
		11. 810
		  −279
			12. 651
			  −268

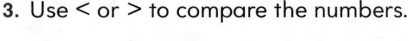

Challenge — Number Sense

Read Adriana's party invitation. She has an interesting rule about how to respond.

1. Diego wrote back with this problem. Solve.

   $752 - 356 = $ _____

2. Can Diego come to Adriana's party?

   _____

3. Use < or > to compare the numbers.

   _____ ◯ 380

> You're invited to my birthday party on May 5th.
>
> Please let me know if you can come.
>
> Write back with a subtraction problem.
>
> If you can come, the difference should be greater than 380.
>
> If you can't come, the difference should be less than 380.
>
> I hope you can make it!
>
> Adriana

KEY **NS 2.2** Find the sum or difference of two whole numbers up to three digits long.
Also KEY **NS 1.3**

five hundred sixty-three **563**

Math Music

Check What You Subtract

🎧 **Math Music,** Track 10
Tune: original

You can check what you subtract
When you add—and that's a fact!

How much money will I have left
If I buy this space toy now?
I'll subtract, then check my answer.
Come and look. I'll show you how!

You can check what you subtract
When you add—and that's a fact!

You can add to check subtraction.
Add the difference first, you see,
With the number you subtracted.
Find the sum. Does it agree?

You can check what you subtract
When you add—and that's a fact!

KEY NS 2.1 Understand and use the inverse relationship between addition and subtraction (e.g., an opposite number sentence for 8 + 6 = 14 is 14 − 6 = 8) to solve problems and check solutions.

Name _____

Concepts and Skills

Use the table to solve.
Write the sum or difference. KEY **NS 5.1**, KEY **NS 5.2**

Toy Sale	
Car	$3.45
Train	$9.75
Boat	$4.99

1. How much more is the train than the car?

_____

Write the total value of the amount shown. KEY **NS 5.2**

2.

_____

Find the difference.
Check by using addition. KEY **NS 2.1**

3. 706
   −287   + _____

Round each number to the
nearest hundred. Subtract. NS 6.0, KEY **NS 2.2**

4. 770
   −248

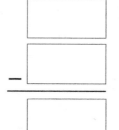

Problem Solving KEY **NS 2.2**

Write a number sentence. Solve.

5. Amy spent 164 minutes last
   week jumping rope. She spent
   158 minutes this week. How long did
   she spend jumping rope in all?

_____ ◯ _____ ◯ _____

Spiral Review and Test Practice

1. What is the sum?

787
+156

843 ○   833 ○   933 ○   943 ○

KEY **NS 2.2**, NS 2.0 Page 501

---

2. What is the difference?

578
− 99

KEY **AF 1.1** 1–2

471 ○   479 ○   481 ○   521 ○

KEY **NS 2.2**, NS 2.0 Page 533

---

3. What is the total value of the amount shown?

$3.02 ○ $2.81 ○ $2.02 ○ $1.02 ○

KEY **NS 5.1**, KEY **NS 5.2**, NS 5.0 Page 551

---

4. Which addition problem can be used to check this subtraction?

706
−487

706   467   219   219
+487   +487   +487   +706
○   ○   ○   ○

KEY **NS 2.1**, KEY **NS 2.2** Page 555

Education Place
Visit **www.eduplace.com/camap/** for
Test-Taking Tips and Extra Practice.

Spiral Review

Name _____

Greg Tang's Go Fast, Go Far

Unit 10 Mental Math Strategies

Divide by 4

Divide by 4? This way's shorter.
Half of half, it's called a quarter.

I have a fast way to do 20 ÷ 4.
Dividing by 4 is the same as dividing
by 2 twice. Dividing in two steps is
easier than dividing in one.

1. 20 ÷ 4 → [10] → [5]
   Divide 20 by 2.   Divide by 2.

2. 12 ÷ 4 → [ ] → [ ]
   Divide 12 by 2.   Divide by 2.

3. 24 ÷ 4 → [ ] → [ ]
   Divide 24 by 2.   Divide by 2.

4. 36 ÷ 4 → [ ] → [ ]
   Divide 36 by 2.   Divide by 2.

5. 28 ÷ 4 → [ ] → [ ]

6. 32 ÷ 4 → [ ] → [ ]

Go Faster!

Take It Further: Now try doing all the steps in your head!

7. 16 ÷ 4 = [ ]

8. 40 ÷ 4 = [ ]

Reading and Writing Math

Choose a word from the word bank for each blank.

1. When you rewrite 150 + 340 by lining up the digits, you are using _____.

2. The _____ of subtraction is addition.

3. When you subtract 308 − 255, you have to regroup _____.

Add or subtract. Then match each example with a think cloud.

4.   300
   +600

    a. I'll regroup 1 ten as 10 ones.

5.   342
   +183

    b. I'll use 3 + 6 to help me add.

6.   282
   − 57

    c. I'll regroup 10 tens to make 100.

7. **Writing Math** Add. Then write a think cloud to explain the addition.

    $2.15
   +$3.54

KEY NS 2.2 Find the sum or difference of two whole numbers up to three digits long.
Also **NS 2.3, MR 1.1, MR 2.1**

Name _____

Concepts and Skills

Write the sum or difference. KEY NS 2.2

1. 8 hundreds   800
   +2 hundreds   +200
   _____ hundreds

2. 9 hundreds   900
   −3 hundreds   −300
   _____ hundreds

Add or subtract. Decide if you need to regroup. KEY NS 2.2

3. 409
   +268

4. 623
   +167

5. 967
   −378

6. 707
   −459

Subtract. KEY NS 2.2

7.

H	T	O
8	6	6
− 3	4	9

8.

H	T	O
8	4	7
− 2	2	8

9.

H	T	O
7	2	8
− 3	4	9

10.

H	T	O
9	4	4
− 3	7	9

Subtract. KEY NS 2.2

11. 700
  − 370

12. 601
  − 298

Rewrite to subtract. KEY NS 2.2

13. 482 − 113

Use the table to solve.
Write the sum or difference. KEY NS 5.2, AF 1.3

14. How much more is the doll
than the puppet?

_____

Toy Prices	
Teddy Bear	$3.45
Doll	$9.75
Puppet	$4.99

Find the difference.
Check by using addition. KEY NS 2.1

15. 902
  − 147

  + _____

Problem Solving

Solve. MR 2.0, KEY NS 2.2

16. On his vacation, Mr. Stein drove
36 miles, flew 709 miles, and biked
162 miles. How many miles is that
in all?

_____

Draw or write to explain.

□□□□□|||||||

Name _____

THIS YEAR
I learned to . . .

 NUMBER SENSE

compare and order numbers

Circle the number sentence that is true.

243 < 239   243 < 256   243 < 243   243 > 243

KEY **NS 1.1**, KEY **NS 1.3**

add and subtract

```
  42          75
+ 29        - 32
----        ----
```

KEY **NS 2.2**

multiply and divide

8 groups of 5 = _____

_____ × _____ = _____

KEY **NS 3.1**, KEY **NS 3.3**, KEY **NS 3.2**

_____ ÷ _____ = _____

THIS YEAR
I learned to . . .

 GRAPHS AND DATA   make bar graphs

Use the tally chart to complete the graph.

Favorite Color	
Red	‖‖‖	
Yellow	‖
Blue	‖‖‖ |||
Green	‖‖‖

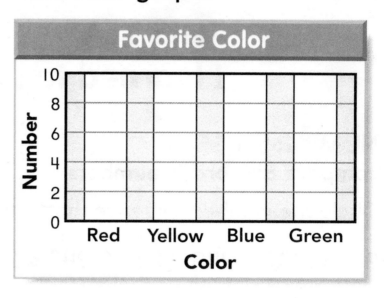

SDAP 1.2

 GEOMETRY
count the faces, edges, and vertices of solid shapes

		Faces	Edges	Vertices
	cube	———	———	———
	sphere	———	———	———
	pyramid	———	———	———

KEY **MG 2.1**

NEXT YEAR
I will learn more about . . .

- place value
- multiplying and dividing whole numbers
- geometry and measurement
- probability

I can use the Review/Preview worksheets to get ready for next year.

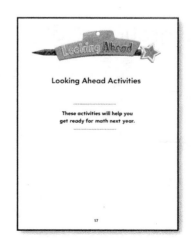

Glossary

A

A.M. The hours between midnight and noon.

A.M. Las horas comprendidas entre la medianoche y el mediodía.

---

add $5 + 2 = 7$

sumar $5 + 2 = 7$

---

addend

$5 + 6 = 11$
↑   ↑
addends

sumandos

sumando

---

addition A mathematical operation that tells how many things there are in all when two sets are put together.

suma Operación matemática que dice cuántas cosas hay en total cuando dos conjuntos se unen.

---

after 98, 99
99 is after 98

después 98, 99
99 viene después de 98.

---

array Objects or numbers arranged in rows and columns. This is a 3 × 5 array.

matriz Objetos o números ordenados en filas y columnas. Ésta es una matriz de 3 × 5.

Associative Property of Addition Changing the grouping of the numbers does not change the sum.

$$(3 + 4) + 5 = 3 + (4 + 5)$$

$$7 + 5 = 3 + 9$$

$$12 = 12$$

Propiedad asociativa de la suma Al cambiar la forma en que se agrupan los números no cambia la suma.

bar graph

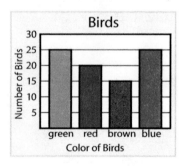

gráfica de barras

before 31, 32
31 is before 32

antes 31, 32
31 viene antes de 32.

between 54, 55, 56
55 is between 54 and 56.

entre
55 está entre 54 y 56.

calendar

March

Sunday	Monday	Tuesday	Wednesday	Thursday	Friday	Saturday
		1	2	3	4	5	6
7	8	9	10	11	12	13
14	15	16	17	18	19	20
21	22	23	24	25	26	27
28	29	30	31			

calendario

centimeter (cm) A unit of length in the metric system. 100 cm = 1 m

centímetro (cm) Unidad de longitud del sistema métrico. 100 cm = 1 m

centimeter ruler A centimeter ruler measures length in centimeters.

regla en centímetros Una regla en centímetros mide longitud en centímetros.

change In a money situation, the amount returned to the customer after the seller has subtracted the price from the amount of money given.

cambio En una situación relacionada con dinero, la cantidad que se devuelve al cliente después de que el vendedor le resta el precio a la cantidad de dinero entregado.

---

coin A penny, a nickel, a dime and a quarter are all examples of coins.

moneda Una moneda de un centavo, una moneda de cinco centavos, una moneda de diez centavos y una moneda de veinticinco centavos son todas ejemplos de monedas.

Commutative Property of Addition Changing the order of the addends does not change the sum.

$$5 + 9 = 9 + 5$$
$$14 = 14$$

Propiedad conmutativa de la suma Cambiar el orden de los sumandos no cambia la suma.

Commutative Property of Multiplication Changing the order of the factors does not change the product.

$$3 \times 7 = 7 \times 3$$
$$21 = 21$$

Propiedad conmutativa de la multiplicación Cambiar el orden de los factores no cambia el producto.

---

compare To examine two or more things or numbers to determine which are greater or less than the others.

comparar Examinar dos o más cosas o números para determinar cuál es mayor o menor que los otros.

---

cone

cono

cube

cubo

---

cylinder

cilindro

---

data a set of information

Favorite Snacks	
cheese	|||
pretzels	~~||||~~

5 choose pretzels. 3 choose cheese.

5 eligen pretzels. 3 eligen queso.

datos Conjunto de información

---

day One day is 24 hours. There are 7 days in one week.

November

Sunday	Monday	Tuesday	Wednesday	Thursday	Friday	Saturday
			1	2	3	4
5	6	7	8	9	10	11
12	13	14	15	16	17	18
19	20	21	22	23	24	25
26	27	28	29	30		

Each box shows one day.

día Un día tiene 24 horas. Una semana tiene 7 días.

---

decimal point

$1.00

↑ decimal point

punto decimal

punto decimal

---

difference The result of a subtraction.

$$11 - 3 = 8$$

↑ difference

diferencia

$$\begin{array}{r} 11 \\ -3 \\ \hline 8 \end{array}$$

diferencia El resultado de la resta.

digit

39
↑ ↑
digits

39 has two digits: 3 and 9.

39 tiene dos dígitos: 3 y 9.

dígitos

dígito

---

dime   10¢, 10 cents or $0.10

moneda de diez centavos

10¢, 10 centavos ó $0.10

---

divide

$$6 \div 3 = 2$$

number in all | number of sets | number in each set

dividir

---

division   One of the four basic operations of arithmetic; fair shares.

división   Una de las cuatro operaciones básicas aritméticas; partes iguales.

---

division sentence

$$15 \div 5 = 3$$

15 divided by 5 equals 3.

15 dividido entre 5 es igual a 3.

enunciado de división

---

dollar   100¢ or $1.00

dólar   100¢ ó $1.00

---

dollar sign

$2.00
↑
dollar sign

signo de dólar

signo de dólar

E

edge An edge is where two faces meet.

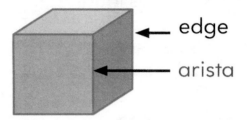

edge

arista

arista Una arista es donde se encuentran dos caras.

---

equal These amounts are equal. Their difference is zero.

$$4 + 4 = 8$$

4 plus 4 is equal to 8

4 más 4 es igual a 8

igual Estas cantidades son iguales. Su diferencia es cero.

---

equal groups Equal groups have the same number of things. 3 equal groups of 2.

grupos iguales Los grupos iguales tienen el mismo número de objetos. 3 grupos iguales de 2.

---

equal sign 4 plus 1 is equal to 5

$$4 + 1 = 5$$

equal sign

signo de igual

signo de igual 4 más 1 es igual a 5

---

estimate An estimate is an answer that is close to an exact amount. You can estimate a sum. You can estimate the number of objects in a set.

$$\begin{array}{r} 28 \\ + \ 23 \\ \hline \end{array} \qquad \begin{array}{r} 30 \\ + \ 20 \\ \hline 50 \end{array}$$

estimación Una estimación es una respuesta cercana a una cantidad exacta. Puedes estimar una suma. Puedes estimar el número de objetos en un conjunto.

---

even number A number is even when you make groups of 2 and none are left over. 8 is an even number.

número par Un número es par cuando al hacer grupos de 2 no sobra nada. 8 es un número par.

expanded form

$$283 = 200 + 80 + 3$$

forma extendida

---

face One of the flat surfaces used to form a solid.

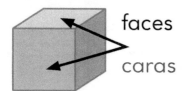
faces
caras

cara Una de las superficies planas usadas para formar un cuerpo geométrico.

---

fact family

$$9 + 7 = 16$$
$$7 + 9 = 16$$
$$16 - 9 = 7$$
$$16 - 7 = 9$$

familia de operaciones

---

five-dollar bill 500¢ or $5.00

billete de cinco dólares 500¢ ó $5.00

---

fraction A way to express a part of a whole or a part of a set.

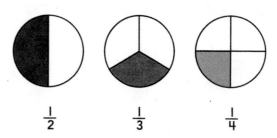

$\frac{1}{2}$ $\frac{1}{3}$ $\frac{1}{4}$

fracción Manera de expresar una parte de un entero o una parte de un conjunto.

---

greater than (>)

$$34 > 25$$

mayor que (>)

---

greatest

25 41 63
63 is the greatest number.

mayor, el mayor de todos

63 es el número mayor de todos.

H

half-dollar 50¢ or 50 cents.

medio dólar 50¢ ó 50 centavos.

hexagon

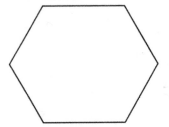

hexágono

hour 60 minutes = 1 hour

2:00

hora 60 minutos = 1 hora

hour hand

hour hand

manecilla de la hora

manecilla de la hora

hundred 1 hundred. 100.
centena 1 centena. 100.

hundreds

3 hundred 300

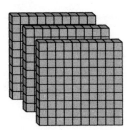

centenas

3 centenas 300

inch (in.) A unit of length in the customary system.

pulgada (pulg) Unidad de longitud en el sistema usual.

inch ruler An inch ruler measures length in inches.

regla en pulgadas Una regla en pulgadas mide longitud en pulgadas.

---

inverse operation An operation that reverses or undoes another operation. Subtraction is the inverse operation of addition. Addition is the inverse operation of subtraction.

$$14 + 23 = 37$$
$$37 - 23 = 14$$

operación inversa Operación opuesta a otra operación. La resta es la operación inversa de la suma. La suma es la operación inversa de la resta.

L

least

14   7   63

7 is the least number.

7 es el número menor de todos.

el menor de todos

---

less than (<)

$$45 < 46$$

menor que (<)

M

meter (m) 100 centimeters = 1 meter

metro (m) 100 centímetros = 1 metro

---

minute 60 seconds = 1 minute

minuto 60 segundos = 1 minuto

mode The number that appears most often in a set of data.

$$3 \; 4 \; 5 \; 4 \; 5 \; 4 \; 2$$

4 is the mode.

4 es la moda.

moda El número que aparece con más frecuencia en un conjunto de datos.

---

month

	June					
Sunday	Monday	Tuesday	Wednesday	Thursday	Friday	Saturday
			1	2	3	4
5	6	7	8	9	10	11
12	13	14	15	16	17	18
19	20	21	22	23	24	25
26	27	28	29	30		

mes

---

multiplication

$$2 \times 5 = 10$$

2 times 5 equals 10

2 por 5 es igual a 10

multiplicación

---

multiply

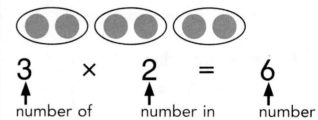

$$3 \quad \times \quad 2 \quad = \quad 6$$

number of groups   number in each group   number in all

multiplicar

$$3 \quad \times \quad 2 \quad = \quad 6$$

número de grupos   número en cada grupo   número total

---

nickel 5¢, 5 cents, or $0.05

moneda de cinco centavos

5¢, 5 centavos ó $0.05

---

number line

0 1 2 3 4 5 6 7 8 9 10

recta numérica

---

number sentence

$$2 + 4 + 5 = 11$$

enunciado numérico

odd number A number is odd when you make groups of two and have one left over. 9 is an odd number.

número impar Un número es impar cuando al hacer grupos de dos sobra uno. 9 es un número impar.

---

one-dollar bill 100¢ or $1.00

billete de un dólar 100¢ ó $1.00

---

ones Counting a set of objects one-by-one

unidades Contar un conjunto de objetos de a uno

---

order The numbers 2, 5, and 6 are in order from least to greatest.

orden Los números 2, 5 y 6 están en orden de menor a mayor.

P.M. The hours between noon and midnight.

P.M. Las horas entre el mediodía y la medianoche.

---

penny 1¢, 1 cent, or $0.01

moneda de un centavo 1¢, 1 centavo, ó $0.01

---

picture graph

Playground Toys			
soccer ball	★	★	★
jump ropes	★		
soft ball	★	★	

Key: Each ★ stands for 5 toys.

pictografía

place value The value of each digit in a number.

315
3 hundreds = 300
1 tens = 10
5 ones = 5

valor de posición El valor de cada dígito en un número.

315
3 centenas = 300
1 decena = 10
5 unidades = 5

---

place-value chart

Hundreds	Tens	Ones

tabla de valor de posición

---

plane shape A 2-dimensional shape such as a square, triangle, or rectangle.

figura plana Figura de dos dimensiones como el cuadrado, el triángulo o el rectángulo.

product

$3 \times 2 = 6$

↑
product
producto

producto

---

pyramid

pirámide

---

quarter 25¢, 25 cents or $0.25

moneda de veinticinco centavos 25¢, 25 centavos ó $0.25

quarter hour

15 minutes = 1 quarter hour

cuarto de hora

15 minutos = 1 cuarto de hora

range

1 4 3 1 3 2 5

5 − 1 = 4

↑   ↑   ↑

greatest   least   range

mayor   menor   rango

rango

rectangle

rectángulo

rectangular prism

prisma rectangular

regroup

10 ones = 1 ten

10 unidades = 1 decena

reagrupar

related facts

9 + 4 = 13   13 − 4 + 9

operaciones relacionadas

9 + 4 = 13   13 − 4 + 9

remainder

9 ÷ 4 = 2 remainder 1

residuo

Glossary

second 60 seconds = 1 minute
It takes about one second to raise your hand.

segundo 60 segundos = 1 minuto
Te toma más o menos un segundo levantar tu mano.

side Triangles have 3 sides.

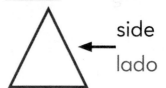

side
lado

lado Los triángulos tienen tres lados.

solid shape A 3-dimensional shape such as a cube, pyramid or cylinder.

cuerpo geométrico Figura de tres dimensiones como el cubo, la pirámide o el cilindro.

sphere

esfera

square

cuadrado

subtract

$5 - 3 = 2$

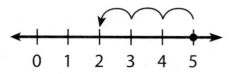

0 1 2 3 4 5

restar $5 - 3 = 2$

subtraction One of the four basic operations of arithmetic. It is the opposite of addition.

resta Una de las cuatro operaciones básicas aritméticas. Es el opuesto de la suma.

sum

$4 + 3 = 7$

$$\begin{array}{r} 4 \\ +3 \\ \hline 7 \end{array}$$

↑
sum

sum →

suma

suma

586 Glossary

tally chart

Favorite Color	Tally Marks	Number of Students
red	IIII	4
blue	ʰʰʰ I	6
yellow	ʰʰʰ II	7

tablero de conteo

tally marks

stands for I.   stands for 5.

representa I.   representa 5.

marcas de conteo

ten-dollar bill 1,000¢, $10.00

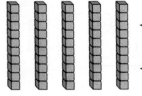

billete de diez dólares 1,000¢, $10.00

tens

←5 tens; 50

←5 decenas; 50

decenas

thousand one thousand, 1,000

mil un millar, 1,000

triangle

triángulo

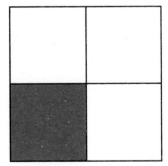

unit

unidad

unit fraction A unit fraction names one of the parts of a whole.

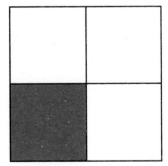

unidad fraccionaria Una unidad fraccionaria representa una de las partes de un entero.

V

vertex/vertices

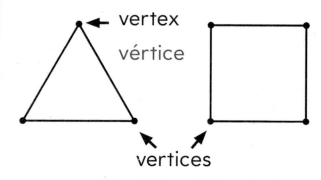

vertex
vértice

vertices

vértice/vértices

W

week A week is 7 days.

March

Sunday	Monday	Tuesday	Wednesday	Thursday	Friday	Saturday
			1	2	3	4
5	6	7	8	9	10	11
12	13	14	15	16	17	18
19	20	21	22	23	24	25
26	27	28	29	30	31	

semana Una semana tiene 7 días.

whole

$\frac{4}{4}$ are green. $\frac{4}{4} = 1$
One whole is equal to 1.

entero

$\frac{4}{4}$ son verdes. $\frac{4}{4} = 1$
Un entero es igual a 1.

width

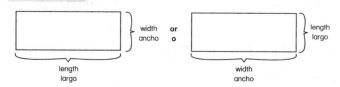

width
ancho   **or**
o

length
largo

length
largo

width
ancho

ancho

Y

year A year is 12 months.

January

Sunday	Monday	Tuesday	Wednesday	Thursday	Friday	Saturday
			1	2	3	4
5	6	7	8	9	10	11
12	13	14	15	16	17	18
19	20	21	22	23	24	25
26	27	28	29	30	31	

año Un año tiene 12 meses.

zero The absence of any numbers in a set. None.

cero Ausencia de números en un conjunto. Nada.